HB 241 FIR

D1647153

SCASSS

THE SWEDISH COLLEGIUM FOR ADVANCED STUDY IN THE SOCIAL SCIENCES

QMW LIBRARY
(MILE END)

edited by
Masahiko Aoki,
Bo Gustafsson and
Oliver E. Williamson

 SAGE Publications

London ● Newbury Park ● New Delhi

© SCASSS 1990

First published 1990

All rights reserved. No part of this publication may
be reproduced, stored in a retrieval system,
transmitted or utilized in any form or by any means,
electronic, mechanical, photocopying, recording or
otherwise, without permission in writing from the
Publishers.

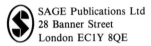

SAGE Publications Ltd
28 Banner Street
London EC1Y 8QE

SAGE Publications Inc
2111 West Hillcrest Drive
Newbury Park, California 91320

SAGE Publications India Pvt Ltd
32, M-Block Market
Greater Kailash – I
New Delhi 110 048

British Library Cataloguing in Publication Data

The firm as a nexus of treaties.
  1. Business firms. Organisation structure.
  Econometric models.
  I. Aoki, Masahiko, *1938–*   II. Gustafsson, Bo
  III. Williams, Oliver E. (Oliver Eaton, *1932–*)
  338.7

ISBN 0-8039-8244-5
ISBN 0-8039-8245-3 Pbk

Library of Congress catalog card number 89-062697

Filmset by Mayhew Typesetting, Bristol, England
Printed in Great Britain by Dotesios Printers Ltd, Trowbridge, Wiltshire

Contents

Foreword

In the recently published *New Palgrave Dictionary of Economics* we read in the opening paragraph, under the entry 'firm, theory of': 'It is doubtful if there is yet general agreement among economists on the subject matter designated by the title "theory of the firm", on, that is, the scope and purpose of the part of economics so titled.'

This assessment by a leading authority on the theory of the firm is probably too cautious. There is certainly no such general agreement and considering the centrifugal forces operating in this field one may doubt whether general agreement will be reached in the foreseeable future. The lack of general agreement, moreover, includes not only the scope and purpose of the theory of the firm but also the proper orientation and content of the theoretical core as well.

In view of the role of the modern firm in practical as well as in theoretical economics one may deplore this state of things. As testified inter alia by the contributions to this volume, part of the explanation lies in the swift advances taking place. But there are also other explanations. The term 'firm' is within economics almost as general as the term 'mammal' within zoology, covering many species. Due to varying institutional settings, structural peculiarities and differences in behavioural rules, different kinds of firms – large corporations, financial institutions, worker-controlled firms etc. – may not be profitably analysed by one and the same theoretical construct. Further, and related to this fact, different theories move on different levels of generality depending upon the number of assumptions made and variables modelled. For the purpose of general equilibrium theory it may be irrelevant whether entrepreneurs should be included as a factor of production or not, and whether the revenues of the firm should be divided between owners and managers or not. Such issues are clearly of prime importance for a theory focusing on the firm as such trying to account for what is going on inside firms. But even then approaches may differ because of conflicting cognitive attitudes. For some economists firms are real-world entities, while others conceive the firm as only a theoretical link, a mental construct for explaining how one gets from cause to effect.

Moreover, theories of the firm may differ because they focus on different aspects of the firm. Some theories may have their strong point in explaining conditions of existence, others in pricing, distribution, managerial behaviour or growth. To this extent, theories of the firm are inherently complementary rather than substitutes. In any case, only after a period of peaceful co-existence and competition will it be possible to see whether one of the different approaches could be taken as the point of departure for a generalization, or whether a completely new paradigm may be created, incorporating the earlier approaches as special cases.

Looking at the theory of the firm from the point of view of economic history it is, lastly, manifest that theories of the firm are born, flower and give way to new theories not only because existing theories are destroyed by new and superior ones but because historical reality, in this case the institutional settings, structure and behaviour of firms, is changing, making old theories outmoded and creating a demand for new ones. If these changes are sufficiently sweeping, the old theory may not just be refor-mulated by some new assumptions or by the incorporation of some new arguments, but must be replaced by new constructs.

Let me take a few examples. The capitalist firm as, for example, Marx conceived it, had no room for conflicts between owners and managers, workers were in unlimited supply and they were power-less and worked at maximum intensity. This model may have been realistic for some British industries at this time and may also have produced interesting results. But when historical reality changed, the model had to be modified or discarded. Marshall's view of the firm is complex and in some respects very sophisticated, making allowance for varying returns to scale, external and internal economies, quasi-rents, bargaining and primacy for management in relation to owners. Still, his 'representative firm' in its short-run behaviour did little more than expand output until the U-shaped cost curve hit the exogenously given price line from below. Maybe this was what most firms did and could do in contemporary Britain. But surely the rise and growth of the large corporation from the late nineteenth century and the creation of distinct segments of firms of different kinds eroded the realism of this approach, and by the 1930s the scene was set for big changes. Joan Robinson, anticipated by Zeuthen, concluded her *Economics of Imperfect Competition* with a chapter on 'A World of Mono-polies', and her German contemporary, Stackelberg, visualized firm behaviour as an internecine struggle between oligopolistic giants. Parallel to this Berle and Means, as well as Yntema and others, in the USA investigated the large corporations with new results and new concepts as a consequence.

This opened the way for the post-1945 thinking on the modern capitalist firm as an extensive organization with several interlocked blocs of interest – shareholders, management, employees, suppliers, customers etc. – temporarily summed up in the behavioural theory of the firm. After this the new theory of the firm was firmly set on its own road leading towards complex, conflicting and complementary theories of organization. Aspects of the most recent history of these developments are admirably summarized by Oliver E. Williamson in his introduction (Chapter 1) which attempts to promote a dialogue between economics and sociology. Williamson has, in another context, pertinently characterized the present situation:

> The intellectual appeal of a single, unified theory of organization notwithstanding, we are presently operating in a pre-unified stage of development. Even if a comprehensive, integrated theory were in prospect, which it is not, our understanding of some complex organizational phenomena may be better served by working out of several well-focused perspectives. Exposing the power and limits of each of the leading approaches and the tensions and complementaries between them can be and often is a productive enterprise. (Williamson, 1988)

Exactly this view was guiding the initiators of the conference, 'The Firm as a Nexus of Treaties', which took place in Uppsala 6–8 June, 1988 under the auspices of the new Swedish Collegium for Advanced Study in the Social Sciences (SCASSS). The idea was brought up by Masahiko Aoki at the first SCASSS conference in June 1986 within the research programme 'Property Rights, Organizational Forms and Economic Behaviour'. Oliver E. Williamson consented to join Masahiko and myself as a promoter of the conference, which was attended by more than thirty participants from the USA, Japan, Denmark, Finland, Norway and Sweden, representing not only economics and business studies but also economic history, law and sociology. The approach to the agenda of the conference was thus truly inter-disciplinary and in accordance with the objective of SCASSS: to promote theoretically innovative multidisciplinary research. Even if the conference did not map out a new battlefield – the proverbial prerogative of gods – it hopefully succeeded in placing some banners where a banner never flew.

In conclusion I would like to thank Masahiko Aoki and Oliver

E. Williamson – both of them in the forefront of theoretical advance within the theory of the modern firm – for their efforts to make the conference into a success and for bringing this volume to a larger audience. In this I also include other contributors to this volume as well as discussants at the conference. David Hill of Sage in London made an amazingly fast and craftmanlike publishing job. The Tercentenary Fund of the National Bank of Sweden (Riksbankens Jubileumsfond), which sponsors the research programme indicated above, generously provided funds for the conference.

Bo Gustafsson
Director of Economic Studies
The Swedish Collegium for Advanced
Study in the Social Sciences (SCASSS)

Reference

Williamson, Oliver E. (1988) 'The Economics and Sociology of Organization: Promoting a Dialogue' in George Farkas and Paul England (eds), *Industries, Firms and Jobs*. New York: Plenum.

1
The Firm as a Nexus of Treaties:
an Introduction

Oliver E. Williamson

The past decade has witnessed a renewal of interest – of conceptual, theoretical and empirical kinds – in the study of economic organization. The modern corporation is the central economic institution with which this research is concerned. An interesting but controversial new term – 'nexus of contracts' – is sometimes used to describe the modern business firm. Economists interested in corporate finance and corporate governance have found the term nexus of contracts especially congenial.

The term nexus of treaties is somewhat broader and is the theme around which the 1988 Uppsala conference was organized. Some of the reasons for supplanting nexus of contract by nexus of treaties are sketched in Section 1. The rudiments of the transaction cost economics approach to economic organization, with which much of my own research has been concerned, are set out in Section 2. The conference papers and some of the more important and recurrent conference themes are briefly described in Section 3. Concluding remarks follow.

1. Why treaties?

The theory of the firm is one of the two key analytical constructs on which microeconomic theory rests (the other being the theory of consumer behaviour). Whereas the neoclassical theory of the firm mainly withstood assaults by new managerial theories of the firm (Baumol, 1959; Marris, 1964; Williamson, 1964; Alchian, 1965) and the behavioural theory of the firm (Cyert and March, 1963), more recent work, in which a quasi-contractual approach to the theory of the firm is employed, has made substantial headway.

Major changes in the way in which a subject is treated invariably make their way, with a time lag, into the textbooks. A comparison of the theory of the firm in the third edition of James Henderson and Richard Quandt's *Microeconomic Theory* (1980) with that in Jean Tirole's *The Theory of Industrial Organization* (1988) is pertinent. Thus whereas the neoclassical theory of the firm works entirely out of a production function setup (Henderson and Quandt, 1980: 64–134), which is mainly a technological conception, Tirole examines the firm from both technological and contractual points of view – with special emphasis on the latter (1988: 15–60). The comparative contractual approach to the study of economic organization, to include a reconceptualization of a firm as a governance structure, has plainly made inroads.

As discussed in Section 2, and as illustrated by the chapters in this volume, the new theories of the firm address issues that were never raised by and were even alien to the neoclassical tradition. Questions of the boundaries of the firm (or, in more prosaic terms, the 'make or buy' decision), of the factors responsible for limits to firm size, of when to use debt rather than equity and why, of corporate governance, the organization of labour and the like – all of them matters that deeply implicate issues of *both* economics and organization – were posed. These are addressed, moreover, from a variety of contractual points of view – including transaction costs (Williamson, 1971, 1975, 1979, 1985; Klein et al., 1978; Grossman and Hart, 1986), team organization (of both communication (Marschak and Radner, 1972) and technological nonseparability (Alchian and Demsetz, 1972) kinds), nexus of contracts (Jensen and Meckling, 1976; Fama, 1980) and co-operative games (Aoki, 1984).

To be sure, the neoclassical theory of the firm purported to and does deal with the issue of vertical integration. In the absence, however, of market power (at one or both of two successive stages of production) or of taxes or quotas on the sale of intermediate product, the neoclassical theory has little to say about whether a firm should buy or make a good or service. There being huge numbers of transactions for which a make or buy decision is needed for which market power, quotas, and taxes are all absent, the neoclassical apparatus is plainly limited. The issue of firm size is similarly beyond the reach of the neoclassical production function setup.[1] And while the neoclassical proposition that the cost of capital is independent of the choice of financial instruments has been enormously instructive, a huge number of financial puzzles are nevertheless posed. Many anomalies likewise arise in attempting to understand labour organization (including the purposes served by internal labour markets, unions, and the like) within a strictly neoclassical framework.

The new theories of the firm to which I refer were initially regarded as rivals to the neoclassical theory. Increasingly, however, they are coming to be treated as complements. Kenneth Arrow's remarks about the New Institutional Economics are pertinent:

> the New Institutional Economics movement . . . [does] not consist primarily of giving new answers to the traditional questions of economics – resource allocation and degree of utilization. Rather it consists of answering new questions, why economic institutions have emerged the way they did and not otherwise; it merges into economic history, but brings sharper nanoeconomic . . . ('nano' is an extreme version of 'micro') reasoning to bear than has been customary. (Arrow, 1987: 734)

Tirole's treatment of the older (neoclassical/production function) and newer (more microanalytic/contracting) theories as complements is consonant.

To be sure, this presents a need to pick and choose. Roughly, if the issues are ones of price, output, efficient factor proportions and the like, the production function setup applies. If, however, the object is to assess the *comparative* efficacy of alternative economic and organizational instruments (make or buy; debt or equity; piece rates or time rates; reciprocal trade or not; etc.), recourse to the newer theories, which expressly engage the relevant microanalytics, is indicated.

The term nexus of treaties is meant to apply to this entire set of non-neoclassical work on the theory of the firm. But the substitution of treaties for contracts does more than simply encompass the recent work to which I refer. More importantly, it (1) has conceptual benefits, (2) invites both politics and sociology to join the dialogue, and (3) helps to expand the research agenda.

Conceptual benefits

As Jeffrey Gordon recently remarks, to regard

> the corporate entity [as] nothing more than a gathering point for a series of contracts, express and implied . . . rankles some sensibilities, because the economist's conception of 'contract' as an arrangement between two or more actors supported by reciprocal expectations and behavior is far broader than a lawyer's, which looks for the standard indicia of contract formation, offer and acceptance, ideally reflected in an explicit bargaining process (Gordon, 1988: 2).

Were it only, however, that the sensibilities of lawyers were at stake, this would scarcely warrant substituting the term treaties for contracts. That is mere form, and what concerns us is substance.

The fact is that the term contract often carries *unwanted* legal meanings. A legalistic view of contract can deter rather than promote an understanding of complex economic organization. Note in this connection that most studies of exchange assume that efficacious rules of law regarding contract disputes are in place and are applied by the courts in an informed, sophisticated, and low-cost way. Those assumptions are convenient, in that lawyers and economists are relieved of the need to examine the variety of ways by which individual parties to an exchange 'contract out of or away from' the governance structures of the state by devising private orderings. Thus arises a division of effort whereby economists are preoccupied with the economic benefits that accrue to specialization and exchange, while legal specialists focus on the technicalities of contract law.

The 'legal centralism' tradition reflects the latter orientation. It maintains that 'disputes require "access" to a forum external to the original social setting of the dispute [and that] remedies will be provided as prescribed in some body of authoritative learning and dispensed by experts who operate under the auspices of the state' (Galanter, 1981: 1). The facts, however, disclose otherwise. Most disputes, including many that under current rules could be brought to a court, are resolved by avoidance, self-help, and the like (Galanter, 1981: 2). This is because in 'many instances the participants can devise more satisfactory solutions to their disputes than can professionals constrained to apply general rules on the basis of limited knowledge of the dispute' (Galanter, 1981: 4).

The substitution of the term treaty for contract brings private ordering forcefully to the fore. The limits of legal centralism being so transparent for treaties – since the parties may refuse a legal forum and/or ignore legal sanctions – there is a clear need from the outset for the parties to craft specialized governance structures within which to embed a treaty. The 'Standing Consultative Committee' created by the parties to the SALT agreement is an example: 'The SCC is not an independent third party, and it has no authority with respect to enforcement; rather, it is a forum in which the two parties can meet to work out ambiguities stemming from the implementation of arms control treaties' (Davis et al, 1987: 25). Plainly, the SCC is an instrument of private ordering, there being no legal forum to which the parties would be willing to present their concerns and contest differences.

Political science and sociology
A new 'science of organization' in which all of the social sciences have a stake is in prospect. To be sure, such an aspiration goes beyond the purposes of the 1988 conference, and not all of the participants would agree that such is needed. There is at least a possibility, however, that an interdisciplinary science of organization – in

which economics, sociology and political science are all joined – is in progress. In the degree to which the term contract is congenial to economics while treaty opens the dialogue up, added benefits could result from using the broader term. Issues of power, embeddedness, bureaucracy, coalitions and the study of political institutions are all implicated.

I have examined some of the relations between economics and sociology elsewhere (Williamson, 1988). The lack of an adequate theory of bureaucracy, however, warrants further remark. And the appearance of political science on the scene deserves mention.

Bureaucracy Oskar Lange, in what is still regarded as the classic contribution to the theory of socialism, set himself the task of showing that rules could be devised whereby efficient pricing and resource allocation could be realized in a socialist economy. To be sure, some of Lange's assumptions were heroic (Kornai, 1986). But the relevant efficiency criteria can be derived and planners and managers can be asked to implement them.

Lange goes on to observe, however, that:

> [an argument] might be raised against socialism with regard to the efficiency of public officials as compared with private entrepreneurs as managers of production. Strictly speaking, these public officials must be compared with corporation managers under capitalism, and not with private small-scale entrepreneurs. The argument thus loses much of its force. The discussion of this argument belongs in the field of sociology rather than of economic theory and must therefore be dispensed with here. By doing so we do not mean, however, to deny its great importance. It seems to us, indeed, that *the real danger of socialism is that of a bureaucratization of economic life*, and not the impossibility of coping with the problem of allocation of resources. (Lange, 1938: 109; emphasis in original)

Lange thus makes three points: (1) bureaucratization is a basic problem of economic organization; (2) it needs to be assessed comparatively; and (3) this is beyond the purview of economics, belonging instead to the field of sociology. Interim progress notwithstanding, it is now fifty years later and we are still waiting. As compared with the study of markets, where an extensive literature on 'market failure' has developed, a parallel literature on 'bureaucratic failure' has not resulted from the study of internal organization. There is growing agreement that this disparity needs to be corrected. I submit that bureaucracy needs to be examined firstly in comparative institutional terms, and secondly through the lens of economizing.

The comparative institutional test is not whether internal organization experiences a bureaucratic cost of one sort or another but rather whether a *differential* cost can be shown to exist by organizing a task one way rather than another. Put differently, bureaucratic costs that attend every feasible mode of economic organization are, as a comparative institutional matter, neither here nor there. That the study of bureaucracy has languished for so long is partly because a comparative orientation has not been regularly applied.

Consider, for example, the question, 'Why can't a large firm do everything that a collection of small firms can do and more?' This is *a comparative and operational* way of addressing the ancient puzzle of: What is responsible for limitations to firm size? Whereas the latter appropriately calls attention to costs, the mere fact that large firms incur added bureaucratic costs when they grow does not suffice. Rather, the cutting edge is whether large firms incur *added* costs in comparison with the best feasible alternative, the composition of activity to be organized being held constant.[2] Adopting and insistently employing a comparative institutional test, wherein one mode is always assessed in relation to another, has been lacking but is vitally needed to ascertain the costs of bureaucracy.

Virtually everyone now agrees that economic organization is very complex and services many purposes. Considering the primitive state of our understanding, there is much to be said for working out of a 'main case framework' in which one goal is held to be salient and other goals are treated as qualifications or extensions. The pressing need of a predictive theory of organization is to focus on core features – or, as Lon Fuller put it much earlier, the need is to sort the 'essentials' from the 'tosh' (Fuller, 1978: 356). Although tastes and predilections may well vary on what qualifies as essential, I join Frank Knight (1941: 252) in his suggestion that economizing be made the main case.

But I furthermore assert that sociology, including the comparative analysis of bureaucracy to which I refer above, is pertinent to economizing assessments. The microanalytics of organization is where sociologists enjoy a comparative advantage – provided the appropriate lenses are employed.

Political science   Political scientists have displayed a longstanding interest in the study of organization. Albeit usually with reference to political and public sector organization, many of their concerns carry over into the private economic arena. But there is also a reverse flow, as political scientists have expressly taken notice of 'the new economics of organization' (Miller and Moe, 1984; Keohane, 1984; Weingast and Marshall, 1988). Among the 'political' issues to which the study of economic organization can relate with benefit are (1) coalitions, (2) alliances, (3) life cycle transformations, and (4) power. Consider these seriatim.

Coalitions may be purely instrumental (Barnard, 1938); they may also be highly strategic (Cyert and March, 1963; Williamson, 1967; Tirole, 1986). Also, coalitions can occur within firms and between firms. The factors that favour and disfavour coalitions and the associated economic consequences (benefits and costs) are greatly in need of explication.

The alliance is a hybrid form of organization that is located between coalitions and mergers in its economic properties and differs from both in political respects. As compared with coalitions, alliances are more formal, have longer projected durations, and are normally thought of as taking place between rather than within firms (although certain internal forms of co-operation might usefully be described as alliances). As compared with mergers, alliances preserve a greater degree of autonomy among the membership. (The optimal degree of autonomy and the factors on which it depends have not, however, been systematically investigated.)

Aspects of Japanese economic organization display interesting alliance properties. Indeed, Michael Gerlach characterizes the relation between firms joined in 'enterprise groups' in Japan as 'alliance capitalism' (1987). Albeit driven by commercial considerations – in which banking and, more generally, complex financing (including cross-ownership of equity) play the key roles – the successful operation of these groups also implicates politics. Thus Gerlach remarks that one of the three integrating mechanisms on which these alliances rely is 'the creation of high-level executive councils which symbolically identify group members and the boundaries of the social unit, as well as provide a forum for interaction among group firms' (1987: 128). More concerted study of alliances, in both economic and political respects, is greatly needed.

Although most studies of organization focus on immediate consequences, predictable future consequences plainly deserve to be counted in as part of the decision calculus. Allowance for life cycle effects, in the context, for example, of regulation, may be vital. Thus, if regulation is predictably given to 'creeping ancillariness,' in that it goes beyond original intent to include additional purposes and otherwise takes on a life of its own (Bernstein, 1955), and if an understanding of such process transformations requires a sensitivity to politics, then the political science point of view is essential.

Power is a term to which non-economists, especially political scientists, frequently appeal for explanation. Power, however, is an exceptionally elastic term and is often used in ways that are either tautological or confuse power outcomes with efficiency. Delimiting the uses of power reasoning and establishing when and how the concept of power adds to rather than confuses our understanding of economic organization would be major contributions. Manipulating the political process by established economic actors, thereby better to insulate themselves against new competition – by new entrants or smaller rivals (foreign or domestic) – is a common use of power for which further analysis is needed. Concerted study of the 'power of incumbency,' to include an examination of the propensity of incumbents to favour oligarchy (Michels, 1962), is needed.

2. Transaction cost economics[3]

As previously remarked, the orthodox approach to the theory of the firm is to describe it as a production function. The allocation of activity between firm and market (whether to make or buy) is thus taken as given. The firm, thus regarded, is a monad.

The contracting approach proceeds differently. A 'comparative dyadic' approach is employed instead. Whether to make or buy is thus taken as problematic. Holding the activity to be organized constant, the object is to assess the efficacy of alternative means of contracting. Interfirm contracting is well suited for some transactions; intrafirm contracting is well suited for others. Hybrid modes are superior in still others. The object is to establish which transactions go where. Posing the vertical integration issue in comparative dyadic terms represents the first step in what is hereafter referred to as transaction cost economics (Coase, 1937; Williamson, 1971).

Transaction cost economics is part of a renewal of interest in the New Institutional Economics. As recently as twenty years ago the economics of institutions was thought to be a relic living mainly in the pages of the history of economic thought. That has changed. R.C.O. Mathews asserts that the 'economics of institutions has become one of the liveliest areas in our discipline' (1986: 903). That is a remarkable transformation.

The New Institutional Economic turns on two propositions: institutions (1) matter and (2) are susceptible to analysis (Mathews,

1986: 903). Both the older and newer approaches to institutional economics are in agreement on the first of these. Where they differ is with respect to the second. Thus whereas the older institutional economics made little effort to operationalize the argument that institutions matter, the New Institutional Economics insists that reconceptualization and operationalization proceed in tandem. Indeed, but for this commitment to operationalization it is doubtful that institutional economics would have been awarded a new life.[4]

Albeit related, two branches of the New Institutional Economics – institutional environment and institutional arrangement – are usefully distinguished. Lance Davis and Douglass North, in an early and important contribution to the renewal of institutional economics, distinguish between these two as follows:

> The *institutional environment* is the set of fundamental political, social and legal ground rules that establishes the basis for production, exchange and distribution. Rules governing elections, property rights, and the right of contract are examples . . . .
> An *institutional arrangement* is an arrangement between economic units that governs the ways in which these units can cooperate and/or compete. It . . . [can] provide a structure within which its members can cooperate . . . or [it can] provide a mechanism that can effect a change in laws or property rights. (Davis and North, 1971: 6–7; emphasis in original)

Transaction cost economics is predominantly concerned with institutional arrangements, normally referred to as governance structures. Interestingly, R.C.O. Mathews treats the 'economics of institutions and the economics of transaction costs [as] . . . a single approach' (1986: 907). That is evidently because the transaction cost economics branch has developed so rapidly with applications 'to many areas: industrial organization and corporate governance; labor economics; public choice; development; and economic history' (1986: 907). The fruitfulness of studying economic organization from a comparative contractual perspective and the fact that so many issues either arise as or can be reformulated in contracting terms are responsible for this richness of applications.

Foundations

I have examined the intellectual foundations of transaction cost economics elsewhere (Williamson, 1975, 1985). As therein described, transaction cost economics is an interdisciplinary undertaking in which law, economics and organization theory are joined. Karl Llewellyn's examination of contract law (1931) – where he urged that the usual legal rules approach was narrow and even misleading and that it was more instructive to view contract as framework with emphasis on the purposes to be served – was and remains important. A purposive approach to organization theory in which bounded rationality and both formal and informal organization are featured (Barnard, 1938; Simon, 1947) likewise figures prominently in the transactions cost economics scheme of things. But it is to economics that transactions cost economics is especially indebted.

John R. Commons both ascribed economic importance to non-market institutions and proposed that the transaction be made the basic unit of analysis (1925; 1934). It was Ronald Coase (1937), however, who went to the nub. He posed two classic (and related) puzzles with which the theory of the firm must come to grips: 'What factors are responsible for the boundaries of the firm?' And 'Why is not all production carried on in one big firm?' (Coase, 1937/1952 edn: 340). Coase asserted that the answers resided in differential transaction costs between firm and market, but the underlying factors responsible for these differences remained obscure.

Also pertinent was Frank Knight's view that economizing was the main case to which economics should appeal in attempting to understand economic organization:

> Men in general, and within limits, wish to behave economically, to make their activities *and their organization* 'efficient' rather than wasteful. This fact does deserve the utmost emphasis; and an adequate definition of the science of economics . . . might well make it explicit that the main relevance of the discussion is found in its relation to social policy, assumed to be directed toward the end indicated, of increasing economic efficiency, or reducing waste. (Knight, 1941: 252; emphasis added)

But the research ramifications of these remarks were likewise unclear.

Kenneth Arrow's numerous contributions to the study of organization helped to unpack and explicate the issues. The market failure literature – including especially his probing treatment of information asymmetries and the limits of markets for information (Arrow, 1962; 1963; 1969; 1974) – provided important links. Thus Arrow observed that market failure is a more general category than externalities and it is better still to consider a 'broader category, that of transaction costs, which in general impede and in particular cases completely block the formation of markets' (1969: 48) – where transaction costs are defined as the 'costs of running the economic system' (1969: 48). Arrow, also advanced the hypothesis that non-market institutions (as well as redefinitions of property rights) often had the purpose and effect of relieving market failures (1963: 947).

Operationalization

Transaction cost economics is informed by and attempts an integrated treatment of these insights. But added content was needed. Of special importance in the effort to evolve a transaction cost economics theory of organization were (1) stating the behavioural assumptions and displaying the organizational ramifications that accrue thereto; (2) dimensionalizing transactions and displaying the differential transaction cost consequences; (3) taking the microanalytics of organization seriously, including an effort to discover the 'process consequences' of alternative forms of contract and organization; (4) featuring and developing the organizational importance of 'credible commitments'; (5) explicating the basic trade-off between markets and hierarchies; and (6) developing the implied new theory. Consider these seriatim.

Behavioural assumptions   Transactions cost economics employs two critical behavioural assumptions – bounded rationality and opportunism – both of which differ from orthodoxy.

Although it is sometimes believed that Simon's notion of bounded rationality is alien to the rationality tradition in economics, Simon actually enlarges rather than reduces the scope for rationality analysis. Thus he defines bounded rationality as behaviour that is '*intendedly* rational, but only *limitedly* so' (1947: xxiv). Both parts of the definition warrant respect. An economizing orientation is elicited by the intended rationality part of the definition, while the study of institutions is encouraged by acknowledging that cognitive competence is limited: 'It is only because individual human beings are limited in knowledge, foresight, skill, and time that organizations are useful investments for the achievement of human purpose' (Simon, 1947, p. 199).

The recent development of the theory of incomplete contracting is a concession to the infeasibility of comprehensive *ex ante* contracting. Although frequently unexpressed, bounded rationality has become the operative behavioural assumption out of which the economics of contracting increasingly works.

Transaction cost economics pairs the assumption of bounded rationality with a self-interest seeking assumption that makes allowance for guile. Specifically, economic agents are permitted to disclose information in a selective and distorted manner. Calculated efforts to mislead, disguise, obfuscate and confuse are thus admitted. This self-interest seeking attribute is variously described as opportunism, moral hazard and agency.[5]

These two behavioural assumptions – individually, but especially in combination – have profound ramifications for economic organization. Given bounded rationality, *all complex contracts are unavoidably incomplete*. Given opportunism, *contract-as-promise unsupported by credible commitments is hopelessly naive*. Taken together, the following organizational imperative obtains: organize transactions so as to economize on bounded rationality while simultaneously safeguarding transactions against the hazards of opportunism.

Dimensionalizing transactions   Transaction cost economics not only adopts John R. Commons's argument that the transaction is the basic unit of analysis but it also asks and attempts to answer the logically posterior question: What are the principal dimensions with respect to which transactions differ?

As developed elsewhere (Williamson, 1985), transaction cost economics provisionally (or preliminarily) identifies three key dimensions: asset specificity, uncertainty and frequency. Of the three, asset specificity is the most important and most distinctive.

Asset specificity has reference to the degree to which an asset can be redeployed to alternative uses and by alternative users without sacrifice of productive value.[6] The condition was noted by Alfred Marshall, in conjunction with his discussion of quasi-rents (1948: 626). And Michael Polanyi's discussion of embedded human assets (1962: 52–3) as well as Jacob Marschak's remarks about the importance of unique assets (1968: 14) are pertinent. The possibility, however, that asset specificity is a widespread condition with pervasive organizational importance went unremarked. Indeed, the quasi-rent condition to which Marshall referred played a lesser rather than a greater role as neoclassical economics progressed.

The distinction between *ex ante* bilateral monopoly and *ex post* bilateral dependency is pertinent in this connection. The first is correctly perceived to be a rare condition, on which account it was widely but incorrectly assumed that the latter condition was rare as well. As it turns out, *ex post* bilateral dependency is a common condition with pervasive organizational ramifications.

An examination of the contracting process is needed to ascertain if and why a large numbers bidding competition at the outset is transformed into a bilateral dependency condition thereafter. The presence (or not) of a non-trivial degree of asset specificity is the underlying economic factor chiefly responsible for this transformation condition. (Actually, it is more complicated. It is asset specificity in conjunction with bounded rationality, opportunism and uncertainty that poses the contractual/organizational strains.)

Displaying the complications and working out the organizational ramifications of these behavioural and transactional factors describes much of what transaction cost economics has been up to. The following 'discriminating alignment' hypothesis is a direct outgrowth of the dimensionalization exercise: align transactions (which differ in their attributes) with governance structures (which differ in their costs and competencies) in a transaction cost economizing way.[7] Repeated application of this hypothesis is responsible for much of the predictive content of the transaction cost economics agenda.

Microanalytics Transaction cost economics is more microanalytic than orthodoxy in three respects. First, and most obviously, the transaction is a more microanalytic unit of analysis. The relevant data are not the prices and output with which orthodoxy is preoccupied (Arrow, 1971: 180). Instead, much more detail about the attributes of transactions comes under scrutiny. Second, transaction cost economics maintains that organization form matters. For example, the business firm is not regarded as a neoclassical production function but it described instead as a governance structure – the internal structure, incentives and controls of which matter. Third, transaction cost economics locates many of the 'problems' of economic organization in the process transformations that attend intertemporal contracting.

To be sure, this focus on microanalytics comes at a cost, the justifications for which are sometimes questioned. Thus David Kreps and Michael Spence observe that 'if one wishes to model the behaviour of organizations such as firms, then study of the firm as an organization ought to be high on one's agenda. This study is not, strictly speaking, necessary: one can hope to divine the correct "reduced form" for the behaviour of the organization without considering the micro-forces within the organization' (1985: 374–5).

The Kreps–Spence approach thus relegates the study of microanalytics to others or, alternatively, turns on the hope that economists will be lucky. The main risks with the first of these are that those to whom the study of the details are relegated will either make the wrong observations or will report the right observations in ways that mask their economic significance. Since hoping to get lucky is even more problematic, the need for economists to take the study of organization seriously is herein suggested.

Herbert Simon's contrast between the physical sciences and economics in microanalytic respects is instructive. As he observes:

> In the physical sciences, when errors of measurement and other noise are found to be of the same order of magnitude as the phenomena under study, the response is not to try to squeeze more information out of the data by statistical means; it is instead to find techniques for observing the phenomena at a higher level of resolution. The corresponding strategy for economics is obvious: to secure new kinds of data at the micro level. (Simon, 1984: 40)

Transaction cost economics subscribes to Simon's prescription in both conceptual and empirical respects.

Both the Fundamental Transformation (which is responsible for *ex post* bilateral dependency in circumstances where transactions are supported by investments in specific assets) and the 'impossibility of selective intervention' (which is responsible for limits to vertical integration – and, more generally, for limits to firm size) are illustrations of microanalytic economic reasoning.[8]

Credible commitments   As compared with the study of credible threats, which has played a huge role in the recent industrial organization literature, the study of credible commitments has been slight. To be sure, some of Common's interests in harmonizing trade and crafting 'going concerns' can be reconstrued in credible commitment terms. But this was not the prevailing orientation. More often a spot contracting and/or legal rules approach to contract was employed.

Recall that Machiavelli advised his prince that 'a prudent ruler ought not to keep faith when by so doing it would be against his interest, and when the reasons which made him bind himself no longer exist . . . . [L]egitimate grounds [have never] failed a prince who wished to show colourable excuse for the promise' (Gauss, 1952: 92–3). But reciprocal or pre-emptive opportunism is not the only lesson to be gleaned from an awareness that human agents are not fully trustworthy. Indeed, that is a very primitive response.

The more important lesson, for the purposes of studying economic organization, is this: transactions that are subject to *ex post* opportunism will benefit if appropriate safeguards can be devised *ex ante*. Rather than reply to opportunism in kind, therefore, the wise prince is one who seeks both to give and to receive 'credible commitments'. Incentives may be realigned, and/ or superior governance structures within which to organize transactions may be devised.

Whereas credible threats are designed to *deter* rivalry, those who make credible commitments are attempting to *support* exchange. Different investments will be made, better prices will obtain, and transactions will proceed more smoothly if cost-effective credible commitments are made in support of asset-specific exchange.

Interestingly, pecuniary bonding and legal sanctions are severely limited in credible commitment respects (Williamson, 1983). The crafting of credible commitments through complex contracting (such as reciprocity) and non-market organization (such as vertical integration) arise for this reason.[9] Private ordering rather than legal centralism becomes the operative orientation.

The governance trade-off The basic trade-off that characterizes the choice between markets and hierarchies – or, more generally, between the use of rules governance and discretion – is between high-powered incentives and bilateral adaptability. Rules governance supports high-powered incentives but sacrifices adaptability. Discretionary governance (administration) reverses this relation. Which governance structure to employ where is the comparative institutional issue of interest. The issues are complicated and are developed elsewhere (Williamson, 1985; 1988).

The new theory of incomplete contracting The premises out of which transaction cost economics works have been adopted (sometimes implicitly) by the recent and growing theory of incomplete contracting. Not only would (1) incomplete contracting vanish were it not for bounded rationality, but (2) most interesting incomplete contracting problems implicate bilateral dependency, which is to say that asset specificity is present in non-trivial degree, and (3) the critical contracting issue is how to effect adaptations to changing circumstances, whence uncertainty is a key feature. Also, although the limits of contract as promise often goes unmentioned, opportunism is implicitly taken as given.

Although the formal analysis of discrete structural alternatives sometimes employs a neoclassical set-up (as in Riordan and Williamson, 1985), new solution concepts have also been proposed (as in Grossman and Hart, 1986). The very real importance of these new solution concepts notwithstanding, it is noteworthy that Grossman and Hart (and related papers of this kind) work from transaction cost economics premises – albeit with terminological differences. Thus Grossman and Hart employ the terms non-contractibility and nonverifiability rather than bounded rationality. And they refer to 'relationship-specific investments' rather than asset specificity. Unanticipated state realizations, and the need to adapt thereto, are what pose contractual strains in their model. So uncertainty makes an appearance. Only opportunism goes un-remarked, presumably because the limits of contract as promise are believed to be transparent.[10] Subsequent work by Hart and John Moore (1988) as well as the survey of the theory of contracts by Hart and Bengt Holmstrom (1987) are broadly consonant.

Useful though it is to think about economic organization from the standpoint of 'incomplete contracting in its entirety' – whereupon provision is made for both *ex ante* incentive alignment (of an incomplete kind) and *ex post* governance (to effect adaptations) – there are also limitations. The distinction between prospective changes and retrospective changes is pertinent. As John Pratt and Richard Zeckhauser argue, parties crafting a prospective agreement are engaged 'predominantly [in] a search for efficiency rather than a struggle over distribution' (1985: 18). Once agreements are struck, however, and especially if politics intrudes in the process, redistributive purposes become more salient (Pratt and Zeckhauser, 1985: 19).

To be sure, parties to a contract will make allowance for all of the pertinent hazards at the outset – including, for example, refusal to commit specialized assets if expropriation by courts or legislatures is in prospect. The fiction of efficient contracting nevertheless experiences considerable strain as the length of the contract increases and unanticipated shocks accumulate.

Thus although, as a comparative institutional matter, the parties to a long-term contract may have crafted the most efficient feasible agreement, a redistributive logic may better explain outcomes at late stages. Who wins and who loses may bear little relation to the initial agreement if a series of political, technological or economic 'surprises' intrude.[11]

3. A summary of contributions to this collection

The chapters are organized into four groups. Part I is concerned with knowledge – its acquisition, sharing, and/or asymmetry. Part II deals with vertical integration and the strategic management of the enterprise. Part III addresses issues of labour organization. And Part IV is concerned with the political structure and finance.

Masahiko Aoki, whose work on the 'co-operative game theory

of the firm' has had widespread influence, addresses related issues in his chapter, 'The Participatory Generation of Information Rents and the Theory of the Firm'. He takes as his main concern the need to develop a theory of the firm that features 'organizational co-ordination', and argues that new forms of organization are emerging that rely on the participation of workers to communicate and process information. Although these forms are commonly associated with Japanese firms, he observes that the condition is very general and is attracting a worldwide response. As compared with earlier rule-governed modes of organization, the newer modes are more discretionary and participatory. The key trade-off on which Aoki focuses entails an assessment of the added value through participatory learning and communication in relation to the sacrifice of productive efficiency through expert skill. Information rents arise in the participatory mode (as a consequence of collective firm-specific learning among the workers), and from this arises the need to craft a governance structure whereby these rents will be credibly shared between workers and owners.

Jacques Crémer likewise focuses on information sharing in his chapter, 'Common Knowledge and the Co-ordination of Economic Activities'. Crémer observes that while the contractual model of the firm has many attractions, there are also serious needs in working through the interactions among contracts. Given that agents are subject to bounded rationality, there are both benefits and costs in developing 'common knowledge'. These are difficult matters to work through, whence Crémer sets aside incentive differences. His model thus works out of the team theory tradition in which opportunism is suppressed. The trade-off on which he focuses is between accumulating more knowledge about the nature of the environment and increasing the degree of common knowledge within the firm. This trade-off naturally depends on the benefits associated with knowledge of each kind. The homogeneity of the work force, understandably, is a relevant factor.

Matti Pohjola's is the third chapter in Part I. 'Profit sharing, Information and Employment: Implications of the Utilitarian Monopoly Union Model' examines the way in which optimal profit sharing varies as a function of the distribution of information and differential risk aversion.

Michael Riordan's chapter, 'What is Vertical Integration?' contrasts vertical integration with requirements contracting. Riordan describes a requirements contract as one that involves contracting for outputs, while vertical integration involves contracting for inputs. The basic trade-off, in his formulation, is between better quantity decisions (where vertical integration has the advantage) and incentive intensity to reduce costs (where the requirements contract has the advantage). Limited ability to make credible commitments – both between and within organizations – is crucially implicated by Riordan's analysis of these contracting alternatives.

Kurt Lundren is also concerned with vertical integration, with special emphasis on technological innovation. His chapter, 'Vertical Integration, Transaction Costs, and "Learning by Using"' works out of an incomplete contracting set-up and calls attention to hybrid forms of organization. Examples of Swedish industry (ball bearings and automobile manufacture) are used to illustrate the changing relations between suppliers and buyers of intermediate product over time. A duopoly model is used to examine the complex incentive and information problems that innovation presents.

Torger Reve focuses entirely on internal organization. His treatment of 'The Firm as a Nexus of Internal and External Contracts' links recent work on the theory of the firm with the business strategy literature. Reve uses a combined economics and organizations approach to define and assess the strategic core of the enterprise and strategic alliances. The study of strategy is complicated and often undisciplined. Reve's framework helps to supply some badly needed definition. Unsurprisingly, asset specificity plays an important role in defining the core while intertemporal and interfirm economies are important to alliances.

Henry Hansmann's treatment of 'The Viability of Worker Ownership: an Economic Perspective on the Political Structure of the Firm' is the first chapter in Part III. He examines both the benefits and the costs of worker ownership. Among the latter are the costs of collective decision making. Although, with the benefit of hindsight, many will regard his main result as 'obvious', this is only because he develops the argument in such a compelling way. Hansmann argues and documents that political mechanisms within firms work well only in 'simple settings' – mainly in smaller firms with mature products and a homogeneous work force. Hansmann predicts that workers and investors who are joined in more complex settings will in the future, as they have in the past, remain separate (rather than combined) polities, each with its own interests joined by a nexus of treaties.

Kazuo Koike examines 'Intellectual Skill and the Role of Employees as Constituent Members of Large Firms in Contemporary Japan'. Japanese labour organizations being of such widespread interest, a careful examination and explication is greatly needed. Koike does this in both conceptual and empirical respects. He argues that Japanese culture is not the distinctive feature but that the development and remuneration of firm-specific skills are what distinguish employment in large Japanese firms. The combination of long-term employment with assessments and promotions are vital to the development of shop floor efficiency based on intellectual skills. Widely held views to the contrary notwithstanding, Koike interprets Japanese employment practices in individualistic rather than group terms.

Ronald Gilson and Robert Mnookin examine 'The Implicit Contract for Corporate Law Firm Associates: *Ex Post* Opportunism and *Ex Ante* Bonding'. Surprisingly, the literature on worker-managed firms usually ignores professional organizations and focuses on manufacturing. But the law firm plainly qualifies as a worker-managed enterprise. Although professional organizations are usually small (as firms go), worker management in such organizations can be complicated. A special puzzle in the law firm is the 'up-or-out' system, whereby associates in the law firm are either promoted to partnership at the end of an 'apprenticeship' period or are terminated. Why would partners and associates find such a contract in their mutual interest? Gilson and Mnookin trace the 'solution' to this puzzle to the development of firm-specific human capital and the associated need to craft credible commitments. The up-or-out system – severe as it may appear – serves credibility purposes.

Part IV begins with an emphasis on finance and moves progressively to introduce issues of organization. As it turns out, finance and organization are not independent issues but actually need to be studied jointly. Erik Berglöf's chapter deals with 'Capital Structure as a Mechanism of Control: a Comparison of Financial Systems'. He works out of an incomplete contracting framework and asks what is it that explains different debt to equity ratios in different countries. Six countries – two of which (the United States and United Kingdom) are 'market oriented', three of which (France, Japan and the Federal Republic of Germany) are 'bank oriented', and the sixth (Sweden) being 'much smaller than the others' – are included in his study. Berglöf finds that bank oriented systems have higher debt–equity ratios and ascribes this to differences in financial controls between bank and market oriented systems.

Håkan Lindgren examines 'Long-term Contracts in Financial Markets', with special reference to the operations of the Stockholms Enskilde Bank from 1900 to 1970. Lindgren discovers close networks of relationships that have lasted over long periods of time between banks and commercial enterprises. Both oral and written contracts were used. In either case, private ordering was normally employed, with appeals to the courts being rare. Minority ownership of firms by the bank was sometimes used to buttress the informal and formal contracts. Majority ownership was less common but, when it occurred, was more intrusive.

Herbert Gintis poses and investigates 'The Principle of External Accountability in Competitive Markets'. He asks what type of 'political structure' in the firm is apt to be preferred by a principal dealing with the firm as an agent, focusing especially on the principal as one who supplies finance. He shows that lenders will commonly prefer to deal with a compact leadership group rather than the diffuse membership of the entire enterprise. He also argues that if private and social valuations of bankruptcy differ, then the private preference for hierarchy may run contrary to a social preference for democracy.

Karl Ove Moene works out of a strategic game theory set-up to examine 'Union Militancy and Plant Designs'. Contrary to the standard view that threats to strike induce capital intensive methods, Moene's model shows the reverse. He then goes on to compare worker co-operatives with capitalist firms that have strike-prone workers. Again, contrary to earlier views, his analysis contradicts the proposition that the stronger the union in the capitalist firm, the more the capitalist firm resembles a worker co-operative. The basic (counter-intuitive) result is that capitalist firms 'favour' inputs that have greater bargaining power, the effect of which is to reduce that power.

The final chapter in Part IV and in the volume is by Marc Schneiberg and J. Rogers Hollingsworth, who ask 'Can Transaction Cost Economics Explain Trade Associations?' They answer that it can help in some respects but that strategic relations between the industry and the state also play a key role. Life cycle considerations also complicate the study of these matters. A more general theory of governance, in which these and other complications are taken into account, is, in their judgement, needed.

4. Concluding remarks

The neoclassical theory of the firm treats the firm as a monad. The dyad is the basic relation on which the firm as a nexus of contracts focuses. Of course this dyadic construction can be qualified and extended to make provision for interaction effects. If, however, the contracts in question are normally governed by private ordering, and if further the interactions of importance involve coalitions, alliances and the like, then the substitution of treaties for contracts is both natural and appropriate. Not only are sociology and political science invited to join the dialogue, but the continued neglect of private ordering for the study of economic organization becomes much more difficult to sustain.

This book both opens the dialogue and begins the reshaping. But work on the firm as a nexus of treaties has just begun. A fully developed theory of the firm as a nexus of treaties will require a great deal more work – at least some of which will be both inter-disciplinary and microanalytic, which is a daunting combination. Whether the follow-on work invokes the nexus of treaties imagery or not, the important thing is that work of this kind get under way. The contributions to this volume accomplish precisely that.

Notes

1. Since technologies can always be replicated, the obvious candidate for size limitations is management. But if management can intervene 'selectively', then this argument also fails (Williamson, 1985, Chapter 6).

2. This is a simplification. For a more general treatment, see Riordan and Williamson (1985).

3. This section is based on Section 2 of my paper, 'Operationalizing the New Institutional Economics: the Transaction Cost Economics Perspective' (presented at the December 1988 meeting of the American Economic Association).

4. Thomas Kuhn's examination of scientific change led him to conclude that criticism of orthodoxy does not suffice and that it takes a theory to beat (or join) a theory (1970: 77).

5. H.L.A. Hart's remarks help to put opportunism in perspective:

> Neither understanding of long-term interest, nor the strength of goodness of will . . . are shared by all men alike. All are tempted at times to prefer their own immediate interests . . . 'Sanctions' are . . . required not as the normal motive for obedience, but as a *guarantee* that those who would voluntarily obey shall not be sacrificed by those who would not. (Hart, 1961: 193; emphasis in original)

6. See Williamson (1971, 1975, 1979, 1983) and Klein, Crawford and Alchian (1978). Note that asset specificity can take several forms – site specificity, human asset specificity, physical asset specificity, and dedicated assets – and that these have different contracting ramifications (Williamson, 1985).

7. To be sure, this oversimplifies. Economizing on the sum of production costs and transaction costs is a more general statement of the hypothesis (Riordan and Williamson, 1985).

8. The first of these conditions has already been described. To repeat, trans-actions that begin as large numbers bargaining relations but thereafter become small numbers dependency conditions undergo process transformations that vitiate neoclassical market contracting. The breakdown of incentive intensity within

bureaucracies as compared with markets contributes to the impossibility of transferring a transaction from market to firm (or the reverse) without attendant costs. Selective intervention – which contemplates gain without cost – is therefore impossible. The Fundamental Transformation is elaborated in Williamson (1985: 61–3). The impossibility of selective intervention is treated in Williamson (1985, Chapter 6).

9. Aoki's work on the corporation as a co-operative game is also concerned with credible commitments.

10. The alignment of asset returns and asset ownership to which Hart (1988) refers reflects opportunism concerns.

11. The term surprise is used in the sense of Nicholas Georgescu-Roegen (1971). Although contract 'excuse doctrine' can relieve some of the redistributive strains if surprises have economic or technological origins, political surprises may be beyond the reach of the courts.

References

Alchian, Armen (1965) 'The Basis of Some Recent Advances in the Theory of Management of the Firm', *Journal of Industrial Economics*, 14 (Dec.): 30–41.

Alchian, Armen and Harold Demsetz (1972) 'Production, Information Costs, and Economic Organization', *American Economic Review*, 62: 777–95.

Aoki, Masahiko (1984) *The Cooperative Game Theory of the Firm*. London: Oxford University Press.

Arrow, Kenneth (1962) 'Economic Welfare and the Allocation of Resources for Invention', in *The Rate and Direction of Economic Activity*. Princeton: Princeton University Press.

Arrow, Kenneth (1963) 'Uncertainty and the Welfare Economics of Medical Care', *American Economic Review*, 53 (Dec.): 941–73.

Arrow, Kenneth (1969) 'The Organization of Economic Activity: Issues Pertinent to the Choice of Market versus Nonmarket Allocation', in *The Analysis and Evaluation of Public Expenditure: The PPB System, Vol. 1, US Joint Economic Committee, 91st Congress, 1st Session*, pp. 59–73. Washington, DC: US Government Printing Office.

Arrow, Kenneth (1971) *Essays in the Theory of Risk-Bearing*. Chicago: Markham.

Arrow, Kenneth (1974) *The Limits of Organization*. New York: W.W. Norton.

Arrow, Kenneth (1987) 'Reflections on the Essays', in George Feiwel (ed.) *Arrow and the Foundations of the Theory of Economic Policy*, pp. 727–34. New York: NYU Press.

Barnard, Chester (1938) *The Functions of the Executive*. Cambridge, MA: Harvard University Press.

Baumol, William (1959) *Business Behavior, Value and Growth*. New York: Macmillan.

Bernstein, Marver (1955) *Regulating Business by Independent Commission*. Princeton, NJ: Princeton University Press.

Coase, Ronald (1937) 'The Nature of the Firm', *Economica N.S.*, 4: 386–405. Reprinted in G.J. Stigler and K.E. Boulding (eds) (1952) *Readings in Price Theory*. Homewood, IL: Richard D. Irwin.

Commons, John (1925) 'Law and Economics', *Yale Law Journal*, 34: 371–82.

Commons, John (1934) *Institutional Economics*. Madison: University of Wisconsin Press.

Cyert, Richard and James March (1963) *A Behavioral Theory of the Firm*. Englewood Cliffs, NJ: Prentice-Hall.

Davis, Gerald, Robert Kahn and Mayer Zald (1987) 'Contracts, Treaties, and Joint Ventures in Organizational Theory and International Relations', unpublished manuscript.

Davis, Lance and Douglass North (1971) *Institutional Change and American Economic Growth*. Cambridge, UK: Cambridge University Press.

Fama, Eugene (1980) 'Agency Problems and the Theory of the Firm', *Journal of Political Economy*, 88: 288–307.

Fama, Eugene and Michael Jensen (1983) 'Separation of Ownership and Control', *Journal of Law and Economics*, 26: 301–26.

Fuller, Lon. (1978) 'The Forms and Limits of Adjudication', *Harvard Law Review*, 92: 353–409.

Galanter, Marc (1981) 'Justice in Many Rooms: Courts, Private Ordering, and Indigenous Law', *Journal of Legal Pluralism*, 19: 1–47.

Gauss, Christian (1952) 'Introduction' to Niccoló Machiavelli *The Prince*, pp. 7–32. New York: New American Library.

Georgescu-Roegen, Nicholas (1971) *The Entropy Law and Economic Process*. Cambridge, MA: Harvard University Press.

Gerlach, Michael (1987) 'Business Alliances and the Strategy of the Japanese Firm', *California Management Review*, 30 (Fall): 126–42.

Gordon, Jeffrey (1988) 'The Mandatory Structure of Corporate Law', unpublished manuscript.

Granovetter, Mark (1985) 'Economic Action and Social Structure: The Problem of Embeddedness', *American Journal of Sociology*, 91 (Nov.): 481–501.

Grossman, Sanford and Oliver Hart (1986) 'The Costs and Benefits of Ownership: A Theory of Vertical and Lateral Integration', *Journal of Political Economy*, 94 (Aug.): 691–719.

Hart, H.L.A. (1961) *The Concept of Law*. Oxford: Oxford University Press.

Hart, Oliver (1988) 'Incomplete Contracts and the Theory of the Firm', *Journal of Law, Economics and Organization* 4 (Spring): 119–40.

Hart, Oliver and Bengt Holmstrom (1987) 'The Theory of Contracts', in Truman Bewley (ed.) *Advances in Economic Theory*. Cambridge UK: Cambridge University Press.

Hart, Oliver and John Moore (1988) 'Property Rights and the Nature of the Firm', unpublished manuscript.

Hayek, Friedrich (1967) *Studies in Philosophy, Politics, and Economics*. London: Routledge & Kegan Paul.

Henderson, James and Richard Quandt (1980) *Microeconomic Theory*, 3rd ed. New York: McGraw-Hill.

Jensen, Michael and William Meckling (1976) 'Theory of the Firm: Managerial Behavior, Agency, Costs, and Capital Structure', *Journal of Financial Economics*, 3 (Oct.): 305–60.

Keohane, Robert (1984) *After Hegemony: Cooperation and Discord in the World Political Economy*. Princeton, NJ: Princeton University Press.

Klein, Benjamin, Robert Crawford and Armen Alchian (1978) 'Vertical Integration, Appropriable Rents, and the Competitive Contracting Process', *Journal of Law and Economics*, 21 (Oct.): 297–326.

Knight, Frank (1941) 'Review of Melville J. Herskovits's *Economic Anthropology*', *Journal of Political Economy*, 49: 247–58.

Kornai, Janos (1986) 'The Hungarian Reform Process', *Journal of Economic Literature*, 24 (Dec.): 1697–737.

Kreps, David and Michael Spence (1985) 'Modelling the Role of History in Industrial Organization and Competition', in George Feiwel (ed.) *Issues in Contemporary Microeconomics and Welfare*, pp. 340–79. London: Macmillan.

Kuhn, Thomas (1970) *The Structure of Scientific Revolutions*. Chicago: University of Chicago Press.

Lange, Oskar (1938) 'On the Economic Theory of Socialism', in Benjamin Lippincott (ed.) *On the Economic Theory of Socialism*, pp. 57–141. Minneapolis: University of Minnesota Press.

Llewellyn, Karl (1931) 'What Price Contract? An Essay in Perspective', *Yale Law Journal*, 40: 704–51.

Marris, Robin (1964) *The Economic Theory of Managerial Capitalism*. New York: Free Press.

Marschak, Jacob (1968) 'Economics of Inquiring, Communicating, Deciding', *American Economic Review*, 58: 1–18.

Marschak, Jacob and Roy Radner (1972) *The Theory of Teams*. New Haven, CT: Yale University Press.

Marshall, Alfred (1948) *Principles of Economics*, 8th edn. New York: Macmillan.

Mathews, R.C.O. (1986) 'The Economics of Institutions and the Sources of Economic Growth', *Economic Journal*, 96 (Dec.): 903–18.

Michels, Robert (1962) *Political Parties*. Glencoe, IL: The Free Press.

Miller, Gary and Terry Moe (1984) 'The New Economics of Organization', *American Political Science Review*, 78 (Nov.).

Polanyi, Michael (1962) *Personal Knowledge: Towards a Post-Critical Philosophy*. New York: Harper & Row.

Pratt, John and Richard Zeckhauser (1985) *Principals and Agents*. Boston: Harvard Business School Press.

Riordan, Michael and Oliver Williamson (1985) 'Asset Specificity and Economic Organization', *International Journal of Industrial Organization*, 3: 365–78.

Simon, Herbert (1947) *Administrative Behavior*, 2nd edn 1961. New York: Macmillan.

Simon, Herbert (1978) 'Rationality as Process and as Product of Thought', *American Economic Review*, 68 (May): 1–16.

Simon, Herbert (1984) 'On the Behavioral and Rational Foundations of Economic Dynamics', *Journal of Economic Behavior and Organization*, 5: 35–56.

Tirole, Jean (1986) 'Hierarchies and Bureaucracies: On the Role of Collusion in Organizations', *Journal of Law, Economics, and Organization*. 2 (Fall): 181–214.

Tirole, Jean (1988) *The Theory of Industrial Organization*. Cambridge MA: MIT Press.

Weingast, Barry and William Marshall (1988) 'The Industrial Organization of Congress; or, Why Legislatures, Like Firms, are Not Organized as Markets', *Journal of Political Economy*, 96 (Feb.): 132–63.

Williamson, Oliver (1964) *The Economics of Discretionary Behavior: Managerial Objectives in a Theory of the Firm*. Englewood Cliffs, NJ: Prentice Hall.

Williamson, Oliver (1967) 'The Economics of Defense Contracting: Incentives and Performance', in *Issues in Defense Economics*, pp. 217–56. New York: National Bureau of Economic Research.

Williamson, Oliver (1971) 'The Vertical Integration of Production: Market Failure Considerations', *American Economic Review*, 61: 112–23.

Williamson, Oliver (1975) *Markets and Hierarchies: Analysis and Antitrust Implications*. New York: Free Press.

Williamson, Oliver (1976) 'Franchise Bidding for Natural Monopolies – In General and With Respect to CATV', *Bell Journal of Economics*, 7 (Spring): 73–104.

Williamson, Oliver (1979) 'Transaction Cost Economics: The Governance of Contractual Relations', *Journal of Law and Economics*, 22 (Oct.): 233–61.

Williamson, Oliver (1983) 'Credible Commitments: Using Hostages to Support Exchange', *American Economic Review*, 73: 519–40.

Williamson, Oliver (1985) *The Economic Institutions of Capitalism*. New York: Free Press.

PART I

KNOWLEDGE: ITS ACQUISITION, SHARING AND/OR ASYMMETRY

2

The Participatory Generation of Information Rents and the Theory of the Firm

Masahiko Aoki

In a conference held at Yale in the spring of 1987 to celebrate the fiftieth anniversary of the publication of a seminal paper entitled 'The Nature of the Firm', its author, Ronald Coase, delivered a series of lectures about the paper's 'origin', 'meaning', and 'influence'. In his final lecture (Coase, 1988), which looked to the future, he remarked that his exposition in that article had 'weaknesses' which 'commentators that [he has] read do not seem to have detected'. He recognized that one of the main weaknesses 'stems from the use of the employer–employee relationship as the archetype of the firm' (1988: 37). He defended his exposition as adequate for his purpose fifty years ago, which was to explain the emergence of the firm in the market system. But he expressed his concern that for the further development of the theory of the firm, the way in which he presented his idea had 'led to, or encouraged, an undue emphasis on the role of the firm as a purchaser of the services of factors of production and on the choice of the contractual arrangements which it makes with them'. Indeed the prevailing state of the theory of the firm has become such that the firm is nothing but a 'nexus of contracts' (Jensen and Meckling, 1976).

As a consequence of this concentration on the contractual aspect of the firm, Coase argued, economists have tended to neglect the main activity of a firm, organizational co-ordination. The key idea in 'The Nature of the Firm' was the comparison of costs of organizational co-ordination within the firm with the costs of market transactions. But the mature Coase maintained that this is no longer adequate. In his words:

I did not investigate the factors that would make the costs of organizing lower for some firms than for others. This was quite satisfactory if the main purpose was, as mine was, to explain why there are firms. But if one is to explain the institutional structure of production in the system as a whole it is necessary to uncover the reasons why the cost of organizing particular activities differs *among firms* (1988: 47; emphasis added).

I consider the research agenda he proposed in this passage to be of great theoretical and practical significance; in this chapter I initiate my modest attempt to respond to his call.

Section 1, as an introduction, briefly describes a recent phenomenon, the emergence of a new mode of intra-organizational co-ordination which is somewhat at odds with the traditional economists' modelling of the firm as a hierarchy. This emerging mode relies more upon participatory information processing by, and the communications among, workers (shops) than does the traditional hierarchical structure, which is characterized by the specialized separation between co-ordination and operating tasks as well as among different operating tasks. As I have argued elsewhere (Aoki, 1986; 1988, Chapter 2), this emerging mode is a relatively more conspicuous feature of Japanese firms. Some authors (for example, Abegglen and Stalk, 1985) have alleged that this mode is responsible for the increasing competitiveness of Japanese firms in the ever integrative, and consequently more volatile, global markets. But I submit that the tendency towards the delegation of decision making to the lower levels of organizational hierarchies, where economically useful on-the-spot information is available, as well as the non-hierarchical communication among operating units, is becoming a more discernible phenomena on a world-wide scale, wherever conditions permit.

I speculate that the participatory mode is not just an Oriental cultural phenomenon, but that it also reflects a rational response of universal relevance by competing firms to their changing environment: increasing educational and intellectual achievements of employees and their democratic aspirations, the unprecedented development and accessibility of communication and information processing technology at the grassroots level, ever-intensifying global competition in which quick adaptation to market signals and continual introduction of innovation are becoming crucial conditions for their survival, and so on. I maintain, therefore, that a serious theoretical attempt by economists to model and analyse performance characteristics of the new emerging mode of organizational co-ordination, as well as to compare them with those of the traditional, hierarchical mode, is now overdue.

In Section 2, I analyse a model which captures a certain aspect of the new participatory mode of organizational co-ordination. The production side of the model is essentially the same as the one developed by Crémer (1980) and Geanakopolos and Milgrom (1985) and as employed in my previous work (Aoki, 1986). I incorporate the Bayesian inference theory into the model to analyse how information processing and communications at the shop level can generate value. There is a trade-off, however, between productive efficiency derived from functional specialization, on one hand, and the generation of value involving time-consuming participatory information processing, on the other. I derive a condition for the equilibrium level of investment of time in learning to maximize the net value of the firm and examine how this equilibrium value reacts to various changes in parametric values representing employees' learning capabilities and uncertainties.

What Section 2 shows is that the cost of producing a certain mix of outputs through a complex process involving interrelated activities of many shops cannot be regarded as exogenously given by a technological blueprint, but should be regarded as partly contingent on a co-ordination mode internalized within the firm. Section 3 defines the cost underrun (overrun) of the participatory mode vis-a-vis the hierarchical mode as information rents attributable to that particular co-ordination mode. Depending upon conditions of output market as well as the technological nature of the industry, information rents may be positive or negative. In any case, I emphasize that the generation of informational rents in the participatory mode of organizational co-ordination is truly *firm-specific* in that employees' information processing and communicative capacity to generate such rents is a collective one nurtured in the organizational framework and that it cannot be embodied in, nor be portable by, individual employees. Consequently its distribution cannot be written into individual contracts. In other words, the firm cannot be dissolved into a bundle of individual employment contracts. Rather it should be regarded as a co-operative venture in which the provision of capital by the owners (stockholders), of an organizational framework by management, and of information processing capacities by employees can generate rents in co-operation, the distribution of which is susceptible to intrafirm bargaining among those agents. I hope that the micro-micro (or endo-) analysis of organizational co-ordination attempted here will provide a solid foundation for the bargaining game approach to the theory of the firm.

1. The Motivation for the Study

Various recent economic and sociological studies have come to recognize that there are two major modes of work organization and inter-workshop co-ordination practised within modern firms: one traditional and the other emerging. In the traditional mode, workers are normally assigned to specific operating jobs and are expected to perform those jobs according to predetermined plans, manuals, customs, etc. Workers are not authorized to respond ad hoc to unexpected emergencies – such as malfunctions of machines, defective in-process products – beyond their job jurisdictions. These emergencies are dealt with only by corresponding specialists (e.g., repairmen, inspectors). Co-ordination among shops is a specialized task of management, which designs efficient flow of intermediate good among interrelated shops for a certain period of time, according to prior knowledge of shop floor technology as well as of external market conditions. New information may be utilized at intervals for new planning, but within a planned period uncertain exigencies are mostly dealt with by changes in precautionary buffer inventories. Learning by doing in this mode is essentially directed toward the development of specific expertise, operating and managerial.

In the emerging mode, one characteristic is a more ad hoc approach to problem solving. Job demarcation among workers is relatively fluid and ambiguous. They are encouraged to respond to uncertain emergencies autonomously within their capabilities: for example, if operating workers spot defective in-process products, they are authorized to institute necessary remedies on their own initiative – to stop a line for example. Such an approach may sacrifice economies of specialization. In uncertain environments, however, the quick utilization of economically useful on-the-spot information may generate gains unavailable in rigid adherence to a priori job assignments. Autonomous and ad hoc problem solving at the shop floor level necessitate fine tuning of prior inter-shop transaction plans. Other characteristics of this mode parallel to the quick utilization of on-the-spot information at the shop floor level, therefore, are the horizontal exchange of information regarding emergent events and the flexible, co-ordinated readjustments of planned work schedules among shops. A larger proportion of the time of operating workers may thus be diverted from direct production to information processing and communication. Learning in this mode may be directed more toward the development of information processing and communicative capacities than exclusively to the development of expert skills in specific tasks.

The hierarchy-cum-specialism feature of the first mode has been widely considered by economists to be a generic element of the firm as an alternative transaction mode to the market mechanism, and its performance characteristics have been analysed with rigour by many authors (e.g., Williamson, 1985, Chapter 9; Crémer, 1980; Geanakopolos and Milgrom, 1985). But the growing recent literature in comparative economic and sociological systems has come to recognize that Japanese firms tend to cluster more toward the second mode, while the first mode is relatively more typical of unionized Anglo-American firms: Aoki (1986; 1988), Cole (1979), Dore (1973; 1987), Koike (1984; 1987a) and Lincoln et al. (1986) may be cited as examples. Further, there are indications that the delegation of decision making to the lower levels of hierarchy, as well as various non-hierarchical modes of communication (such as the *kanban* system (to be discussed later), the matrix management system and interdisciplinary project teams) are instituted in and/or experimented with on ever larger scales elsewhere as well, with the aid of the development of communication–information processing technologies and systematic personnel development programmes.

The comparison of performance characteristics of the two modes may be performed on various dimensions. In a previous work (Aoki, 1986), I have attempted to analyse them from the perspective of 'vertical vs. horizontal' information structures of the firm. In a series of insightful works, Koike has presented the perspective of 'specialized vs. integrative skills' (see, for example, 1987a; 1987b). By the latter he means that workers' skills are not specialized in certain well defined jobs, but rather that skills for operating tasks and for coping with exigencies tend to be developed in an integrated way in the second mode. Itoh (1987) has also analysed the comparative performances of 'specialist type vs. generalist type' of information processing capacities at the shop floor level. I understand that Riordan's work (1987) is not unrelated to the issue and hints at another important dimension of comparing the two modes: 'monitoring by the supervisor vs. the autonomy of the agent (the worker) in the use of expertise'.

In this chapter, I would like to focus on yet another dimension of comparison, although not unrelated to some of the dimensions mentioned above, 'prior planning vs. ad hoc adaptation based on posterior information'. By (prior and posterior) information I refer to information about local random events affecting individual shop floor technologies (costs) rather than about global random events affecting market conditions for outputs of the firm. In fact I will argue later that these two types of uncertainties can be dealt with separately by the firm under certain conditions.

Suppose that planning of production co-ordination among shops is made by management – the central planning office – based upon its prior knowledge (that is, prior distribution) of local events, which I refer to as prior planning. Suppose that actual events may be observed only at relevant shops with certain levels of noise. The central planning office may monitor those events, but suppose that it can process and utilize this information in a consistent way only with certain time lag because of the complexity of production process. On the other hand, a shop may observe its own local events and utilize the information on the spot, but its capability to do so with increased precision also requires the investment of time in learning and mutual communication.

There are two ways of responding to the evolution of local events. In one mode – the participatory mode – prior planning only sets a general framework of reference, with respect to which implementable operating schedules may be adjusted in response to posterior information as this becomes available. The adjustment is delegated to the level where on-the-spot information is available and horizontal communications then become necessary to make such decentralized adjustments mutually consistent with the organizational goals.

In the other mode – the hierarchical mode – the centralization of information and decision making is an essential structural element. The central planning office monitors information about random events affecting productivities of shops, revises prior distributions, and utilizes them in a systematic way to calculate a rational plan for the next round of planning. Meanwhile, operations at the shop floor level are conducted according to prior planning.

The use of posterior information in the first mode as it arises and where it arises may generate certain economic value (cost savings) to the firm, which may be called information value. However, as implied already, this is not costless. Productive time at the shop floor level needs to be diverted for information processing and communication, as well as for the development of capacities for performing such activities (what Koike would call 'integrative skills'), at the sacrifice of the development and use of expert skills. The comparative efficiencies of the two modes are therefore likely to depend on various structural values defining each mode as well as on parameter values characterizing environments of firms, institutional framework for job assignments, and learning capabilities of workers. Let us therefore move on to an analysis of the comparative performance of the two modes on the basis of a simple model of prior planning vs. ad hoc adaptation.

2. The Model

Information value
The firm is composed of m technologically interrelated subunits called shops identified by index, $i = 1, \ldots, m$. There are two types of goods. One type is composed of those goods of which internal and/or external flow needs to be co-ordinated among shops or form the firm-wide perspective (for example, final outputs to be marketed, in-house intermediate goods, and in-house collective capital goods); and the other, those goods of which uses may be controlled by individual shops (for example, quasi-fixed labour assigned to a particular shop, machines, energies and materials of external sources). Suppose that there are n goods of the first type and let $x_i \in R^n$ denote a vector of the rate of production of goods of this type at the ith shop per unit time, with the usual convention that negative components indicate inputs from other shops, and positive components, outputs to other shops and/or markets (possibly there are many zero elements). The rate of net production of the firm is

$$x = \sum_i x_i, \qquad (2.1)$$

where zero components of x indicate intermediate goods transacted within the firm (the accumulation of inventories is assumed away) and its positive components indicate goods supplied to markets by the firm. Denoting a market price vector of these goods by $p \in R^n$ (components corresponding to intermediate goods may be zero), the gross revenue of the firm is given by px.

Suppose that the cost incurred by shop i per unit time to realize x_i is represented by a quadratic function:

$$C_i(x_i, u_i) = [x_i - u_i]'B_i[x_i - u_i] + \overline{C}_i \quad (i = 1, \ldots m)$$

where B_i is a positive semidefinite matrix with at least one diagonal element being strictly positive, $\overline{C}_i$ is a constant matrix, and $u_i \in R^n$ is a random vector representing cost uncertainty. The cost C_i includes expenditures for market inputs, monetary evaluation of disutility of effort expenditure by quasi-fixed labour, maintenance costs of machines, etc.; and it depends upon such uncertain factors as conditions of input markets, workers' health condition and infrequencies of machine breakdown. It is assumed that the prior distribution of u_i is multivariate normal distribution with mean vector $\bar{u}_i$ and positive definite variance matrix Σ_i, independent of other u_j's $(j \neq i)$. The inverse of Σ_i is called precision matrix.

Given a net output vector x, the expected aggregate cost

$$E[C(x, u)] = \sum_i E[C_i(x_i, u_i)], \tag{2.2}$$

where $u = (u_1, ..., u_m)$, depends upon ways in which inter-shop transactions are co-ordinated. One way is for the production planning department to specify a set of vectors $x^a = (x_1^a, ... x_m^a)$ that minimizes the expected aggregate cost (2.2) subject to (2.1) relative to the prior distribution of u. Then each shop is required to implement the prior plan;

$$x_i^a = \bar{u}_i + B_i^{-1}B[x - \sum_k \bar{u}_k] \qquad (i = 1, ..., m)$$

where

$$B = [\sum_k B_k^{-1}]^{-1}.$$

The expected cost per unit time is

$$C^a(x) = \sum_i E\{[x_i^a - u_i]'B_i[x_i^a - u_i]\} + \sum_i \bar{C}_i$$
$$= C(x) + \sum_i \text{tr}[B_i \Sigma_i],$$

where

$$\bar{C}(x) = [x - \sum_i \bar{u}_i]'B[x - \sum_i \bar{u}_i] + \sum_i \bar{C}_i$$
$$\text{tr}[B_i \Sigma_i] = E\{[u_i - \bar{u}_i]'B_i[u_i - \bar{u}_i]\}$$

Expected profit maximizing output x^* may be chosen by setting

$$\bar{p} - \bar{C}_x(x^*) = 0,$$

where $\bar{p}$ is expected price and $\bar{C}_x(x)$ is the gradient vector of $\bar{C}(x)$.

There can be an alternative way of intrafirm co-ordination in which shops learn from their experiences, communicate with each other and act accordingly. Such a process takes time, which I will model shortly. For the moment, assume that shops have attended to, and communicated with each other, information about u_i's, but they have only come to share noisy signals $\xi_i = u_i + v_i$ ($i = 1, ..., m$), where v_i is a multivariate random variable vector, representing observation and communication error. The vector v_i is assumed to be normally distributed, independently of u_i's (for all i) and v_j's (for all $j \neq i$), with mean zero and a specified precision matrix (the inverse of covariance matrix) H_i. Applying the Bayes' rule, the posterior distribution of u_i is a normal distribution with mean

$$E(u_i | \xi_i) = (I - A_i)u_i + A_i\xi_i$$

and precision matrix

$$\Sigma_i^{-1}(u_i | \xi_i) = \Sigma_i^{-1} + H_i,$$

where

$$A_i = (\Sigma_i^{-1} + H_i)^{-1}H_i.$$

Let

$$h_i = |H_i|^{1/n} \text{ and } \eta = H_i/h_i, \ |\eta| = 1.$$

Here the precision of posterior information is factored into two parts; a scalar h_i, which may be called *information processing capacity* of shop i according to H. Itoh, and a matrix η relative precision, which signifies the relative allocation of information processing capacity. The weight given to new information ξ_i, matrix A_i, is an increasing function of h_i and

$$\lim_{h_i \to o} A_i = 0 \quad \text{and} \quad \lim_{h_i \to \infty} A_i = I$$

where I is the identity matrix. To achieve a total net production x with the minimum expected total cost after information $\xi = (\xi_1, ..., \xi_m)$ is available, each shop ought to implement the following production schedule,

$$x_i^p = E(u_i | \xi_i) + B_i^{-1}B[x - \sum_k (u_k | \xi_k)] \quad (i = 1, ..., m) \quad (2.3)$$

The achieved minimum expected total cost is given by

$$C^p(x) = \mathrm{E}[C(x; u | \xi_1, ..., \xi_m)]$$

$$= \overline{C}(x) + \sum_i \{\mathrm{tr}[(I - A_i)B_i \Sigma_i] + \mathrm{tr}[A_i B\Sigma_i]\}$$

$$= C^a(x) - \sum_i \mathrm{tr}[A_i(B_i - B)\Sigma_i]. \tag{2.4}$$

(See Appendix 1). Define

$$V = \sum_i \mathrm{tr}[A_i (B_i - B)\Sigma_i],$$

which may be interpreted as the *information value*. As the information processing capacities h_i increases, A_i increases and so does V. As h_i's approach the infinity, A_i's approach to the identity matrix and

$$C^p(x) \rightarrow \overline{C}(x) + \sum_i \mathrm{tr}[B\Sigma_i].$$

Note that the information value depends only on the prior precision Σ_i's and the information processing capacity of shops h_i's, but not on the net product mix per unit time x. Given an expected price vector $\overline{p}$, therefore, the profit maximizing product mix under positive information value is proportional to that derived in the prior planning (which corresponds to the case in which $h_i = 0$), that is x^* such that $\overline{p} = \overline{C}_x(x^*)$. As far as the precision of market information remains invariant, the decision concerning net product of final outputs may be made independently of information available at the shop level. Below, we use the following simplified notation:

$$\pi^* = \overline{p}x^* - C^a(x^*),$$

Equilibrium investment in information processing
capacity
We have seen that once the level of information processing capacities of shops and their relative uses are given, the value of information is determined independently of the *rate* of net production of final outputs per unit time. But this does not mean that the net revenue of the firm within *a certain period* is also independent of the level and use of information processing capacities of the shops. They can be accumulated and used only with costs.

Suppose that the length of period for which the firm plans to accumulate information processing capacities ('learn') and use them in production is T. During this period, the market information regarding price vector p is invariant. Assume that T can be decomposed into three parts: t_1, time devoted by shops to accumulating information processing capacities (learning time), t_2 fixed time needed for communicating learning results among shops, and the remaining time $T - t_1 - t_2$, time in which shop attention can be devoted to production.

Assume that each shop has identical information processing capacity $h(0)$ initially and can develop it uniformly according to the following 'Gompertz' learning curve:

$$h(t_1) = Q\exp(-\beta e^{-kt_1})$$

where $\beta = \log Q/h(0)$. Differentiating this logarithmically, we have

$$\frac{1}{h(t_1)} \frac{dh(t_1)}{dt_1} = k\log \frac{Q}{h(t_1)} = k\beta e^{-kt_1} \qquad (2.5)$$

and

$$\lim_{t_1 \to \infty} h(t_1) = Q.$$

[5]...3 0⁴⁴⁴X₃₅₃₄ k may be identified with the efficiency rate of learning and the parameter Q with potential capability. As (2.5) indicates, the time rate of accumulation of information processing capacity gradually diminishes as learning accumulates (See Figure 2.1).

Next, let us introduce a simplifying assumption regarding the internal allocation of accumulated information processing capacities. First, factor the prior covariance matrix Σ_i into two parts, as we did for the posterior precision matrix H_i, as follows:

$$\sigma_i^2 = |\Sigma_i|^{1/r} \text{ and } s_i = \Sigma_i/\sigma_i^2, \ |s_i| = 1.$$

Assume that

$$\eta_i \equiv s_i^{-1}, \qquad (i = 1, ..., m)$$

that is, accumulated information processing capacities are utilized to enhance the posterior precision equiproportionally to the prior precision. Then, by setting

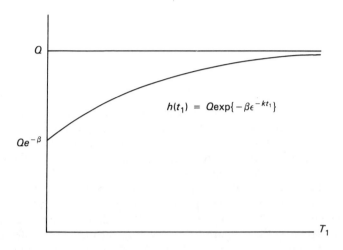

Figure 2.1 *The Gompertz Learning Curve*

$$\alpha_i(t_1) = \frac{h(t_1)}{h(t_1) + \dfrac{1}{\sigma_i^2}} \qquad (i = 1, ..., m)$$

the expression for information value can be simplified as the function of t_1 as

$$V(t_1) = \sum_i \alpha_i(t_1)\overline{V}_i, \qquad (2.6)$$

where

$$\overline{V}_i = \sigma_i^2 \text{tr}[B_i - B]s_i.$$

Net expected revenue of the firm within the period T is now written as follows:

$$R(t_1, t_2) = [T - t_1 - t_2] [\pi^* + \sum_i \alpha_i(t_1) \overline{V}_i]$$

Maximizing $R(t_1, t_2)$ requires the values of (t_1, t_2) to be set at such levels that

$$\pi^* + V(t_1^*) = [T - t_1^* - t_2^*] \sum_i \alpha_i'(t_1^*) \, \overline{V}_i \qquad (2.7)$$

$$t_2^* = \bar{t}_2,$$

if

$$[T - t_1^* - \bar{t}_2] V(t_1^*) > (t_1^* + \bar{t}_2) \, \pi^*; \qquad (2.8)$$

$$t_1^* = t_2^* = 0 \text{ otherwise.}$$

The condition (2.8) requires that the value of information is large enough relative to the rate of profit in prior planning so that the sacrifice of production time is rationalized for the sake of accumulation and use of information processing capacities. Otherwise no time should be allocated either to learning ($t_1^* = 0$) nor communication ($t_2^* = 0$), and the full period should be devoted to production according to the prior plan (2.2) with $x = x^*$.

The condition (2.7) is a usual marginal condition with respect to learning time t_1 (See Figure 2.2). Dividing through both sides by (2.6), it can be reformulated in the following economically interesting form:

$$\frac{\pi^* + V(t_1^*)}{V(t_1^*)} = [T - t_1^* - t_2^*] \, \frac{\sum_i \alpha_i'(t_1^*)\overline{V}_i}{\sum_i \alpha_i(t_1^*)\overline{V}_i}$$

that is, investment in information processing capacities should proceed up to the point where the ratio of profit to information value is equalized with the production-time elasticity of information value. Since the left-hand side is greater than one, this implies that a percentage reduction in production time must increase information value more than equiproportionally at the equilibrium.

Learning capabilities and uncertainties
How does the equilibrium rate of investment of time t_1^* for improving information processing capacities of shops change in response to shifts of parametric values of the model? In considering this problem below, we assume that $t_1^* > 0$.

First consider the effect of changes in those parameters signifying various aspects of learning capabilities. The results of comparative statics is summarized below (see Appendix 2 for proof):

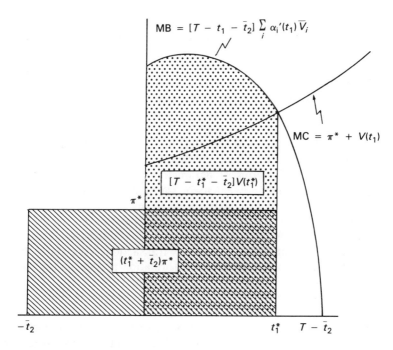

Figure 2.2 *The equilibrium investment in learning time* t_1^*

Proposition 1
- (a) $dt_1^* / dQ > 0$
- (b) $dt_1^* / dh(0) < 0$
- (c) $dt_1^* / dk \gtreqless 0$ according as $kt_1^* \gtreqless 1$
- (d) $dt_1^* / d\bar{t}_2 < 0$

Propositions (a) and (b) are intuitively obvious. Namely, the lower the initial level of information processing capacities $h(0)$ is and/or the higher the potential learning capability Q is, the more time should be allocated for learning and improving upon prior information to enhance the rate of information value. The initial capacity and the potential capability are mutually compensatory in our model in the sense that an equiproportional increase (decrease) in the value of $h(0)$ and Q will not change the equilibrium value of t_1^*.

Proposition (c) is less obvious, but in order to understand its meaning, note that the value kt_1 is equal to the time elasticity of the rate of accumulation of information processing capacity

$(1/h)(dh/dt_1)$. Therefore, (c) can be interpreted to say that, if a percentage increase in learning time enhances the rate of accumulation of information processing capacity more than equiproportionately at the equilibrium $t_1 = t_1^*$, a parametric increase in learning efficiency k should lead to decrease in learning time t_1. That is, if learning efficiency is *already* high (*yet* low) in the said sense, then a further improvement in learning efficiency ought to lead to the reduction (increase) of learning time. Unfortunately, proposition (c) involves an assumption about the equilibrium value of the endogenous value t_1. But noting that $t_1 < T$ for any positive profit, a sufficient condition for $dt_1^*/dk > 0$ can be formulated only in terms of parameters of the model. That is, if $kT < 1$, then an improvement in learning efficiency rationalizes further diversion of production time to learning.

Proposition (d) is also obvious. It says that the shorter the time required for communicating learning results and agreeing on the required adjustments of inter-shop transactions, the more time should be spent in developing the information processing capacities of the shops.

Next, let us examine the effects of changes in parameters representing uncertainties. For this, I take: (a) prior (scalar) variance σ_i^2 representing the level of prior uncertainty (ignorance) about random variable u_i ($i = 1, \ldots, m$); and (b) new parameter ϱ representing the degree of volatility of random variable u_i's from one period to the next. Suppose that the value of random variable $u_i(\tau)$ of this period and that of the next period $u_i(\tau + T)$ is expected to be correlated by the following formula:

$$\mathrm{E}\{[u_i(\tau) - \bar{u}_i]\,[u_i(\tau + T) - \bar{u}_i]\} = e^{-\varrho T}\Sigma_i(t), (i = 1, \ldots, m)$$

where ϱ is a known parameter representing the degree by which the random environment u_i 'forgets' its past history, assuming that the movement of u_i from one period to the next is susceptible to mutually independent exogenous shocks (that is, it constitutes a first order autoregressive process). Suppose that in such an environment learning in one period to improve on the precision of prior information about u_i can be utilized only in the next period of production. Then, after observing noisy signals ξ_i's in this period, in order to maximize profit in the next period shops ought to implement the following production schedule:

$$x_i(\tau + T) = (1 - \alpha_i)\bar{u}_i + \alpha_i\xi_i(\tau)$$
$$+ B_i^{-1}B\sum_k [(1 - \alpha_k)\bar{u}_k + \alpha_k\xi_k(\tau)]$$

with

$$\alpha_i = \frac{h}{h + \dfrac{1}{\sigma_i^2}} e^{-kT}. \qquad\qquad (i = 1, ..., m)$$

(Here the effect of accumulation of information processing capacity on the generation of information values beyond the next period is ignored.)

The results of comparative statics regarding σ_i^2 and ϱ are summarized as follows (See Appendix 2.2):

Proposition 2
(a) $dt_1^* / d\sigma_i^2 > 0$.
(b) $dt_1^* / d\varrho < 0$.

Proposition 2(a) dictates that, the less precise the prior information is, the more time should be devoted to learning. That is, greater uncertainty in terms of prior distribution under a stable environment warrants a higher level of learning.

Proposition (b) indicates that if the external environment is more volatile and if there is a time lag in the use of posterior information, the expected gross value of information resulting from learning will decline. The same proposition also implies that as time elapsing between the availability of posterior information and the implementation of a plan based on new information is shortened, proportionately more time may be allocated to learning.

3. Discussion

The generation of information rents

In the previous section I compared the efficiency of ad hoc adaptation based on posterior information vs. prior planning within a certain period. It is not a direct comparison between hierarchical and participatory (horizontal) co-ordinative modes. The hierarchical mode may also utilize posterior information available from shop floor experiences for the improvement of its prior planning. But the point is that such centralization of information about shop floor experiences is time-consuming and that during hierarchical communication and centralized computation, direct production needs to take place at the shop floor level according to prior planning. Let us assume that the length of a period T in the model is taken to be equal to the length of time which is required for the hierarchical mode to learn from shop floor experiences to revise its prior planning. In other words, during this period production takes place according to prior planning.

Suppose, on the other hand, that in the participatory coordinative mode, learning can occur at the shop floor level even within this period in a manner modelled in Section 2. Namely, the precision of prior distributions of random variables regarding shop floor technology is improved as shops devote more time $t_1 < T - \bar{t}_2$ to learning and the results of learning can be communicated among shops for fine tuning the prior plan by investing some fixed time, $\bar{t}_2$. Then the analysis in Section 2 may become relevant to the comparison of the two co-ordinative modes.

It is interesting to note that at least in our model the decision concerning aggregated (let us say 'global') variable x and the decisions concerning disaggregated (respectively 'local') variables x_i's can be made disjointly without losing organizational efficiency as long as the time dimension of learning about the market condition (months, say) is greater than that about shop floor conditions (days, say). This suggests that, while decisions regarding policies of organizational importance (for example, the level of aggregative outputs, diversification, and so on) may be specialized by management in processing market and other important information concerning global environments of the firm, decisions concerning work at the shop level and inter-shop transactions may be delegated to that level which attends to relevant local information, once the global framework is set by management. There is no inherent reason why organizational co-ordination must be centralized by management. On the contrary, under certain conditions the separation of global and local decisions may contribute to informational efficiency (the generation of information value).

Whether participatory learning and communication are worth the sacrifice of productive efficiency through expert skill may be assessed by condition (2.8). If the total sum of potential information value within a period (its left hand side) is greater than the productive losses due to learning and communications (its right hand side), the emerging participatory mode performs better than the traditional mode in the short run (within a period) and vice versa. We may call the difference:

$$R = [T - t_1 - \bar{t}_2] V(t_1) - (t_1 + \bar{t}_2)\pi^*$$

as *information rents*. Note that these rents depend upon, among other things, the learning capabilities of employees at the shop floor level, the initial level of precision of prior knowledge implicit in V, and the rate of market profits $\pi^* = \bar{p}x^* - \bar{C}(x^*)$ relative to the magnitude of information value V. The last factor indicates that the greater the monopolistic market power of the firm, the less the information rents. For a sufficiently large market power, information rents can well become negative and the traditional hierarchical mode based on prior planning and operating task specialization would dominate the participatory mode. This is consistent with a frequent allegation that flexible adaptation is a rational response of firms in the increasingly competitive global market environment and that the hierarchical mode of co-ordination, while having a clear advantage under the stable oligopolistic market environment which prevailed up to the early 1970s, may be in a gradually weakening position (see for example Piore and Sabel, 1984).

On the other hand, a reinterpretation of the model suggests that if the market environment becomes too volatile, economic rents from learning diminish and finally become negative (Proposition 2(b)).[1] This observation is consistent with that of Itoh (1987) who explicitly considers optimal relationships between the degree of volatility of the product market and the kinds of shop floor expertise required. He proved that it is more profitable to develop specialized skills at the shop level under a very volatile market environment, as well as a very stable one, while it is more desirable to nurture wide-ranging skills under the intermediate range of output market volatility.

Propositions 1(d) and 2(b) indicate that the shorter the time required for participatory communication, the more the relative advantage of the participatory mode would increase vis-a-vis the hierarchical mode. This suggests that cultural factors contributing to the ease of communication, such as the ethnic homogeneity of employees, the custom of dense communication among employees and so on, may affect the relative efficiency of the two modes. But as I have argued elsewhere (Aoki, 1988, Chapter 9), 'small groupism' (the development of a coherent small group) per se may not contribute to the organizational efficiency in the context of a large production system, because the coherent small group may develop its own local goal and divert its resources (such as time and information processing capacity) for the promotion of group-centric goals at the sacrifice of the organizational goals. (This problem is also discussed by Milgrom and Roberts, 1987.)

In the case of a large organization, time needed for inter-shop communication may be reduced by improvements in information methods. Such an improvement may come not only from techno-logical development in the narrower sense, but also from organiza-tional innovation as exemplified by the *kanban* system. The *kanban* system, a participatory communication method originally developed at the Toyota factory and then propagated widely to other factories, is characterized by large-scale and intricate assembly work processes. In this system, neighbouring shops are connected directly with each other through the chain-linked circula-tion of *kanban* (cards). Downstream shops in the large-scale assembly factory periodically issue order forms called *kanban* to immediate upstream shops for the delivery of parts, in-process products, etc., at specified times in specified quantities. Those *kanban* in turn are returned to the original issuers as delivery notices by supplying shops. This functions as a device for checking the implementation of processed information. The automatized and periodical chain-linked circulation of the *kanban* is known to be effective for fine tuning a prior production schedule, and the production system can generate information rents by reducing time needed for inter-shop communication and negotiations as well as reducing buffer stocks of parts and in-process inventories under continually changing output market conditions. For this reason, the method is sometimes referred to as the zero-inventory method or the just-in-time method (See Aoki, 1988, Chapter 2 for further details of the *kanban* system).

Bargainability of information rents
Given positive information rents in the participatory mode, the next interesting question is: who appropriates these rents? I would argue that their distribution is subject to collective bargaining (implicit or explicit) between the employee and the provider of finance. Note that the generation of information value, different from that of productive rents resulting from expert skills of individual employees, is truly *collective*. Its generation involves 'com-munication' of posterior information (learning results) among shops and among workers. Unless posterior information is communicated and utilized in the aggregative manner as formally expressed by (2.3), the result of learning about shop floor technology cannot be economically exploited. Although potential learning capability as

formalized by the Gompertz learning function (2.5) may be individually embodied, it can be activated within the organizational context and may lead to the generation of information value only through the filter of communication. The traditional view among economists has been that intrafirm communication is institutionalized only in the formal hierarchical structure of management, but the view which I am here trying to advance is that economically valuable on-the-spot information may be processed and communicated more efficiently in a participatory manner.

The collective nature of employees' capability to generate information rents then implies two things: one, employees' threat to collectively withhold their co-operation for information processing and mutual communications unless they are guaranteed sharing of information rents becomes credible and effective. Second, learning and communication of employees take place only within the organizational framework, their knowledge, as well as their capacities to communicate with each other are not individually portable. Therefore, the providers of the organizational framework can also threaten the withdrawal of co-operation unless they too can participate in the sharing of the rent. This is a typical bargaining situation, the consequence of which may be analysed with the aid of bargaining game theory.

In the 1980s, we have seen growing interest among economists in the bargaining game approach to the theory of the firm. One may say that there are two major streams of thought about why the bargaining game approach is appropriate for the analysis of wage determination and other behaviour of the firm; that is, why it is appropriate to consider how the employees can and do internally influence the firm's behaviour directly or implicitly rather than that the profit-maximizing entrepreneur alone can decide on the firm's behaviour subject only to market constraints.[2] The prevailing view attends to the institutional power of the union which forces the firm to bargain on wages and possibly on other variables affecting the welfare of its members. Works such as McDonald and Solow (1981), Grout (1984) and Strand (1987) may be cited as representative of this view. The other view emphasizes the firm-specificity of employees' skills, which are not transferable on the market, or can be replaced only at a cost. For this, Aoki (1984) and Shaked and Sutton (1987) may be referred to.

These two views are not necessarily incompatible, but whether or not firm-specificity is involved in the use of human resources may have quite different efficiency implications. Without it, the bargaining power of the union will disturb the allocative efficiency, if not internal efficiency between the incumbent employees and the firm owner (See McDonald and Solow, 1981 and Aoki, 1984). The first type of modelling may be more realistic when the oligopolistic firm can gain market rents based on its market power and afford to share them with the monopsonic union. But, as I have already argued, such a condition is rapidly being eroded under the intensified competition on the global scale. Instead, the employees' capacity to generate different type of rents, the information rents, is becoming an important means for the firm to gain competitive edge in such market environment.

On the other hand, the firm-specificity of an employee's skill alone may not immediately rationalize the bargaining approach. An interesting two-period contractual model by Riordan (1987), in which investment in firm-specific skill ('reliance investment', in his words) is an important ingredient, illuminates the point. In his model, investment in an employee's firm-specific skill takes place in the first period. In the second period, through the control of the use of his/her firm-specific skill, the employee appropriates information rents due to the asymmetry of information existing between him/her and the firm about random events affecting idiosyncratic technology. The firm can, however, design a two-period contract in which the firm extracts all anticipating rents from the employee in the first period. The firm is dissolvable again into a 'nexus of contracts'. In other words, bargaining is reduced to that between management and the marginal worker, and the labour market condition, perfectly competitive or monopsonic, determines the essence of the contracts. Unless there is some *collective* element involved, it may still be hard to rationalize the bargaining approach only on the concept of firm-specificity. I have argued that capacities of shops to process and communicate relevant local information and thereby generate information rents are nurtured within the organizational context and are accumulated in a collectivity. They are not dissolvable into individual pieces marketable in isolation.

Once the bargaining game approach is accepted in lieu of a single-minded profit-maximizing hypothesis, whether one should adopt the co-operative game approach or the non-co-operative game approach may not be of primary significance. Thanks to a recent development in strategic game approach (non-co-operative game approach) by Binmore, Rubinstein and Wolinsky (1986), the perfect sub-game equilibrium of a non-co-operative game played between two rational players is expected to yield a qualitatively similar outcome to the one that a neutral and fair arbiter may dictate (i.e., the Nash bargaining solution). A factor which has a crucial impact on the outcome of bargaining is instead the range of bargainable subjects. As a classic paper by Leontief (1946) showed, and as recent works by Grout (1984) and Aoki (1984) discussed in the context of the firm, if the bargainable subjects remain a partial set of entire variables affecting the well-being of employees, then the (internal) efficiency of a bargainable outcome may be lost. But is any variable other than the usual distributive variable crucial enough to be included as a bargainable subject for the efficiency of internal bargaining? The model of Section 2 suggests an answer to this question as well.

The model is devoted to the short-run analysis, that is, it is concerned only with the generation of information rents within a period. But doubtless, the accumulated information processing capacities of the shop and the employee may be utilized beyond one period subject only to depreciation due to the obsolescence of technological knowledge, human wear, and so on. Indeed Proposition 1(b) in Section 2 indicates that the accumulation of information processing capacities may save on future learning time. Then it is not straightforward to decide whether jobs of employees incorporating, and/or being trained for, information processing capacities are to be secured or not in the face of a short-run downturn in monopolistic profits. While the employees may be willing to trade off the current wage level for the utility of job security, the decline in the market rate of profit under such a circumstance may reduce the relative cost of training and learning (the right hand side of (2.8)). Thus there ought to be mutual interest between the employer and the employee, if they are rational, to include the level of employment bargainable, together with the traditional subject of wages, and to reach an agreement on a higher rate of employment than the short-run profit maximizing rule would warrant. It would contribute to an internally efficient, as well as allocatively efficient, bargain outcome, through the accumulation of economically useful information processing capacities.[3]

Because the firm is assuming aspects of an information processing institution, and as employees become indispensable resources therein, the traditional theory and practice of the firm as envisioned in the neoclassical profit maximizing paradigm seems to need more serious scrutiny.

Appendix 2.1: the derivation of (2.4)

Substituting the expression x_i^p into (2.2) and utilizing the mutual independence of u_i's $(i = 1, ..., m)$, we have

$$C^p = \overline{C}(x) + \mathrm{E}\{\sum_i [u_i - \overline{u}_i]' A_i B_i A_i [u_i - \overline{u}_i] + \sum_i v_i' A B_i A v_i$$

$$+ (\sum_i [u_i - \overline{u}_i]' A_i) B (\sum_i A_i [u_i - \overline{u}_i])$$

$$+ (\sum_i v_i' A_i) B (\sum_i v_i A_i)\}$$

$$= \overline{C}(x) + \sum_i \mathrm{tr}[A_i B_i A_i (\Sigma_i + H_i^{-1})]$$

$$+ \sum_i \mathrm{tr}[A_i B A_i (\Sigma_i + H_i^{-1})].$$

By the definition of A, we have

$$[I - A_i]\Sigma_i = A_i H_i^{-1},$$

so that

$$A_i(\Sigma_i + H_i^{-1}) = \Sigma_i. \qquad\qquad (i = 1, ..., m)$$

Hence

$$\mathrm{tr}[A_i B_i A_i (\Sigma_i + H_i^{-1})] = \mathrm{tr}[A_i B_i \Sigma_i] \qquad (i = 1, ..., m)$$

$$\mathrm{tr}[A_i B A_i (\Sigma_i + H_i^{-1})] = \mathrm{tr}[A_i B \Sigma_i] \qquad (i = 1, ..., m)$$

Substituting these relations into the above expression of C^p, we can arrive at the expression (2.4) in the main text.

Appendix 2.2: proof of propositions 1 and 2

Set

$$\mathrm{MC}(t_1) = \pi^* + \sum_i \alpha_i(t_1) \overline{V}_i,$$

$$\mathrm{MB}(t_1) = [T - t_1 - t_2^*] \sum_i \alpha_i'(t_1) \overline{V}_i,$$

where

$$\alpha_i'(t_1) = \frac{\dfrac{1}{\sigma_i^2}}{h(t) + \dfrac{1}{\sigma_i^2}} \frac{dh(t_1)}{dt_1}$$

$$= \alpha_i(t_1)[1 - \alpha_i(t_1)]k\beta e^{-kt_1}.$$

Assume $MC(0) < MB(0)$. Then, since $MC'(t_1) = \sum_i \alpha_i'(t_1)\overline{V}_i > 0$ and $MB(T - t_2^*) = 0$, there exists $t_1^* = 0$ such that $MC(t_1^*) = MB(t_1^*)$. See Figure 2. Differentiating $MC(t_1^*) = MB(t_1^*)$ logarithmically with respect to β, we have

$$\frac{1}{MB(t_1^*)} [MC'(t_1^*) - MB'(t_1^*)] \frac{dt_1^*}{d\beta} = \frac{1}{\beta}.$$

Hence $dt_1^*/d\beta > 0$. As $\beta = \log Q/H(0)$, Propositions 1(a) and (b) follow. (Below, let us omit the variable notation t_1^*.)
    Likewise,

$$\frac{dt_1}{dk} = \frac{MB}{MC' - MB'} [\frac{1}{k} - t_1].$$

Therefore $dt_1^*/dk \lessgtr 0$ according as $kt_1^* \gtreqless 0$.
    It is easy to show that

$$\frac{dt_1}{dt_2} = \frac{-MB}{[\bar{1} - t_1 - \bar{t}_2]MC' - MB'}$$

so that $dt_1^*/d\bar{t}_2 < 0$.
    For the proof of Proposition 2, we assume $\alpha_i(t) \equiv \alpha(t)$ for some $\alpha(t)$ for all t. This is only a simplifying assumption and a proof can be carried through in an essentially same way for the general case.

$$\frac{dt_1}{d\sigma_i^2} = \frac{MB}{MC' - MB'} [\frac{\alpha_i'}{\sum_k \alpha_k'\overline{V}_k} - \frac{\alpha_i}{\pi^* + \sum_k \alpha_k\overline{V}_k}] \frac{d\overline{V}_i}{d\sigma_i^2}$$

$$= \frac{MB}{MC' - MB'} \left[\frac{1}{\alpha \sum_k \overline{V}_k} - \frac{1}{\pi^* + \alpha \sum_k \overline{V}_k} \right] \alpha \mathrm{tr}[(B_i - B)s_i].$$

Hence $dt_1 / d\sigma_i^2 > 0$ at $t_1 = t_1^*$.
Finally, set

$$\alpha_i(t_1) = \tilde{\alpha}(t_1) = \frac{h}{h + \dfrac{1}{\sigma^2}} e^{-\varrho T}$$

and

$$\tilde{\alpha}_i'(t_1) = \tilde{\alpha}(t_1) \left(1 - \frac{h}{h + \dfrac{1}{\sigma^2}} \right) k\beta e^{-kt_1}$$

for all i. Differentiating the corresponding MC = MB with respect to ϱ and after suitable arrangements, we have

$$\frac{dt_1}{d\varrho} = \frac{MB}{MC' - MB'} \left[\frac{1}{MB} \tilde{\alpha} \sum_i \overline{V}_i T + \frac{1}{\tilde{\alpha}'} \frac{d\tilde{\alpha}'}{d\varrho} \right]$$

$$= \frac{-\pi^* T}{MC' - MB'}.$$

Therefore $dt_1 / d\varrho < 0$ at $t = t_1^*$.

Notes

1. Suppose that one of shops, say m, represents the sales department, using diversified products as 'inputs' and generating sales revenues as negative 'cost', while x is to be zero (i.e., no unsold product). In this interpretation the corresponding stochastic variable u represents market uncertainty.

2. In fact, the profit-maximizing *cum* perfectly-competitive-market hypothesis regarding the firm can be subsumed under the bargaining game approach as a special case. See Aoki (1984) and Shaked and Sutton (1987).

3. The relative decline of training costs in the depressed stage may also rationalize the layoffs of skilled senior workers rather than unskilled junior workers. See Carmichael (1983).

References

Abegglen, James C. and George Stalk Jr. (1985) *Kaisha, the Japanese Corporation*. New York: Basic Books.

Aoki, Masahiko (1984) *The Cooperative Game Theory of the Firm*. Oxford: Oxford University Press.

Aoki, Masahiko (1986) 'Horizontal vs. Vertical Information Structure of the Firm', *American Economic Review*, 76: 971–83.

Aoki, Masahiko (1988) *Information, Incentives and Bargaining in the Japanese Economy*, New York and Cambridge: Cambridge University Press.

Binmore, Ken, Ariel Rubinstein and Asher Wolinsky (1986) 'The Nash Bargaining Solution in Economic Modeling', *Rand Journal of Economics*, 17: 176–88.

Carmichael, Lorie (1983) 'Does Rising Productivity Explain Seniority Rules for Layoffs?' *American Economic Review*, 73: 1127–31.

Coase, Ronald (1988) 'Lecture on "The Nature of the Firm"', III: Influence', *Journal of Law, Economics, and Organization*, 4: 33–47.

Cole, Robert E. (1979) *Work, Mobility, and Participation: A Comparative Study of American and Japanese Industry*. Berkeley: University of California Press.

Crémer, Jacques (1980) 'A Partial Theory of the Optimal Organization of a Bureaucracy', *Bell Journal of Economics*, 11: 683–93.

Dore, Ronald, (1973) *British Factory–Japanese Factory: The Origin of National Diversity in Industrial Relations*. Berkeley: University of California Press.

Dore, Ronald (1987) *Taking Japan Seriously*. London: Athlone.

Geanakopolos, John and Paul Milgrom (1985) 'A Theory of Hierarchies Based on Limited Managerial Attention', unpublished manuscript.

Grout, Paul A. (1984) 'Investment and Wages in the Absence of Binding Contracts: A Nash Bargaining Approach', *Econometrica*, 52: 449–60.

Itoh, Hideshi (1987) 'Information Processing Capacities of the Firm', *Journal of the Japanese and International Economies*, 1: 299–326.

Jensen, Michael and William Meckling (1976) 'Theory of the Firm: Managerial Behavior, Agency Costs, and Capital Structure', *Journal of Financial Economics*, 3: 305–60.

Koike, Kazuo (1984) 'Skill Formation Systems in the US and Japan: A Comparative Study', in M. Aoki (ed.) *The Economic Analysis of the Japanese Firm*, pp. 47–76. Amsterdam: North-Holland.

Koike, Kazuo (1987a) 'Skill Formation Systems, A Thai–Japan Comparison', *Journal of the Japanese and International Economies*, 1: 408–40.

Koike, Kazuo (1987b) 'Human Resource Development and Labor–Management Relations', in Kozo Yamamura and Yasukichi Yasuba (eds) *The Political Economy of Japan: Volume 1, Domestic Transformation*, pp. 289–330. Stanford: Stanford University Press.

Leontief, Wassily (1946) 'The Pure Theory of Guaranteed Annual Wage Contract', *Journal of Political Economy*, 54: 392–415.

Lincoln, James, Mitsuyo Hanada and Kerry McBird (1986) 'Organizational Structures in Japanese and US Manufacturing', *Administrative Science Quarterly*, 31: 384–64.

McDonald, Ian and Robert Solow (1981) 'Wage Bargaining and Employment', *American Economic Review*, 71: 896–908.

Milgrom, Paul and John Roberts (1987) 'Bargaining Costs, Influence Costs, and the Organization of Economic Activity'. Stanford University: mimeograph.

Piore, Michael, and Charles E. Sabel (1984) *The Second Industrial Divide*. New York: Basic Books.

Riordan, Michael (1987) 'Hierarchical Control and Investment Incentives'. Stanford University: mimeograph.

Shaked, A. and John Sutton (1987) 'Involuntary Unemployment as a Perfect Equilibrium in a Bargaining Model', in Ken Binmore and Partha Dasgupta (eds) *The Economics of Bargaining*, pp. 106–20. Oxford: Basil Blackwell.

Strand, Jon (1987) 'Monopoly Unions Versus Efficient Bargaining: a Repeated Game Approach'. University of Oslo: mimeograph.

Williamson, Oliver E. (1985) *The Economic Institutions of Capitalism*. New York: Free Press.

3

Common Knowledge and the Co-ordination of Economic Activities

Jacques Crémer

I

For the last fifteen years or so, economists have studied the consequences of asymmetric information, and in organization theory the contractual framework has become the dominant paradigm. The firm is viewed as a form of generalized one principal–many agents structure. However, agents in a firm are in reality part to many contracts, or treaties: the firm is 'a nexus of treaties' rather than one large all-encompassing contract.

Two modelling methodologies can be used to approach this issue. First we can make the following mental experiment: each employee has signed a contract directly with the stockholders. But once they have signed these contracts, employees may, if there is a positive payoff, deviate by forming coalitions, that is by signing between themselves side contracts (see Tirole, 1986 and Lee, 1987). In this case the nexus of treaties is composed of the contracts signed by each of the employees with the stockholders and the contracts that they have signed between themselves in order to form coalitions. Alternatively, we can think directly of the firm as a web of contracts. In this approach, each agent signs, implicitly or explicitly, contracts with other members of the organization, and we study the existence of an equilibrium in contracts, as well as its properties.

If we choose any of these two approaches, we must study the influence of each contract on others. Employees of the firm have implicit or explicit contractual relationships with the stockholders (through their employment contracts), their supervisor, their subordinates, and some of their co-workers. These contracts interrelate at two levels. First, through incentives considerations. During contract execution, an agent's incentives in his relationships with subordinates will depend on the developments in his relationship with his superiors. Because he and his subordinates will take this into consideration when designing the contracts that link them, this will influence the type of contracts that are signed. A complete analysis of this phenomenon requires the development of a concept of 'general equilibrium in contracts', that is of a set of contracts such that no pair of contracting parties has any incentives to resign their contract. (See Crémer and Riordan, 1987, for a preliminary analysis along these lines.)

Note that this type of problem is not specific to the theory of internal organization, nor to industrial organization. In macro-economics for instance the theory of implicit contracts has studied bilateral contracts in set-ups where each agent is party to only one contract, but, in reality, a firm is involved in contractual relation-ships with its labour force, its suppliers and its customers, and these contracts will influence each other.

Although there is much interesting analysis to be carried out on these topics, the focus of this chapter will be different. I will not study the interrelationships between contracts linked to incentives considerations, but rather the interrelationships linked to the presence of bounded rationality. A familiar example of this inter-relationship can be found in the literature in the discussion of coding (Arrow, 1974; Williamson, 1975). In a complex organiza-tion, a number of specialized terms are used to describe specific objects, rules or facts. Names of buildings are an obvious example. I do not know of any formal analysis of the concept, but the basic idea is clear. The fact that only one word is necessary to describe a complex reality makes communications cheaper. Although this point is not usually made explicitly, coding can only be important if each agent has regular communications with many different interlocutors in the organization, for otherwise there could be no benefit in developing a firm-wide code.

In a previous paper (Crémer, 1987), I have argued that, more generally, certain common ways of 'doing things' have efficiency inducing properties for organizations. For instance, the presence of rules that describe the type of relationships that individuals, acting on behalf of the organization, should have with customers will enable each employee to predict better the actions of other members of the organization, and will therefore improve co-ordination.[1] The presence of these common ways of doing things can improve incentives. For instance, they provide well understood rules for the games that agents of different services play against each other. They also help economize on bounded rationality. This has led me to define corporate culture as 'the stock of knowledge that is common to a substantial portion of the employees of the firm, but not to the general population from which they are drawn', and to show that such a common knowledge will ease the computations and communications within the organization.

In this chapter, I will explore the possibility of modelling this common knowledge. I will abstract from any incentive consideration, and furthermore assume away communications between the members of the organization, by using a straightforward team theoretical framework. Agents will make observations relevant to the decisions that they have to take, and the problem here will be to study the trade-offs faced by a firm between accumulating a diversified knowledge about the environment and providing common ground for decisions. The next section discusses in more detail the notion of common knowledge and the difficulties associated with its modelization. Section III studies a formal model and some of its consequences. In Section IV, I turn my attention to the random interactions between agents in a firm and discuss their importance, while Section V develops a model of common knowledge in this set-up. Finally, Section VI discusses some paths for future research.

II Common knowledge in a fixed group

This section will discuss the concept of common knowledge by focusing attention on a fixed group of agents who meet repeatedly and take decisions with imperfect information. Because I am neglecting incentive questions, each agent tries in good faith to maximize some social utility function. However, because the payoff to the organization as a whole depends on individual decisions in a non-additive way, the optimal decision for one agent will in general depend on the way in which the other members of the organization take their decisions. For instance, a salesman takes decisions on the type of orders to accept while, at the same time, a production manager takes decisions that will affect his ability to meet these orders. The strategy that the salesman should follow will depend on the way in which the production manager takes decisions, even if it cannot depend on the actual decisions, which may be unobservable.

This interdependence of payoffs would create no difficulty in a world where agents could communicate without cost, or alternatively could collect perfect information about the environment faced by others. When this is not the case, the agents must choose, or the organization must choose for them, decision rules based on the imperfect information that they possess. In this chapter, where I ignore incentive considerations, this defines a team theoretical model (see Marschak and Radner, 1972, for a classic and very complete survey).

This section reviews the importance of a set of commonly known facts in an organization. It turns out to be convenient to decompose this knowledge into three parts: first, a common knowledge of 'hard facts', that is of facts as usually understood in common language, secondly a common knowledge of, and adherence to, a number of rules, and finally knowledge of a language, or coding. What we call culture in ordinary language is composed in part, but certainly not exclusively, of such knowledge and if societies have found it efficient to develop such common knowledge, it seems reasonable to assume that we can also find it in organizations.

General description

Knowledge of facts   In the rubric of hard facts I put two types of information: first, information about the physical environment in which the organization is functioning, location of plants and offices, physical processes of production, telephone codes, and information about society at large. Each of the members of the organization can only know a limited number of the facts that it would be useful to know. The organization must decide what facts it would like each of its members to learn. In general, it will be profitable for the sets of facts with which the different members of the organization are knowledgeable to overlap. This will take two forms.

Knowledge of same facts   Agents who work together and communicate regularly will naturally acquire some overlap in their information about the environment. As they discuss and come to joint decisions they communicate new facts to their partners and in the process acquire some knowledge that these partners possess. Once this information has been shared, it facilitates future common decisions, as information need not be retransmitted. In some cases, agents can even economize totally on communications, as they can predict each other's action because they have most of the relevant information on hand. Given this efficiency inducing property of common knowledge of facts, organizations will not wait for its spontaneous appearance, and will systematically promote a common basis of knowledge. Indeed, part of the orientation to which firms subject employees is actually spent teaching them facts which are generally known within the organization.

An example of this phenomenon can be found in armies where field officers receive a rather standardized training, and where the schooling of the future elite is generally concentrated in one school. Of course, given the similarity of the positions held by these officers, there exists a normal overlap in their training, but the rigidity of the requirements goes far beyond this. This common training also teaches each officer what the other officers know. It enables them to communicate efficiently without undue repetition and also to predict the reactions of others to the changes in the environment, which can be important in battle when communications are hindered.

Same knowledge of facts There is another interesting facet of this common knowledge of fact: members of an organization will often acquire the same information about a particular phenomenon. For instance, some decisions must be based, at least in part, on a forecast of the future of the economy. This is the case not only in firms, but also in governments, for instance in the determination of national budgets. A priori, one might think that it would make sense to ask the different divisions of a firm, or committees of Congress, to use different forecasting services, so that if one of these services is off the mark only part of the firm will suffer. In reality, of course, firms and also governments choose an official forecast on which all decisions will be based. This is clearly done to improve the co-ordination of actions.

Knowledge of rules Employees must know the rules they must follow (remember, we are neglecting incentive considerations, knowing a rule and following it are synonymous). But we can go further: first, many of the rules that different agents must follow are similar; second, agents know which of the rules that they themselves follow are common to much of the organization and which are specific to their position. This common knowledge of rules has an important role in co-ordinating the actions of the agents. First, it allows each agent to predict well the actions of the other agents, and therefore to take actions that will mesh well with theirs. Second, it provides for easier communications as each agent knows the constraints under which the others act, and therefore can choose precisely the information that they should receive. Co-ordination is improved if the agents know the rules followed by others. The communality of rules is an instrument by which agents limited by bounded rationality can acquire this knowledge at reasonable cost. Rules are implemented in part in order to make the acquisition of knowledge about the functioning of the organization easier.

Knowledge of language The last element of the common knowledge that we can find in organizations is knowledge of a common language. This has been extensively discussed in the literature under the name of 'coding', as mentioned earlier.

Importance of communality of knowledge

After this brief survey, it may be worthwhile to reflect on the precise meaning of 'common knowledge'. This concept has been extensively explored in the recent theoretical literature, which describes precisely the idea that I know, and I know that you know, and I know that you know that I know, and so on. For our present purposes, it suffices to note that the efficiency inducing properties of common knowledge will be larger if agents also know that it is common. This is clear for codes: a code will be used only if the speaker knows that his audience knows it. But consider rules. We have argued that they enable agents to predict better the actions of others, and to focus communications more precisely. But this co-ordination and this communication will be all the more efficient if both agents understand what the other agents know. Indeed the actions of the other agents become more understandable, and each of them can limit the facts that he communicates. Similarly, if an agent knows the facts that others know he will not restate them when communicating with them.

Trade-offs between communality and extent of knowledge

From the point of view of the organization, there is a trade-off between the extent of knowledge in the organization and the possession of a vast store of common knowledge that will facilitate co-ordination of actions, and Sections III and V will present some formal models designed to explore this issue. The general story line is simple. We model the bounded rationality of agents by assuming that they can only know a given number of facts. Then, we may want to have each agent know a different set of facts, so as to maximize the total amount of knowledge embedded in the organization. On the other hand, this will create difficulties of co-ordination. A trade-off has to be accepted. We would expect that firms who face very uncertain environments, and for whom co-ordination of activities is less important, would put less stress on the development of a common culture.

Another set of issues, which will not be studied formally here, arises upon consideration of the trade-offs between the different forms of common knowledge just described. For instance, if a varied knowledge is important, the firm might impose very strict and simple rules, which would translate into economical but rigid co-ordination, in order to liberate the bounded rationality of the agents so that they can learn more different facts about the environment.

Consequences for the behaviour of firms

From the discussion above, it is clear that corporate culture has something of the nature of job-specific human capital. But, only that part of job-specific human capital common to a substantial proportion of the members of the organization belongs to the corporate culture. If my analysis is correct, the firm has a substantial investment in its corporate culture, the total amount of time spent by its employees learning facts, rules and codes that constitute it. If the culture is adapted to a certain strategy, that strategy will be costly to change. Expansion of the activities of the firm and diversification will be easier in directions which are consistent with existing culture. For instance, if the culture is heavily oriented toward a large set of common knowledge, with extensive rules to know and follow, diversification in industries that require much attention to the different demands of many outside agents will be costly. Much more work is needed before these insights can be made totally clear, but following this research path may help describe in standard economic terminology such phenomena as the competence of firms in specific activities. We might also be able to make more precise statements on the limits to diversification of firms. The recent contractions and refocusing of a number of conglomerates cast doubt on the thesis that the central office can allocate capital efficiently among many different industries. The industries in the portfolio should be chosen in such a way that the same culture can, without too great a loss of efficiency, be used throughout the activities of the firm.

In the next section I will also argue that the amount of common knowledge within the firm influences both the randomness of output and the 'forecasting errors' of the firm. A firm which spends much of the energy of its employees on internal matters will have less information about its environment and will therefore miss the mark more often (this is compensated by smaller costs). In the next section I show that we can also expect it to have greater variance of output.

III A model of common knowledge

The model

Decisions and payoffs We construct a simple team theoretical model in which each of two agents is in charge of a decision. The decision taken by agent i is the value, a real number x_i, of some parameter. In a first step, we focus our attention on symmetrical functions, more general quadratic cases will be considered below, so that the payoff to the team composed of agents 1 and 2 is:

$$A(x_1 + x_2) - \frac{B}{2}(x_1 + x_2)^2 - \frac{C}{2}(x_1 - x_2)^2. \tag{3.1}$$

As usual in term theoretical models, there is no allocation of the payoffs between the two players, each of whom is interested only in maximizing the welfare of the team.

The payoff function described by (3.1) can be thought of as an approximation: it is the result of the Taylor's expansion of a payoff function f such that, for all (x_1, x_2), $f(x_1, x_2)$ is equal to $f(x_2, x_1)$. If the expansion is around some $\bar{x} = (\bar{x}_1, \bar{x}_2)$, B is equal to $-(f''_{11}(\bar{x}) + f''_{12}(\bar{x}))/2$ and C is equal to $(f''_{12}(\bar{x}) - f''_{11}(\bar{x}))/2$. (For a discussion of the difficulties created by such approximations see the discussion between Malcomson, 1978, and Weitzman, 1978.)

To develop intuition about the interpretation of our parameters, think of x_i as the output of the 'shop' directed by agent i. If the co-ordination problem for the two agents consisted only in finding the optimal aggregate level of output, C would be equal to zero. On the other hand, when there are benefits to co-ordinating the levels of output C becomes positive. B cannot be equal to zero, because the optimal output would be in general unbounded, but if it is small in comparison to C, an error in the level of aggregate output will have minor consequences compared to a deviation of x_1 from x_2.

Uncertainty will be represented by the ignorance of the agents of the parameter A at the time at which they take decisions. Our problem will be to determine the optimal information that they should collect about this parameter. On the other hand, as is standard in team theoretical problems, the quadratic parameters B and C are known with certainty. Finally, without loss of generality, we assume that the mean of A is equal to zero.

Observations We want to determine endogenously the information which it will be optimal for the agents to collect. To do so, we assume that there is a large pool of observable variables η, each equal to $A + \epsilon$, where the ϵ's are independent from each other and from A. We also assume that all the random variables ϵ are identically distributed, so that our only problem will be to determine whether the agents should observe the same or different information. In future work, it may be of some interest to relax this hypothesis to determine whether the value of more precise information changes in organizations with more common knowledge.

We assume that each of our two agents can observe only one η, and that he bases his choice of action only on the basis of this observation. In particular, there is no transmission of information between the two agents. A few words are in order to defend these hypotheses. First, if we grant the fact that individuals do have limits on the amount of information that they can gather, because unearthing the information is costly, the reader will accept the simplification that an agent can observe only one such variable as a useful theoretical short cut. In future work, I plan to let the agents be able to observe many variables. Then we will be able to ask questions of the type: 'what proportion of the information used by an agent is common?'.

I find it more difficult to accept the hypothesis that the agents cannot communicate with each other. After all η is, in our model, but a number. An agent should be able at low cost to transmit this number to another agent, and if this were impossible he could certainly transmit his planned production x_i. To understand what is happening, think about the real phenomenon that we are trying to model. In most organizations agents make a very large number of decisions so we would have to represent x_i as a very large vector. Furthermore, summary statistics of the components of x_i can be of little use in order to help co-ordination. I need to know whether you will have use for the foundry facility at this specific time, or whether the engineers will tomorrow be busy on one of your projects. In such complex environments, communications become very costly. It would be more desirable to model directly the process by which such interrelated decisions are taken, but I feel that in a first approach to our problem, we are justified in making the extreme assumption of no communication.

Finally, for technical reasons, we assume that A and the ϵ's are all normally distributed, with means $\overline{A}$ and 0 and variances σ_A^2 and σ_ϵ^2, respectively. This implies that η will also be normally distributed and, more importantly for our purposes, that, conditional on a given value of η, A will also be normally distributed, with the mean of this conditional distribution a linear function of η.

The problem of the organization   The organizational problem faced by the firm is the following. It must tell each of the agents which observation it should make (which η it should observe), and the decision that it should take given his observation of η. The function that links the observation to the decision will not be the same when the observation has been common to the two agents and when it has not. So the organizational problem must be solved in the following way. For each possible pattern of organization, the management of the firm computes the optimal decision rules for each of the agents, and the associated (expected) payoffs. Then it chooses the pattern which yields the higher payoff.

In this framework, we first want to determine under which conditions it will be optimal to instruct the agents to observe the same η. Furthermore, we will study the difference in the response of the firm to changes in its environment induced by different modes of organization.

Comparison with standard team theoretical models   The model studied in this chapter is a very special case of the model studied by Marschak and Radner (1972): we have fewer agents, and a very specific specification of the uncertainty. On the other hand, the results that we present on the comparison of information structure are, to the best of my knowledge, new. After presenting their general model, and some interesting and useful general results which are mostly concerned with technical problems in the computation of solutions, they compare some information structures in a special case that is different from ours. Basically, they assume that the linear term in (3.1) is of the form $A_1 x_1 + A_2 x_2$, where the random variables A_i are independent. Then, they assume that the observations of the agents are also independent.

Notwithstanding the differences in the assumptions, my technique of analysis follows theirs, and I ask the same questions, although my interpretation has a different focus and my description of the accumulation of information is more explicit.

Analysis
We first study the optimal decision rules under undifferentiated information and then turn our attention to the case of differentiated information.

Undifferentiated information With undifferentiated information, each of the agents observes the same η. A decision rule associates to a common η decisions $x_1(\eta)$ and $x_2(\eta)$. The problem of organizational design consists in identifying these functions that maximize:

$$E_{A,\eta}\left[A(x_1(\eta) + x_2(\eta)) - \frac{B}{2}(x_1(\eta) + x_2(\eta))^2 - \frac{C}{2}(x_1(\eta) - x_2(\eta))^2\right]$$

For every η, the derivatives of this function, with respect of $x_1(\eta)$ and $x_2(\eta)$ must be equal to zero, and we get, for all η:

$$E_{A|\eta}[A - B(x_1(\eta) + x_2(\eta)) - C(x_1(\eta) - x_2(\eta))] = 0$$

$$E_{A|\eta}[A - B(x_1(\eta) + x_2(\eta)) + C(x_1(\eta))] = 0$$

This implies that $x_i(\eta)$ is a linear function of $E[A|\eta]$ for $i = 1,2$. By our normality assumptions, $E[A|\eta]$ is a linear function of η, and therefore so are the $x_i(\eta)$'s.

Let therefore $x_i(\eta)$ be equal to $\lambda\eta$ (it is clear that $x_1(\eta)$ and $x_2(\eta)$ must be equal to each other, and that $x_i(0)$ must be equal to 0). Substituting in (3.1), we get a payoff of:

$$E_{A,\eta}[2A\lambda\eta - 2B\lambda^2\eta^2] = E_{A,\epsilon}[2\lambda A(A + \epsilon) - 2B\lambda^2(A^2 + 2\epsilon A + \epsilon^2)]$$

$$= 2\lambda\sigma_A^2 - 2B(\sigma_A^2 + \sigma_\epsilon^2)\lambda^2.$$

We maximize this last expression with respect to λ, and get a payoff of

$$\frac{\sigma_A^4}{2B(\sigma_A^2 + \sigma_\epsilon^2)}.$$

Differentiated information Turn now to the case of differentiated information. Agent i observes η_i. In the same manner as above, it is possible to show that the optimal decision rule is linear, and $x_i(\eta_i)$, the decision of agent i when he observes $\eta_i = A + \epsilon^i$, is therefore equal to $\lambda\eta_i$ (again, the symmetry of the decision rules, and the fact that $x_i(0)$ is equal to 0, can easily be proven). The payoff becomes:

$$E_{A,\epsilon^1,\epsilon^2}[A\lambda(2A + \epsilon^1 + \epsilon^2) - \frac{B}{2}\lambda^2(2A + \epsilon^1 + \epsilon^2)^2$$

$$- \frac{C}{2}\lambda^2(\epsilon^1 - \epsilon^2)^2] = 2\sigma_A^2\lambda - \lambda^2(2B\sigma_A^2 + \sigma_\epsilon^2(B + C)).$$

The maximum payoff is

$$\frac{\sigma_A^4}{2B\sigma_A^2 + \sigma_\epsilon^2(B + C)}.$$

Comparisons of information structures
Comparing the two payoffs above we get:

> *Proposition 1. Undifferentiated information dominates differentiated information if and only if C is strictly greater than B.*

Under differentiated information, the two agents observe different η_i, therefore it is more difficult to co-ordinate their decisions. This is optimal when the importance of co-ordination is relatively small compared to the importance of an accurate aggregate decision, that is when C is smaller than B.

We can gain some more insight by comparing the optimal values of λ under the two possible organizations. With undifferentiated information the optimal value of λ is

$$\frac{\sigma_A^2}{2B(\sigma_A^2 + \sigma_\epsilon^2)},$$

whereas under differentiated information it is

$$\frac{\sigma_A^2}{2B\sigma_A^2 + \sigma_\epsilon^2(B + C)}.$$

The optimal organization will allow the choice of the greatest optimal λ. Whatever the organizational form, λ is chosen smaller than would be optimal were there no error in observations (i.e. if σ_ϵ^2 were equal to 0). The imperfect information about the environment induces the firm to restrain its reaction to observed changes. Under differentiated information, when co-ordination is important (relatively greater C), each agent will react relatively little to changes in his observations (small λ), in order to make sure that the two x_i's will not be too different. But then, it becomes better to restrict the amount of information available to the organization by having the two agents observe the same variable, and letting them react more strongly to observed changes in the environment.

It is also of some interest to study the errors in production level associated with the two modes of organization. The optimal aggregate production, with perfect information, would be A/B. Under undifferentiated information, the aggregate production is $2\lambda\eta$, that is

$$\frac{\sigma_A^2}{B(\sigma_A^2 + \sigma_\epsilon^2)} (A + \epsilon),$$

a normal random variable of mean 0 and variance

$$\frac{\sigma_A^2}{B^2(\sigma_A^2 + \sigma_\epsilon^2)}.$$

The error made by the firm is the difference of these two productions, a normally distributed random variable of mean zero and variance

$$\frac{\sigma_A^2 \sigma_\epsilon^2}{B^2(\sigma_A^2 + \sigma_\epsilon^2)}.$$

Similarly, with differentiated information the production and the error have means zero and respective variances

$$2 \frac{\sigma_A^4}{2B\sigma_A^2 + \sigma_\epsilon^2(B + C)^2} (\sigma_A^2 + \sigma_\epsilon^2)$$

and

$$\sigma_A^2 \sigma_\epsilon^2 \frac{2B^2\sigma_A^2 + \sigma_\epsilon^2(B + C)^2}{B^2[2B\sigma_A^2 + \sigma_\epsilon^2(B + C)]^2}.$$

Intuitively, one expects that the variance of error would be greater with undifferentiated information, as the firm uses less information. The variance of production should also be greater because there is less risk in choosing a large λ and obtaining an overwhelmingly large $(x_1 - x_2)^2$. Actually, depending on the relative values of B and C and of σ_A^2 and σ_ϵ^2, we can get any ranking of these variances, but for the most interesting cases, when the benefits of one form of organization do not totally overwhelm the benefits of the other,[2] the intuition is confirmed. More precisely, we get:

> *Proposition 2. The variance of production is greater under undifferentiated information if (but not only if) σ_A^2 is greater than or equal to $\frac{\sqrt{2}}{2}\sigma_\epsilon^2$ or if C is greater than or equal to $\frac{\sqrt{3}}{3}B$.*

> *Proposition 3. The variance of the error in aggregate production is greater under undifferentiated than under differentiated information if (but not only if) B is greater than $\frac{\sqrt{3}}{3}C$ or if σ_ϵ^2 is smaller than σ_A^2 and B is greater than $\frac{\sqrt{5}}{5}C$.*

Extensions

Agent-specific errors in observation The model that we have presented above assumes that if the two agents observe the same variable, they will read the same number. In reality, problems in interpretation often lead agents who observe the same data to draw different conclusions. In our set-up, we can represent this by assuming that when agent i observes the variable $A + \epsilon$, he actually reads, and bases his decision on $A + \epsilon + \delta_i$, where the δ_i's are again normally distributed, of mean zero and variance σ_δ^2. We then have $x_i = \lambda(A + \epsilon + \delta_i)$, and the decisions of the agents can be different even when they observe the same variable. It is easy to show that Proposition 1 is still valid under this assumption, although the payoffs do change.[3]

Arbitrary number of agents Assume that the number of agents is n and that the payoff function is:

$$A \sum_{i=1}^{n} x_i - \frac{B}{2}\left(\sum_{i=1}^{n} x_i\right)^2 - \frac{C}{2}\sum_{i=1}^{n}(x_i - \bar{x})^2,$$

where $\bar{x}$ is the mean of the x_i's, $\sum_{i=1}^{n} x_i/n$. It is easy to show that Proposition 1 still holds, and actually one can show that the payoffs are the same.

Non-symmetrical payoff functions Finally, let us study the consequences of introducing asymmetry in the payoff function. We will see that asymmetries generally increase in the chances of finding optimal the undifferentiated information organization. The focal symmetrical case that we have used is the less favourable to the defence of the benefits of common knowledge. We use the following payoff function:

$$v_1 A x_1 + v_2 A x_2 - \frac{D_{11}}{2}x_1^2 - \frac{D_{22}}{2}x_2^2 - D_{12}x_1 x_2.$$

The variables ν_1 and ν_2 represent the relative weight of the decisions made by the two agents. As above, we assume that A is the only source of uncertainty in the payoff, and the technology of information acquisition does not change. The symmetrical case considered above corresponds to the case $D_{11} = D_{22} = B + C$ and $D_{12} = B - C$.

Going through the same exercise as above, but making sure to consider the possibility that the λ's are different, we obtain the following maximum payoff for the undifferentiated case:[4]

$$\frac{\sigma_A^4[\nu_1^2 D_{22} + \nu_2^2 D_{11} - 2\nu_1\nu_2 D_{12}]}{2(D_{11}D_{22} - D_{12}^2)(\sigma_A^2 + \sigma_\epsilon^2)}.$$

The payoff in the differentiated information case is:[5]

$$\frac{\sigma_A^4[(\nu_1^2 D_{22} + \nu_2^2 D_{11})(\sigma_A^2 + \sigma_\epsilon^2) - 2\nu_1\nu_2 D_{12}\sigma_A^2]}{2[D_{11}D_{22}(\sigma_A^2 + \sigma_\epsilon^2)^2 - D_{12}^2\sigma_A^4]}.$$

The proof of the following proposition is then straightforward:

Proposition 4.   a) if D_{12} is equal to zero the payoffs associated with the differentiated and undifferentiated information structures are equal.

b) if D_{12} is negative, the payoff associated with the undifferentiated information structure is greater.

c) For D_{12} small enough and positive, the payoff associated with the differentiated information structure is greater.

d) For ν_1/ν_2 different enough from 1, the payoff associated with the undifferentiated information structure is greater.

When D_{12} is negative the undifferentiated organization structure is better, the payoffs are equal when it is equal to zero, and for small positive values of D_{12}, the differentiated structure becomes optimal. However, as D_{12} continues to increase, the undifferentiated structure regains the advantage if the two ν_i's are different enough from each other. This last point is interesting and not obvious a priori from the economics of the problem. As ν_1 becomes large compared to ν_2, we want to allow agent 1 to make large adjustments in response to the information that he receives without worrying about co-ordination with agent 2. In order to do this, we restrict agent 2's information in such a way that he can predict well what agent 1 will do, even though the additional information that he could get is of quality equal to that of agent 1.

In the symmetrical case studied above, part (d) of Proposition 4 does not play any role as v_1 and v_2 are equal. The introduction of the asymmetry introduces some new cases when D_{12} (which corresponds to $B - C$) is positive and the undifferentiated information structure is better.

IV Random meetings and the theory of the firm

The importance of non-hierarchical communications

Most of our models of organization focus on hierarchical relationships, whether we are studying incentives or communications. Because incentives are set by one's hierarchical superior, this focus seems a priori perfectly appropriate for their study. On the other hand many, if not most, communications in organizations are not conducted along hierarchical lines. For instance, a foreman does not order parts from a purchasing clerk through their joint hierarchical superior. One can also find some academic evidence of the importance of these lateral communications (see Burns, 1954, and Mulder, 1960, both cited in Gutzkow, 1965).

For very automatic types of communications, this non-hierarchical transmission of information is largely irrelevant. We can imagine that a piece of paper on which the information has been written transits through the office of the hierarchical superior. This would be the case for instance if our foreman orders an item which he knows to be in stock. If we consider less automatic forms of communication or joint decision making, the situation becomes somewhat more complicated. For instance, take the case where the foreman must handle a production problem and one of the alternatives would require ordering some specialized inputs. Consider his call to the purchasing department to ask if the order can be ready within a week. In most cases, joint superiors of the two agents will never even be aware of the transaction, and cannot be involved in more than exceptional cases, given the limits on their time and on their bounded rationality. This creates problems of incentives, such as the determination of the optimal number of checks on the work of agents, which have not been fully treated in the literature, and deserve more attention.

Interesting questions also arise when we keep our focus on our cognitive framework. For one thing, there are many more possible partners in an organization where agents have lateral relationships than in a strictly hierarchical organization. This imposes a greater load on the bounded rationality of agents if they must adapt their mode of behaviour to every one of them. If the web of relationships is dense enough there will also be a strong tendency to develop common modes of behaviour throughout the whole firm.

Flexibility of channels
Another important facet of many organizations is the flexibility of channels of communications. Agents have a core of permanent contacts but also have a very large net of potential interlocutors. Furthermore, even the identity of the permanent contacts changes regularly because of job turnover, promotions and resignations. Agents must be ready to communicate and co-ordinate their decisions with a very large number of colleagues. The communality of knowledge becomes even more important than discussed in Sections II and III. Take coding for instance. It is imperative that a common language be known in the entire organization so that agents newly put in contact with each other can communicate effectively. Common decision rules and knowledge of facts will also take on added importance as the agents must be able to predict the behaviour of agents whose identity they still do not know, as when a salesman must make a decision to refuse or accept a special request of a client based on his prediction of the behaviour of a production engineer.

Up to now I have argued that the flexibility of channels will make the reasons that we have already discussed for the existence of corporate culture stronger. It also brings in a new reason. Agents must be able to find the appropriate interlocutor for the problem that they are facing, and this will require internal knowledge about the organization and the functioning of the firm.

Trade-offs between flexibility of channels and
specialization of knowledge
If the possibility of communicating efficiently with a vast number of potential interlocutors within the organization has benefits, it also has costs. And these costs can easily be identified within our framework: in order for the increase in the number of channels to be fruitful, the amount of common knowledge within the firm must be sizeable, and this will limit the specialization of knowledge. (Masahiko Aoki makes a similar point in the third part of his chapter in this volume: a certain homogeneity of the labour force is necessary for the participatory mode of organization to be optimal.) The optimal trade-off between the two aspects is an important area of future research. Academia has solved it, for instance, by accepting the fact that scholars in different disciplines cannot communicate on professional matters.

The model presented in the next section makes a first attempt at answering these questions and tries to show that they can be given solutions and that their answer does have consequences for our understanding of the behaviour of organizations.

V A model of common knowledge with random meetings

The model
Grouping of agents and meetings Consider an organization with two types of agents, denoted by t, $t = 1,2$, agent i of type t will be denoted by (i, t). In order to produce, two agents, one of each type, must collaborate. Once two agents, $(i, 1)$ and $(j, 2)$ have met, they must independently choose decisions x_i^1 and x_j^2. Contrary to the set-up in Section III, we assume that there is an individual component to productivity, independent of the productivity of the type of the agent: To agent (i, t) is associated the productivity parameter $\pi_i^t = A^t + \gamma_i^t$. The random variables, A^1, A^2, and all the γ_i^t's are normally distributed, with mean zero and variances σ_A^2 and σ_γ^2, and independent of each other. The payoff from the meeting of the agents $(i, 1)$ and $(j, 2)$ is:

$$(A^1 + \gamma_i^1 + A^2 + \gamma_j^2) (x_i^1 + x_j^2) - \frac{B}{2} (x_i^1 + x_j^2)^2$$

$$- \frac{C}{2}(x_i^1 - x_j^2)^2.$$

The agents can only make two observations, one that provides information about their own productivity and one that provides information about the productivity of the agents of the other type. This reflects the following institutional assumption: the agents participate in many productive meetings. At the beginning of the month they observe two variables, and on the basis of the information so acquired, take their decisions during the whole month. Because their information does not change, they take the same decision in each meeting.

An agent of type t can observe two types of variable that carry information about his own productivity. As in Section III, there is a large pool of random variables. Some, denoted by η^{A^t}, provide information on A^t, some, denoted by η^{π_i}, provide information on π_i^t, and therefore the agent faces a trade-off, which we will explore in more detail on pp. 71–3, between acquiring better knowledge on his own specific productivity and acquiring knowledge that will be similar to that of his partners.

Agent (i, t) will also observe a variable $\eta^{A^{t'}}$ that provides information on the productivity of agents of the other type t'. Because agents participate in many meetings, it will never be optimal to gather information on the specific productivity $\pi_j^{t'}$ of one of the agents of the other type.

Each of the observation variables η is equal to the variable on which it provides information plus a random variable ϵ, taken from a large pool of such variables. All the ϵ's are normally distributed with zero mean and variances σ_ϵ^2, and are independent of each other and of the other variables in the model.

Information structures We will study two different information structures/organizations. In the undifferentiated organization all the agents have the same information, one variable η^{A^1} and one variable η^{A^2}. No agent has information about his own specific productivity. In the differentiated organization all agents of one type collect the same information about the productivities of the agents of the other type. For instance, agents of type 1 all observe the same variable η^{A^2}. But each agent observes a variable that provides specific information about his own productivity, that is a η^{π^i}. There are other possible types of information structure and we briefly discuss some of these below.

Our analysis will show that even though agents of a given type never produce jointly, because they belong to the same organization they may find it optimal to slight specific information about their own productivity in favour of more general information. This is an example of organization specific human capital whose possible importance we have stressed in previous discussion.

Analysis

The undifferentiated organization In the undifferentiated organization, two agents who have met have the same information, two variables η^{A^t} of the form $A^t + \epsilon^t$, with of course different ϵ^t's for each type. Because of our normality assumptions, the optimal decision rules are linear in the observations, and we have, for all i and j:

$$x_i^1 = \lambda(A^1 + \epsilon^1) + \mu(A^2 + \epsilon^2)$$
$$x_j^2 = \lambda(A^2 + \epsilon^2) + \mu(A^1 + \epsilon^1).$$

Our problem is to compute the optimal λ and μ. The payoff is equal to:

$$2(\lambda + \mu)\sigma_A^2 - B(\lambda + \mu)^2 (\sigma_A^2 + \sigma_\epsilon^2) - C(\lambda - \mu)^2(\sigma_A^2 + \sigma_\epsilon^2).$$

At the optimum λ and μ are equal to each other[6] and to

$$\frac{\sigma_A^2}{2B(\sigma_A^2 + \sigma_\epsilon^2)},$$

and the maximum payoff is

$$\frac{\sigma_A^4}{B(\sigma_A^2 + \sigma_\epsilon^2)}.$$

The differentiated organization   In the differentiated organization, two agents who have met have different information. Each agent (i, t) has observed some information $\eta_{(i,t)}^{\pi_i^t} = A^t + \gamma_i^t + \epsilon^{(i,t)}$ on his own productivity, and some information $\eta^{A^{t'}} = A^{t'} + \epsilon^{t'}$ on the productivity of agents of the other type. The decisions will be:

$$x_i^1 = \lambda(A^1 + \gamma_i^1 + \epsilon^{(i,1)}) + \mu(A^2 + \epsilon^2)$$
$$x_j^2 = \lambda(A^2 + \gamma_j^2 + \epsilon^{(j,2)}) + \mu(A^1 + \epsilon^1).$$

The payoff is:

$$2\lambda(\sigma_A^2 + \sigma_\gamma^2) + 2\mu\sigma_A^2 - \lambda^2(B + C)(\sigma_A^2 + \sigma_\epsilon^2 + \sigma_\gamma^2)$$
$$- \mu^2(B + C)(\sigma_A^2 + \sigma_\epsilon^2) - 2\lambda\mu(B - C)\sigma_A^2.$$

At this point formulae become messy. Let us define the variable:

$$G = (B + C)^2(\sigma_A^2 + \sigma_\epsilon^2 + \sigma_\gamma^2)(\sigma_A^2 + \sigma_\epsilon^2) - (B - C)^2\sigma_A^4,$$

then, we have:

$$\lambda = \frac{(B + C)(\sigma_A^2 + \sigma_\epsilon^2)(\sigma_A^2 + \sigma_\gamma^2) - (B - C)\sigma_A^4}{G},$$

and:

$$\mu = \frac{B\sigma_\epsilon^2 + C(2\sigma_A^2 + 2\sigma_\gamma^2 + \sigma_\epsilon^2)}{G}.$$

The payoff is:

$$\frac{(B + C)((\sigma_A^2 + \sigma_\gamma^2)^2(\sigma_A^2 + \sigma_\epsilon^2) + \sigma_A^4\sigma_\epsilon^2) + (3C - B)\sigma_A^4(\sigma_A^2 + \sigma_\gamma^2)}{G}$$

Comparison From the comparison of the payoffs above, we can easily prove the following proposition:

> *Proposition 5. (a) If B is equal to C and σ_γ^2 is equal to zero (that is, there is no individual-specific productivity), the differentiated and undifferentiated organizations yield the same payoffs.*
>
> *(b) The payoff[7] to the undifferentiated organization does not vary with C, whereas the payoff to the differentiated organization is inversely related to C.*
>
> *(c) The payoff to the undifferentiated organization does not vary with σ_γ^2. The payoff to the differentiated organization can increase or decrease with σ_γ^2. It increases when B is equal to C, and decreases when σ_A^2 is smaller that σ_ϵ^2, σ_γ^2 is small enough and C is large enough.*

Because the payoffs are continuous in all their parameters in the model, an immediate consequence of parts (a) and (b) of Proposition 5 is that for C greater than B and σ_γ^2 small enough the undifferentiated organization will be optimal. Let us rephrase this in economic terms. If the interdependence between the actions of the two types of agent is strong enough and if the individual-specific components of productivity are small enough, the undifferentiated organization will be better. It is optimal for agents to observe an index of the productivity of their type rather than an index of their own productivity.

Part (c) of Proposition 5 deserves some comment. In quadratic team theoretical models, increases in the variance of the linear term are in general good. If it were always equal to zero, the optimal payoff would always be equal to zero, but as the variance increases, decisions correlated with the linear term enable the agents to generate a strictly positive payoff. In our case, however, once the differentiated organization has been chosen, the increase in the variance of total productivity linked to an increase in σ_γ^2 is only a mixed blessing. The benefits sketched above are offset by the loss of information on the behaviour of the other agents, which is costly when C is large.

One other special case deserves special mention:

> *Proposition 6. If σ_ϵ^2 is equal to zero, the undifferentiated organization is better than the differentiated organization when C/B is very large. However, when C/B is smaller than 3, the differentiated organization is better.[8]*

Contrary to what happened in Section III, the benefit to common knowledge does not become nil when variables can be observed without error. Furthermore, in this case the result of the comparison can be interpreted in a straightforward fashion. If the importance of co-ordination relative to correct determination of aggregate output is large enough (C/B large), then the undifferentiated organization is optimal.

Consequences and extensions

Remember the intuition that launched us on the study of this model. We wanted to show that even though agents did not work directly together, the fact that they collaborated with the same agents would imply benefits to some communality of knowledge. This intuition is confirmed by the very simple model which we have presented.

In the analysis that precedes, we have considered only two types of organization. There are others. For instance, agents of one type could gather agent-specific information, whereas agents of the other type gather type-specific information. We could also imagine that, although all agents gather type-specific information, they differentiate their information by observing different variables. It is possible to show that this option is dominated by the undifferentiated organization described above whenever C is greater than B.

Eventually, a complete exploration of the issues raised in this model would require a more precise description of the types of activities performed by the different types of agent, and of their interrelationships. It is not clear whether there is a theoretically clean way to do this. For instance, it is difficult to model precisely the difference between the tasks of marketing and production personnel.

VI Conclusions

Future work will focus on two issues. First, I would like to develop in more detail the analysis of common knowledge of Section III. In particular, I would like to study a framework in which the quantity of common knowledge can be varied continuously, and where we are not restricted to a binary choice between common or specific knowledge. The techniques introduced by Novschek and Sonnenschein (1982), and also exploited by Li (1985) and Gal-Or (1985), should allow us to do this. These authors consider the decision to collect information by oligopolists, in a market where a demand parameter is unknown. Each of them can observe a certain number of random variables correlated with this parameter, and they study whether they would choose to observe the same variables. In our set-up the game theoretical aspect of the issue is considerably simpler and there should not be too many difficulties adapting this work.

The random meeting model of Section V also deserves some more attention. We might actually be able to introduce incentives in this framework, and study the way in which the organization is able to control the rules of the game that the agents are playing between themselves.

Finally, I would like to stress that there has been much discussion in policy circles about the ability of firms to conduct this or that activity. Hopefully, this chapter will have convinced the reader that it may be possible to build a theory of these abilities, and that the focus on the networks of relationships in organizations and of the communality of the knowledge and incentives is a fruitful research path.

Notes

Comments from Mike Riordan and from the participants at the SCASSS conference are gratefully acknowledged. The work presented here has been supported by NSF grant #8722014.

1. This type of rule would also help the firm establish a reputation, which again can have efficiency inducing aspects (see Kreps, 1984).

2. Take for instance the case when C is much smaller than B. Then the benefits of co-ordination become small and the undifferentiated organization only has the disadvantage of working with less precise information. Then it reacts less to the signals that it receives, and its variance of production is smaller.

3. Add to the denominators of the expressions that give the payoffs under the different organizations the quantity $(B + C)\sigma_\delta^2$.

4. In this case λ_1 is equal to

$$\frac{\nu_1 D_{22} - \nu_2 D_{11}}{(D_{11} D_{22} - D_{12}^2)(\sigma_A^2 + \sigma_\epsilon^2)} \, \sigma_A^2,$$

and of course λ_2 can be obtained by symmetry.

5. In this case λ_1 is equal to

$$\frac{\nu_1 D_{22}(\sigma_A^2 + \sigma_\epsilon^2)^2 - \nu_2 D_{12}\sigma_A^2}{D_{11} D_{22}(\sigma_A^2 + \sigma_\epsilon^2)^2 - D_{12}^2 \sigma_A^4} \, \sigma_A^2.$$

6. This is no surprise once we examine the payoff function. If none of the two agents have information about any of the π_i''s, the problem is totally symmetrical in the x_i''s.

7. I do not recommend trying to prove this part of the proposition by differentiating

the expressions above. Note rather that once the decision rule is fixed, the payoff must be decreasing in C, hence the second part of the statement.

8. More precisely, the undifferentiated organization is better than the differentiated organization if and only if $C^2 - B^2$ is greater than

$$BC\,(3 + \frac{\sigma_\gamma^2}{\sigma_A^2}).$$

References

Arrow, K.J. (1974) *The Limits of Organization*. New York: W.W. Norton.

Burns, T. (1954) 'The Directions of Activity and Communication in a Departmental Executive Group', *Human Relations*, 7: 683–93.

Crémer, J. (1987) 'Corporate Culture: Cognitive Aspects', working paper, Department of Economics, Virginia Polytechnic Institute and State University, E87–10–02.

Crémer, J. and M. Riordan (1987) 'On Governing Multilateral Relationships with Bilateral Contracts', *RAND Journal of Economics*, 18 (3): 436–51.

Gal-Or, E. (1985) 'Information Sharing in Oligopoly', *Econometrica*, 53 (2): 329–44.

Gutzkow, H. (1965) 'Communications in Organizations', in J. March (ed.) *Handbook of Organization*. Chicago: Rand McNally.

Kreps, D. (1984) 'Corporate Culture and Economic Theory', mimeograph. Graduate School of Business, Stanford, CA.

Lee, D. (1987) 'Coalitions Forging Evidence', working paper, Department of Economics, Virginia Polytechnic Institute and State University, E87–90–04.

Li, L. (1985) 'Cournot Oligopoly with Information Sharing', *RAND Journal of Economics*, 16 (4): 521–36.

Malcomson, J.M. (1978) 'Prices vs. Quantities: a Critical Note on the Use of Approximations', *Review of Economic Studies*, 45 (1): 203–7.

Marschak, J. and R. Radner (1972) *Economic Theory of Teams*. New Haven, CT: Yale University Press.

Mulder, M. (1960) 'Communication Structure, Decision Structure, and Group Performance', *Sociometry*, 23: 1–14.

Novschek, W. and H. Sonnenschein (1982) 'Fulfilled Expectations Cournot Duopoly with Information Acquisition and Release', *Bell Journal of Economics*, 13 (1): 214–18.

Tirole, J. (1986) 'Hierarchies and Bureaucracies: On the Role of Collusion in Organizations', *Journal of Law, Economics and Organization*, 2 (2): 181–214.

Weitzman, M.L. (1978) 'Reply to "Prices vs. Quantities: a Critical Note on the Use of Approximations"', *Review of Economic Studies*, 45 (1): 209–10.

Williamson, O.E. (1975) *Markets and Hierarchies: Analysis and Antitrust Implications*. New York: Free Press.

4
Profit Sharing, Information and Employment: Implications of the Utilitarian Monopoly Union Model

Matti Pohjola

1. Introduction

Current economic literature contains a number of well-known arguments for employee remuneration systems which are explicitly or implicitly based on profit sharing.[1] Given the enthusiasm of the profession and of many policy makers, it is appropriate to ask why such schemes are not more common. Arguments against linking pay to company profits can be classified into three broad categories. The first is the free-riding and insider problem associated with the Weitzman (1983) proposal:[2] although all workers could be made better off as a result of the simultaneous adaptation by all firms of profit sharing, the employed workers in any single firm always have an incentive to revert to the fixed wage system. This is because they can gain from the lower price level resulting from the introduction of profit sharing in other firms. The employed workers – the insiders – resist such plans because by increasing employment the firm can dilute their nominal wages. Such action is induced by profit-sharing schemes because, for a given level of employment, the marginal cost of labour can be lowered by making total remuneration consist of a basic wage rate and a share in total value added per employee. The profit component, however, diminishes as the number of employees increases, making the insider workers reluctant to share profits, especially if their employment is secure. Tax incentives aimed at alleviating the free-riding problem may consequently induce employers and insider employees to defraud the taxpayer by devising 'cosmetic' sharing schemes which continue to regard the total remuneration as the marginal cost of labour.

The second argument also emphasizes the role of insiders: they may not be willing to accept an increase in income risk brought about by profit-related pay and in this way to share the risks of entrepreneurship, particularly if their employment is already secured by seniority rules (see, for example, Estrin et al., 1987).

This is because their opportunities of diversifying the risks are more limited than are those of the owners of the firm. Implicit contract theory supports this view, even in the case where employees face unemployment risks, by demonstrating that the optimal contract under symmetric information takes the form of fixed wages if the employees are risk averse but the firm is risk neutral (Azariadis, 1975). The result is, however, based on capital market imperfections: it must be assumed that the firm cannot insure its workers against unemployment due to moral hazard or other reasons (see, for example, Oswald, 1986).

The third argument, put forward by Hollander and Lacroix (1986), is related to the relative bargaining power of employers and employees. They claim that, as profit sharing requires firms to disclose profits to their employees, the implementation of such schemes may have a distributive effect which adversely affects employers. Private information about profitability is thus seen to result in surplus profits – a view shared by Manning (1986) – explaining employers' reluctance to introduce profit-related pay even when it raises workers' productivity.

Since the first argument has already been extensively discussed in the literature (Estrin et al., 1987), this chapter concentrates on the other two. Profit sharing is here analysed in a partial equilibrium framework in which a utilitarian union can impose the parameters of the sharing scheme on a risk-neutral firm but in which the firm has the 'right to manage', that is can set employment levels unilaterally. Three different share contract structures are considered. The first, used as the reference case, is based on the assumption that the union does not know the value of the marginal product of labour when the parameters of the sharing scheme have to be chosen but that it becomes known before the firm makes its employment decision. Consequently, the optimization of union utility has to take place under the constraint that the firm maximizes profits for all realized states of nature. Thus, profits are observable to workers in the *ex post* sense. It is further assumed that the share parameters cannot be indexed to the marginal product of labour. This contract structure is the same as in Atkinson (1977), and may be regarded as the most relevant one in practice. The first alternative to it is the one in which the union is assumed to be able to impose state-contingent share parameters on the firm but in which the firm has still the right to choose employment levels unilaterally. The second alternative is the one in which information about profits is the firm's private information even *ex post*. The firm is not required to disclose profits to the employees, but the question will be raised whether it can be induced to do so by proper incentives devised by the union. The optimal values of the parameters of the 'linear wage' schedule are derived for each contractual framework. To reveal the importance of employees' attitude towards risk, the exercises are also performed separately for the cases where workers are assumed to be risk neutral and risk averse, respectively.

The discussion on profit sharing summarized above clearly shows that any sharing plan should consider its effect on the following factors: (1) worker motivation, (2) production efficiency as measured by the marginal cost of labour, (3) risk sharing and (4) the distribution of value added. Consequently, the model and the optimal linear wage parameters should also reflect these factors. The analysis in this chapter leaves the motivational questions aside and concentrates only on the last three aspects of the problem.

Given the amount of attention that profit sharing has recently received from economists, it is surprising to find how few studies there are specifying the way in which the parameters of such a scheme are chosen. These few include Aoki (1979), Pohjola (1987) and Weitzman (1987). Aoki considers risk sharing in a model in which employment is fixed, the firm is also risk averse, information is symmetric and the parameters are chosen so as to maximize the expected value of the sum of worker and firm utility. In his analysis, the profit share parameter is determined by the relationship between the measures of employers' and employees' absolute risk aversion whereas the basic wage reflects the desired distribution of utilities between the parties. Pohjola's bargaining analysis is based on the assumption that there is no uncertainty and that the firm is risk neutral and has the right to set employment levels unilaterally. The share parameter is here determined on the basis of the parties' relative bargaining power and it consequently takes care of distribution, whereas the basic wage guarantees Pareto-efficiency. Weitzman's study has more macroeconomic flavour in it. A profit-maximizing firm bargains with its existing employees, who are only interested in maximizing wages, in an environment where there is no uncertainty and where the profit share parameter is statutorily fixed by the government. The resulting basic wage rate reflects both distributional and efficiency aspects of the problem, This is his response to the criticism concerning the possibility of devising cosmetic sharing plans: with proper tax incentives the problem can be overcome and the basic result that a share system is more expansionary than a wage economy still holds.

The contract theory literature includes a number of studies which explore the properties of the optimal labour contract. The papers by Manning (1986) and Oswald (1986) consider a utilitarian union which is strong enough to impose a nonlinear wage contract on the firm. The latter, however, possesses private information about the profitability of production. They differ from each other basically in that Manning includes a strong individual rationality constraint in his model whereas Oswald does not. This constraint requires that variable costs of production have to be covered in all states of nature for the firm to produce at all, and its inclusion leads Manning to the conclusion that the union cannot extract all surplus profits from the firm. This chapter follows the approach of these two studies but specifies the form of the wage contract to be linear in the sense meant in profit-sharing literature. It is assumed in the main body of the chapter that profits are observable to workers *ex post*, but the role of private information is also briefly investigated. Consequently, this study differs from the analyses of Manning and Oswald in the same way as analyses of optimal linear income taxation differ from models of optimal nonlinear taxation.

The model is specified in the next section. Section 3 contains the analyses of the optimal profit-sharing scheme. The concluding section presents a summary and a discussion of the results.

2. The model

The utilitarian union (Atkinson, 1977) is considered. It is interested in maximizing the mathematical expectation of the sum of union member utilities

$$EU = \int_0^\infty [n(\theta)u(w(\theta)) + (1 - n(\theta))u(\overline{w})]g(\theta)d\theta \qquad (4.1)$$

with respect to the basic wage rate b and the profit share a of the linear sharing scheme

$$w(\theta) = b + a\,\frac{\theta f(n(\theta)) - bn(\theta)}{n(\theta)}. \qquad (4.2)$$

Here $u(.)$ is the concave, strictly increasing and twice-differentiable utility function of the worker. All employees are identical in terms of their preferences and abilities. Leisure has no value – only a single unit of labour is supplied by each worker. The union is thus assumed to treat members identically and to care about the sum of their utilities. Total per worker remuneration $w(\theta)$ is obtained by those $n(\theta)$ workers employed by the firm whereas the remaining $1 - n(\theta)$ have to be content with the fixed wage rate $\bar{w}$ obtainable elsewhere. Thus there is no private unemployment insurance available. Union membership is scaled to unity so that $n(\theta)$ measures the union' employment rate.

Output price (θ) is given to the firm but is a random variable which is distributed according to the density function $g(\theta)$, taking positive values on the half-open support $[0,\infty)$. The realization of (θ) is not known when the share parameters a and b have to be chosen by the union, but it becomes known before the firm has to make its employment decision $n(\theta)$. Thus, the union has to be content with the knowledge of the distributional properties of the product price. This is the simplest possible way of introducing asymmetry into the union–firm contracting framework, and it can also be regarded as a realistic description of actual profit-sharing schemes. The production function $f(.)$ is assumed to be concave, strictly increasing, twice-differentiable and such that $f(0) = 0$. Equation (4.2) can thus be seen to specify the remuneration per employed union member as the sum of the basic wage rate and the union's share in realized profits per worker.

The maximization of union utility has to take place under the following two constraints. First, given the wage parameters and the output price, the firm is allowed to choose the employment level so as to maximize the profits accruing to the owners. Defining

$$r(b,\theta) = \max_{0 \le n(\theta) \le 1} \theta f(n(\theta)) - bn(\theta)$$

and

$$\pi(a,b,\theta) = (1 - a)r(b,\theta)$$

as the maximum value profit function and the maximum profits received by the owners, respectively, this constraint can be written as

$$n(\theta) = \begin{cases} 1, & \text{for } \theta \ge \bar{\theta} \\ -r_b(b,\theta), & \text{for } \underline{\theta} < \theta < \bar{\theta} \\ 0, & \text{for } \theta \le \underline{\theta}. \end{cases} \tag{4.3}$$

Here $\bar{\theta}$ and $\underline{\theta}$ are obtained from $\bar{\theta}f'(1) = b$ and from $\underline{\theta}f'(0) = b$, respectively. Equation (4.3) is the firm's labour demand function

obtained from conventional duality properties assuming that
$a < 1$. This kind of contract governance is necessary if, as is
assumed here, the value of the firm's short-run production cannot
be observed by the union before employment is determined and if
it is impossible to make the contract parameters conditional on the
realization of θ. As any rational employment decision has to
depend on the marginal revenue product of labour, such a decision
must be delegated to the agent with the necessary information,
namely the firm. The equation corresponds to the standard
specification in the (deterministic) monopoly union model (see, for
example, Oswald, 1985).

The second constraint

$$E\pi = (1 - a) \int_0^\infty r(b,\theta)g(\theta)d\theta \geq \overline{\pi} \qquad (4.4)$$

is called (weak) individual rationality. This specifies that the
optimal profit-sharing scheme must offer the owners of the firm at
least $\overline{\pi}$, which can be interpreted as a market-determined expected
level of profits. A third constraint $\pi(a,b,\theta) \geq 0$, $\forall \theta$, could be
included to reflect strong individual rationality: the optimal
contract must give the firm non-negative profits in every state
because the variable costs of production have to be covered. It is,
however, already implied for any given θ by (4.3) by concavity of
the production function.

3. Optimal profit sharing

The first-order conditions for the problem of maximizing (4.1)
subject to (4.2)–(4.3) are obtained by differentiating with respect to
a, b and λ the Lagrangean

$$L = \int_0^\infty \{n(\theta)u(w(\theta)) + (1 - n(\theta))u(\overline{w})$$

$$+ \lambda[(1 - a)r(b,\theta) - \overline{\pi}]\}g(\theta)d\theta \qquad (4.5)$$

where λ stands for the coefficient associated with the individual
rationality constraint (4.4). Making use of equations (4.2) and (4.3)
these first-order conditions can, after routine calculations, be
expressed as

$$\int_0^\infty [u'(w(\theta)) - \lambda] r(b,\theta) g(\theta) d\theta = 0, \tag{4.6}$$

$$(1 - a) \int_0^\infty n(\theta([u'(w(\theta)) - \lambda] g(\theta) d\theta$$

$$- \int_\theta^{\bar\theta} r_{bb}(b,\theta)[u(w(\theta)) - u(\overline{w}) - u'(w(\theta))(w(\theta) \tag{4.7}$$

$$- b)] g(\theta) d\theta = 0,$$

$$(1 - a) \int_0^\infty r(b,\theta) g(\theta) d\theta \geq \overline{\pi}. \tag{4.8}$$

The second-order conditions are assumed to be satisfied.

Equations (4.6)–(4.7) characterize the risk-sharing, production efficiency and distributional aspects, respectively, of the problem. The first one can be solved for λ to obtain

$$\lambda = \frac{E[u'(w(\theta)) r(b,\theta)]}{Er(b,\theta)} \tag{4.9}$$

where E denotes the mathematical expectation with respect to θ. It is seen that the average marginal utility of worker profit income should be proportional to the expected level of profits. Marginal utilities are not necessarily equated state-by-state, that is optimal risk sharing in the Arrow–Borch sense ($u'(w(\theta)) = \lambda$, $\forall \theta$) is not achieved here because it is assumed that the union cannot index the share parameters to the realization of θ.

Equation (4.7) contains elements of both the insurance and efficiency aspects of the contract problem. The first term on the left-hand side reflects the former while the second term describes the latter because the expression in brackets is the standard contract curve. If the parameters of the sharing scheme could be made conditional on θ, then optimal risk sharing would be achieved. In the case of risk-averse workers and risk-neutral firm, it implies a fixed level of wages. The basic wage rate and the implied employment level determined by $\theta f'(n(\theta)) = b$ should then satisfy the conventional contract curve $[u(w) - u(\overline{w})]/u'(w) = w - b$, making also the second term in (4.7) equal to zero. When state-contingent share parameters cannot be used, it is evident that both optimal risk sharing and Pareto-efficiency may not be achieved simultaneously but have to be traded off against each other. This fact and its implication for the efficiency of production will be considered in detail in the following pages.

Equation (4.9) implies that $\lambda > 0$ if $Er(b,\theta) > 0$. Consequently, constraint (4.8) is binding, and it can be solved for a to obtain

$$a = \frac{Er(b,\theta) - \bar{\pi}}{Er(b,\theta)}. \tag{4.10}$$

The profit-share parameter is positive if $Er(b,\theta) > \bar{\pi}$ and approaches unity as $\bar{\pi}$ goes to zero. This is the first result of the chapter.

Proposition 1. If information is symmetric, the profit-share parameter of the optimal sharing scheme is designed to produce the desired distribution of income. It is not directly affected by either risk-sharing or production efficiency considerations.

Thus, neither workers' risk-aversion nor their lack of information about the profitability of short-run production can be taken as direct arguments against profit sharing. If these considerations enter the analysis, they do so via the basic wage rate b. Namely, it is possible for b to be so large that a becomes negative in (4.10). If the share parameter is confined to non-negative values only, then such a case would mean that the union prefers fixed wages. It will next be considered whether it is optimal for the union to set the basic wage at such a level.

State-contingent share parameters

As the solution for b seems to be very hard to obtain from equation (4.7) at this level of generality, it is instructive to consider some special cases. Assume for the moment that the parameters of the share contract (4.2) can be indexed to θ. Equation (4.6) implies that $u'(w(\theta)) = \lambda$, $\forall\theta$. Total remuneration is now fixed because, in the case of risk-averse workers and a risk-neutral firm, optimal risk sharing entails full insurance for employed workers against fluctuations in income. The wage level $w(\theta) = w^*$ is obtained from $Er(w^*,\theta)$ to guarantee the desired income distribution. The share parameter $a(\theta)$ is chosen to satisfy (4.2), and the basic wage rate is determined by the contract curve part of (4.7) as

$$b = w^* - \frac{u(w^*) - u(\bar{w})}{u'(w^*)} \le \bar{w}. \tag{4.11}$$

The inequality follows from the concavity of $u(.)$ and from the fact that $w^* > \bar{w}$ must hold for the employees to be willing to work in the firm in question.

This is a standard result of early contract theory (Azariadis, 1975; Rosen, 1985). Given that $\overline{w}$ can be interpreted as the social marginal cost of labour and that employment is determined by (4.3) from $\theta f'(n(\theta)) = b$, the lack of private unemployment insurance results in overemployment; production is excessive from the viewpoint of social efficiency. Employed workers are better off *ex post* than the unemployed because $w(w^*) > u(\overline{w})$. Involuntary unemployment prevails in this sense.

This outcome is exactly the same as that of the conventional contract theory in which it is assumed that the union can impose wage-employment contracts $(w(\theta), n(\theta))$ on the firm. If indexation is not too costly, strong unions can thus implement efficient contracts even when firms can set employment levels unilaterally. The overemployment result corresponds to Weitzman's (1983) claim that profit sharing is expansionary because it lowers the marginal cost of labour (see also Pohjola, 1987).

Because total remuneration is fixed here, there is no true profit sharing in this model. However, adopting the artificial contract form (4.2) serves the purpose of a reference solution and illustrates the roles of the parameters in providing information about production efficiency, risk sharing and distribution. The last two aspects of the problem are taken care of here by the fixed level of total remuneration.

Risk-neutral workers

The original model of non-contingent share parameters is next considered by assuming that workers are also risk neutral. Then $\lambda = 1$ in (4.6) and (4.9), and (4.7) immediately yields $b = \overline{w}$. Let us define production to be socially profitable if $Er(\overline{w}, \theta) \geq \overline{\pi}$. The second result can now be summarized.

Proposition 2. If information is symmetric, workers are risk neutral and production is socially profitable, then production is socially efficient and profit sharing optimal from the standpoint of the union in the sense that the share parameter is positive.

The basic wage rate takes care of efficiency whereas the share parameter produces the desired distribution. Risk sharing now plays no role in the determination of the optimal contract parameters because both parties are risk neutral. This solution is equivalent to the one obtained when state-contingent share parameters can be used and the workers are risk neutral because $b = \overline{w}$ in (4.11) and $a(\theta)$ can be chosen to make (4.8) binding for each realization of θ. The only difference lies in the choice of the profit share parameter. When indexation is used, it can be made conditional on θ, and $a(\theta)$ is thus chosen so as to make (4.8) binding for each realization of the random product price. In the absence of indexation, the share parameter a is chosen to satisfy (4.10). Comparing these choices in *ex ante* terms, it can be observed by applying Jensen's inequality that

$$Ea(\theta) = 1 - E(\frac{\overline{\pi}}{r(b,\theta)}) \leq 1 - \frac{\overline{\pi}}{Er(b,\theta)} = a$$

where the first equality comes from (4.8) and the second from (4.10). Consequently, in the absence of indexed share contracts, the union has to commit itself to a value of the share parameter a which is not smaller than the expected value of the indexed share parameters $a(\theta)$.

Linear production function
Let us next consider the original problem with the simplified form of the linear production function $f(n(\theta)) = n(\theta)$. Employment is determined by Equation (4.3) where now $\theta = \overline{\theta} = b$. All workers are simultaneously either laid off ($n(\theta) = 0$) or employed ($n(\theta) = 1$), depending on whether $\theta < b$ or $\theta \geq b$, respectively. First-order conditions (4.6) and (4.8) keep their present forms with the simplification that $r(b,\theta) = \theta - b$ for $\theta \geq b$ and zero otherwise. Equation (4.7) can be simplified considerably to

$$(1 - a) \int_b^\infty [u'(w(\theta)) - \lambda]g(\theta)\,d\theta = [u(b) - u(\overline{w})]g(b). \quad (4.12)$$

It nicely illustrates the insurance and efficiency aspects of the contract problem. The optimal profit-sharing scheme cannot be production efficient ($b = \overline{w}$) unless there is efficient sharing of risks in the Arrow–Borch sense for each realization of the random variable ($u'(w(\theta)) = \lambda$). As mentioned above, this cannot be achieved if state-contingent parameters are ruled out.

Solving (4.7) for λ and (4.8) for a and inserting in (4.12) yields

$$-\int_b^\infty u'(w(\theta))[\theta - \hat{\theta}_b]g(\theta)\,d\theta$$

$$= \frac{u(b) - u(\overline{w})}{1 - a} \frac{g(b)}{1 - G(b)} Er(b,\theta) \quad (4.13)$$

where

$$\hat{\theta}_b = \frac{\int_b^\infty \theta g(\theta) d\theta}{1 - G(b)}$$

and where $G(.)$ denotes the cumulative distribution function of θ. The left-hand side of this equation can be shown to be positive by demonstrating that the integral is negative. The integral measures the covariance between the marginal utility of wages and the output price. As marginal utility is diminishing and as wages increase with the output price, these variables covary in the opposite direction. More formally the result can be proved in the following way. From

$$u'(w(\theta)) - u'(w(\hat{\theta}_b)) = \begin{cases} < 0, & \text{for } \theta > \hat{\theta}_b, \\ > 0, & \text{for } \theta < \hat{\theta}_b, \end{cases}$$

it is seen that

$$u'(w(\theta))[\theta - \hat{\theta}_b] < u'(w(\hat{\theta}_b))[\theta - \hat{\theta}_b], \forall \theta \neq \hat{\theta}_b.$$

This can be integrated to obtain the desired result:

$$\int_b^\infty u'(w(\theta))[\theta - \hat{\theta}_b] g(\theta) d\theta$$
$$< u'(w(\hat{\theta}_b)) \int_b^\infty [\theta - \hat{\theta}_b] g(\theta) d\theta = 0.$$

This conclusion means that $b > \overline{w}$ in (4.13): the basic wage rate is set at a level which is higher than the shadow price of labour. Underemployment results because the firm's marginal cost of labour now exceeds the social cost. Thus, for those realizations of the product price satisfying $\overline{w} < \theta < b$, no production is undertaken although it would be socially optimal to do so. This is the cost of risk aversion in the present framework. Because of the linearity of the production function all workers are simultaneously either laid off or employed: there is no involuntary unemployment in the sense of unequal treatment of identical workers. Given the basic wage rate, the profit share parameter is obtained from equation (4.10). It can be checked that the constraint $a \geq 0$ is not binding if production is socially profitable in the sense that $Er(\overline{w}, \theta) \geq \overline{\pi}$. Profit sharing is thus optimal from the standpoint of the union.

> *Proposition 3.   If information is symmetric, workers are risk averse, production is socially profitable and the production function linear, then profit sharing is optimal in the sense of a positive share parameter, but the basic wage rate exceeds the alternative wage. The resulting underemployment is the social cost of risk aversion.*

To bring out in a clear way the redistributive role of the profit share parameter a, let us briefly consider the suboptimal fixed wage problem. Assume that the union chooses the fixed wage rate b so as to maximize the expected utility (4.1) subject to the constraints of (4.3), (4.4) and $a = 0$. The production function is still assumed to be linear. The first-order conditions are

$$\frac{u'(b) - \lambda}{u(b) - u(\overline{w})} = \frac{g(b)}{1 - G(b)} \tag{4.14}$$

and

$$Er(b,\theta) \geq \overline{\pi} \tag{4.15}$$

where λ is the multiplier associated with the constraint (4.4). Assume $\overline{\pi}$ to be so small that the constraint (4.15) is not binding. Then $\lambda = 0$ in (4.14), and this equation can be easily interpreted. The left-hand side is the union's boldness at b.[3] It is the reciprocal of the marginal risk premium needed to compensate the employees for risking an infinitesimally small probability of layoff when their attained wage level is b. The right-hand side is the hazard rate of the distribution of θ. Roughly speaking, it measures the probability that workers will be laid off at the wage level b, given that they have not already been laid off. Thus, at the margin, the union balances its boldness with the probability of layoffs. It can be seen that $b > \overline{w}$ because the hazard rate is positive. The suboptimality of the fixed wage solution reflects the difficulties of attaining more than one objective with a single parameter. The introduction of profit sharing gives more parameters, and the distributional constraint can be taken care of with a, separately from the risk-sharing and efficiency aspects of the problem.

It was argued above that profit sharing is contractionary in the case of symmetric information and non-contingent share parameters in the sense that the basic wage exceeds the social marginal cost of labour $\overline{w}$. Given that the monopoly union is known to push wages to a level higher than the alternative wage, this may not be the relevant base of comparison. However, it turned out to be impossible to obtain any definite conclusions about the relationship between the basic wage as given in Equation (4.13) and the sub-optimal fixed wage determined by (4.14). It depends on the utility and distribution functions in a rather complicated way. On the other hand, the social marginal cost of labour has some relevance as the point of comparison because in the case of symmetric information and contingent share parameters the private marginal cost of labour falls short of the social one despite the presence of the monopoly union.

Asymmetric information
Let us next turn to consider the case where profits are not even *ex post* observable to the union. In devising the optimal profit-sharing scheme, it now has to rely on the value of profits, or of θ, reported by the firm. Let θ^a denote the value of the product price announced by the firm. Profits then become

$$\pi(\theta,\theta^a) = \theta f(n(\theta^a)) - w(\theta^a)n(\theta^a)$$
$$= \theta f(n(\theta^a)) - bn(\theta^a) - a[\theta^a f(n(\theta^a)) - bn(\theta^a)] \quad (4.16)$$

where use has been made of Equation (4.2).

The union's problem is to find a sharing scheme which, in addition to satisfying the constraints (4.3) and (4.4), ensures that the firm reveals the state to the employees correctly, that is which is incentive compatible. To have this property, the profit-sharing scheme must satisfy the incentive compatibility constraint (see for example Manning, 1986, or Oswald, 1986)

$$\pi(\theta,\theta) \geq \pi(\theta,\theta^a), \forall \theta,\theta^a \in [0, \infty), \quad (4.17)$$

meaning that $\theta^a = \theta$ maximizes (4.16). Thus, for a nonlinear production function, the partial derivative with respect to θ^a of (4.16) should be equal to zero when it is evaluated at $\theta^a = \theta$. But, for $\theta f'(n(\theta)) = b$, it is easily verified that

$$\frac{\partial \pi}{\partial \theta^a} (\theta,\theta) = -af(n(\theta))$$

which is negative for $a > 0$. This means that the firm has always an incentive to say that the state is the worst possible. Consequently, the profit-sharing contract is incentive compatible only if $a = 0$. But then wages are fixed: $w(\theta) = b$.

If the production function is linear, a similar result can be obtained from Equation (4.16) directly. The fixed wage rate is now given by (4.14). The inequality in Equation (4.15) then reveals that the union is not able to extract all surplus profits: private information can be profitable to the firm. This being the case, there are incentives for firms to create and protect private information and thus to resist profit-sharing plans.

> *Proposition 4.   If information is asymmetric, profit sharing is not incentive compatible and fixed wages are optimal to the union. The monopoly union is not able to expropriate surplus profits, meaning that the firm has an incentive to protect private information by resisting profit-sharing plans.*

4. Conclusions

Leaving motivational issues aside, the basic argument in support of profit sharing is that it is more expansionary, in terms of output and employment, than the fixed wage compensation system. This feature follows from the fact that with a two-parameter wage it is possible to separate the marginal cost of labour and total worker remuneration from each other. All the arguments against profit-related pay boil down to the question of whether it is possible, in theory or in practice, to make this separation. It is evident that the answer must be sought in an analytical framework capturing the objectives, actions and information of the two parties involved – the firm and its labour force. This approach has been followed in surprisingly few studies.

Two of the principal arguments against profit sharing have been studied in this chapter in the monopoly union framework, where the union is assumed to be able to impose the parameters of the share contract on the risk-neutral firm but where the latter sets employment levels unilaterally. It was also assumed that the parameters have to be chosen before the value of the marginal product of labour is revealed, whereas employment can be determined after it has been observed. The claim was made that this kind of arrangement corresponds to sharing schemes found in practice (see for example Atkinson, 1977).

The first argument against profit sharing subjected to closer examination was workers' risk aversion. It was shown that its effects cannot be studied separately from efficiency of production and symmetry of information. However, one conclusion emerges in a clear way; the share parameter is not directly affected by employees' aversion to risks – the possible effect comes through the choice of the basic wage rate. If the parameters of the profit-sharing scheme can be made state contingent, then the basic rate is smaller than the alternative wage rate. Production is socially inefficient in the sense that the marginal cost of labour falls short of the shadow price of labour. This corresponds to the expansionary effect of profit sharing discussed earlier. The explanation of this standard contract theory result rests on the unavailability of private unemployment insurance: for risk-averse workers, one way to partially insure against layoffs and unemployment is to work in circumstances where it is socially inefficient to do so. Profit sharing is not achieved in the conventional meaning of the word because total remuneration is known to be fixed in the case where the firm is risk neutral.

If state-contingent share parameters are ruled out – as they seem to be in practice – then the conclusion is significantly different: in the case where the employees are risk averse the basic wage rate exceeds the alternative wage level resulting in underemployment. This is in accordance with the standard theory of the monopoly union setting fixed wages. The finding may, however, be of some interest as it is seen that profit sharing is no longer expansionary because the marginal cost of labour exceeds its shadow price. The resulting social cost, in terms of underemployment and lost production, can be seen as the necessary sacrifice for the union to obtain some efficiency in the sharing of risk.

The second argument examined in detail was the view that profit sharing has a distributive effect which adversely affects the owners of the firm because they have to disclose profits to their employees. It was shown that the linear profit-sharing scheme is not incentive compatible, meaning that fixed wages are optimal to the union. It was also shown that private information can lead to surplus profits, which provides the firm with an incentive to conceal information from the workers. Consequently, profit sharing is difficult to apply in small owner-managed companies, the profits of which are not observable, but is more suitable to public companies or corporations where profit statements are published and dividend payments can be observed. This result can be seen as an explanation of why sharing schemes are not more common. It does not, of course, mean that profit sharing is socially undesirable. Furthermore, the fact that private information is profitable to the owners of the firm may explain workers' and their unions' desire for participation in the firm's decision-making process.

Notes

Without implicating them, I wish to thank Michael H. Riordan and an anonymous referee for helpful comments. This research was supported by a grant to the author from the Yrjö Jahnsson Foundation and by financial assistance provided by the Finnish Ministry for Foreign Affairs to the project 'Unemployment, Inflation and Social Corporatism' being carried out at the Labour Institute for Economic Research.

1. Estrin et al. (1987) survey the literature on both the traditional view, according to which profit sharing enhances labour productivity by improving worker motivation, and the macroeconomic view, originated by Weitzman (1983), according to which it cures stagnation by lowering the marginal cost of labour. Risk sharing, which plays a dominant role in the implicit contract theory (see, for instance, Rosen 1985), is also seen in Atkinson (1977) and Aoki (1979) to give support to explicit schemes linking wages to profits. Pohjola (1987) argues that efficient wage-employment bargains can be made enforceable in union–firm bargaining without any binding contracts on employment if the parties adopt profit sharing. The literature on contract theory also contains many analyses supporting (implicit) sharing schemes, particularly if information is asymmetric (see e.g. Hollander and Lacroix, 1986, for an account).
2. See Estrin et al. (1987) for a thorough discussion.
3. See e.g. Aoki (1984: 71–2) for the definition of boldness.

References

Aoki, M. (1979) 'Linear Wage Contracts vs. the Spot Market in their Risk-bearing Functions', *Economic Studies Quarterly*, 30: 97–106.

Aoki, M. (1984) *The Co-operative Game Theory of the Firm*. Oxford: Clarendon Press.

Atkinson, A.B. (1977) 'Profit-sharing, Collective Bargaining and "Employment Risk"' *Zeitschrift für die gesamte Staatswissenschaft*, 133, Special Issue: Profit-sharing: 43–52.

Azariadis, C. (1975) 'Implicit Contracts and Underemployment Equilibria', *Journal of Political Economy*, 83: 1183–202.

Estrin, S., P. Grout and S. Wadhwani (1987) 'Profit-sharing and Employee Share Ownership', *Economic Policy*, 4: 14–62.

Hollander, A. and R. Lacroix (1986) 'Unionism, Information Disclosure and Profit-sharing', *Southern Economic Journal*, 52: 706–17.

Manning, A. (1986) 'The Profitability of Private Information in Unionised Capitalist Enterprises', *Economic Journal Conference Papers*, 96: 122–33.

Oswald, A.J. (1985) 'The Economic Theory of Trade Unions: An Introductory Survey', *Scandinavian Journal of Economics*, 87: 160–93.

Oswald, A.J. (1986) 'Unemployment Insurance and Labor Contracts under Asymmetric Information: Theory and Facts', *American Economic Review*, 76: 365–77.

Pohjola, M. (1987) 'Profit-sharing, Collective Bargaining and Employment', *Journal of Institutional and Theoretical Economics*, 143: 334–42.

Rosen, S. (1985) 'Implicit Contracts: A Survey', *Journal of Economic Literature*, 23: 1144–75.

Weitzman, M.L. (1983) 'Some Macroeconomic Implications of Alternative Compensation Systems', *Economic Journal*, 93: 763–83.
Weitzman, M.L. (1987) 'Steady State Unemployment under Profit Sharing', *Economic Journal*, 97: 86–105.

PART II

VERTICAL INTEGRATION AND THE STRATEGIC MANAGEMENT OF THE ENTERPRISE

5
What Is Vertical Integration?

Michael H. Riordan

1. Introduction

Vertical integration is the organization of two successive production processes by a single firm. In this definition, a *production process* describes the technical relationships that map inputs into feasible outputs, and two production processes are *successive* if the output from one is an input into the other. A *firm* is a legal entity that owns assets, and enters into commercial and financial contracts. A firm *organizes* a production process if it purchases or owns the inputs used in production.

This definition of vertical integration recognizes the firm as a nexus of contracts, or – to the extent that contracts are incomplete and implicit – a nexus of 'treaties'. These contracts govern relationships with suppliers of inputs and customers of output. The firm also contracts with creditors and shareholders, both of whom have claims on the firm's profits. Nevertheless, it is useful to think of the firm itself as a profit-centre, acquiring productive assets, paying for marketed inputs, and receiving revenues from the sale of outputs.

The definition distinguishes the organization of a production process from its control. Webster's *New Collegiate Dictionary* (1981) defines control as 'the direction, regulation, and coordination of business activities'. As such, control is essentially a managerial function. A manager controls a production process by purchasing inputs and directing, regulating and co-ordinating their use in production. The manager's authority is delimited by a contract with the firm. However, the firm remains responsible for the contractual obligations that the manager incurs on its behalf.

The definition distinguishes vertical integration from market exchange by the nature of contracts. Vertical integration refers to contracts for upstream inputs. Market exchange refers to a contract for upstream output. A crucial consequence of vertical integration is a change in information structure – that is, better information about upstream costs. A vertically integrated firm directly internalizes at least part of the costs of upstream production; for example, standard internal accounting controls monitor expenditures on inputs. In contrast, market exchange requires no information about upstream costs.

In this chapter I develop a formal model of vertical integration, in which a firm's ability to monitor upstream variable input cost matters for two reasons. First, output decisions track cost realizations more efficiently (see Crocker, 1983). Second, costs tend to be higher, because managerial incentives are undermined. This trade-off is similar to that discussed informally in the transaction cost literature: market exchange enjoys advantages of 'high-powered incentives', while internal organization facilitates 'adaptive, sequential adjustments to disturbances' (Williamson, 1985: 90–1; see also Wiggins, 1988).

Before proceeding to this analysis, it is worth noting that my definition of vertical integration differs from Grossman and Hart's (1986). They define a firm by the ownership of assets, and define ownership as the control of residual rights – rights over the use of an asset that are too costly to specify contractually. A firm is vertically integrated if it owns assets used at successive production stages. Important contributions of their analysis are to provide a precise and useful definition of the ownership of assets, and to show that ownership matters for transactions when assets are specific and contracts are incomplete.

In order to contrast these definitions of vertical integration consider the following two situations. *Case A*: a firm buys material inputs and contracts for the specific rights to employ labour and capital services in an upstream production process. *Case B*: a firm contracts for output from a supplier but leases to the supplier some specialized asset used in its production. In each case, a potentially important residual right of control is the right to redeploy assets to other uses. This matters if assets are not fully dedicated, if the contract is cancelled or breached prematurely, and at contract renewal intervals. The downstream firm owns the residual right to redeploy assets only in Case B. Therefore, by the Grossman–Hart definition, Case B is vertical integration, but Case A is not. My definition of vertical integration labels these cases in the opposite way.

My definition of vertical integration reflects the ideas that some productive activity is intrinsic to the notion of a firm, and that the nature of contracts is intrinsic to the notion of vertical integration. Moreover, the ownership of assets is intrinsic to neither. After all, production, spanning one or more vertically related activities, conceivably can be accomplished by purchasing or leasing all inputs. Indeed this way of organizing production is traditionally ascribed to the neoclassical firm.

There is also a narrow sense in which the two definitions of vertical integration are consistent. The outputs of a production process are an inventory, which might be interpreted as an asset for which residual rights of control are well defined. By Grossman and Hart's (1986) definition, vertical integration corresponds to the centralized ownership of output inventories for two successive production processes. Implicit in my definition is the assumption that a firm that organizes a production process owns the resulting output.

In the final analysis, vertical integration is an intuitive concept. More fruitful than debating definitions is identifying organizational features that matter for economic outcomes. Grossman and Hart's (1986) definition of vertical integration emphasizes property rights over the use of physical assets. My definition emphasizes a downstream firm's ability to monitor the use of inputs in an upstream production process. From a general perspective, the two approaches are complementary.

The rest of this chapter is organized as follows. The next section develops a comparative organizational model of an upstream production process that distinguishes vertical integration from requirements contracting by a change in information structure, and features the aforementioned trade-off between efficient output decisions and managerial incentives for cost reduction. In the context of this model, Section 3 argues that some form of limited contractual commitment is crucial for a theory of comparative organizations, while Section 4 argues that the crucial difference between organizational modes lies in their information structures. Section 5 turns to the ownership of assets, and argues that ownership matters because of its consequences for information structure. Section 6 concludes with a brief summary.

2. Vertical integration versus requirements contracting

Consider a downstream firm ('the principal') that is organizing the manufacture and marketing of a unique product. The product requires a component input which might be either standard or non-standard. The standard component can be procured on a competitive spot market, but is less valuable. The non-standard component must be contracted for in advance.

The principal's requirements for production of the component are constant and normalized to unity. That is, either one unit of the non-standard component or one unit of the standard component is to be used in downstream production. The value of non-standard component to the principal is common knowledge and equal to $v > 0$. The net value of the standard component – procured competitively – is fixed and normalized to zero. The trade-off between these two options hinges on cost considerations.

The production technology for the non-standard component has the following features. First, it requires a sunk investment in a specialized physical capital asset, whose cost is fixed and equal to K. This asset has no alternative use value (which assumption is relaxed in Section 5). Second, there is a managerial input. The job of the manager is to study the production process and determine a least cost combination of variable inputs (see Wiggins, 1988). Managerial effort (e) can be interpreted as a complementary investment in a specific asset, namely, knowledge about the technology. There are a large number of identical risk-neutral agents capable of providing managerial effort.

Assume that there is minimal effort level, normalized to zero, that the manager provides simply by 'being there'. Any effort beyond this level is at the discretion of the manager and is not directly observable by the principal. Thus $e \geq 0$. The measurement of this variable is normalized so that the opportunity cost of providing effort level e is equal to e itself.

A given effort level induces a probability distribution over variable cost, $F(c|e)$, which is continuously differentiable in both its arguments. Let $F_c(c|e) > 0$ denote the corresponding density function for $c > 0$. A higher value of e shifts the distribution of variable cost down in the sense of first-order stochastic dominance; $F_e(c|e) > 0$ for $c > 0$. In other words, managerial effort reduces variable input cost, but the extent of cost reduction for any given level of effort is uncertain.

Define

$$M(P,e) = \int_0^P (P - c) \, dF_e(c|e)$$

to be a manager's marginal expected return to effort given a take-it-or-leave-it price P. Assume that $M(P,e)$ is decreasing continuously in e for all $P > 0$, and that $M(P,0) > 1$ for all $P > 0$. Thus, a manager with an option of producing at a positive price has an incentive to devote positive effort to cost reduction.

To interpret this last assumption further, invert $z = F(x|e)$ to obtain $x = \xi(z,e)$. Suppose that production takes place whenever $c \leq \xi(z,e)$. Then the probability of production is z, and expected variable cost is

$$C(z,e) = z. \int_0^{\xi(z,e)} c \, dF(c|e).$$

By assumption, $z > 0$ implies that $[C(z,e) + e]$ is minimized at a strictly positive e. In other words, given a positive probability of production, total expected cost is minimized by a positive level of managerial effort.

For expositional convenience, assume also that the probability distribution over c satisfies the 'regularity conditions' that the inverse hazard rate $H(c,e) \equiv F(c|e)/f(c|e)$ is increasing continuously in e for all $c \geq 0$, and $[c + H(c,e)]$ is increasing continuously in c for all $e \geq 0$. In particular, the probabilities that $v > c$ and that $v < c$ are always strictly positive; that is, production of the non-standard component may or may not be efficient for any level of effort.

I analyse two modes of organizing the potential procurement of the non-standard component: requirements contracting and vertical integration. These modes differ by their information structures, which in turn support different types of contracts. The principal observes variable-input cost (c) under vertical integration but not under a requirements contract. Later, in Section 4, I will interpret this change in information structure as arising from differing incentives of the manager to disclose information to the principal.

The status of the manager differs under these two modes. Under vertical integration, the principal hires an 'employee–manager' at a fixed wage and directly purchases variable inputs. Under a requirements contract, the principal selects an 'owner–manager' as an exclusive supplier. This supplier contracts for variable inputs, and sells the upstream output to the principal.

Contracting under vertical integration proceeds in the following stages. *Stage 1*: The principal hires a manager at a competitive wage, normalized to zero, and purchases specialized capital at a cost of K. The manager provides effort $e = 0$, determining a probability distribution over variable cost for the non-standard component $F(c|0)$. The cost realization c is observed by the principal. *Stage 2*: If $v \geq c$, then the principal pays the variable input cost c and produces the non-standard component. If $v < c$, then the principal procures the standard component.

Under vertical integration, the production of the non-standard component is efficient *ex post*, taking place with probability $F(v|0)$. On the other hand, the managerial input decision is not efficient *ex ante*. The *ex ante* efficient level solves

$$\text{maximize} \atop e \geq 0 \quad \int_0^v [v - c] \, dF(c|e) - e$$

which has an interior solution satisfying $M(v,e) = 1$. However, under vertical integration, the manager has no incentive to provide a positive effort level. Thus the expected net benefits to the principal of vertical integration are

$$B_V = \int_0^v [v - c] \, dF(c|0) - K.$$

Requirements contracting also proceeds in two stages. *Stage 1*: The principal contracts with a manager to sink the specialized investment K for a lump sum transfer payment T. The manager chooses an effort $e \geq 0$, determining a probability distribution over variable cost $F(c|e)$. The manager privately observes realized cost c. *Stage 2*: The principal makes a take-it-or-leave-it offer P for production of the non-standard component. If $c \leq P$, the manager accepts the offer, produces the component, and pays the variable cost. If $c > P$ the manager rejects the offer, and the principal procures the standard component. (This model is a special case of Tirole's, 1986.)

The principal's take-it-or-leave-it offer solves the monopsony pricing problem

$$\text{maximize} \, (v - P) \, F(P|e^*) \atop P \geq 0$$

where e^* is the principal's belief about the level of effort undertaken by the agent, and $f(P|e^*)$ is the corresponding probability of production at price P. The solution to this equation, $P = P(v,e^*)$, solves $v = P + H(P,e^*)$. Clearly $v > P(v,e^*)$, and $P_v(v,e^*) \geq 0$ by the regularity conditions on H.

The solution to this pricing problem implies that production of the non-standard component takes place if $v \geq c + H(c,e^*)$. Thus production is distorted downward, that is fails to take place even when it is efficient *ex post*. This underproduction result derives from the monopsony power of the principal.

At Stage 1 the manager chooses an effort level that maximizes

$$\pi = \int_0^{P^*} [P^* - c] \, dF(c|e) - e.$$

where P^* is the take-it-or-leave-it price anticipated by the manager. The first-order condition for an interior solution is $M(P^*,e) = 1$. As discussed earlier, this is a condition for productive efficiency. The optimal effort for the manager, e^*, minimizes $[C(F(P^*|e^*),e) + e]$, which equals expected total cost given that production takes place with probability $F(P^*|e^*)$.

This investment efficiency result is easily explained. The manager understands that the principal's beliefs about e^* are fixed. Given a knowledge of these beliefs, the manager can predict perfectly the price that the principal will offer. Moreover, given a knowledge of his own optimal production strategy, the manager also perfectly predicts the probability of production. Since he internalizes all of the benefits of cost reduction, the manager is always induced to choose an efficient effort given equilibrium expected quantity. (In this model effort is below the first-best level, but only because of the second-stage quantity distortion; see Tirole's (1986) Proposition 1.)

Let $e(P^*)$ denote the solution to the manager's effort choice problem; second-order conditions imply that $e'(P^*) \geq 0$. A higher price induces more effort from the manager. This is because a higher price increases the probability of production for any given effort level, and therefore increases the marginal return to cost reduction.

In equilibrium, beliefs are correct, that is $e^* = e$ and $P^* = P(v,e)$. These conditions determine equilibrium effort and price as increasing functions of v. Given the equilibrium level of managerial effort, competition in the market for managers will determine a transfer payment to the manager,

$$T = K - \pi,$$

that fully extracts expected rents. The corresponding expected benefits to the principal from requirements contracting are

$$B_R = \int_0^{P*} [v - c] \, dF(c|e^*) - e^* - K.$$

Under requirements contracting, too little production is undertaken *ex post* since $P < v$. However, managerial effort minimizes expected production cost. Thus the trade-off between vertical integration and requirements contracting is between distorted production decisions and distorted managerial incentives. In general, the principal's preferred mode of organization depends on v (but not on K), and in a complicated way on the production technology through the properties of $F(c|e)$.

Organizational mode does have consequences for both the level of output and the cost of producing it. If $F(P^*|e^*) \geq F(v|0)$, then requirements contracting dominates vertical integration. Production of the non-standard component takes place at least as often and at a lower cost. It follows that a necessary condition for vertical integration to be the preferred mode is that $F(P^*|e^*) < F(v|0)$. Therefore, expected output is higher but more costly than under requirements contracting if the principal chooses vertical integration by preference.

These results are suggestive for antitrust policy toward vertical mergers. Williamson (1985: Ch. 14) observes that antitrust doctrine in the 1960s treated vertical mergers suspiciously because of market foreclosure concerns, but the recent Department of Justice's *Merger Guidelines* do accept efficiency arguments as a defence. The theory of strategic entry deterrence makes clear that a commitment to produce more output can deter entry, possibly to the detriment of consumers (Gilbert, 1988). By eliminating output distortions between a customer and a supplier, vertical integration might in fact serve as such a commitment, potentially (but not necessarily) having adverse market foreclosure consequences. Moreover, this output is produced less efficiently – that is, at a higher cost than under requirements contracting, due to a deterioration of managerial incentives. Thus, the only 'efficiency' motivation for vertical merger is that, by eliminating the mark-up paid to a supplier, output is chosen at a higher, more profitable level. This is socially desirable absent any market foreclosure, but may not be otherwise. A full examination of this issue requires embedding the theory of vertical integration in a model of strategic market interaction.

3. Limited commitment and comparative organizations

The above characterizations of vertical integration and requirements contracting each assume a limited ability to make contractual commitments. In the case of vertical integration, the manager
cannot commit to a level of effort beyond a minimum amount, and
the principal cannot commit to compensate the manager as a function of realized cost. Either of these could solve the moral hazard
problem for managerial incentives, leading to a first-best allocation
of resources.

The manager's inability to commit to an effort level is natural
if it is costly for the principal to monitor or supervise the manager.
Even if the principal could monitor managerial effort, enforcement
of a contractual specification of effort would probably encounter
problems. There is no natural metric for effort, and it would be
difficult to stipulate one contractually. Circumstances would
undoubtedly give rise to disputes over whether or not the manager
had complied with contractual stipulations. Third-party verifica-
tion would be hindered by incomplete documentary evidence, and
arbitration would be time consuming and costly in other ways.

Similarly, a contract linking managerial compensation to realized
cost must also rely on incomplete and costly third-party verifica-
tion. There is a potential for disputes over what should be counted
as a cost and what should not, and where lies the responsibility for
cost overruns. An arbitrator or auditor is likely to be treated
suspiciously by one or the other party to the contract. It would be
difficult to completely specify an accounting methodology in
advance. Particularly acrimonious circumstances would leave the
interpretation of the contract to the courts.

To be sure, managers are sometimes paid bonuses contingent on
some measure of a firm's profitability, for example, the stock
market price. Typically, however, these bonuses are a small fraction
of compensation (except perhaps for very high-level managers), and
only distantly related to individual managerial performance. While
such bonuses might improve managerial incentives at the margin, it
is doubtful that they could resolve the managerial moral hazard
problem completely.

In the case of requirements contracting, the owner–manager
cannot commit to report cost truthfully. The only way such a
commitment might be credible is via a contractual obligation for
the owner–manager to 'open his books' to the principal. Understandably, firms are reluctant completely to disclose all internal
accounting information to an outside party. A firm engages in

many different transactions with many different customers. It is often difficult to open the books only partially, to disclose information pertinent to only a single transaction, partly due to the arbitrariness of cost allocations. On the other hand, completely opening the books risks leaking trade secrets, and so on. Moreover, the interpretation of accounting-cost data may be questionable, owing to opportunities for cost shifting both across outputs and across time.

The requirements contracting model also assumes that the principal cannot commit to a price until after investments – including managerial effort – are sunk. Otherwise, a first-best allocation could be achieved by committing to a price equal to value v (Harris and Raviv, 1979; Loeb and Magat, 1979). By such a contract, the principal commits to give the manager all of the *ex post* surplus from production, in exchange for a 'franchise fee' that fully extracts *ex ante* surplus.

Such a long-term contract might appear natural in the model, given that v is certain and common knowledge. The courts, however, would have to enforce such a contract with probability one for it to be fully credible. In practice, judges are fickle enforcers of long-term commercial contracts. Even if v were certain and common knowledge *ex ante*, this might not be apparent to the courts *ex post* and might be impossible to prove. The courts might fail to enforce a long-term contract by appealing, say, to the legal doctrine of commercial foreseeability (Landa, 1986).

By failing to perfectly enforce long-term price contracts, the courts undermine the first-best franchise contract in several ways. First, a 'take the money and run' strategy is potentially attractive to the principal. Suppose, for example, that the value of the transaction to the principal, v, hinged on reliance investments by the principal – for example marketing expenditures, investments in a distribution network, or quality investments at downstream production stages. The principal might simply forgo these reliance investments and cancel the contract. The principal might claim a justification for cancelling the contract because of bad faith compliance by the agent – for example faulty workmanship, delays, and so on. The manager might have trouble recovering fully his franchise fee in court, and further trouble gaining full compensation for damages. The rents ultimately gained by the principal from this opportunistic strategy might well exceed those to be had from good faith compliance.

Secondly, and probably more importantly, the principal could use the threat of going to court as an instrument for renegotiating the contract. A manager with any doubt that the court would enforce the contract would be willing to give up some *ex post* surplus just to avoid expected court costs. An out-of-court settlement would amount to a renegotiation of the contract price.

Moreover, the model is artificially stark in assuming an environment that is completely stable, except for private cost uncertainty. In particular, the common knowledge assumption about v is very unrealistic. Relaxing this assumption – introducing uncertainty and private information of the principal about v – would complicate the exposition of the model but not alter basic comparative organizational trade-offs. Fully efficient contacts – that generalize simple franchise arrangements – are available (Riordan, 1984), but are considerably more complicated and, correspondingly, even more difficult to enforce.

Furthermore, optimal long-term contracts expose one or both parties to risk. Risk-sharing gives rise to underproduction (Moore, 1988). Also, with limited liability, the threat of bankruptcy provides additional opportunities for renegotiating the contract. If limited liability constraints are taken into account when the contract is negotiated initially, then the optimal contract becomes even more complicated (Riordan and Sappington, 1988). Also, these constraints operate essentially like individual rationality constraints in mechanism design problems, also giving rise to underproduction (Myerson and Satterthwaite, 1983). Thus the comparative organizational issues remain similar – vertical integration reduces quantity distortions but undermines managerial incentives.

Finally, casual empiricism suggests that requirements contracts are often short term, easily cancelled, and subject to renegotiation. Where specific assets are at stake, stable commercial relationships may extend over many years. Yet many requirements contracts are negotiated annually, and may even be renegotiated within the contract year.

The assumption that the principal has monopsony power over price is possibly reasonable for some applications. For example, a large corporation such as General Motors certainly has more market power than a small supplier. However, it is mainly an expositional simplification. Allowing more balanced bargaining power at the price negotiation stage need not alter the basic comparative institutional trade-offs identified above (Tirole, 1986). For example, suppose that there were bilateral information asymmetries, and that the principal and manager negotiated the contract price by making alternating offers. The equilibrium of such a bargaining model might feature costly delay (Crampton, 1987), which is just another form of quantity distortion.

The main points of this discourse are two. First, limited commitment is a reasonable assumption. Second, limited commitment is important for a comparative institutional theory. This is clearly true for the model – where perfect commitment gives rise to identical first-best outcomes under both modes, but also more generally. The central role of limited commitment is also featured in the comparative organizational analyses of Grossman and Hart (1986) and Williamson (1985: Ch. 6).

4. Information structure and comparative organizations

It is also true (in the model) that information structure crucially distinguishes vertical integration from requirements contracting. If variable input costs were directly observed by the principal under requirements contracting, then the principal would always offer a price that exactly compensated the manager for these costs. The owner–manager would earn no rent from effort, and so would provide none but the minimum. The outcome would be identical to that under vertical integration.

The idea that information structure distinguishes organizational modes can be traced back to team theory (Marshak and Radner, 1977), although team theory does not examine the strategic consequences of different information structures. In the spirit of team theory, a change of information structure is basic to Arrow's (1975) analysis of vertical integration, Aoki's (1986) comparison of Japanese and American firms, and Sah and Stiglitz's (1986) contrast of hierarchy and polyarchy. Riordan and Sappington (1987) consider some strategic (i.e. incentive) consequences of differing information structures.

The choice of information structure is usefully viewed as a commitment device. This view is supported strongly by Arrow's (1974: 39–40) discussion of information structure as an investment decision:

A second key characteristic of information costs is that they are in part capital costs; more specifically, they typically represent an irreversible investment. I am not placing much weight on the physical aspects of communication, telephone lines and the like, though they are in fact non-negligible in cost and they do provide a concrete, understandable paradigm. Rather I am thinking of the need for having made an adequate investment of time and effort to be able to distinguish one signal from another. Learning a foreign language is an obvious example of what I have in mind. The subsequent ability to receive signals in French requires this initial investment. There are in practice many other examples of codes that have to be learned in order to receive messages;

the technical vocabulary of any science is a case in point. The issue here is that others have found it economical to use one of a large number of possible coding methods, and for any individual it is necessary to make an initial investment to acquire it.

Arrow's argument is that observation of an 'information signal' requires a prior investment in an 'information channel'. The point extends directly to cost accounting in firms. In order to monitor input costs, it is necessary to establish cost accounting standards. Otherwise, relevant cost information might be prohibitively costly to retrieve or interpret, or might not even be kept.

A commitment to an information structure might also be partly contractual. Cost accounting data is proprietary. Moreover, according to Masten (1988: 189–90) an employee has a legal obligation to disclose all cost information to his employer, while an independent supplier retains considerably more latitude (and motive) for opportunistic behaviour:

> (A)n employee is legally accountable for any pecuniary losses sustained by his employer as a result of failing to disclose relevant facts and is liable for damages and the returns of all ill-gotten gains derived from that failure. An independent subcontractor bears no such responsibility and is free, among other things, to exploit profit opportunities that arise in the course of the contract's performance.

Thus vertical integration might be interpreted as the acquisition of proprietary information – precisely as in Arrow's (1975) model.

Grossman and Hart deny that a change in information structure is intrinsic to vertical integration (see also Evans and Grossman, 1983): 'Any audits that an employer can have done of his subsidiary are also feasible when the subsidiary is a separate company' (Grossman and Hart, 1986: 695).

Williamson takes a contrary view.

> An external auditor is typically constrained to review written records and documents and in other respects restrict the scope of his investigation to clearly pertinent matters. An internal auditor, by contrast, has greater freedom of action, both to include less formal evidence and to explore the byways into which his investigation leads (1975: 29–30).

However, these two arguments need not be inconsistent, for as Grossman and Hart note: 'the right to audit is sometimes a residual right rather than a contractible right, in which case the theory . . . can explain the dependence of information on ownership patterns' (1986: fn 3).

For obvious reasons, monitoring and auditing upstream production activity is more important when contracting for inputs than when contracting for output. Thus, it is natural that the choice of information structure varies with contract type. For transaction cost reasons it might be easier to tie monitoring and auditing rights to the ownership of assets, rather than specify these rights contractually.

A final, and somewhat deeper, argument is that a manager's incentive to disclose information changes with vertical integration. An upstream owner–manager is a residual claimant who profits from misrepresenting costs to justify a higher price for output. In contrast, an employee–manager cannot gain from misrepresenting variable cost, because the principal has agreed to pay these costs directly, compensating the manager only with a fixed wage. This argument is reinforced by the aforementioned legal obligations of an employee and by superiority of internal auditing.

4. Does the control of assets matter?

A potentially important residual right of control is the right to redeploy assets to other uses. As noted in the introduction, this could be relevant if a contract is cancelled prematurely, at contract renewal intervals, or if assets are not fully dedicated to their primary use. Does the ownership of this right matter for the outcome of transactions?

I will argue that the ownership of assets matters because of its consequences for information structure. The opportunity value of assets is a component of short-run variable cost. The manager's private information about this cost component is potentially the source of an information rent for the manager. The size of this information rent affects managerial incentives for cost reduction and quantity distortions. However, the information rent exists only if the manager directly internalizes the capital component of variable cost, that is only if the manager owns the assets.

In the model of Section 2, production of the non-standard component is supported by an investment of K in a physical asset. Here the question of ownership is moot because this investment is fully specific, that is the asset has no alternative use value. Thus the right to redeploy the asset when production fails to take place is irrelevant.

However, the model is easily generalized. Suppose that the asset has a value of αK in its next best use, with $0 \leq \alpha \leq 1$. The parameter α measures the sunkness of the investment. Note that even when $\alpha = 1$ there can still be a specific component to the investment, since the value of the asset in producing the non-standard component is $v - c$. Thus *ex post* asset specificity is endogenous, depending on the realization of c.

If α is certain and common knowledge, then the asset ownership has no comparative organizational significance. The only complication is that αK must be treated as an additional component of variable cost. If the principal owns the asset under vertical integration, then the employee–manager would still provide zero effort, but production would take place whenever $v - c - \alpha K \geq 0$. Managerial ownership of the asset would not affect effort and production decisions. The manager would be compensated for the opportunity cost of the asset, αK, when production takes place, and the manager's first period wage would be adjusted to reflect the expected present discounted value of the asset. Similar minor complications arise for requirements contracting, but again the ownership of assets only matters for the structure of compensation, not for resource allocation decisions. The comparative organizational trade-offs between vertical integration and requirements contracting depend only on their differing information structures.

Matters are different if α is uncertain and is privately observed by the manager. Let $G(\alpha)$ denote the probability distribution over α, and assume that the manager observes α at the beginning of Stage 2. This is a natural assumption if a managerial function is the discovery of alternative production opportunities. Two cases of ownership can be distinguished. If the principal (manager) owns the asset, then the principal (manager) internalizes the benefit αK from its redeployment.

Consider vertical integration with the principal owning the asset and observing c as before. The manager's compensation is independent of how the asset is deployed. Therefore the manager has no incentive to misrepresent α to the principal (and is legally culpable for doing so). Moreover, internal accounting controls enable the principal to check directly on a manager's report should the asset actually be redeployed. This is tantamount to the principal observing α directly. Thus, resource allocation is exactly as if αK were certain and common knowledge.

Now suppose that the manager owns the asset, but information structure remains as under vertical integration. What changes? Now the manager will quit production and redeploy the assets elsewhere unless compensated by at least αK. Consequently, the manager has a potential incentive to overstate α in order to justify a greater compensation. The realization αK becomes a variable cost about which the principal is uninformed at the beginning of Stage 2.

Under this information structure, the principal faces a monopsony pricing problem similar to that arising before, under requirements contracting. After observing the realization of c, the principal makes a take-it-or-leave-it offer P to the manager that maximizes $(v - c - P)G(P/K)$.

By second-order conditions, the solution to this problem is monotonically increasing function of $(v - c)$. This potentially gives the manager a positive incentive to undertake cost-reducing effort; by lowering c, the manager earns greater information rents at Stage 2. However, the second-stage quantity decision will be distorted since $P < v - c$ at an optimum. Thus the trade-offs are similar to those for requirements contracting. Improved managerial incentives accompany inefficient production decisions.

Managerial ownership of assets, with the principal monitoring non-capital variable costs c, is an intermediate organizational mode falling between full vertical integration and simple requirements contracting. Under requirements contracting the owner–manager privately observes both components of variable cost, c and αK. Under appropriate regularity conditions, this greater information asymmetry yields better managerial incentives but greater quantity distortions (see Riordan, 1987). In this model, the ownership of assets matters only because it affects information structure.

5. Concluding remarks

I have argued that differing information structures crucially distinguish alternative modes for organizing successive production processes. Vertical integration – contracting for inputs instead of output – conveys better information about upstream variable costs. Consequently, vertical integration yields more efficient quantity decisions but undermines managerial incentives for cost reduction.

Monitoring of upstream non-capital variable costs by a downstream firm, but without acquiring upstream assets, is intermediate between vertical integration and arms-length requirements contracting. In this case, the ownership of assets matters because of its consequences for information structure. The upstream firm retains private information about the opportunity cost of assets employed in production. The resulting information rent improves managerial incentives, but also leads to less efficient production, compared to full vertical integration.

Note

I thank Masahiko Aoki, Albert Ma, Marc Robinson, Steve Wiggins and Oliver Williamson for helpful comments and discussions, and acknowledge research support from the National Science Foundation (grant IRI-8706150).

References

Aoki, Masahiko (1986) 'Horizontal vs. Vertical Information Structure of the Firm', *American Economic Review*, 76: 971–83.

Arrow, Kenneth J. (1974) *The Limits of Organization*. New York: W.W. Norton.

Arrow, Kenneth J. (1975) 'Vertical Integration and Communication', *Bell Journal of Economics*, 6: 173–83.

Crampton, Peter C. (1987) 'Strategic Delay in Bargaining with Two-Sided Uncertainty,' Yale working paper (October).

Crocker, Keith J. (1983) 'Vertical Integration and the Strategic Use of Private Information', *Bell Journal of Economics*, 14: 236–48.

Evans, David and Sanford J. Grossman (1983) 'Integration' in D. Evans (ed.) *Breaking Up Bell*. New York: North-Holland.

Gilbert, Richard J. (1988) 'Mobility Barriers and the Value of Incumbency'. University of California at Berkeley working paper (October); forthcoming in R. Schmalensee and R. Willig (eds) *Handbook of Industrial Organization*.

Grossman, Sanford J. and Oliver D. Hart (1986) 'The Costs and Benefits of Ownership: A Theory of Vertical and Lateral Integration', *Journal of Political Economy*, 94: 691–719.

Harris, Milton and Arthur Raviv (1979) 'Optimal Incentive Contracts with Imperfect Information', *Journal of Economic Theory*, 20: 231–59.

Landa, Janet T. (1986) 'Hadley v. Baxendale Revisited: The Foreseeability and the Mitigation Doctrines in Contract Law'. Hoover Institution working paper E-86-48, Stanford University.

Loeb, Martin and Wesley Magat (1979) 'A Decentralized Method for Utility Regulation', *Journal of Law and Economics*, 22: 399–404.

Marshak, Jacob and Roy Radner (1977) *The Theory of Teams*. New Haven: Yale University Press.

Masten, Scott E. (1988) 'A Legal Basis for the Firm', *Journal of Law, Economics and Organization*, 4: 181–98.

Moore, John (1988) 'Contracting between Two Parties with Private Information', *Review of Economic Studies*, 105: 49–70.

Myerson, Roger B. and Mark A. Satterthwaite (1983) 'Efficient Mechanisms for Bilateral Trading', *Journal of Economic Theory*, 29: 265–81.

Riordan, Michael H. (1984) 'Uncertainty, Asymmetric Information and Bilateral Contracts', *Review of Economic Studies*, 101: 83–94.

Riordan, Michael H. (1987) 'Hierarchical Control and Investment Incentives in Procurement'. Hoover Institution working paper E-77-44, Stanford University (September).

Riordan, Michael H. and David E.M. Sappington (1987) 'Information, Incentives, and Organizational Mode', *Quarterly Journal of Economics*, 102: 243–64.

Riordan, Michael H. and David E.M. Sappington (1988) 'Commitment in Procurement Contracting', *Scandinavian Journal of Economics*, 90: 357–72.

Sah, Raaj Kumar and Joseph E. Stiglitz (1986) 'The Architecture of Economic Systems: Hierarchies and Polyarchies', *American Economic Review*, 76: 716–27.

Tirole, J. (1986) 'Procurement and Renegotiation', *Journal of Political Economy*, 94: 235–59.

Wiggins, Steven N. (1988) 'The Comparative Advantages of Long Term Contracts and Firms', Texas A&M working paper (January).

Williamson, Oliver E. (1975) *Markets and Hierarchies: Analysis and Antitrust Implications.* New York: The Free Press.

Williamson, Oliver E. (1979) 'Transaction-cost Economics: the Governance of Contractual Relations', *Journal of Law and Economics*, 22: 3–61.

Williamson, Oliver E. (1985) *The Economic Institutions of Capitalism.* New York: The Free Press.

6

Vertical Integration, Transaction Costs and 'Learning by Using'

Kurt Lundgren

A classic question in transaction cost analysis is whether a transaction should be carried out in a hierarchy, that is, inside one single firm, or through the market. This question is discussed here with respect to the interaction for product development and innovation between the user of a product and the producer, 'learning by using'.

Intuitively, *vertical integration could*, in the presence of transaction costs, *protect valuable knowledge* developed in a 'learning by using' process. In Section 1 this intuitive reason for vertical integration is illustrated as well as questioned.

The main problem discussed in this chapter is the interdependence of *the incentives for the users to transmit their knowledge* to the producer and *the institutional relations* between the agents. In Section 2 a model is constructed of a network consisting of three firms, two manufacturers (the users) competing with each other in the final goods market, and one input producer whom the users have in common. Our findings indicate that in general vertical integration can be a useful tool to establish property rights to knowledge and to avoid the losses of successive monopolies. In the analysis these results are qualified with respect to (1) the condition where the market conditions in the input market restrict the possibilities of the input producer to set the (input) prices which maximize his own profit, and (2) the rate of substitutability in the final goods market.

In Section 3 a patent race model is applied to our network which is now assumed to be threatened by external rivals. How will increased rivalry from external producers affect the incentives of the users in our network to increase their efforts in R&D? And how does the answer to this question depend on one of them being vertically integrated with the input producer? In particular we analyse the possibilities for a change in the institutional relations between the agents to achieve a more efficient result in the generation of R&D. Is, for example, a dissolution of an integration an advisable measure to meet this external threat?

Studying vertical integration from a learning-by-using perspective yields new insights into the nature of vertical integration that are not revealed in traditional transaction cost analysis. In particular, the phenomenon of the *temporary, cyclical character of vertical integration* becomes visible.

1. Vertical integration, transaction costs and learning by using

Why do firms integrate?
Many reasons for vertical integration are presented in the literature. (For an overview see for example Williamson, 1971). Arrow (1975) emphasizes 'the role of uncertainty in the supply of the upstream good and the need for information by the downstream firm'. Such effects of information asymmetries are referred to by Oliver E. Williamson (1975, 1985) as 'information impactedness' in a more general framework. In the transaction cost approach the abilities of different institutional designs to reduce transaction costs are compared. In the approach developed by Williamson the market relation can create 'high-powered incentives', but vertical integration can reduce the level of transaction costs in the presence of complexity/uncertainty, opportunistic behaviour and small exchange numbers.

A neglected aspect of vertical integration is, in my opinion, the problems of *the relation between product innovation and institutional design*. The problem of innovation is treated by Williamson (1975) where the most discussed variable seems to be the size of the firm. In this chapter we focus on *the institutional design* under which product innovation takes place.

Learning by using
Product innovation is a concept which covers a broad field. It is a process which does not take place in isolation but in interaction between different agents in the economy. Often new products are introduced by new, emerging firms, where the entrepreneur interacts with basic research or, if the product is not too complicated, develops new knowledge himself. In other cases the interaction takes place between existing firms where the interaction between the users and producers ('learning by using') is of special importance. In von Hippel (1976) a sample of 111 scientific instrument innovations was studied. In approximately 80% of these the innovations were 'invented, prototyped and first-tested by the users

of the instruments rather than by an instrumental manufacturer'. Why is it that this process, 'learning by using', is so important for product innovation? One of the reasons is that 'many significant characteristics are revealed only after intensive or, more significantly, prolonged use' (Rosenberg, 1982: 122). Thus the user can detect shortcomings in the functioning of the product, he can suggest improvements or, together with the producer, engage in a project to improve the product.

Can the institutional design affect the user/producer interaction?

The user and the producer can either be independent firms linked together by the market or different departments (subsidiaries) of one single firm (vertical integration). Why the first or why the second variant? Is it, for example, reasonable to assume that a user (F II) will transmit his confidential information to an independent producer (F III) who is also the deliverer of his competitors (F I), or even worse – if the producer (F III) is vertically integrated with one of his competitors (F I)?

If it were possible for the parties in a product development project to write and enforce a market contract which could guarantee them an outcome of a co-operation which is better for them than their best alternative solution, such contracts would be concluded. In fact, contracts of that type also exist. Let us assume that the independent user (F II) transfers knowledge to the producer (F III) and that the result of that will be an improved functioning of the products made not only by F II but also of the products of F I, a subsidiary of F III who competes with our user F II in the final goods market. The improved functioning of the products of F I will have a negative effect on the sales of F II, a result which makes the initial transfer of knowledge from F II to F III doubtful.

Now if the outcomes could be forecast and a market contract concluded F II could be compensated for this loss. In such a case the institutional relation between the agents would be of less interest. In many cases, however, the transaction costs of concluding contracts of this type are prohibitive. Thus, if these transactions were connected with high costs, if opportunistic behaviour would be hard to detect, and so on, *vertical integration matters*. In this case we would expect the user primarily to transmit information to the user with whom he is vertically integrated and to be very careful in revealing confidential information to producers integrated with competing firms.

But we know that competing firms may co-operate. Confidential information is sometimes revealed to independent producers although the latter may sell their products to competing firms. How is it that the user in these cases can trust the producer? There are mechanisms which can provide the (vertically integrated) input producer with incentives to behave honestly in relation to a customer competing with his own subsidiary. Let us shortly mention two of these mechanisms.

In one-shot games the producer can benefit from an opportunistic strategy. But if the transactions can be expected to be *repeated* it could be important for the producer to behave co-operatively.

For similar reasons the integration with a known and well reputed customer can be an advantage and not a disadvantage in absorbing the experiences of other users. *The brand name* of the partner can serve as a hostage to facilitate co-operation. The costs of opportunistic behaviour will now include the potential losses in the value of the brand name of the well reputed partner.

Vertical integration as a method for the protection of knowledge

Let us return to our user who is assumed to have developed a piece of knowledge which, if transferred to the producer, can improve the functioning of his products. If this knowledge is transferred to the producer, the latter can earn more money if he reveals this confidential information to other users as well, thus making our first user worse off. But given that the user can forecast this behaviour on the part of the producer, he will not transmit any information to the producer in the first place. The outcome where the user reveals the knowledge to the producer and the latter keeps it to himself is therefore disequilibrium. By giving up his independence, allowing hierarchical control and thereby voluntarily giving up the possibility to spread the information to other users as well, thus inducing the user to transmit his knowledge, the producer can do better than the outcome of the initial equilibrium which meant that no information was transmitted.

In this case the user has two options:

1. To build up an input department of his own.
2. To integrate backward with an existing producer.

The first solution demands the necessary skills to be developed inside the new department, probably making this solution rather expensive. If so, backward vertical integration with an already existing producer can be the solution to guarantee property rights to knowledge. Is this aspect of vertical integration important? In real life many reasons related to transaction cost interfere. Among these can be the desire to protect knowledge. Let us study an example of this which also indicates some of the factors which must be present to induce an integration.

SKF's purchase of Hofors – an example

When the Swedish ball bearing producer Svenska Kullagerfabriken (SKF) acquired the steel mill Hofors in 1916, SKF had for many years made use of modern science to develop the understanding of how reliability in ball bearing work could be improved. For this reason SKF started a laboratory for research on the material problems in 1911. At the SKF laboratory chemical and metallurgic investigations were initiated in order to localize the shortcomings of the steel. But 'those different shortcomings could only be eliminated gradually and to the degree that it was possible to persuade the steel mill in question about the desirability of a more scientific control of all the stages in the production process' (Wingquist quoted in Steckzén, 1957b: 132)

The task of inducing the mills to follow the descriptions was not easy. Their metallurgic know-how was not especially developed, yet they could find a market for their products without being forced to satisfy the quality demands of SKF. Given the bad experience of arguing with independent mills, the founder of SKF, Sven Wingquist, began to consider the possibility of *acquiring* an iron mill which could be controlled by SKF and which could guarantee deliveries of high-quality ball bearing steel. At the SKF board meeting, Wingquist presented a report on the steel issue. He forecast a rapidly growing demand for high-quality steel which would make it possible for the mills to raise the prices or force SKF to drop its quality requirements.

> 'The only possibility of improving this situation and guaranteeing our supply of high-quality steel for the future seems to be if the company acquire a mill of its own with sufficient access to ores suitable for us, enough energy supply and the possibility of a smooth adjustment to our growing demand. . . . Another advantage is that with a mill at our own disposal we might totally control the character and quantity of production according to what is most advantageous for us. We might not only control the technical part of the production, for example regarding the chemical compositions of the products, heat-treatment etc., but we could also arrange the breeding of the material which would be more advantageous to carry out at the mill than at the ball bearing factory.' (Steckzén, 1957b, 392).

Up to this point the arguments for the purchase are of a 'traditional' transaction cost character. An integration could reduce the haggling over prices and qualities. But there are also arguments for the purchase that are not considered in traditional transaction cost analysis.

According to Wingquist, the experiences developed by SKF, partly in laboratory work and partly during the production process, had to be transferred to the producers. 'Furthermore, all our findings and experiences will be kept to ourselves, which means that the considerable profits we otherwise would be obliged to renounce to the mills, would be utilized by ourselves' (Steckzén, 1957b: 392–3). After analysing the laboratory protocols from different suppliers the board later decided to make an offer to buy the Hofors mill.[1]

Alternative to vertical integration
But was there *no alternative way of making this arrangement?* Might SKF have *patented* the process and might satisfactory results have been achieved through the bargaining power of the patents?

SKF's problem was to develop a reliable bearing steel and to improve its endurance fatigue properties. These properties are determined by the contents of slag, sulphur, phosphorous and other contaminations, how processes like decarbonization and annealing have been carried out, and so on.

Some processes for removal of slag are patentable, but for patenting a certain level of the invention is demanded. Much of the skill required for developing such a steel might have been classified as 'obvious to person skilled in the art' by the patent authorities; nevertheless a whole collection of such 'obvious findings' taken together can be very valuable. It was know-how rather than a discernible innovation that was important. There was also another reason, however, why patenting was not a suitable method of protecting the knowledge. In order to get a patent the findings must be published, and in many cases the costs for prosecuting encroachments on process technology patents are prohibitive. So patenting in such cases does not give any protection.

Is this case exceptional? Many studies in innovation seem to indicate that the role of patenting in protecting property rights to knowledge is limited. ('In fact, managers placed greater faith in secrecy as a means of protecting their property right' – quoted from a summary by Katz and Shapiro, 1987: 403.) The conclusion of such an analysis is that vertical integration can be one possible solution to the problem of how the initiator could safeguard for himself the maximum returns to his investments in the development of knowledge. However, this method seems to be favourable only in certain circumstances – for example, the knowledge must be difficult to patent. Of course vertical integration cannot mean total protection; trade secrets can be leaked by engineers or skilled workers who leave the company. On the whole, however, corporate law offers more possibilities of protecting the knowledge inside an integrated firm than do transactions between independent firms.

The role of firm specificity in vertical integration
In Williamson (1985) *investments in firm specific assets* is the most importance factor in explaining vertical integration: 'The importance of asset specificity to transaction cost economies is difficult to exaggerate' (Williamson, 1985: 56).

But what is the role of asset specificity in the transaction we have discussed? Of course there were investments of specific character made by the contractual parties, among which the building up of a specific information and communication system to facilitate discussion between the experts on bearings and metallurges, might have been the most important. (For a discussion of investments in information channels see Arrow, 1974, or Lundvall, 1985.)

One of the most important features of the transaction, however, was the need for protection of the metallurgic knowledge. This 'good' was not of a specific character; it was because of its *general* applicability that it needed protection. But even if the asset in this case was general in character, *it had the same function as firm-specific investments in Williamson's examples*, that is, in a world of bounded rationality it provided the agents (in this case the Hofors part) with the possibility to behave opportunistically.

This means that investments in 'firm-specific assets' do not seem to be a necessary condition for vertical integration. If the asset we study is knowledge, it has other properties which make it difficult to carry out transactions with it in the market; difficulties in convincing the customer of its value without revealing the trade secret, difficulties in preventing resales and so on.

Vertical integration and the loss of external user information
So far we have studied an example of how vertical integration in certain circumstances could serve the purpose of preventing competing firms from getting access to knowledge, and in that way could provide the user with incentives to transmit his experiences to the producer.

order to achieve compatibility and profitability.

In this section the four types of strategic alliance corresponding to the four different strategic paths have been discussed as pure types. It was mentioned though that one type of alliance is sometimes formed to increase bargaining power in other alliances, for example using horizontal alliances to influence vertical relationships (Reve, 1986). More complex sets of strategic alliances are found in Japanese *keiretsu* relationships of the major corporate groups (Imai and Itami, 1981). Here all four types of alliance constitute one big network organization (Imai, 1985). Similar patterns can be found for some of the major European corporations, for example Swedish Volvo, although the amount of capital control is typically higher.

While *keiretsu* relationships are built around a strong corporate core, such as Mitsui or Mitsubishi, network organizations are also found among smaller firms (Miles and Snow, 1986). In fact, the core skills which keep some of these network organizations together are simply the networking management capacity. An example has been given by Imai (1985) in the case of Dainichi's R&D efforts in robotics. Dainichi is neither a robot manufacturer nor a robot user, but it is an integrator of manufacturers and users. Here interface skills become the strategic core of the network organization, and the full range of strategic alliances are activated to attain strategic goals.

These two types of network organizations – those which centre on a dominant corporate group and those which are built on interface skills – represent, in this author's view, business organizations of the future.

The role of incentives

In the sections on strategic core and strategic alliances attention centred on core skills and complementary skills. In the initial contract formulation incentives represented the second component that needs to be attended to. The main difference between internal and external contracts is the range of incentives available for governance of exchange. In principle internal contracts rely on hierarchical controls, and external contracts rely on relational controls. In the first case, authority and fiat can be used for making decisions. In the second case, negotiations and consensus are resorted to. What is typically found in both cases is a mixture of hierarchical and relational elements (Stinchcombe, 1985) or a mutual penetration of the organization principle and market principle

(Imai and Itami, 1981; Arndt, 1979).

Let us first discuss the two pure cases of organizational and interorganizational incentives. In the agency formulation an internal contract is established between a principal (for example a manager) and an agent (for example a subordinate). In order for the principal to get the agent to perform organizational tasks, an inducement–contribution balance has to be established defining what the agent is expected to do and what s/he receives in return (Barnard, 1938; Simon, 1955). The inducement–contribution balance also defines the limits of the authority relation available to the principal and within which the agent will comply. Under opportunism conditions shirking behaviour is likely to occur among agents, such as holding down productivity or on-the-job consumption. If performance can be monitored and measured, results-based incentives can be used. Examples include piece-rate wage systems, profits-based bonuses, and stock options plans.

When asset specificity is high and performance is difficult to monitor and measure, other types of organizational incentive have to be resorted to. In bureaucracies internal labour markets represent an organizational incentive to perform, given that people seek promotions that usually involve both higher pay and higher status, and sometimes even more rewarding work. This also suggests a whole range of motivational measures which are commonly used by organizations (see, Porter and Lawler, 1972; Steers and Porter, 1975). Participation in decision making and industrial democracy plans should probably also be considered as some types of organizational incentive, as can also be much of recent human resource management techniques.

More significant from a contract point of view are the efforts to infuse the organization with shared values (Selznick, 1957) which seem to be the essence of organizational culture (Ouchi, 1981, Schein, 1985). What is important for contracting in organizational culture is that trust replaces monitoring and control, thus creating transaction cost-efficient governance structures compared to traditional hierarchical contracts.

Currently, there seem to be two trends in business organizations, at least in Europe and the United States, when it comes to organizational incentives and control. The first is an increased reliance on market-based incentives within organizations, for example, in the use of profit centres, transfer pricing, results-based remuneration, and other types of decentralization measures. The second is an increased interest in organizational culture and governance through shared values and trust. Both developments supplement the traditional hierarchical authority systems as means of organizational governance, and the range of 'organizational incentives' has been broadened.

Although most managers know which organizational incentives are available, the challenge is often to find which incentives are appropriate for which core skills. A simple notion of economic man may lead to a predominance of economic incentives, while some organizational perspectives may overemphasize psychological and social incentives. It is a fine mix, and no final answers can be given here. The field of organization behaviour should have much to offer in increasing our understanding of organizational incentive issues. What is stressed here is simply that organizational incentives should depend on the asset specificity of the skills involved.

When it comes to external contracts, the range of incentives available is much narrower than in internal contracts. Traditional hierarchical governance cannot be used as there is no well defined authority relation between the contracting parties. Thus the agency problem of the alliance is more complex than the agency problem of the organization.

There are basically two approaches to the agency problems of alliances. One is the economic approach in which self-interested actors choose a co-operative solution to increase joint profits. Transactions have to be protected by safeguards, and relations remain impersonal and unstable. Typically a game formulation is used for analysing such bilateral contracting.

The other approach is more behavioural in nature and attaches a value to the relationship between the parties. Under this approach the identity of the exchange party is critical, and relations tend to be long-lasting. Contracts do not only apply to a particular transaction, thus both prior and future exchange matters. Social ties are built, and trust and solidarity develop between the parties. The exchange situation can best be described in terms of relations contracts (Macneil, 1980). Relations contracts are characterized by relational norms such as role integrity, trust, preservation of relation, conflict resolution and supracontract norms.

In the economic approach bilateral exchange is formulated as a bargaining problem. In bargaining the pattern of dependence between the parties is often the determining factor, and the various bases of power available are activated by both parties. This does not mean that the parties cannot reach co-operative agreements, but they will search for the best solution to the game, exploiting fully their game position.

In the behavioural approach bilateral exchange can also be seen as a bargaining situation, but a more long-range view is taken. As is the case in repeated, co-operative games, transactions can be undertaken using trust, and long-lasting, transaction cost-efficient contracts develop.

In the first case, the pattern of dependencies may define imbalanced power which allows for the use of authority and organization-like incentives. In the second case, shared values and exchange norms tend to develop as interorganizational incentives. In both cases, skills in negotiations and relationship management may have an impact on the terms obtained.

Comparing governance in internal and external contracts shows organizational governance to be hard and authority based, while interorganizational governance tends to be soft and negotiation based. In reality, the two modes of governance penetrate each other. Thus negotiation supplements authority in organizations, and power supplements negotiations in bilateral governance. Industrial democracy and participatory management is an example of the first, while auto franchising may be an example of the second (John, 1984).

In terms of strategic management the role of organizational and interorganizational incentives in maintaining core and complementary skills should be emphasized. Incentives need to be tailor-made to the assets in question depending on the asset specificity involved. Negotiations and relational skills tend to be more and more common in strategic management given the importance of strategic alliances and mixed modes of organizational governance.

An integrated model of strategy

The simple model of strategy developed here has two major elements: strategic core and strategic alliances. The strategic core is governed by internal contracts relying on organizational incentives, while the strategic alliances are governed by external contracts relying on interorganizational incentives. Core skills are high in asset specificity and are governed internally, while the complementary skills are of medium asset specificity and governed through alliances. All other assets of low specificity are obtained in the market.

Strategic management according to this model is the alignment of strategic core and strategic alliances to obtain sustainable competitive advantage. The model is a normative model arguing that efficiency gains can be obtained by drawing the efficient

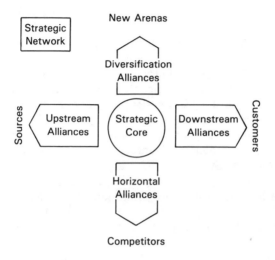

Figure 7.3 *Contracting model of strategic management*

boundaries of the firm. Thus there is an optimal set of internal and external contracts which define the ideal strategic position of the firm under given external conditions. The model does not argue that this strategy optimum can easily be found, but at least it gives some guidance in distinguishing between efficient and non-efficient strategies. In addition to providing a theoretical under-pinning of important aspects of strategic management, the concepts involved can easily be translated into managerial language. Strategy consists of critical skills and relationships held together by appropriate incentives. Skills and relationships need to be created, maintained and developed, and efficient boundaries have to be established to economize on transaction costs.

Using the notion presented that strategic core can be identified within the value chain, there are four types of economies to be obtained – downstream and upstream integration, scale and scope. When asset specificity is medium, such economies can most effi-ciently be obtained through strategic alliances, also of four types

– downstream alliance, upstream alliance, horizontal alliance, and diversification alliance (Figure 7.3)

Diversification alliances are limited to an exploitation of economies of scope, thus only include related diversification. Unrelated diversification to exploit internal capital market economies is not considered further, given the economic rationale against this type of diversification.

Horizontal alliances are limited to an exploitation of economies of scale, thus do not include the formation of cartels or monopolies, given that such alternatives are typically banned by antitrust legislation. In principle, all types of market imperfections can be exploited strategically, as strongly argued by Porter (1980).

The contracting model of strategy developed in this chapter primarily deals with governance issues of efficient boundaries, arguing that governance advantages produce an advantageous strategic position. Such a mode, I argue strongly, can fill in the organizational void of Porter's competitive positioning model. Pedagogically, the positioning model and the contracting model can be integrated into one figure (see Figure 7.4).

Putting the two strategy models into one figure does not necessarily produce an integrated model of strategy. Some would even prefer to keep the two models separate and not make things even more complex. If positioning and contracting are the two major elements of strategy, positioning being the external component, and contracting the internal and bridging component, it should be possible to suggest linkages between the two.

Going back to the figure of the integrated model, we see how downstream and upstream alliances are ways of positioning the firm relative to its customers and suppliers. In fact, vertical alliances may be ways in which entry barriers are erected and market imperfections are exploited. At the same time, there are integration economies to be obtained from vertical alliances, for example by superior logistics and marketing.

Horizontal alliances clearly have a role to play when it comes to potential invaders. Horizontal alliances may be formed with firms which are likely to be future invaders in order to pre-empt invasion. Furthermore they may be formed to create entry barriers which make it more difficult for potential invaders to succeed.

Diversification alliances basically have the objective of taking the firm into another competitive arena, thus going beyond Porter's industry-type analysis. If diversification means forming technology contracts with other firms, it may also be a way of meeting substitutes in the existing competitive arena. Thus

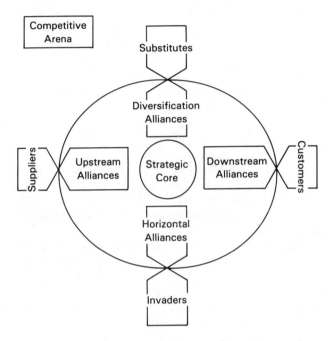

Figure 7.4 *Integrated model of strategic management*

diversification alliances may be one way of technology transfer which makes the firm ready to meet challenges from substitutes in an existing competitive arena, or such alliances may be a way of moving the firm out of a mature competitive industry and into new arenas when new technology takes over.

The illustrative propositions show the directions in which an integrated model can be developed. It is, however, beyond the scope of this chapter to develop the full set of more detailed propositions which will extend the integrated model of strategy proposed here into a full-fledged theory of strategic management. The purpose of this chapter is to take a first step suggesting some direction in theory development. First of all, a contract theory of strategy needs to be more precisely developed, for example in operationalizing asset specificity, core and complementary skills, and organizational and interorganizational incentives.

Fully developed, an integrated model of strategy should capture the full repertoire of strategies a firm can activate. The model should point out the strategic expansion paths available, and it should demonstrate how the various alternatives interact. Furthermore, the model should allow for external changes to guide the firm in its adaptation to changing markets. This final factor shows the importance of joining the positioning model of strategy with the contracting model of strategy to stay with the original notion of strategy as the adaptation between organization and environment to attain strategic and economic goals.

Conclusion

This chapter has two ambitious objectives. First, it sets out to develop a contract theory of strategic management. Second, it points toward an integrated model of strategy in which the positioning model and the contracting model are integrated into a common framework.

In reaching for these two ambitious objectives a number of complex concepts have been used. Although often imprecisely defined with much ambiguity to be resolved, the concepts advanced suggest a managerial language of core and alliances which is useful in working with firms, but also an interdisciplinary language of contracts which is useful in strategy research. The value of the framework presented ultimately rests on its ability to provide strategic guidance for firms and managers, and on its ability to provide some research guidance to the field of strategic management.

The research agenda is overwhelming. It includes further theory development, and more work in the area of contracts and incentives. It includes derivation of research propositions, in the vein initiated by researchers such as David Teece (1987). It includes more precise operationalizations of variables, and it requires empirical testing of predictions. There is a need for comparative empirical studies of efficient boundaries, skills and incentives. And finally, more research rigour is needed within the field of strategic management, in terms both of theory and of methods. The present chapter takes a small step on the theory development avenue. Others need to fill in the subsequent steps.

Note

Helpful comments from Oliver Williamson are acknowledged.

References

Ansoff, J. Igor (1965) *Corporate Strategy*, New York: McGraw Hill.

Arndt, Johan (1979) 'Toward a Concept of Domesticated Markets', *Journal of Marketing*, 43: 69–75.

Barnard, Chester I. (1938) *The Functions of the Executive*. Cambridge, Mass.: Harvard University Press.

Chandler, Alfred D. Jr (1962) *Strategy and Structure*. Cambridge, Mass.: MIT Press.

Chandler, Alfred D. Jr (1977) *The Visible Hand*. Cambridge, Mass.: Harvard University Press.

Coase, Richard, H. (1937) 'The Nature of the Firm', *Economica*, 4: 386–405.

Cyert, Richard M. and James G. March (1963) *A Behavioural Theory of the Firm*. Englewood Cliffs, NJ: Prentice Hall.

Daft, Richard L. and Karl E. Weick (1984) 'Toward a Model of Organizations as Interpretation Systems', *Academy of Management Review*, 9: 284–96.

Doeringer, Peter B. and Michael J. Piore (1971) *Internal Labor Markets and Manpower Analysis*. Lexington, Mass.: Heath.

Duncan, Robert B. (1972) 'Characteristics of Organizational Environments and Perceived Environmental Uncertainty', *Administrative Science Quarterly*, 17: 313–27.

Fama, Eugene F. (1980) 'Agency Problems and the Theory of the Firm', *American Economic Review*, 76: 971–83.

Fama, Eugene F. and Michael C. Jensen (1983) 'Agency Problems and Residual Claims', *Journal of Law and Economics*, 26: 327–49.

Grönhaug, Kjell and Geir Kaufmann (eds) (1988) *Innovation: A Cross-disciplinary Perspective*. Oslo: Norwegian University Press.

Hart, Oliver and Bengt Holmstrom (1987) 'The Theory of Contract', in T. Bewley (ed.) *Advances in Economic Theory*, pp. 71–155. Cambridge: Cambridge University Press.

Imai, Ken-ichi (1985) 'Network Organization and Incremental Innovation in Japan', Discussion paper No. 122, Institute of Business Research, Hitotsubashi University, Tokyo.

Imai, Ken-ichi (1988) 'The Corporate Network in Japan', *Japanese Economic Studies*, 16: 3–37.

Imai, Ken-ichi and Hiroyuki Itami (1981) 'The Firm and Market in Japan – Mutual Penetration of the Market Principle and Organization Principle', Discussion paper No. 104, Institute of Business Research, Hitotsubashi University, Tokyo.

Itami, Hiroyuki (1987) *Mobilizing Invisible Assets*. Cambridge, Mass.: Harvard University Press.

Jensen, Michael C. and William H. Meckling (1976) 'Theory of the Firm: Managerial Behavior, Agency Costs, and Ownership Structure', *Journal of Financial Economics*, 3: 305–60.

John, George (1984) 'An Empirical Investigation of Some Antecedents of Opportunism in a Marketing Channel', *Journal of Marketing Research*, 21: 278–89.

Jones, Gareth R. and Charles W.L. Hill (1988) 'Transaction Cost Analysis of Strategy–Structure Choice', *Strategic Management Journal*, 9: 159–72.

Kay, Neil M. (1984) *The Emergent Firm: Knowledge Ignorance and Surprise in Economic Organization*. New York: St Martin's Press.

Klein, B., R. Crawford and A.A. Alchian (1978) 'Vertical Integration, Appropriate Rents and the Competitive Contracting Process', *Journal of Law and Economics*, 21: 297–326.

Lippman, S.A. and R.P. Rumelt (1982) 'Uncertain Imitability: An Analysis of Interfirm Differences in Efficiency under Competition', *Bell Journal of Economics*, 13: 418–38.

Macneil, Ian R. (1974) 'The Many Futures of Contract', *Southern California Law Review*, 47: 691–748.

Macneil, Ian R. (1980) *The New Social Contact: An Inquiry Into Modern Contractual Relations*. New Haven, Conn.: Yale University Press.

March, James G. (1981) 'Footnotes to Organizational Change', *Administrative Science Quarterly*, 26: 563–77.

March, James G. and Johan P. Olsen (1975) *Ambiguity and Choice in Organizations*. Bergen: Norwegian University Press.

Miles, Raymond E. and Charles C. Snow (1986) 'Network Organizations: New Concepts for New Forms', *California Management Review*, 28: 62–73.

Nelson, Richard R. and Sidney G. Winter (1982) *An Evolutionary Theory of Economic Change*. Cambridge, Mass.: Harvard University Press.

Ouchi, William G. (1981) *Theory Z: How American Business Can Meet the Japanese Challenge*. Reading, Mass.: Addison-Wesley.

Pfeffer, Jeffrey and Gerald R. Salancik (1978) *The External Control of Organizations*. New York: Harper & Row.

Porter, Lyman W. and Edward E. Lawler III (1972) *Behavior in Organizations*. New York: McGraw Hill.

Porter, Michael E. (1980) *Competitive Strategy*. New York: The Free Press.

Porter, Michael E. (1985) *Competitive Advantage*. New York: The Free Press.

Reve, Torger (1986) 'Organization for Distribution', *Research in Marketing*, 8: 1–26.

Rumelt, Richard P. (1982) 'Towards a Strategic Theory of the Firm', in Robert Boyden Lamb (ed.) *Competitive Strategic Management*, pp. 556–70. Englewood Cliffs, NJ: Prentice-Hall.

Schein, Edgar H. (1985) *Organizational Culture and Leadership*. San Francisco: Jossey-Bass.

Selznick, Philip (1957) *Leadership in Administration*. Evanston, Ill.: Row.

Simon, Herbert A. (1955) *Administrative Behavior*. New York: Macmillan.

Simon, Herbert A. (1960) *The New Science of Management Decision*. New York: Harper.

Steers, Richard M. and Lyman W. Porter (1975) *Motivation and Work Behavior*. New York: McGraw Hill.

Stern, Louis W. and Adel. I El-Ansary (1988) *Marketing Channels*. Englewood Cliffs, NJ.: Prentice-Hall.

Stern, Louis W. and Torger Reve (1980) 'Distribution Channels as Political Economies: A Framework for Comparative Analysis', *Journal of Marketing*, 44: 52–64.

Stinchcombe, Arthur L. (1959) 'Bureaucratic and Craft Administration of Production: A Comparative Study', *Administrative Science Quarterly*, 4: 168–87.

Stinchcombe, Arthur L. (1985) 'Contracts as Hierarchical Documents', in Arthur L. Stinchcombe and Carol Heimer (eds) *Organization Theory and Project Management*, 121–71. Oslo: Norwegian University Press.

Teece, David J. (1985) 'Applying Concepts of Economic Analysis to Strategic

Management', in Johannes Pennings (ed.) *Organizational Strategy and Change*, 35–63. San Francisco: Jossey-Bass.

Teece, David J. (1987) *The Competitive Challenge: Strategies for Industrial Innovation and Renewal*. Cambridge, Mass.: Ballinger.

Thompson, James D. (1967) *Organization in Action*. New York: McGraw Hill.

Thorelli, Hans B. (1986) 'Networks: Between Markets and Hierarchies', *Strategic Management Journal*, 7: 37–52.

Williamson, Oliver E. (1975) *Markets and Hierarchies*. New York: The Free Press.

Williamson, Oliver E. (1979) 'Transaction-Cost Economics: The Governance of Contractual Relations', *Journal of Law and Economics*, 22: 232–61.

Williamson, Oliver E. (1981) 'The Economics of Organization: The Transaction Cost Approach', *American Journal of Sociology*, 87: 548–77.

Williamson, Oliver E. (1985) *The Economic Institutions of Capitalism: Firms, Markets and Relational Contracting*. New York: The Free Press.

PART III

ISSUES OF LABOUR ORGANIZATION

8

The Viability of Worker Ownership: an Economic Perspective on the Political Structure of the Firm

Henry Hansmann

1. Introduction

Both scholars and reformers have long been fascinated by worker ownership of enterprise. Nevertheless, existing analyses fail to explain adequately the observed distribution of worker ownership across industries – a phenomenon that Williamson has described as 'the producer cooperative dilemma' (1986: 165–8). I have suggested elsewhere that an important reason for this is that previous analyses have largely neglected a critical consideration: the cost of collective decision making, or what we might term the internal politics of the firm (Hansmann, 1988).[1] I wish to expand on that theme here, and to explore its implications for the full range of alternative means through which transactions between labour and other participants in the firm can be structured, including collective bargaining, employee stock ownership plans, and codetermination.

The issue is of interest not simply in the context of worker ownership, but more generally as well. All firms in which ownership is shared among a numerous group of individuals – including publicly held business corporations as well as most forms of co-operative and mutual enterprise – involve not just hierarchical control mechanisms but political mechanisms as well. And, while the efficiency of hierarchies has long been the subject of study within the theory of the firm, from Coase (1937) through to Simon (1947) and Williamson (1975), the internal politics of the firm has been much neglected.

An important general implication of this enquiry is that political mechanisms work well within firms only in relatively simple settings. In more complex environments, it appears that markets, perhaps supplemented by various forms of complex contracting, offer more efficient representation of the interests of the parties involved.

2. The existing pattern of worker ownership

If market forces tend to select for efficient organizational forms, then, in free-enterprise economies, we should expect to find worker-owned firms in those industries in which they have efficiency advantages over investor-owned firms, and to find investor-owned firms elsewhere. Thus, by observing the existing pattern of worker ownership across industries, we should be able to test theories about the relative efficiency of investor-owned and worker-owned firms.

Taking the American economy as an example, we find that worker-owned firms are rare in the industrial sector. If we exclude firms that have adopted employee stock ownership plans in recent years – a subject to which we shall return later – there have been only a few industries in which worker-owned industrial firms have proven themselves viable over the long run. The most conspicuous example today is the plywood industry, in which more than a dozen worker co-operatives have maintained substantial market share for a number of decades (Berman, 1967; Greenberg, 1984).

In the service sector, on the other hand, worker-owned firms are common. In particular, they are the dominant mode of organization among firms of service professionals: law and accounting firms are almost universally owned by the professionals who work for them, and firms of investment bankers, doctors, engineers and management consultants are frequently organized this way as well. Moreover, although this is less common, such firms also appear occasionally where the workers involved are not professionals. In particular, taxi-cab companies are often worker-owned, and there have long been a number of worker-owned refuse collection companies on the West Coast of the US (Russell, 1985b).[2]

To some extent, of course, this particular distribution of worker-owned firms is a response to peculiar features of the American economy and American law.[3] In general respects, however, it appears typical of the pattern of worker ownership in other developed market economies as well.[4]

In order to understand the reasons for this pattern, it helps to view it in light of the potential costs and benefits that worker ownership might bring.

3. The benefits of worker ownership

As compared with the standard business corporation, in which investors own the firm and workers are hired through market contracting, worker ownership offers several potentially important efficiencies.

A. *Worker monitoring*

Because of the difficulty of monitoring individual workers, a degree of moral hazard necessarily infects market contracting for all but the simplest types of labour. Making the workers the owners may succeed in internalizing some of these costs, and hence improve productivity. Strong empirical evidence on this point is lacking (see Jones and Svejnar, 1982), although there is anecdotal evidence – for example, from the plywood industry – that worker ownership indeed has this effect (for example Greenberg, 1984).

Following this logic, it has sometimes been argued – most prominently by Alchian and Demsetz (1972) – that worker ownership can be understood largely as a response to moral hazard in labour contracting, and thus that worker ownership tends to arise in those situations in which workers are unusually hard to monitor. As it is, however, the existing pattern of worker ownership seems to be just the reverse of what one would expect if this were the case. In the service professions, for example, where worker ownership is the norm, the productivity of individual workers can be, and generally is, monitored quite closely (McChesney, 1982), while in most enterprises in which individuals work in large teams, so that their individual productivity is very difficult to determine, investor ownership predominates.

B. *Worker lock-in*

Workers often must make firm-specific investments in job skills and in personal living arrangements in the community where their firm is located. This locks them into the firm to a degree, and opens up the possibility that their employer will act opportunistically toward them in setting wages or other terms of employment. Worker ownership reduces the incentive for such opportunism, just as other forms of vertical integration do in other industrial settings (Williamson, 1985). This might lead one to expect worker ownership to arise where the problem of lock-in is most severe. Yet this consideration, too, fails to explain the existing pattern of worker ownership, since the types of worker found in worker-owned firms – taxi-cab drivers, refuse collectors, the semi-skilled labourers in the plywood co-operatives and, arguably, service professionals as well – are relatively mobile as workers go.[5]

C. Strategic behaviour in contracting

With investor ownership, management often has information about the firm's prospects that labour lacks, and this creates the incentive and the opportunity for strategic behaviour in bargaining over terms of employment. Strategic behaviour of this sort – for example, strikes and lock-outs – may increase significantly the transaction costs of reaching agreement. Again, worker ownership has the potential to reduce or eliminate the problem by eliminating the conflict of interest and the asymmetry of information between management and labour. Yet this consideration, too, fails to explain the existing pattern of worker ownership, since the potential asymmetry of information between management and workers seems unusually low, relatively speaking, in the types of firm in which worker ownership is common – such as small service firms in which the workers in question are professionals.

D. Agency costs of delegation to management

Finally, the problem of the separation of ownership and control – that is, the agency cost of policing management (Jensen and Meckling, 1976) – is potentially much less acute in worker-owned firms than it is in investor-owned firms. In contrast to investors – who are often widely dispersed, have no sources of information about the firm beyond publications, and hold the firm's securities as only one of a number of investments – workers have both the opportunity and incentive to acquire information about the effectiveness of management, or to appoint and hold accountable representatives who will do this for them, and then to act collectively to hold management accountable to their will. Nor is it necessary to forgo entirely the benefits of the market for corporate control when a firm is worker-owned: the workers can retain the right to sell the firm to outside investors at any point they wish, and in fact such transactions are relatively common (for example, among plywood co-operatives and investment banking firms).

But while this consideration may contribute to the success of worker-owned firms, it also fails to explain the existing distribution of worker ownership, since worker-owned firms tend to be sufficiently small so that, if investor-owned, they would most likely be closely held firms and thus not unusually subject to agency costs of this type.

E. Summary

In short, there is a variety of important respects in which one might expect worker-owned firms in general to face lower costs than investor-owned firms. The magnitudes of these potential efficiency gains across different industries do not, however, correlate well with the observed pattern of worker ownership; in general, they seem most important in large-scale, hierarchical firms and considerably less significant in the type of small-scale service enterprise where worker ownership is in fact most common. To explain the existing pattern of worker ownership we must, therefore, turn to the relative liabilities of worker ownership.

4. Costs of worker ownership

Worker ownership can, of course, often be a costlier governance structure than investor ownership. If this were not so, then the considerations just surveyed would presumably lead to the complete dominance of worker-owned over investor-owned firms in all industries.

A. Liquidity and risk-bearing

Most obvious among the costs of worker ownership are the problems associated with raising capital. Owing to the incentives for opportunism that arise when a firm borrows the capital needed to finance firm-specific assets (Klein et al., 1978), worker-owned firms must either pay a high cost to borrow such capital, or else require the workers to contribute some or all of that capital themselves and incur the attendant high costs of illiquidity and poorly diversified risk.

Clearly this consideration helps in explaining the existing distribution of worker ownership, which seldom appears in firms, such as those in the industrial sector, that require large amounts of firm-specific capital per worker.[6] Two further observations are important here, however. First, worker-owned firms are evidently viable even in relatively capital-intensive industries so long as the capital is not firm-specific and thus can be financed in large part by debt secured by a lien on the firm's assets. Risk bearing itself does not appear to be a major obstacle to worker ownership; evidently workers are prepared to bear a substantial amount of risk. Family farms are a familiar example. Investment banking firms organized as partnerships are another. And yet a third example, and one that we shall return to, is the recently proposed corporate take-over of United Air Lines under which its 6500 pilots have offered to purchase a controlling interest in the firm. Although it is not yet clear whether this plan will come to fruition, it appears sufficiently viable to have been taken seriously by all parties.[7] An important consideration here, presumably, is the fact that while airlines are relatively capital intensive, most of their assets – primarily planes – are not firm-specific.

Yet, while low amounts of firm-specific capital may be a necessary condition for worker ownership to be viable, it is not sufficient. There are many industries in the service sector that involve low amounts of firm-specific capital but in which worker ownership has never taken hold, such as hotel and restaurant services, the construction trades, and retailing.

B. Collective decision making

A second potential disadvantage of worker ownership vis-a-vis investor ownership is that which is our principal interest here: the costs of using some form of collective choice mechanism to aggregate the preferences of the owners of the firm. Jensen and Meckling have referred to this as 'the control problem' (1979: 488–9), though neither they nor subsequent authors have explored the issue in any detail.

We noted earlier that, as contrasted with investors, workers are often well situated to engage in effective oversight of management. They are on the spot, they have a proportionally large personal stake in the fortunes of the firm, and they are easily organized and assembled. Yet the political processes by which their preferences are aggregated and transformed to action can evidently engender substantial costs. In an investor-owned firm, the owners generally have highly homogeneous preferences; all essentially wish to maximize the net present value of the firm's future earnings.[8] Consequently, there is relatively little room for disagreement over the policies to be pursued by the firm. Workers within a given firm, in contrast, may have highly divergent interests in various aspects of firm policy.

There are various potential sources of conflict among the workers within a firm. To begin with, there can of course be disagreement over relative wages among different workers. Further, workers may also have different stakes in any pattern of investments chosen by the firm such as which plants to keep open, which processes to automate, or where to make further investments in safety. The extent to which workers' investments diverge in these respects is likely to be greater as the division of labour within the firm increases; where all workers do essentially the same job, they will be similarly affected by most decisions. But there may also be conflicts of interest among workers that have other sources besides differences in job assignments. For instance, if the amount of equity capital invested in the firm differs among workers – as will dramatically be the case, for example, if the firm's pension fund is the principal vehicle through which the workers invest in the firm – this may become a source of conflict: workers with disproportionately large amounts of capital invested (for example, older workers) will wish to have a larger amount of the firm's earnings attributed to capital (and hence distributed, for example, as earnings on amounts invested in the pension fund), and a smaller amount attributed to labour (and hence paid out as wages), than will other workers.

To be sure, none of these potential sources of conflict would probably be very troublesome in practice if there were obvious objective criteria to serve as focal points for making the decisions in question – for example, if wages or return on capital could simply be set on the basis of marginal productivity. But such objective criteria are usually absent or unmeasurable, and thus in each case there is generally considerable latitude for judgement and discretion, and hence room for active disagreement.

Existing theory in both political science and economics does not pinpoint well the sources of the costs of collective decision making. We know from public choice theory that the possibility of a voting cycle among alternatives increases as preferences among the electorate become more heterogeneous (Plott, 1976); that, even if individuals vote non-strategically, seriously inefficient decisions can result when the median voter's preferences are not those of the mean (Shepsle and Weingast, 1984); and that, while committee structures can inhibit cycling and facilitate the vote trading necessary to mitigate the median voter problem, committees themselves can be the source of seriously inefficient decisions (Weingast and Marshall, 1988). But the costs of political mechanisms may go well beyond these. For example, information biases may be a problem too: the high salience of wages and working conditions to workers may make them myopic in their role as owners. And the process costs of collective choice mechanisms can themselves be high: even if workers seek in all cases to exercise their collective control rights as owners efficiently and without opportunism, they may need to invest considerable time and effort in knowledge about the firm and about other workers' preferences, and in the meetings and other activities necessary to reach and implement effective collective decisions.

These costs of collective decision making appear to be extremely important in determining where worker ownership succeeds and how it is organized, and in fact appear to go far toward explaining the large residual in the existing pattern of worker ownership that is left unexplained by the other considerations reviewed above. The following section discusses some of the evidence.[9]

5. Evidence of the costs of collective decision making

A. Which firms succeed?

Striking evidence of the high costs of collective decision making comes from the fact that worker ownership is extremely rare in firms in which there is any substantial degree of heterogeneity in the work force. Most typically, the workers who share ownership within worker-owned firms all do extremely similar work and are of essentially equivalent status within the firm. This is evident in the professional service firms, where worker ownership seems best established. The partners in a law firm, for example, are all lawyers of roughly equal skill and productivity who work more or less independently of each other; rarely does one partner have substantial supervisory authority over another. And the same pattern is found in other industries in which worker ownership is common. Taxi-cab drivers and refuse collectors obviously also fit this mould, as do the pilots of United Air Lines. And the workers in the plywood co-operatives, who are only semi-skilled and unspecialized, commonly rotate through the various jobs in the mill; the only person in the firm with specialized skills, the manager, is in nearly all firms not a member of the co-operative but rather hired as a salaried worker (Berman, 1967; Greenberg, 1984).

The reason for this pattern, evidently, is that such circumstances provide the minimum opportunity for conflicts of interest among the worker–owners. Presumably greater diversity of interest among the workers involved severely compromises the viability of worker ownership.[10]

B. Structures to avoid the costs

Another indication that collective governance can be costly for worker-owned firms lies in the strong tendency of such firms to adopt rules and practices that tend to promote homogeneity of interest among the worker–owners where this might not otherwise exist.

For example, the plywood co-operatives nearly all adhere rigidly to a scheme under which all members of the firm receive the same rate of pay (Berman, 1967: 151–6). Even more striking, many of America's largest and most prosperous law firms have long followed a practice of sharing the partnership's earnings equally among all partners of a given age, regardless of individual productivity. Gilson and Mnookin (1985) seek to explain this practice as a mechanism for risk sharing. Yet, while this may be among the functions the practice serves, it seems implausible that risk sharing is the principal motivation for it. It is difficult to believe that lawyers who have already succeeded so well as to have been selected for partnership in one of the nation's most prosperous law firms, in which expected earnings per partner may well exceed half a million dollars per year, are so risk averse that, for that reason alone, they will abandon all financial incentives toward productivity just to assure that their own income will always be equal to the mean of others their age. Rather, it seems likely that these equal sharing schemes are adopted in important part to reduce conflicts in collective decision making by simply removing from the agenda, crudely but effectively, the potentially troublesome question of how the pie is to be divided.[11]

Law firms that do not adopt equal sharing rules commonly employ formulas under which a partner's share is determined according to specified indicia of productivity, such as hours billed or number and value of new clients brought to the firm. Such formulas – as opposed to less formal approaches under which a manager or committee has discretion to set relative shares as it thinks appropriate – are evidently an alternative effort to establish more or less objective, and hence uncontroversial, criteria for dividing the pie where equal sharing is too difficult to justify.[12] Even so, there is considerable dissension within firms about the structure of these formulas, and the resulting disagreements are an important source of instability among law partnerships.

Indeed, worker ownership seems to thrive only where, if equal sharing is not practicable, individual worker productivities are sufficiently easy to measure so that some relatively objective, and hence uncontroversial, method of pay based on that measure can be employed. Thus we find worker co-operatives among taxi drivers and refuse collection crews, where members of the co-operative bill clients individually and can simply be compensated with a fraction of those billings.

Worker-owned firms also commonly strive hard to assure that not only pay, but also work, is equalized among the members of the firm. The worker–owners in the plywood factories, as already noted, commonly rotate through the different jobs over time, so that there is little long-run specialization of work among them. Law firms strongly resist admitting to the partnership any lawyer who is not of roughly the same competence and productivity as the other partners; less qualified partners, if valuable to the firm, are kept on as permanent salaried associates rather than as partners who simply receive a smaller share of earnings. Similarly, law firms strongly resist letting some partners work fewer hours than average in exchange for a smaller share. The recent rapid increase in the number of women lawyers, for example, has created considerable pressure for part-time work arrangements to permit time for child-rearing. Many law firms now willingly accept such arrangements for young salaried associates, but refuse to permit women to be partners on a part-time basis.[13] This refusal is sometimes explained on the grounds that clients demand that attorneys be available full time, or that attorneys must practise full time to keep up their skills (Sorenson, 1983). But these explanations seem a bit forced. Rather, it appears likely that such inequalities among members of the firm are also resisted in considerable part because they tend to destabilize the co-operative governance structure.[14] A simple rule under which everyone does essentially the same amount and kind of work is by far the easiest to agree upon and to enforce, and these advantages are evidently often sufficient to outweigh the costs such rules engender in the form of inflexibility, poor incentives, and lack of diversification among the work force.[15]

To be sure, it is possible that such tendencies toward equality are adopted at least in part for other reasons. For example, workers who share ownership of a firm may be more inclined than they would otherwise be to consider themselves as a collective reference group for purposes of judging their individual welfare, and this could in turn create an incentive to flatten out the wage structure (Frank, 1984) and to determine levels of effort collectively in order to avoid an inefficient rat race (Frank, 1985). We cannot clearly conclude, therefore, that a high degree of heterogeneity in the work force will necessarily raise the transaction costs of decision making to an unmanageable level. We can, however, conclude that, whatever the reason may be, a highly homogeneous work force seems important to the viability of worker ownership.

C. Representative versus participatory democracy

In a large and complex firm, worker control must presumably be exercised through a representative rather than a highly participatory form of democracy (see Putterman, 1984; Russell,

1985a; Williamson, 1985). This is in fact the approach taken in the most prominent example of successful industrial worker co-operatives in a free enterprise economy, namely the well established group of roughly eighty affiliated worker co-operatives at Mondragon, Spain, which have a total of approximately 20,000 worker–members. In those firms, worker participation in control is largely confined to electing nine members to a supervisory board for terms of four years; the supervisory board, in turn, is responsible for appointing the firm's managers, who are appointed for a minimum of four years and cannot be removed except for cause (Thomas and Logan, 1982; Bradley and Gelb, 1983). This parallels the control structure employed in most publicly held investor-owned corporations, in which – aside from the right to vote directly on major corporate changes such as merger or liquidation – shareholder control is exercised only indirectly, through the election at large of a small number of directors at intervals of a year or more.

One might think that such a system of representative worker democracy would avoid or mitigate many of the costs that might be engendered by more direct or participatory systems of democracy when the work force is heterogeneous. And indeed the Mondragon experience demonstrates that worker co-operatives with such a governance structure can operate successfully in industrial enterprise.[16] Yet Mondragon remains a unique case, and it is unclear how easily it can be replicated. In general, successful worker ownership remains largely confined to small firms in which a highly participatory form of democracy is feasible. And even in the few worker-owned firms that are large, such as the major accounting firms with thousands of partners, there is generally a high degree of homogeneity among the worker–owners.

This pattern suggests that simply employing a representative form of democracy does not suffice to make the costs of collective decision making acceptable for worker-owned firms with a heterogeneous work force. Why might this be? Three possible reasons come to mind. First, representative democracy may be affected by some of the same inefficiencies, whether of biased decisions or high process costs, that affect more direct forms of democracy in the context of a heterogeneous work force. For example, there may be a tendency for election of directors to become highly politicized. Or, second, representative forms of democracy may attenuate the worker's participation in control to the point where worker ownership loses some of its important potential advantages over investor ownership, such as closer supervision of management or reduction in opportunistic behaviour on the part of the firm toward its workers. Or, as yet a third (and rather speculative) possibility, when electing directors in a large firm workers may tend to have in mind principally their interests as investors in the firm rather than their interests as workers. If so, they would tend to elect much the same type of directors that would be elected if the firm were investor owned. And, in that case, ownership might as well be assigned to investors, since management will not be much different and the firm would gain improved access to capital.

D.   Evidence from other types of co-operatives
The conclusion that heterogeneity of participants is inimical to the governance of worker-owned firms is reinforced by the experience with other types of co-operative. Both producer and consumer co-operatives are in fact common in the American economy in industries ranging from hardware wholesaling to dairy product marketing to electric utilities. In virtually all situations in which they have prospered, however, they are characterized by extreme homogeneity among the members. In the few situations in which this is not the case – such as among the larger mutual insurance companies – the firms are typically operated as purely managerial entities, with the members exercising no meaningful voice whatever in the control of the firm (Hansmann, 1988).

6. Other mechanisms for worker participation

So far we have been considering just two polar forms for organizing the firm: full investor ownership or full worker ownership. As we have seen, both forms are subject to inefficiencies. Indeed, Aoki (1980; 1984a) has argued plausibly that, since suboptimization is likely to result if either investors or workers alone have control over decision making concerning variables that cannot be explicitly governed by contract between them, greater efficiency is likely to be achieved if some mechanism for shared decision making between workers and investors can be arranged.

The preceding discussion suggests that there are likely to be serious problems in any effort to share control of the firm between two groups with such heterogeneous interests as investors and workers. With this in mind, it is instructive to survey the forms of worker participation that have most commonly been implemented or proposed.

A. Codetermination

The most direct approach to sharing decision making between investors and workers is to establish joint control formally by having workers and investors participate equally in electing representatives to the firm's board of directors. German-style codetermination has essentially this objective. From all that has already been said, however, one would expect that any true sharing of formal control, through the firm's internal political process, between two such heterogeneous groups as workers and investors might be highly inefficient. And indeed this seems consistent with the German experience: codetermination in itself does not in general seem to have brought true worker participation in control of the corporation at the board level, which effectively remains in the hands of investors. Rather, as Aoki has noted (1984a: 167), the real value of codetermination apparently lies in the access it gives workers to accurate information about the firm that would otherwise be confined to management. This information can then be used by the workers when bargaining with management in contexts other than decision making at the board level – as when the firm's management bargains with individual workers, with the works councils, and with the unions – where shared information presumably reduces the incentive for, and hence the costs of, strategic bargaining behaviour. But if this is so, then there may not be much difference in practice between German-style codetermination and a system, such as that which has been in effect in Sweden since 1976, in which workers are simply entitled to one or two representatives on the board of directors.

B. Unions

In collective bargaining conducted through labour unions, workers have their own separate political process that is not involved in selecting the firm's management but rather selects representatives to bargain with the firm's management.

It might at first seem that unions have most of the costs and few of the benefits of worker ownership. On the one hand, because unions do not involve full worker ownership, they do not entirely remove the possibility that the management of the firm will behave opportunistically toward the workers (or vice versa). Yet on the other hand, they potentially have all the costs of collective decision making among workers.

There is probably some truth to this view, and this may help explain the declining importance in the United States today of the model of collective bargaining that was adopted in American law in the 1930s. Whatever the overall efficiency of that model of worker representation, however, we can see many ways in which it has been adjusted in apparent recognition of the problems of collective representation that are our focus here.

To begin with, white-collar workers, and particularly workers with managerial or supervisory responsibilities, are generally not unionized; it is usually only the workers who comprise the lowest, most horizontal stratum among the firm's employees who belong to a union. Further, where the jobs held by the unionized workers are particularly diverse, the workers are frequently split up into separate bargaining units. As a consequence, there is in fact a fair degree of homogeneity of interest among the workers represented by any given union.

Further, unions typically bargain with management over only a relatively narrow range of issues immediately touching on the employees' interests, such as wages, hours and job classifications. Other issues, such as the firm's investment policies or even its policy on layoffs, are seldom bargained over even though, as Aoki suggests, it might be more efficient if workers were to be more actively involved in deciding such issues. Indeed, the unions themselves seem to wish to avoid broader involvement of this sort, and to keep the scope of bargaining narrowly confined. There may be a variety of reasons for this. But, whether it is cause or consequence, by adopting this strategy the union avoids some possibilities of costly internal conflict; expanding the scope of bargaining might bring substantial transaction costs that would outweigh the concomitant benefits.

Finally, it is conventional wisdom that unions are seldom democratic (Lipset et al., 1956). This is commonly deplored in both the social science and policy literature, much as the general absence of genuine shareholder democracy in publicly held business corporations was deplored twenty years ago. But it may be that greater democracy would bring much higher governance costs without much offsetting improvement in the accuracy with which the members' preferences are represented. Michels' (1949 [1911]) iron law of oligarchy may in fact be an economic law, at least where unions are concerned.

Similar considerations may help explain why it is that bargaining between a union and a firm is so often conducted in large part by representatives from the union's national office, rather than just by local union officials: it helps defuse even further the problem of local internal politics.[17]

C.   Employee stock ownership plans

Beginning about fifteen years ago, large numbers of American business corporations began to adopt so-called employee stock ownership plans (ESOPs) under which most or all of the firm's employees receive a portion of their annual compensation in the form of stock in the firm. In essence these plans are structured as deferred compensation plans, in which the employer deposits stock in a trust fund that holds the stock for the benefit of the participating employees. By 1986, 4700 companies had adopted such plans. Twenty-five percent of these plans owned more than 25% of the stock in their firms, and something less than 2% owned all of the stock (US GAO, 1986: 18, 39). One author estimates, perhaps generously, that today approximately 1000 to 1500 companies with a total of one million workers are 51% to 100% employee-owned through ESOPs (Blasi, 1988: 4).

The widespread adoption of these plans is not an unbiased indicator of their efficiency. Although the ESOP concept has been actively promoted since the 1950s, it did not become popular until ESOPs were granted substantial federal tax subsidies beginning in 1974 – tax subsidies that have since been broadened and deepened – and until it was discovered that creation of an ESOP could be a useful defensive tactic for management in an attempted corporate take-over.[18] It is entirely possible that, without these special advantages, ESOPs would remain rare. The numerous studies that have sought to measure directly the effect of ESOPs on worker productivity and firm profitability, though not conclusive, have to date failed to present clear evidence of improvements once tax subsidies have been controlled for.[19] Thus the only inference we can draw about the efficiency of ESOPs from their current popularity is that the magnitude of any inherent *in*efficiencies associated with them probably do not exceed, in general, the size of the tax subsidies given them.

For present purposes, however, the most interesting fact about ESOPs is that, whatever the motivation for adopting them, they generally provide for participation only in earnings, and not in control. Only rarely are they structured to give the workers a voice in the governance of the firm. To begin with, about half the stock held by ESOPs is non-voting stock (US GAO, 1986: 39). Further, the tax law provides that the power to vote an ESOP's stock need not be passed through to the workers in a privately held corporation, but rather can be voted by the plan's trustee.[20] And the trustee, in turn, can be appointed by the firm's management without consultation with the workers who are the plan's beneficiaries. In publicly held corporations in contrast, voting power must be passed through to the workers on all ESOP stock actually allocated to the workers – which is to say, not purchased through borrowing, as in the popular 'leveraged' ESOP.[21] These provisions are evidently important in understanding the pattern of ESOPs that has evolved. If we exclude so-called tax credit ESOPs – that is, ESOPs created under a special (and now repealed) provision effectively providing for a 100% tax subsidy to the plan – roughly 90% of all ESOPs are in privately held firms. Moreover, there are very few publicly traded firms in which an ESOP has more than 20% of the firm's stock, and perhaps none in which the plan has a majority of the stock (Blasi, 1988: 90–3, 103).[22] Firms in which a majority of the stock is held by an ESOP are virtually all privately held. And, although the law permits (but does not require) that votes on ESOP stock be passed through to employees in privately held firms, it appears that this is rarely done. A common pattern in privately held firms in which an ESOP holds a majority of the stock is for a small group of managers to own the rest, with which they control the firm through their power to appoint the ESOP's trustee (who is often, in fact, a manager). Thus, in neither publicly nor privately held firms is it the case that ESOPs permit much worker participation in the control of the firm. Indeed, an extensive 1986 survey found no firms with ESOPs in which employee representatives constituted a majority of the board of directors (US GAO, 1986: 40).

What is particularly interesting here is that voting rights are not passed through to workers even in firms in which the ESOP owns 100% of the firm's stock. Rather, voting rights are held by the ESOP's trustee, who in turn is appointed by a self-perpetuating board.[23] In effect, these firms are operated as nonprofits, in which directors with control but no claim on residual earnings are charged with managing the firm as fiduciaries for the benefit of the workers. Evidently those who have structured these firms have concluded[24] that any reduction in agency costs that might result from making management directly accountable to the firm's beneficial owners would be outweighed by the costs – perhaps in the form of inefficient decisions or high process costs – that would be engendered by the political process required for such accountability.[25]

Widespread experimentation with ESOPs is still too new to permit strong conclusions about worker ownership to be drawn from them. But we can at least say that they provide little affirmative evidence that direct worker participation in the control of enterprise through ownership can be made both effective and efficient with a heterogeneous work force, and considerable circumstantial evidence that such participation may be quite costly.

D.   Management buyouts

Recent years have brought rapidly increasing numbers of management buyouts of firms whose stock had previously been publicly traded. In these transactions, the firm is converted to private ownership through the repurchase of all of its stock by a group led by the firm's management. The resulting firms might appear to be instances of a reductive form of worker ownership in which the worker–owners are confined to the firm's managers. As it is, however, these firms do not provide much evidence concerning the viability of worker ownership. Typically only a very small number of managers participates in ownership of these firms. Further, the managers' share in ownership is often modest. In one sample of fifty management buyouts, for example, the officers of the median firm already owned 11.5% of the firm's equity before the transaction, and increased this only to 16.7% afterwards (Smith, 1988); other investors continued to hold the great bulk of the firm's stock. And finally, although experience with management buyouts has been too brief for a clear pattern to emerge, the conventional wisdom is that a substantial number of the firms involved return to public ownership around five years after the transaction takes place, casting some doubt on the proposition that management participation in ownership is a major source of efficiency.

E.   The Meidner Plan

A very different approach to worker participation in the control of enterprise was offered by the original Swedish Meidner Plan, under which a controlling interest in large firms would eventually come to be held in a mutual fund controlled by the labour federation. The plan provided that workers in individual firms would be given the right to vote the shares initially accumulated by the fund up to a total of 20% of the firm's total stock; shares accumulated by the fund beyond that would be voted by a labour board covering the entire industrial sector in which the firm operated (Meidner, 1978). By thus providing for only a limited degree of worker control at the level of the firm, the plan might have avoided some of the internal political costs associated with simple worker ownership, while it still promised to reduce to some extent any incentive for the management of the firm to behave opportunistically with respect to labour. On the other hand, control of firms by labour-dominated boards at a sectoral level may have engendered some inefficiencies of its own. In any event, any effort to use such a device to affect corporate control seems to have been abandoned in 1984 when, instead of the original Meidner Plan, a much more modest scheme was enacted that created five regional wage earners' funds, none of which is permitted to own more than 8% of the stock of any single firm (Flanagan, 1987).

In summary, the experience with each of the alternative structures for worker participation described here seems consistent with the conclusion that direct involvement of a heterogeneous work force in control of the firm is not promising as a route to efficiency.

7. Conclusion

The classical model of the business corporation, under which formal control of the firm is confined to the firm's equity investors while management in turn deals with workers through simple individual market contracts, leaves room for considerable inefficiency in terms of agency costs between owners and managers, and in terms of opportunistic behaviour between managers and workers. Worker participation in control might be thought to offer substantial efficiency improvements in both respects. And indeed it arguably does in those circumstances where the workers involved are as homogeneous as most economic models of the firm assume they are. But the evidence suggests that direct worker involvement in control through ownership of the firm, whether this ownership is complete or partial, is quite costly where workers' interests are heterogeneous. Consequently, other types of alternative governance structures, such as collective bargaining, works councils, or quality circles, may be more promising mechanisms for improving on the efficiency of the classical model.

In short, although there remains much that we do not know about the internal politics of the firm, it seems reasonable to predict that investors and workers, and even subgroups among the workers, will generally remain separate polities within the firm, and will deal with each other principally through, as it were, a complex nexus of treaties.

Notes

I am grateful to the participants in the conference on 'The Firm as a Nexus of Treaties' for helpful comments on an earlier draft.

1. An exception is Jensen and Meckling (1979), who refer to the issue as 'the control problem'. They suggest briefly the importance of homogeneity of interest among owners, discussed in this chapter, but offer little analysis.

2. For a survey of worker co-operatives throughout American history, see Jones (1984).

3. It is not obvious that organizational law or, until recently, tax law has had an important influence on the distribution of worker-owned versus investor-owned firms in the United States. In the few instances in which there is an explicit legal preference for one of these firms over the other, it generally runs in favour of worker ownership. For example, law firms in every state must be owned by the lawyers who practise in them; investor-owned law firms are prohibited (Hansmann, 1981). And see Section 6C below on employee stock ownership plans.

4. for example, worker co-operatives in Sweden are particularly prominent in taxi-cabs (100% of all services) and truck transport (50% of all services) (Commission 1979: 16–17).

5. This is not to deny that service professionals, and particularly those not sufficiently prominent to achieve substantial individual reputations outside their firms, may experience a substantial degree of lock-in (see Gilson and Mnookin, 1988).

6. It is sometimes argued that labour co-operatives are plagued by a 'horizon problem', under which such firms have too little incentive to invest in projects that will pay off only over long periods of time; the sources of the problem, it is said, is the workers' lack of transferable residual claims (Furubotn, 1976; Jensen and Meckling, 1979). As it is, however, most worker-owned firms with any significant amount of invested capital give their workers residual claims that are transferable. For example, shares in the plywood co-operatives can be freely sold to new workers by departing ones, subject only to a right of first refusal by the firm (Berman, 1967: 148). And even if this were not the case, and workers could never withdraw capital from the firm, the workers as a group might be expected to have a long time horizon since the median worker's expected length of tenure with the firm may often be as long as fifteen or twenty years, or even longer if pension payoff periods are included.

7. 'United's Pilots are Inching Closer to a Coup', *Business Week*, 31 August, 1987: 32.

8. There is, to be sure, room for disagreement among investors concerning risk and practices, such as dividend payout, that affect taxes. But even these differences can to some extent be eliminated if investors sort themselves across firms.

9. The high costs of collective decision making in the face of heterogeneous interests are apparent elsewhere as well. See, for example, Libecap and Wiggins (1984).

10. This inference gains support from the recent well documented conversion of the investment banking house of Lehman Brothers from a partnership into a firm owned by outside investors. Although the need for more capital is evidently important in explaining this conversion, as well as the many others that have taken place in the investment banking industry in recent years, the precipitating event was a breakdown in internal governance attributable, it appears, to the growth of

specialized divisions within the firm and the resulting feuds among them concerning the division of the pie and the direction the firm should take (Auletta, 1986).

11. This inference is reinforced by the tendency of lawyers to gather in firms in which they share the same speciality and have similar clients – as in firms of patent lawyers, labour lawyers, and so on. If lawyers were so highly risk averse, one would expect to see a much stronger tendency toward firms that are highly diversified in terms of both specialities and clients.

12. Gilson and Mnookin (1985) observe that all productivity formulas are necessarily imperfect, and thus create incentives for suboptimization by the lawyer at the expense of the firm as a whole. And this, they suggest, adds to the attractiveness of equal sharing rules. This is surely true so far as it goes, but it gives emphasis to the question – not explicitly addressed by Gilson and Mnookin – of why it is that firms do not adopt the third alternative mentioned here of permitting earnings to be adjusted to each partner's productivity, but in a discretionary fashion that does not involve a precise formula that can be gamed.

13. This is true, moreover, of some of the firms that hold themselves out as being among the most progressive in their flexibility in permitting associates to work part time. See, for example, the testimony of Antonia Grumbach of New York's Patterson, Belknap, Webb & Tyler before the American Bar Association Commission on Women in the Profession, 6–7 February 1988.

14. In this vein, it is interesting to note that Aoki (1984b: 26–9) has suggested that a 'preference for a relatively homogeneous labor force' (p. 28) on the part of both management and the union may be among the most important reasons why leading Japanese firms such as Toyota have chosen a low level of vertical integration with their suppliers.

15. Members of university faculties, which are worker-governed enterprises of a sort, are familiar with similar phenomena. There is, for example, a strong tendency to equalize teaching loads within a given faculty, as to both number and nature of courses, regardless of the relative productivities of different individuals as teachers and scholars. Individuals, such as clinical faculty at professional schools, who must for curricular reasons be assigned a different mix of teaching responsibilities, may be given tenure but are generally denied voting rights (see Hazard, 1985).

16. In light of the observations above about the tendency of worker-owned firms to adopt equal sharing rules, it is interesting to note that, although the Mondragon co-operatives have not done this, they have until recently deliberately kept the spread between the highest and lowest wages in the firm compressed to a three-to-one ratio – even though this has caused some difficulty in retaining skilled managers. This ratio has recently been increased to 4.5 to one, with consequences that are not yet clear.

17. These observations help inform a prediction about the proposed pilot takeover of United Air Lines described earlier. In an effort to broaden their base, the pilots' union approached the company's machinists' union to explore the possibility that they might join the pilots in the latter's bid for ownership. But if reigning patterns of worker ownership are a guide, such a sharing of control between two such distinct classes of workers would be likely to prove unworkable. It seems more probable that the pilots and the machinists would find it in their collective interest to have ownership confined to the pilots, and for the machinists' union then to deal with the pilot–owners through collective bargaining, and thus exercise influence on the firm not through the political process associated with ownership but rather by

means of the treaties, as it were, that such bargaining yields.

18. For a review of the tax and corporate finance advantages of ESOPs prior to the Tax Reform Act of 1986, see Doernberg and Macey (1986). With the exception of the tax credit ESOPs, which were already slated for extinction after 1986, the 1986 Act reaffirmed and extended somewhat the pre-existing tax subsidies to ESOPs (primarily in the form of partial exclusion from tax of interest income from loans to ESOPs), and added some new subsidies (including, prominently, a 50% exclusion from estate tax for gains on stock sold to an ESOP).

19. For a review of the literature, see Blasi (1988, Ch. 8 and Appendix D).

20. More precisely, this is the case for election of directors and other routine matters subject to vote. The tax code requires that, even in closely held corporations, the votes be passed through to workers on major corporate restructurings such as merger or liquidation (Internal Revenue Code Section 409(e)(3)). Even these voting rights, it should be noted, can be evaded by management through such measures as elimination or conversion of the plan itself.

21. Internal Revenue Code Section 4975(e)(7).

22. Furthermore, ESOPs in publicly held companies are commonly so-called leveraged ESOPs, in which a substantial fraction of the stock held by the plan has been purchased with funds borrowed by the plan. And in such ESOPs the tax law permits the trustee rather than the workers to vote that portion of the stock that has been financed with debt, thus diluting the workers' voice.

23. This has been the case, for example, in the much-publicized Weirton Steel Company since it was purchased on behalf of its workers through an ESOP in 1982. In 1988–9, full voting rights – that is, the right to elect the board of directors – are scheduled to be passed through to Weirton's workers. At that time, however, there is reason to believe that the firm may revert to public ownership in order to accomplish necessary capital financing (Blasi, 1988: 211–15; Lynd, 1985).

24. There is, of course, the alternative explanation that the structure of these firms has been chosen by its managers, who have simply arranged to perpetuate their control.

25. This is not to say that it is inefficient to make the workers the nominal owners of such firms. It is often worthwhile to give nominal ownership of a firm to a class of individuals who transact with it even when those individuals cannot effectively exercise control. In particular, this is the case where ordinary contractual devices are insufficient in themselves to protect the individuals in question from highly costly opportunistic behaviour on the part of the firm – for example, where there is severe asymmetry of information between the firm and the individuals in question, or where the individual must make substantial transaction-specific investments for which the firm cannot easily supply hostages. In such circumstances, making the individuals in question the beneficial owners of the firm, even if they are protected only by fiduciary obligations and not by direct control, may be less costly than leaving them to rely on contracting alone and assigning ownership to someone else (Hansmann, 1988).

References

Alchian, Armen, and Harold Demsetz (1972) 'Production, Information Costs, and Economic Organization', *American Economic Review*, 777.

Aoki, Masahiko (1980) 'A Model of the Firm as a Stockholder–Employee Cooperative Game', *American Economic Review*, 70: 600.

Aoki, Masahiko (1984a) *The Cooperative Game Theory of the Firm*. London: Oxford University Press.

Aoki, Masahiko (1984b) 'Aspects of the Japanese Firm', in Masahiko Aoki (ed.) *The Economic Analysis of the Japanese Firm*. Amsterdam: North-Holland.

Auletta, Ken (1986) *Greed and Glory on Wall Street*. New York: Warner Books.

Berman, Katrina (1967) *Worker-Owned Plywood Companies*. Pullman, Washington: Washington State University Press.

Blasi, Joseph (1988) *Employee Ownership: Revolution or Ripoff?* Cambridge, Mass.: Ballinger.

Bradley, Keith and Alan Gelb (1983) *Cooperation at Work: The Mondragon Experience*. London: Heinemann.

Commission on the Swedish Cooperative Movement and its Role in Society (1979) *The Co-operative Movement in Society*.

Coase, Ronald (1937) 'The Nature of the Firm', *Economica N. S.*, 4: 386–405.

Doernberg, Richard and Jonathan Macey (1986) 'ESOPs and Economic Distortion', *Harvard Journal on Legislation*, 23: 103.

Flanagan, Robert (1987) 'Efficiency and Equality in Swedish Labor Markets', in Barry Bosworth and Alice Rivlin (eds) *The Swedish Economy*. Washington, DC: The Brookings Institution.

Frank, Robert (1984) 'Are Workers Paid Their Marginal Products', *American Economic Review*, 74: 549.

Frank, Robert (1985) *Choosing the Right Pond: Human Behavior and the Quest for Status*. New York: Oxford University Press.

Furubotn, Eirik (1976) 'The Long-Run Analysis of the Labor-Managed Firm: An Alternative Interpretation', *American Economic Review*, 66: 104.

Gilson, Ronald, and Robert Mnookin (1985) 'Sharing Among the Human Capitalists: an Economic Inquiry into the Corporate Law Firm and How Partners Split Profits', *Stanford Law Review*, 37: 313.

Gilson, Ronald, and Robert Mnookin (1988) 'Coming of Age in a Corporate Law Firm: the Implicit Contract for Associates'. Stanford Law School working paper.

Greenberg, Edward (1984) 'Producer Cooperatives and Democratic Theory: The Case of the Plywood Cooperatives' in Robert Jackall and Henry Ledin (eds) *Worker Cooperatives in America*. Berkeley: University of California Press.

Hansmann, Henry (1981) 'Reforming Nonprofit Corporation Law', *University of Pennsylvania Law Review*, 129: 497.

Hansmann, Henry (1988) 'Ownership of the Firm', *Journal of Law, Economics, and Organization*, 4: 267.

Hazard, Geoffrey (1985) 'Curriculum Structure and Faculty Structure', *Journal of Legal Education*, 35: 326.

Jensen, Michael and William Meckling (1976) 'Theory of the Firm: Managerial Behavior, Agency Costs and Ownership Structure', *Journal of Financial Economics*, 3: 305.

Jensen, Michael and William Meckling (1979) 'Rights and Production Functions: an Application to Labor-Managed Firms and Codetermination', *Journal of Business*, 52: 469.

Jones, Derek (1984) 'American Producer Cooperatives and Employee-Owned Firms: a Historical Perspective', in Robert Jackall and Henry Ledin (eds) *Worker*

Cooperatives in America. Berkeley: University of California Press.

Jones, Derek and Jan Svejnar (1982) *Participatory and Self-Managed Forms*. Lexington, Mass.: Lexington Books.

Klein, Benjamin, Robert Crawford and Armen Alchian (1978) 'Vertical Integration, Appropriable Rents, and the Competitive Contracting Process', *Journal of Law and Economics*, 21: 297.

Libecap, Gary and Stephen Wiggins (1984) 'Contractual Responses to the Common Pool', *American Economic Review*, 74: 87.

Lipset, Seymour, Martin Trow and James Coleman (1956) *Union Democracy*. Glencoe, Ill.: The Free Press.

Lynd, Staughton (1985) 'Why We Opposed the Buy-Out at Weirton Steel', *Labor Research Review*, 6: 41.

McChesney, Fred (1982) 'Team Production, Monitoring, and Profit Sharing in Law Firms: an Alternative Hypothesis', *Journal of Legal Studies*, 11: 379.

Meidner, Rudolph (1978) *Employee Investment Funds*. London: Allen & Unwin.

Michels, Robert (1949) [1911] *Political Parties*. Glencoe, Ill.: The Free Press.

Plott, Charles (1976) 'Axiomatic Social Choice Theory: An Overview and Interpretation', *American Journal of Political Science*, 20: 511.

Putterman, Louis (1984) 'On Some Recent Explanations of Why Capital Hires Labor', *Economic Enquiry*, 22: 171.

Russell, Raymond (1985a) 'Employee Ownership and Employee Governance', *Journal of Economic Behaviour and Organization*, 6: 217.

Russell, Raymond (1985b) *Sharing Ownership in the Workplace*. Albany: State University of New York Press.

Shepsle, Kenneth and Barry Weingast (1984) 'Political Solutions to Market Problems', *American Political Science Review*, 78: 417.

Simon, Herbert (1947) *Administrative Behavior*. New York: Macmillan.

Smith, Abbie (1988) 'Corporate Ownership Structure and Performance: the Case of Management Buyouts', unpublished, University of Chicago.

Sorenson, Laurel (1983) 'Life Beyond the Law Office', *American Bar Association Journal*, 70 (July): 68.

Thomas, Henk and Chris Logan (1982) *Mondragon: An Economic Analysis*. London: Allen & Unwin.

US General Accounting Office (1986) *Employee Stock Ownership Plans: Benefits and Costs of ESOP Tax Incentives for Broadening Stock Ownership*.

Weingast, Barry and William Marshall (1988) 'The Industrial Organization of Congress; or, Why Legislatures, Like Firms, Are Not Organized as Markets', *Journal of Political Economy*, 96 (Feb): 132.

Williamson, Oliver (1975) *Markets and Hierarchies: Analysis and Antitrust Implications*. New York: Free Press.

Williamson, Oliver (1985) 'Employee Ownership and Internal Governance: A Perspective', *Journal of Economic Behavior and Organization*, 6: 243.

Williamson, Oliver (1986) *The Economic Institutions of Capitalism*. New York: Free Press.

9

Intellectual Skill and the Role of Employees as Constituent Members of Large Firms in Contemporary Japan

Kazuo Koike

1. Introduction

This chapter examines the roles of the employee and, accordingly, of the labour union, in large contemporary Japanese firms, and tries to clarify how employees become constituent members of the firm. The major feature of this analysis is an emphasis on the nature of skill. Since workers' skill can be considered as a type of 'software' technology, and since technology, unlike cultural traits, is transferable, the following explanation is largely contrary to the prevailing opinion that Japanese culture makes the employee a constituent member of the firm.

The greatest reason why this chapter highlights workers' skill is that it is a key factor in explaining the behaviour of contemporary Japanese firms. This explanation offers more than the transaction theory does; the firm is a nexus of long-term relationships in which efficient skill can be developed. The next section analyses the content of workers' skill, ways in which it produces high efficiency, and how long it takes to achieve this.

Section 3 examines the incentive system that induces workers to acquire this skill. This analysis affords a counter-argument to the conventional one that Japanese workers are group-oriented. Instead, individual assessment of skill development as well as of remuneration is the core of the incentive system of the shop floor in contemporary large Japanese firms. Because of the long-term character of skill formation workers share risk with shareholders. Workers pursue internal careers in order to advance firm-specific intellectual skill, and hence the decline of the firm causes great damage to its employees, in the form of delays in promotion or, at worst, redundancy; often robbing workers of the opportunity to utilize their acquired skills fully. Section 4 discusses such risk sharing by employees, which makes them constituent members of the firm.

Since workers' interest is at stake in the business situation of the firm, an important part of the function of so-called enterprise unionism is found in the firm's decision-making process. Section 5 examines the voice of employees or the labour union in the decision making of the firm.

Another notable feature of the role of employees in contemporary large Japanese firms is a constraint provided by competitive markets. The argument so far seems to imply that there may be considerable 'rent' specific to a particular firm which should be shared between employees and shareholders, and that consequently there would be a substantial variance in the wage level among competing firms in the same industry. And this appears more likely in the presence of enterprise unionism. In-depth examination reveals, however, that the reverse holds; the wage level and the extent of its change are extremely similar among competing firms producing similar products. This does not imply that no rent exists, rather that rents may take the form of differential career progression.

In addition, intense competition in product markets increases the size of risk borne by the employees. This is a crucial aspect of the role of the employee as a member of the firm and is dealt with in Section 6.

2. Intellectual skill

Dealing with changes

Intensive examination of work on the shop floor reveals that intellectual skill is the very foundation on which high efficiency in contemporary large Japanese firms is grounded. Intellectual skill is knowledge that workers can utilize to deal efficiently with various changes occurring on the shop floor. Changes and problems occur so frequently that efficiency relies heavily on how skillfully workers handle them. It is necessary, therefore, to explain what types of change and problem occur, how often they occur, with what knowledge workers manage them, and how employees acquire the necessary knowledge to cope with them.

Through looking closely at the work and intensive interviews with veteran workers,[1] two major components of work on the shop floor can be distinguished in our conceptual framework: (a) 'usual operations' and (b) 'unusual operations'. 'Usual operations' means routine, repetitive and monotonous work, in which past observation tends to be confirmed, and so workers' skills in this work may be measured by the speed and exactness with which work is conducted. Since the requirements of speed and exactness are being transferred to the operation of machinery, people are inclined to conclude that, after all, little skill is necessary in automated workshops. But, even in mass production workshops which seem to be extremely repetitive, changes and problems on a minor scale are constantly occurring, far more frequently than is imagined. In order to maintain the usual flow of production, therefore, much work dealing with changes and problems is necessary, which is here called 'unusual operations'.

'Unusual operations' consist of two parts – one dealing with changes, and the other treating problems. Changes on the shop floor occur in five ways: variation in product mix, in the amount of production, in production methods, the introduction of new products, and changes in labour mix. To save space, only two examples are considered here: changes in product mix and the introduction of new products.

Even in one production line it is not uncommon for several kinds of product with minor variations to flow through in one day. Naturally this requires changes in jigs and tools which in turn requires further small adjustments after these changes. Not only the speed with which such changes are made but also the skillful adjustments afterwards distinctly contribute to the degree of efficiency in production in terms both of amount and of quality of products. The ability to deal with such changes and adjustments is definitely one of the major elements of a worker's skill that is indispensable on the shop floor.

It is crucial for the level of efficiency that procedures of production, as well as jigs and tools, are properly selected when new products are introduced. Of course production engineers or designers are in charge of these matters. If there are production workers, however, who can point out any part to be modified according to their own experience when they actually use them, then efficiency would definitely be promoted. In order to do this, production workers have to know the structure of the machine and the mechanism of production, which is a necessary component of skill.

Dealing with problems
The second part of 'unusual operations' is dealing with problems. There can hardly be a production line without any problems, particularly if we include those of minor scale. To deal with problems efficiently is definitely an essential part of work skills. Operations to cope with problems efficiently are composed of three steps. Step one is to locate problems or defects in goods or parts as soon

as possible, so as to save time working on defective parts. It requires long experience to acquired knowledge of the various patterns of unusual problems. Step two, which is of central importance, is to reason out the cause of problem. This is crucial in order to prevent the recurrence of the problem, and the first preventive measure is to identify the cause of the problem. If workers can reason out cause correctly and speedily, then economic damage from the defect will be minimized. The ability to reason out causes is, therefore, clearly one of the most important components of skill. Step three is to rectify the cause of the problem or defects. Since the cause may lie in machinery, dealing with problems can often lead to the repair of the machine. Overall maintenance is clearly outside the job demarcation of the operators, but minor maintenance can be entrusted to the worker. These second and third steps require some knowledge of the structure, function and mechanism of machinery and products. This can be called intellectual skill, because it is shared at least in part with engineers or technicians, whose formal role is to know the mechanism of the machine and to improve its efficiency.

This intellectual skill becomes more essential as mechanization proceeds. It is commonly said that less skill is needed under mechanization. But in practice what machinery replaces is repetitive, usual operation, but not unusual operation, and the latter occupies the more important part of human work. As the mechanism of machinery becomes more complicated, a higher degree of intellectual skill is naturally required.

Integrated system vs. separated system
A question of crucial importance can now be raised: is it always necessary for production workers to conduct such difficult jobs as unusual operations, which require intellectual skill? This question is divided into two different points – the possibility of standardization of usual operation, and the possibility of division of labour to allocate unusual operation to engineers or technicians other than production workers. Let me begin with the first point.

Some might argue that a careful study of unusual trouble would reveal several patterns, and that standard ways of dealing with these could be described in a manual, so that little time or skill would be required to cope with them. According to veteran workers, however, potential problems are so varied that standardization in the form of a manual is not completely feasible. And even if it were possible to compile a manual analysing problems in terms of standard patterns, the number of patterns to be consulted would be too large to enumerate.

More importantly, standardization conceivably decreases efficiency. An example may be illustrative. In a biochemical plant, the volume of oxygen is crucial to the entire process, and subtle adjustment of the inflow of oxygen to the tank is vital. Ordinary standardization cannot practically formalize these subtle and delicate adjustments; at best it can merely set upper and lower limits; only when the figure exceeds this permissible range would the volume of oxygen be adjusted. If workers are highly skilled, however, minute adjustment of the volume of oxygen can be made within these two limits.[2]

The second point is by and large more crucial: why cannot unusual operations be allotted to engineers or technicians, instead of burdening production workers with such difficult work? Clearly, two types of division of labour are conceivable: the integrated system and the separated system. The separated system divides work between two work groups – usual operations to production workers and unusual operations to higher-grade workers, such as engineers or technicians, while in the case of the integrated system both operations are mainly in the hands of production workers.

With one important qualification, we can discuss which type is more efficient as a system of division of labour. The important consideration is whether production workers have the aptitude to acquire intellectual skill. Once this condition is met, then the integrated system would definitely supersede the separated system in terms of efficiency. Three reasons should be stressed. First, the integrated system has more workers to deal with unusual operations. Second, it has workers who can perform unusual operations on the post, that is, beside the machine; when there is any sign of unusual trouble, these workers can handle it immediately. Compare this with the scene where production workers have to call in technicians or engineers every time they feel something is wrong. Third, the integrated system can promote higher morale among production workers. If production workers are confined only to routine jobs for a long period without any hope of challenging advanced work, it is very natural that their morale should deteriorate.

Broad on-the-job training (OJT)

Then what are main means of acquiring intellectual skill? Once we observe the shop floor, it is undoubtedly clear that broad OJT is the main way of developing these skills, supplemented by two other measures. One is additional OJT – participating in repairmen's work when machines are in trouble – and the other is short off-JT inserted during broad OJT.

Broad OJT in practice means a broad job career. A broad job career is one where a production worker starts his career with one of the easiest jobs in the workshop, proceeding to slightly more difficult jobs in the shop and extending his experience to cover major positions in neighbouring workshops producing closely related goods. This broad career affords workers the best opportunity of understanding and grasping the mechanism of production, the technicalities of machinery and the nature of the products. This understanding is the very essence of the development of workers' intellectual skill. Without understanding the mechanism, structure and function of machines, workers cannot deal with problems that arise on the shop floor. Job careers developed in a single workshop are not peculiar to Japan, and are often seen in heavy industries in the US, in large Thai firms, as well as in Malaysian firms.[3] Japanese careers are called broad because they extend even to neighbouring workshops.

Another type of OJT for acquiring intellectual skill is to participate in repairmen's work when machinery is in trouble. Operators at first just watch the repairmen's work, then work as helpers and finally engage themselves in coping with minor problems. These processes are seen not only in Japanese plants but also in indigenous Thai and in some Malaysian firms.[4]

Intellectual skill cannot be fully developed through OJT alone. It needs to be supplemented by short, inserted off-JT. Inserted off-JT implies that it is inserted between periods of OJT, say once every three years. This is different form the ordinary off-JT commonly described in textbooks, which is given at the start of workers' careers; it is doubtful if new employees unfamiliar with the content of a job could understand this type of detailed off-JT. On the contrary, workers' capacity effectively to understand off-JT is greatly expanded after several years of experience on the job. Thus, short, inserted off-JT affords a worker an opportunity to theorize or systematize his job experience and to build intellectual skill.

The in-house character of skill
The general applicability of broad OJT can be explained as follows. A vital point is that the cost of OJT is less than that of off-JT. Under OJT workers can acquire skill while working. Moreover, OJT becomes less costly by career-making. Needless to say, OJT cannot be free of cost. The cost of OJT appears in the

form of inefficiency or defective products until the worker becomes accustomed to a job. This cost would be enormous when the job is extremely difficult. There is a way, however, to lessen the cost even for the most difficult job. That is to have workers experience closely related but less difficult jobs before conducting the most difficult one. In this way inefficiency caused by unfamiliarity with a difficult job is lessened. Thus emerges the formation of the career in which workers start from the easiest job, and progress through slightly less easy ones, to more difficult jobs which are closely correlated in job content.

Through examining career formation, two very important features of skill become clear, the long-term nature of its formation and its in-plant character. The latter requires explanation. Careers are apt to be enterprise-specific.[5] Even though each job content may be the same between rival companies, there is a degree of freedom as to how to organize jobs into careers. Where there are more veteran workers, firms will organize broad career patterns, while narrow ones might be preferred by other firms with less veteran workers. Broad variety in the extent of career breadth is the content of enterprise-specific skills.[6]

3. Long-term competition

Even though intellectual skill is efficient, workers may be reluctant to invest a long time in acquiring this skill because of the risk involved, unless there is a proper incentive system. This is long-term competition, another feature of large contemporary Japanese firms.

Let us begin with explaining 'long-term'. This is contrary to the ordinary concept of spot market competition, in which the quality of goods to be sold and bought is assumed constant. Here we take away this assumption. This is quite natural if we recall a simple fact – that a worker tends to improve his skill while conducting the same job. Or we can say that this definition of long-term has some similarity with the concept of long-term in ordinary economics: a time span during which capital, K, can grow. Capital in the work force is skill.

The central question here is how to encourage the formation of skill over this long term. As in any competition, it is of prime importance to arrange fair judgement in promotion. This is the more important because a simple job rate system cannot fit the situation. Firstly because even though a worker is conducting the same job he is expected to improve his skill, which is absent from

Table 9.1   *Job map*

	Usual operations			
	Job 1	Job 2	Job 3	Job 4
Mr A	c	c	c	b
B	c	b	b	a
C	b	b	b	a

a = can perform functions temporarily when others are absent.
b = can perform functions by himself.
c = can teach fellow workers how to perform functions.

simple job rate plans. Secondly, and more importantly, the most crucial part of work is the handling of problems, which cannot feasibly be standardized. Consequently, we cannot assess workers simply by the position to which they are deployed. All these points make it difficult to set up a system of fair judgement, and without fair judgement, no effective competition can be maintained.

A practical measure employed in production workshops in large firms in contemporary Japan is to utilize job maps. Usually there are two job maps: one indicates span of experience and the other shows depth of job experience. A job map of the span, as shown in Table 9.1, lists the positions each worker has held and the level of skill with which he conducts them; whether he handles the job by himself or can instruct his fellow workers. A different job map, of depth, pictures each of the major unusual operations concerning problems in the workshop, and whether a worker is capable of handling them. Similarly to the former map, this depicts the level of skill with which the worker conducts unusual operations. Through updating these two job maps, say every three months, we can identify the level and improvement of skill of individual workers in the workshop. These updated job maps are the only practical way of surveying skill accurately in the situation of flexible job deployment. With these measures and apparatus, fair judgement is secured.

These assessments should be connected to the level of compensation. Here again, long-term relationship is of more importance than spot market connection. While every yearly assessment is reflected in a small difference in wages, its long- or medium-range accumulation has a large effect: it causes a difference in the speed with which employees are promoted to a higher class over a long period. Every five or six years, for example, workers have an opportunity to be promoted to a higher class, and promotion ensures larger yearly increments in wages.

The arrangements stated so far are the systems that make Japanese blue-collar workers in large firms constituent members of the firm. In other words, they are paid wages in a manner similar to white-collar employees or banking employees in Western European countries, in terms of salary structure. This is the very reason why large Japanese firms have successfully built up a seemingly enterprise-oriented organization.

4. Risk sharing and redundancy[7]

Once the in-house character of skill is established, then naturally workers have to bear considerable risk through fluctuation of the firm's business. When the firm prospers, all things being equal, the worker could quickly be promoted to more demanding jobs and consequently could acquire higher skills. When the firm declines, however, his promotion could be delayed, or he could be demoted or even (in the worst case) be made redundant. Redundancy is extremely costly to those workers with in-house skill. Even if he finds a new job in another firm, he will be paid less than his former wages to the extent that his skill is enterprise specific.

In addition to this commonly recognized consequence of enterprise-specific skill, institutional characteristics of Japanese redundancy greatly increase the risk shared by workers. Almost reverse seniority in redundancy is usual in contemporary large Japanese firms. In practice this means that those workers whose loss would be the greatest if they were made redundant tend to be laid off first.

A lengthy explanation is needed, because strong myths prevail that redundancy has rarely been made in large Japanese firms and that seniority systems are deeply rooted on the shop floor in Japan. We have to examine these myths.

Redundancy is not rare
It has often been said that large Japanese firms rely, in the face of decline in demand, on measures other than redundancy, such as internal transfer from declining departments to growing ones, layoffs of temporary workers, and reduction of orders to suppliers. A questionnaire sent to individual firms to survey their adjustment measures to decrease employment largely confirms this. Internal transfers, temporary layoffs, and recruitment cutbacks are distinctly more frequent in large firms than in small firms. And the ratio of firms that conducted redundancy measures is far smaller in large firms than in small firms. At first glance, this low figure for large firms seem to support the common perception of

Table 9.2 *Diffusion of redundancy measures**

	Percentage of establishments conducting redundancy measures
Total	19.4
1000	20.3
300–999	30.7
100–299	29.5
30–99	26.1
5–29	16.9

*The percentage of establishments conducting redundancy measures during the period January 1975 to June 1978, by size of manufacturing establishment.

Source: Rōdōshō (Ministry of Labor), *Koyō Hendō Sōgō Chōsa* (Survey on Changes in Employment), 1979

'permanent employment'. It must be considered, however, that these figures related to short-term responses. Once a recession lasts longer, say for one year, which is not exceptional, these measures that try to avoid redundancy become less effective.

Extremely valuable statistics exist on the diffusion of redundancy measures by size of firm, covering a period of three and a half years, from January 1975 to June 1978, the period just after the first oil shock. Table 9.2 shows first, that even among large firms with 1000 or more employees, nearly 20% conducted redundancy measures, and that this figure differs little from that of small firms. The figure 20% is far from negligible, so that no one can say redundancy is exceptional, even for large firms in Japan, and the small gap between large firms and small firms is in striking contrast to the popular argument that employees in large firms enjoy 'permanent employment' even during recessions.

Who are to be made redundant

Now we return to the most crucial issue of who are to be made redundant. Figure 9.1 shows the age distribution of those who are made redundant, regardless of the size of firm. No figures by length of service are available. Age can, however, be a substitute for experience, and can suggest skill grades, although only approximately. From Figure 9.1 it is clear that redundant workers are slightly older than those remaining employed. In both 1977 and 1979 for age groups older than 45 the percentage of the redundant figure becomes larger than that of the employed group.

To investigate in more detail we must rely on case records, as no statistical source is available. Fortunately, the Ministry of Labour

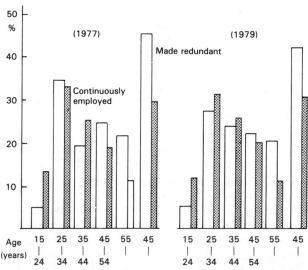

Figure 9.1 *Redundancies by age of worker (males: 1977 and 1979, percentage distribution by age)*

Those made redundant are the persons who have separated from a job since 1974 and whose reasons for separation are redundancies and bankruptcy, among the employed, the unemployed and non-participants in the labour market.

Source: Rōdōsyō (Ministry of Labor), *Rōdōryoku Tokubetsu Chōsa* (*Special Report of Labor Force Survey*)

has compiled documents of industrial disputes of importance in the *Documentary History of the Labor Movement*. In order to utilize this document, the Japanese practice of redundancy must be outlined. Two periods can be identified in the history of industrial disputes after the Second World War: one is the first half of the 1950s when redundancy, even in large firms, was not rare but rather frequent. The other is the period after the oil shock. In the first period, management in large firms usually proposed to advertise for 'volunteers' to apply for 'retirement', offering a large premium of redundancy payment. Here, 'volunteers' meant that no nomination of who was to be considered for redundancy was offered by management. Without exception, Japanese labour unions in this first period strongly opposed the companies' call for volunteers. In the severe economic situation of the 1950s, management declared criteria for redundancy. After this, even the weakest labour unions of the time went into long strikes, some longer than six months. Strikes cannot be effective, particularly in a situation of recession, when management wants to decrease output, and this was so with the strikes in the 1950s. In almost all cases, labour unions exhausted their power through long strikes, and were forced to accept redundancy measures in the final phase without any negotiation concerning who was to be dismissed. In practice the criteria offered by management were applied to most cases.

An examination of cases described in detail in *The Documentary History of the Labor Movement* for the period 1953–5, indicates that there is a distinct tendency for those who bear greater costs in redundancy to be dismissed, because the first-ranked criterion is 'old age'. Second, this document suggests that the 'performance' of workers is one of the important criteria, but there is always a tendency to managerial subjectivity or 'vagueness' in the assessment of performance. Vagueness is enough to cause conflict between labour and management, since management is apt to dismiss those employees who are not loyal to management, in the name of bad performance. It is understandable that disputes of long duration should occur in the first stage.

The lessons were carried over from the first period to the second. Management was careful not to resort to the nomination of candidates for redundancies, but maintained instead a system of advertising for volunteers. The labour union, unlike in the first period, did not reject the advertisement, but negotiated minutely over conditions involved. Thus, reference to who is to be made redundant becomes unclear. Analysis of the cases makes clear the crucial criterion, 'old age, 50 and above'.

To sum up, Japanese redundancy measures are inclined to concentrate on those workers whose loss is relatively large when they are dismissed, quite unlike the United States. This characteristic is strengthened by another institutional feature of crucial importance.

Small shock absorber

Another difference of prime importance in the institutional comparison between the United States and Japan concerns the extent of internal production. Compare, for example, Toyota and Ford. The number of employees is far larger in Ford than in Toyota, although the number of cars produced by each company per year does not differ much. This results in a large gap in apparent labour productivity. The most crucial cause of this large gap is the variation in the extent of internal production: Toyota depends far more on outside suppliers, most of which are independent companies, while Ford prefers to produce relatively more components within its own production complex. Although there is no statistical evidence to confirm the difference in this ratio between the two countries, it seems to be true.[8]

When we connect this difference to redundancy with or without seniority, then a result of crucial importance emerges: the shock absorber in the labour market in the United States is greater than in Japan. This is the opposite of a popular conception. Let us take the case of a 20% reduction in output and, accordingly, a reduction in labour demand in both Ford and Toyota. At a glance, Ford has a smaller shock absorber for employment adjustment because its ratio of internal to total production is high. As Ford follows strict seniority practice, however, the actual effect of redundancy is exactly the reverse. Since redundancy is strictly conducted in reverse of seniority, those workers who have worked in the lowest 20% of job grades are made redundant. As a result, experienced workers in main production lines of Ford have such a degree of protection that it requires an enormous reduction of output for redundancy measures to reach them.

In large Japanese firms the story is completely different. Workers doing jobs similar to those who are most vulnerable to redundancy in Ford are not employed by Toyota, but by suppliers of components. These Japanese suppliers are in most cases independent in terms of ownership as well as in their discretion to sell their products to other auto makers. Since most of them are not owned by Toyota, they are not compelled to function as shock absorbers for Toyota employees. Hence, both Toyota and the suppliers share the burden of employment adjustment. In short, although large firms generally hold surplus labour within the company, if depression in demand lasts for long, say for a year or so, the firm is compelled to conduct redundancy measures.

To sum up, three factors increase the risk shared by workers in large Japanese firms: (a) job careers more broadly and deeply built into a firm; (b) no seniority protection from redundancy, or almost the reverse of those in the US; and (c) smaller shock absorber. This large risk to be borne by employees necessarily strengthens the need for them to have a voice in decision making in the firm.

5. The workers' voice in the decision making of a firm

The need for workers' voice in management policy
Since employees with intellectual skill in a firm have to bear risk to a considerable extent, it is natural for them to realize the need to monitor management decisions which might heavily affect their careers, and accordingly their benefits as well as losses. In order to monitor management policy, they have to know the business

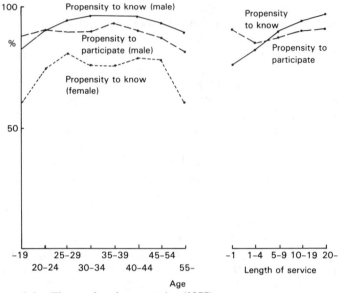

Figure 9.2   *The need to have a voice (1977)*

Source: Rōdōsyō (Ministry of Labor, *Rōshi Cummunication Chōsa (Survey on Labor–Management Communication)*, 1977

situation of the firm and participate in the decision making of the firm. Fortunately, an appropriate survey is available for examining these needs of employees in contemporary Japanese firms. This is a Ministry of Labor questionnaire survey of 5000 establishments with more than 100 employees in all industries: the response rate is nearly 80%. More precisely, one part of the questionnaire is aimed at 20,000 individual employees of those firms, and obtains answers from them directly. The survey was conducted twice, in 1972 and 1977, and here the latter is used because of its larger scale.

Figure 9.2 describes both the propensity to know and the propensity to participate of individual workers. 'Yes' answers to the question, 'Do you want to know management policy?' are used to measure the extent of the propensity to know, and 'yes' answers to the question, 'Do you think it necessary for employees to have a voice in decision making of management policy?' measures the propensity to participate. Clearly the figures are extremely high. More importantly, the propensity to know in particular increases as workers' service becomes longer and the figure for men is distinctly higher than that for women. This evidently suggests that workers of intellectual skill have a larger need to know and to participate.

Table 9.3 *Employees' interest in those items handled in joint consultation schemes, 1977 (percentage of individual workers)*

	Male	Female
Total	100.0	100.0
Business situation of the firm	71.9	34.6
Personnel matters	42.3	32.3
Working conditions	80.1	75.4
Fringe benefits	56.9	53.8
Others	1.4	0.9
No interest in any items	1.3	4.7

Source: Rōdōsyō (Ministry of Labor), *Rōshi Cummunication Chōsha* (*Survey on Labor–Management Communication*), 1977

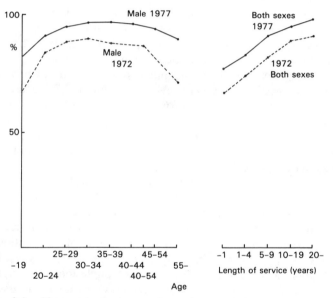

Figure 9.3 *Changes in the propensity to know (1972, 1977: individual workers)*

Source: Rōdōsyō (Ministry of Labor), *Rōshi Cummunication Chōsa* (*Survey on Labor–Management Communication*), 1977

Great interest in managerial issues is indicated in Table 9.3, which describes the percentage of those employees who have an interest in issues handled in joint consultation machinery. Joint consultation machinery is the most prevalent channel through which workers have a voice in various matters including management policy and working conditions. From the table it is evident that the figure relating to the business situation of the firm is nearly as high as that on working conditions and much higher than those on personnel matters and on fringe benefits.

Figure 9.3 compares the propensity to known between 1972 and 1977. According to the hypothesis already stated, the propensity to know would increase as the extent of the risk borne by employees becomes larger. Risk becomes greater when the labour market is slack and redundancy occurs more frequently. The year 1972 is before the oil shock, and has least redundancy, while 1977 is after the shock. If the above hypothesis is correct, the figures should increase for 1977 over 1972. Figure 9.3 distinctly shows this.

Machinery for having a voice
The major channel through which employees have a voice in management policy is undoubtedly joint consultation machinery, so a brief description will be given here. Unlike the Western European situation, contemporary Japanese industrial relations lack any legal machinery for giving employees a voice in management policy. In practice, however, there is a remarkable diffusion of voluntary machinery in the form of joint consultation schemes. These are the machinery through which management and representatives of relevant labour unions, or those of the employees where there is no labour union, discuss both working conditions and management issues.

Where there are labour unions, such joint consultation machinery plays two roles: one is to discuss management issues, and the other is as a preliminary step to collective bargaining. The latter role needs more explanation. 'Preliminary step' does not necessarily imply that it occupies only a small part of overall negotiation, in fact it is a major portion in many cases. In practice, most working conditions can usually be negotiated through joint consultation machinery and when any problem remains unsettled, the issue is submitted to collective bargaining, because the participants of the two channels (collective bargaining and joint consultation) are almost identical. It is also true that a minority of labour unions do not submit the subject of working conditions to joint consultation. This is reflected in Table 9.4, which reveals that the percentage of joint consultation machinery handling working conditions never reaches 100 but stays at nearly 80. Joint consultation machinery where there are no labour unions conducts both roles, talking on managerial policy and negotiation of working conditions.

According to the 1977 survey, first, the majority of firms of large and middle size have joint consultation machinery; second,

Table 9.4 *Topics in joint consultation plans (1977: 1000–4999 employees)*

| | Percentage of establishments | |
	To negotiate	To discuss at all grades
1. Major management policy	8.2	69.5
2. Major plan of production and sales	10.0	69.1
3. Changes in company organization	19.9	76.8
4. Mechanization of production and office work	38.3	77.6
5. Transfer	41.1	72.7
6. Redundancy	14.9	82.1
7. Working hours and holiday plans	79.6	85.0
8. Retirement benefits	74.4	80.5
9. Administration of fringe benefits and benefits	54.5	83.3

Source: Rōdōsyō (Ministry of Labor), *Rōshi Cummunication Chōsa* (*Survey on Labor–Management Communication*), 1977

the larger the firm, the more likely is such machinery to exist; third, firms with labour unions are more likely to have this machinery; and fourth, the diffusion of such machinery to non-union firms is substantial, being present in nearly 40% of these firms.

The working of joint consultation schemes can be assessed by reference to Table 9.4. This shows the percentage of establishments which negotiate or consult through joint consultation on each topic indicated. The original data in the 1977 survey classifies four grades of voice: (a) co-determination, which means that without the work force's consent, no decision can be made; (b) negotiation of issues, but management retains the final say; (c) explanation by management; and (d) the workforce simply listens to talks by management. In practice, the difference between (a) and (b) seems obscure. Even if the language in the formal agreement stipulates that no consent from employees is necessary, practice in the firm often shows clearly that without obtaining 'yes' from the employee side, no decision is taken by management. Similarly the difference between the latter two is not evident. Consequently, Table 9.4 adopts derived indicators: one is the aggregate figure of (a) and (b), and another is the total percentage of establishments which discuss the matter irrespective of grade. Although the original data includes thirteen items, we focus on nine, sufficient to review the extent of the voice.

Firstly, it is clear that employees have a voice in almost all issues. The nine topics in the table fall into three categories – management policy, working conditions and fringe benefits. The figures in the table are high in each category and for all items. For management policy issues, the figures are around 70–78%, while those for working conditions are 73–85%, and for fringe benefits, 80–83%, the difference being small.

Second, the grade of voice or the strength of voice in management issues is less than for others. The percentage of establishments negotiating on working conditions is as high as 75–80%, while under 20% negotiate on managerial issues.[9] A word of caution is necessary. The low figures for redundancy and for transfer do not imply weakness in the employees' voice on these issues. Since these two are the most important, many labour unions, as stated earlier, do not want to submit them to joint consultation, but rather keep them subject to collective bargaining.[10]

6. Strong market constraints

Intra-industry diffusion

The argument so far might, at a glance, seem to imply that there may be considerable 'rent' which could be shared between employees and shareholders, and that, consequently, there would be significant variance in the wage level among competing firms in the same industry. And this argument seems more likely because of enterprise unionism; labour unions are thought to negotiate on wages with individual firms, without any influence from, or even in the absence of, industrial unions.

In-depth examination reveals, however, that the reverse is true: wages and the extent of their changes are extremely similar between competing firms producing similar products. We have extremely important, and rarely available data on the size of yearly wage changes for individual firms, including nearly 300 large firms with labour unions, collected by the Ministry of Labor since the mid-1950s.[11] The Ministry of Labor also publishes the figure of coefficient of variation, both intra- and inter-industry, for each year. As is well known, Japanese wage levels are negotiated in April every year, so this yearly data is important.

Iron and steel

An insight into each industry reveals an interesting situation. Let us begin with iron and steel because it is the leader in the Spring labour offensive. There are at least two groups of firms in the iron and steel industry in terms of products: one is the 'Big Five', which are integrated firms, while the other group consists of specific steel-making, rolling mills and miscellaneous. If we confine our

Table 9.5 *The content of wage settlements (Steel, Big Five, 1983)*

---

(1) Wage increase
   1. Wage increments ¥ 6,800 for a 'standard worker' (aged 35, 15 years of service)
     (a) Increments in basic rate ¥ 3,200
     (b) Yearly increments   ¥ 3,600
   2. Distribution*
     (a) ¥ 1600 for non-job rate
     (b) ¥ 1600 for job rate

---

(2) Retirement pay (Lump-sum payments)
   Increment ¥ 400,000 for production workers (aged 57, 32 years of service)
   (i.e., from ¥ 11,400,000 to ¥ 11,800,000)

---

(3) Supplementary compensation for industrial injury

Grade of injury	increments	amount of compensation
Grade 1,2,3 & death	¥ 1,000,000	¥ 19,000,000
Grade 4	¥ 700,000	¥ 3,500,000
Grade 5	¥ 600,000	¥ 2,900,000
:		
" 14	¥ 100,000	¥ 250,000

---

*For Sumitomo only, a very small difference exists:
(a) increment for non-job rate ¥ 1613, and
(b) increment for job rate ¥ 1587.

Source: Rōdōshō (Ministry of Labor), *Shiryo Rodo Undoshi* (*Documentary History of the Labor Movement*), Tokyo: Romu Gyosei Kenkyujo, 1983

observation only to the Big Five, then tremendous conformity is revealed. Table 9.5 shows the contents of the wage settlement of the Big Five for the year 1983. (There is little difference between years, at least so far as these systems are concerned.)

In order to understand this table, it may be appropriate to describe the process of wage negotiation in the iron and steel industry. In the second week of April in almost every year, the Big Five conduct wage negotiations separately and arrive at a settlement at the same time on the same day with precisely the same content, as Table 9.5 shows. And the other groups in the industry similarly arrive at a settlement through individual negotiation with one or two days delay as well as very small differentials in the extent of wage increase.

Now look at the table. First, the extent of wage increase is precisely the same between the Big Five; 6800 yen for 'a standard worker', which formally means a 35-year-old worker with 15 years of service. Needless to say, this does not guarantee that workers aged 35 who have 15 years service will automatically be paid this amount; a certain amount of performance is required. And allocation of this wage increase is basically regulated. A half of the wage increment is 'basic rate' and the other half is 'yearly increment'. Though it would need many pages to explain the difference between the two, here it suffices to say that the former does not include merit rating, while the latter does. Moreover the distribution of the former is more stipulated: half should be an increase outside the job rate. Except for a very nominal deviation of only one firm, Sumitomo, all these details are completely the same between the Big Five.

Similarity extends to other components of compensation. The extent of increase and the level of retirement payments are uniformly settled among the Big Five; supplementary compensation for injuries through industrial accidents is also uniform. This is a supplement to social security, which itself of course never differs by firm. This clearly shows the existence of 'industry-wide negotiation'. Without intensive talk between management of the Big Five and between their labour and management, one could not expect such conformity of wage increments at the same time on the same day.

This may differ little from the practical procedure of wage negotiation in the iron and steel industry in the US. Wage negotiation is conducted in the US by the group of integrated firms which consists of nearly ten firms, all integrated. In the sense that major collective bargaining consists only of integrated firms and their relevant local unions, no difference between the two countries can be seen.

This is not the whole story of wage negotiation. A lot of other issues are handled in collective bargaining, such as wage structure, rating for each job or each position, and the detailed content of payments by results. All these matters are negotiated either at the enterprise or the plant level, which is common in the US as well as in Japan.

Electrical machinery and automobiles

Another key player in wage negotiation is the electrical machinery industry. Although firms in the industry are composed of various groups with various product lines, the extents of the rate of wage increase converge to precisely the same figure, 4.9%, except in one instance. These firms can be divided into five subgroups; (a) integrated firms which produce almost all major products of

Table 9.6 *Diffusion of wage increases (automobile, 1983)*

	No. of employees	Date of increase	Content of settlement	
			Amount of increase (yen)	Rate of increase
Toyota	63,890	12 April	9900	5.0
Nissan	54,573	12 April	9700	4.96
Honda	30,708	12 April	9600	5.39
Tōyōkōgyō	28,429	12 April	9900	4.80
Isuzu	16,064	13 April	8000	4.46
Fuji Zyūkō	14,524	12 April	9450	4.96
Daihatsu	11,147	19 April	9450	4.96
Suzuki	12,857	13 April	8000	4.53
Hino	8476	12 April	9000	4.83

Source: See Table 9.5

electrical machinery from those for industry use and computer-related products to home appliances; (b) firms which concentrate on products for industry use; (c) the computer-related goods group; (d) the home appliance group; and (e) the telephone and communications group. In spite of this variation in products, both the rate of wage changes and the date of settlement are the same. The only exception is one firm which suffered from a serious decline in output, and from redundancy.

The automobile industry is an example of an industry with a weak industrial union. Conversely to iron and steel, as shown in Table 9.6, dispersion in the rate of wage changes inside the industry is not nil even if we divide it into similar subgroups. The first four are ordinary car assemblers, whose wage increases do not converge perfectly. Others are either the smallest car assemblers or non-passenger car makers. These differ a little. However, the extent of diffusion is just as nominal if we take car assembly makers: Toyota and Toyokogyo obtain 9900 yen, Nissan 9700, and Honda, 9600. No one can find any economic significance in the tiny difference between 9900 yen for Toyota and 9700 yen for Nissan. For reasons of space our observation has focused on the year 1983, but it is true that almost the same story is applicable to other periods.

Incidence
All these facts strongly suggest an extremely competitive situation in product markets in contemporary Japanese industry. What is the result of this competitive situation? Does this competition

destroy the systems in which workers share risk and benefits with other constituent members of the firm, because no extra benefits to be shared with employees could remain? Or in order for this system to survive, how can rent be shared with employees under the condition of such similarity in wage changes among competing firms?

Two things are to be noted; one is to strengthen the employee's character of the constituency membership of the firm, and the other is to say that the rent to be shared is mostly in the form of the speed with which employees are promoted. Needless to say, competitive product markets undoubtedly enlarge the risk borne by the employees. The more competitive the product markets, other things being equal, the more the firms decline or grow. Decline of a firm might lead to redundancy, and if no changes in redundancy practice in contemporary Japan occur, the loss through redundancy will be enormous. Moreover intense competition increases the need for intellectual skill in order to survive, and again this expands losses in the event of redundancy. Larger risk invites the larger need for a voice.

The incentive driving this system is not only the fear of redundancy. Only with the fear of redundancy, motivation for implementing it seems weak. The greatest incentive is the speed with which employees can be promoted to higher positions with higher pay as well as a higher level of skill. This is how rent is shared by employees as constituent members of the firm. While wages are equal among competing firms, the speed of promotion can differ greatly. The workers in growing firms enjoy quicker promotion than others. And promotion offers the most crucial opportunity for gaining higher skill, which is the source of high compensation in the long term.

This naturally strengthens the employees' interest in promotion, which endangers the functioning of the labour union and, accordingly, employees' voice. Promotion is not limited to the sphere of union demarcation. Employees who want to be promoted to a position higher than the union demarcation have to depend on assessment by the manager, rather than on union officers who might protect them from management discretion. If employees do not feel much need to rely on the labour union, the labour union loses bargaining power. This in turn definitely weakens union power and the employees' voice. Here is a problem which has no effective solution.

Notes

1. This is based on two series of field work conducted by the author and collaborators. One is a comparative study of twenty indigenous Japanese, Thai and Malaysian firms, of which six are Japanese. In each case two workshops were visited at least twice (Koike and Inoki, 1987; Koike, 1987). The other field work covers two large and six medium-sized firms; in each case two workshops were also intensively interviewed (Koike and Muramatsu, 1987). Since the practical procedure for increasing skill normally takes the form of shopfloor practice, as will be shown, interviews with veteran workers and foremen are vital in obtaining important information. The analysis in this chapter is based completely on these field studies. No statistical evidence directly illustrating the point is available, though statistical material of some relevance will be utilized here.

2. This reasoning could be said to be along the line of Frank Knight (1971) and to explain efficiency under the grass-roots type of workshop organization. See Aoki (1988).

3. Koike (1977). Examples in English are found in Koike (1984) and Koike (1988). Cases in indigenous Thai and Malaysian are described in Koike and Inoki (1987) and Koike (1987).

4. Koike and Inoki (1987).

5. It should be noted that in practice the extent of enterprise specificity is not large. Although there is no exact way to assess its extent, a rough guess would be 10–20% at most of the job skills, even in jobs called enterprise specific. And 10–20% of enterprise specificity would be enough to let workers stay within a firm.

6. A difference from Doeringer and Piore's theory should be noted. Their theory seems to be too general to explain internal labour markets and enterprise-specific skill. According to their theory, enterprise-specific skill is mainly based on the following two factors: 'individual operating characteristics' of each machine and 'personalities' of work team members (Doeringer and Piore, 1971: 16–17). Every machine, even those made by mass production, has individual characteristics, and whether workers know it or not, this heavily affects efficiency. Any job has a team element, and so those workers who know the personalities of members can work more efficiently. Since these two factors are undoubtedly true of most jobs, internal labour markets were really founded only on these factors. In practice, however, they are concentrated in large firms or heavy industries, and are rarely found in small firms. Moreover, it is also difficult to explain why internal labour markets have emerged after, say, the First World War, and not at an earlier stage. Another hypothesis developed in Koike (1977) tries to account for these features.

7. This section relies heavily on Koike (1986).

8. Asamuma (1988) has made the most insightful analysis of the relationship between the core firm and parts suppliers.

9. This statement is an overall view based on statistical data. Insights into individual cases could afford more informative description, but cannot be given here for reasons of space. Case studies are available on this issue; for example, Koike (1985) analyses in detail one of the most noted cases in the electrical machinery industry.

10. Nitta (1988) has investigated the union voice in the Japanese steel industry in detail.

11. Ministry of Labor, *Shiryo Rodo Undoshi* (*Documentary History of the Labor Movement*), annual.

References

Aoki, Masahiko (1988) *Information, Incentives, and Bargaining in the Japanese Economy*. Cambridge: Cambridge University Press.

Asamuma, Banri (1988) 'Manufacturer–Supplier Relationships in Japan and the Concept of Relation Specific Skill', *Journal of the Japanese and International Economies*, vol. 3, no. 1, pp. 1–30.

Doeringer, Peter and Michael Pioire (1971) *Internal Labor Markets and Manpower Analysis*. Lexington: D.C. Heath.

Knight, Frank H. (1971) *Risk Uncertainty and Profit*, 1st edn 1921. Chicago: University of Chicago Press.

Koike, Kazuo (1977) *Shokuba no Rōdō Kumiai to Sanka–Rōshi Kankei no Nichibei Hikaku* (*A Comparative Study of Industrial Relations on the Shop Floor in the US and Japan*). Tokyo: Tōyō Keizai.

Koike, Kazuo (1980) 'Inter-industry Wage Spillover in Japan – An Insight into Shunto', *Keizai Kagaku* (*Economic Science*), 28 (2): 30–73.

Koike, Kazuo (1984) 'Skill Formation Systems in the US and Japan', in M. Aoki (ed.) *The Economic Analysis of the Japanese Firm*. Amsterdam: North-Holland.

Koike, Kazuo (1985) 'Denki Sangyō' ('Electrical Machinery Industry') in Mikio Sumiya (ed.) *Gijitsu Kakushin to Rōshi Kankei* (*Innovation in Technology and Industrial Relations*). Tokyo: Japan Institute of Labour.

Koike, Kazuo (1986) 'Japanese Redundancy: the impact of Key Labor Market Institutions on the Economic Flexibility of the Japanese Economy', in Peter Chinloy and Ernst Stromsdorfer (eds) *Labor Market Adjustments in the Pacific Basin*, pp. 79–101. Boston: Kluwer-Nijhoff.

Koike, Kazuo (1987) 'Skill Formation Systems: a Thai–Japanese Comparison', *Journal of the Japanese and International Economies*, vol. 1, pp. 408–44.

Koike, Kazuo (1988) *Understanding Industrial Relations in Modern Japan*. London: Macmillan.

Koike, Kazuo and T. Inoki (1987) *Jinzai Keisei no Kokusai Hikaku–Tonan Asia to Nihon* (*An International Comparison of Skill Formation – South East Asia and Japan*). Tokyo: Toyō Keizai.

Koike, Kazuo and K. Muramatsu (1987) *Chiteki Jukuren no Keisei* (*Intellectual Skill Formation*). Nagoya: Aichiken.

Nitta, Michio (1988) *Nihon no Rodosha Sanka* (*The Workers' Voice in Industrial Relations in Japan*). Tokyo: Tokyo University Press.

10

The Implicit Contract for Corporate Law Firm Associates: *Ex Post* Opportunism and *Ex Ante* Bonding

Ronald J. Gilson and Robert H. Mnookin

The traditional American corporate law firm, long an oasis of organizational stability, in recent years has been the subject of dramatic change. The manner in which firms divide profits, perhaps the most revealing aspect of law firm organization because it displays the balance the firm has selected between risk sharing and incentives, has changed in a critical way. From a long-standing reliance on seniority that emphasizes risk sharing, profit division is shifting to a system based on the productivity of individual partners that emphasizes incentives (Gilson and Mnookin, 1985). Now with what seems to be only a short time lag from the change in how profits are divided, a second pillar of traditional corporate law firm organization is the object of assault. The 'up-or-out system' – the long dominant career pattern by which employee (associate) lawyers are either promoted to partnership or fired – also appears to be changing. From a structure in which there were only two categories of lawyer – partner and associate – firms are creating new categories of employee lawyer that, whatever the euphemism – permanent associate, staff lawyer, non-equity partner, junior partner – flaunt the traditional career pattern by retaining associates who are not promoted to partner.[1]

This change in the structure of corporate law firms presents two interesting questions. The first is why the up-or-out policy was dominant for so long when, on initial analysis, it appears to work to the advantage of neither the firm nor the employee lawyer. On the other hand, the system forces the firm to fire lawyers simply because they are not thought qualified for promotion even though they may be performing competently (and profitably) at their present level. On the other hand, the system denies employee lawyers the additional career opportunity of remaining with the firm without being promoted, an opportunity that some may prefer to being fired.

If the historical dominance of the up-or-out system can be

explained, the second question is what accounts for the seemingly sudden change in so central an element in law firm organization. What in the organizational environment has triggered the shift away from the up-or-out system? In this chapter we seek answers to these questions by understanding the economics of the implicit contract governing associate career patterns in corporate law firms.

The puzzle of the up-or-out system

For a firm whose dominant input is human capital, the selection, evaluation and retention of new employees is critical. In effect, these elements comprise the firm's capital budgeting process. And the most peculiar aspect of the corporate law firm's capital budgeting process is that a special pattern – the up-or-out system – appears to have dominated practice over the entire period in which the institution of the corporate law firm has existed.[2] This career pattern is easy enough to describe. Over a period of up to some ten years an associate progresses toward a decision concerning whether he or she will be promoted to partner. This status conveys lifetime tenure and the right to participate in the profits of the firm based, over most of the relevant period, on what we have called a sharing model in which profits are divided based on a lock-step seniority system with regard to the actual productivity of any particular partner (Gilson and Mnookin, 1985: 341–6.

The peculiar characteristic of this career pattern is what happens if the associate is not promoted to partner. However close the associate may have come, if the partnership standard is not met the associate is fired rather than retained as an associate. And what is fascinating about this result is that, at least at first cut, it is difficult to understand from the perspective of either the firm or the associate. Simply put, the up-or-out system seems to work in no one's interest.

The puzzle from the firm's perspective

The law firm's problem in devising an efficient career pattern for young lawyers is familiar in the labour economics literature. At the time of the initial hiring decision the law firm is unable to tell which among its pool of new associates possess the personal attributes that the firm requires in those whom it will make a partner. The firm is uncertain not only about an associate's legal skills,[3] but also about more subjective personal characteristics – for example, co-operativeness, maturity, ability to gain respect of clients and colleagues – that traditionally have been important to the partnership decision.[4] Similarly, during the bulk of the period in which the modern corporate law firm has existed, firms have followed a sharing model of dividing their profits, which requires for success that partners have yet another subjective characteristic: a personal commitment to 'professionalism' – an internally driven strong work ethic – that overcomes the absence of incentives in an income division method that emphasizes risk sharing (Gilson and Mnookin, 1985: 374–9). The solution to the firm's uncertainty concerning its associates at the time they are hired is an apprenticeship: a period between initial hiring and the partnership decision that gives the associates the opportunity to demonstrate that he or she has both the legal skills and the personal characteristics for which the firm is looking.[5]

The apprenticeship period also provides an incentive for the associates to invest in firm-specific human capital. Familiar human capital theory specifies that the firm must pay for the employee's investment in firm-specific human capital.[6] The problem for the firm, however, is to assure that, after it pays for the employee's investment, it actually receives the returns. Once the employee has been paid to make the investment, the employee is in a position to behave opportunistically by threatening to quit unless the returns from the investment are shared in a manner more favourable to the employee. A straightforward resolution of this problem is to pay for the employee's investment in firm-specific human capital by deferred compensation. Then the employee actually receives the compensation for acquiring firm-specific human capital only as, or after, the firm has had the benefit of it (Becker, 1975: 29–31; Bulow and Scholes, 1984; Leazer, 1979). In the law firm setting, the promise of partnership (in effect, the right to share in the future returns from firm-specific capital) as compensation to those associates who successfully acquire firm-specific human capital serves to constrain employee opportunism.[7]

Thus, the employment pattern selected by the firm – an initial hire followed by a lengthy apprenticeship period before the partnership decision is made – makes perfect sense. The apprenticeship period serves to sort out the best and the brightest, provides an incentive for the associate to acquire the firm-specific human capital necessary for the firm's success, and constrains opportunistic behaviour concerning the distribution of returns from that investment.[8]

What does not make sense, however, is the firm's behaviour at the time of the partnership decision. Senior associates are a source of substantial income for the firm.[9] Moreover, those associates who are still with the firm at the time a partnership decision is actually made have already been determined by the firm to be competent lawyers.[10] Those associates who lack that level of competence would have been fired at a much earlier point in the apprenticeship period. Yet, a corporate law firm behaves very differently after making the promotion decision than other businesses. A law firm fires those associates it does not promote, rather than merely retaining them in the position in which they already have been shown to be competent and profitable. From the perspective of the firm, the puzzle is why it gives up the potential profits from continuing to employ the associate in a capacity other than partner. Why would the *firm* select an up-or-out system?

The puzzle from the associate's perspective

Economic theory teaches that individuals are risk averse. Moreover, individuals are likely to be even more risk averse the greater their investment in human capital, which is difficult to diversify. Now assume that a prospective associate has a choice between jobs at two different firms. Both jobs have the same rewards for success – identical salaries and an identical chance of making partnership after an apprenticeship period of identical length. The jobs differ, however, in an important respect: one of the jobs presents a risk, and the other does not. In one firm, associates who do not meet the standards for partnership are given the option of remaining in the firm's employ, but with no chance of ever becoming a partner. In the other firm, those who are not promoted to partnership are fired – the up-or-out system. Although one could understand that some associates who do not make partner would choose not to remain with the firm in a less than first-class capacity, that result is hardly certain. Indeed, the possibility of remaining an associate simply increases the options available to the associate at the time that the firm makes the partnership decision. So long as there is a non-zero probability that, in some state of the world, the associate would elect to remain with the firm despite not being promoted to partner, the option to do so is valuable. Thus common sense suggests that, other things being equal, a job with a firm that offers the opportunity to remain an associate if one is not made a partner would be preferred to one in a firm that has an up-or-out system. Why, then, might would-be *associates* willingly accept, let alone prefer, a firm that did not offer a consolation prize in the partnership race?

A framework to unravel the puzzle: the interaction of dual uncertainty

To this point our discussion of the up-or-out system has focused on the time when the firm makes the partnership decision. The puzzle from the firm's perspective is why it would fire otherwise valuable associates who did not meet partnership standards. The puzzle from the associates' perspective is why they would prefer a system that denied them the option of remaining as associates if they did not meet partnership standards. Taken together, the puzzle is the historical persistence of the up-or-out system when an initial pass at analysis suggests that both the firm *and* the associate are better off with a system that contemplates the possibility of retaining in some capacity an associate who does not make partner.[11]

This dual puzzle begins to unravel when we move back the chronological focus of our attention from the time of the partnership decision to the time when the associate is first hired. At this time the associate and the firm each face a different kind of uncertainty with respect to the associate's career path.[12] The up-or-out system begins to make sense when considered as an organizational response to the dual-sided uncertainty existing at the time when the associate is initially hired.

The firm's uncertainty: associate characteristics

We have already described the uncertainty confronting the firm when the associate is initially hired. The firm is unable to tell who among the pool of associates hired possesses the ability and personal attributes thought necessary to partnership. The organizational response to this uncertainty is an apprenticeship period during which, through their work, the associates can reveal their abilities. For this solution to the firm's uncertainty to be stable, however, it must also be consistent with the associates' interests at the time of initial hire. The difficulty is that, without more, the organizational response to the problem of the firm's uncertainty itself creates the problem of the associates' uncertainty.

The associate's uncertainty: opportunism by the firm

The deal the firm offers the associate is the opportunity to spend seven or eight or nine years working hard to reveal to the firm his or her real abilities. Those who do so and whose revealed abilities meet the firm's standards receive a large incentive payment: partnership. The associate's uncertainty at the time of initial hire is whether the firm will play fair at that future time when the partnership decision is actually made. Analysis of the law firm's incentives at the time of the partnership decision reveals substantial basis for associate concern. The firm has significant incentives to behave opportunistically in evaluating the associate's performance.

Consider the firm's position at the time of the partnership decision. The firm is making a substantial profit from the associate's labour. Promoting the associate to partner – paying off on the promise of an incentive payment if the associate makes the grade – rather than continuing the associate as an employee is costly to the firm; it diminishes the profits accruing to existing partners. At the same time, the associate is in a difficult position to insist that the firm keeps its promise because during the apprenticeship period the associate has made a substantial investment in firm-specific human capital.

The central characteristic of firm-specific capital is that it is worth significantly less in its best use outside the firm (Williamson, 1985: 51–6).[13] An associate who has made a substantial investment in firm-specific capital is in an unenviable position at the time of the partnership decision. Suppose the firm opportunistically offers only a permanent associate position even though the associate has actually met the partnership standards. So long as the firm's non-partnership offer is more lucrative than what the associate could receive in alternative employment, an easily satisfied condition because the associate's firm-specific capital is by definition significantly less valuable to any other employer, the associate is better off taking less than the original promise despite the firm's opportunistic behaviour. From the associate's perspective, the unfortunate thing about the apprenticeship period is that its very purpose is to allow the associate to invest in firm-specific capital.

Recall that the apprenticeship period responds to the firm's uncertainty concerning associate attributes by allowing the associate to reveal her or his abilities over time. This effort yields valuable information because an associate whose abilities are accurately known by the firm is a very different asset than one about whose abilities there is significant uncertainty. It is critical to a firm's successful practice that it knows which associates can be trusted, which are adept at what types of work, which can deal directly with clients, and the like. Thus, an associate's value increases during the apprenticeship period as the firm learns about the associate's ability and, as a result, the associate requires less supervision and can be given more important work.

From the associate's perspective, the problem is that the information concerning the associate's ability is largely firm specific; because of an adverse selection problem, it *cannot* be transferred effectively to a different employer.[14] If the associate tries to leave her current firm after not being promoted to partner, any other potential employer receives an obvious signal about the associate's abilities. The firm with the best knowledge concerning the associate's abilities *declined* to make her a partner.[15] This information asymmetry concerning the associate's abilities between her existing employer and alternative employer thereby turns even investment in ordinary legal skills, which otherwise would be general human capital because they are equally valuable in any legal position, into firm-specific human capital. Thus, an associate is disadvantaged in seeking alternative employment if the firm cheats on the partnership decision, and she is left with little choice but to allow the firm to get away with it.[16]

Our analysis thus far of the solution to the firm's uncertainty concerning associates' ability – an apprenticeship period with a promise of partnership to those who are successful – suggests that, without more, the solution may not work because of the associates' uncertainty. Indeed, the apprenticeship period is the very thing that creates the associate's uncertainty: that the firm may behave opportunistically at the time of the partnership decision. It is a little like the annual fall ritual in the 'Peanuts' comic strip when Lucy holds the football for Charlie Brown to kick. We all wonder why he continues to make the run at the ball knowing that she will pull it away just when he gets close. If the associate's uncertainty cannot be solved, the apprenticeship solution to the firm's uncertainty is not viable.

A solution: the up-or-out system as a bonding device

Once we recognize that the problem facing the law firm and associate at the time of the initial hire is uncertainty over whether the firm will behave opportunistically at the time of the partnership decision, the problem of organizational design becomes clear. For the apprenticeship period to be a viable response to the firm's uncertainty, the firm must have some bonding mechanism that will assure associates when they are hired that the firm will treat them fairly at the time they are considered for partnership.

The most straightforward approach to the problem would be a written contract. The difficulty, however, is that the terms of the partnership decision could not workably be made part of an explicit contract. Consider the usual array of attributes firms describe as desirable in new partners. Traits like good judgement, being a team player, working well with clients, or working hard despite the absence of performance incentives, are all the sort of amorphous, subjective qualities about which reasonable people can differ and behind which opportunistic people can hide. They cannot be specified with any real clarity, and a decision whether an associate possesses them could not be subject to predictable review by a third-party enforcement agent. Thus, a written contract would provide no certainty for the associate, and would introduce substantial uncertainty for the firm.[17] Indeed, in our view a central determinant of when an implicit contract will be observed is that its terms cannot be specified with sufficient precision to allow predictable formal enforcement.[18]

That implicit contracts like that governing associate career patterns are not enforceable by formal legal methods, however, does not mean that they are unenforceable. Rather, it means only that enforcement is informal, either through the market by way of a reputation effect or through the design of the structure of the relationship itself.[19]

Unfortunately, a reputation model confronts substantial barriers with respect to the implicit contract governing associate career patterns. In a setting without repetitive dealings between the same parties, a reputation model requires that past breaches of the implicit contract be communicated effectively to those who will deal with the breaching party in the future (Plaut, 1986; Bull, 1983; Klein and Leffler, 1981; Telser, 1980). The problem in our setting is that the firm's application of the subjective partnership standards to the associate's performance during the apprenticeship period cannot be monitored effectively by third parties. How does anyone know whether the associate really lacked 'judgement' or whether the firm is behaving opportunistically? Thus, determining whether a breach has even occurred, let alone effectively communicating that determination to existing or future associates, would be quite difficult. Under these conditions, a reputation model will not operate.[20]

The unavailability of a reputation model suggests looking to a structural technique – what Oliver Williamson has called a 'credible commitment' – so that the promise to treat the associate fairly at the time of the partnership decision is *self*-enforcing through the very design of the relationship (Williamson, 1983, 1985: 163–205). Our thesis is that the up-or-out system, seemingly foolish from the perspective of both the firm and associate when evaluated at the time when the partnership decision is made, is revealed to provide an effective structural bonding technique when evaluated at the time when the associate is initially hired.

To see this, recall precisely how the firm behaves opportunistically at the time of the partnership decision: it seeks to continue earning profits from the associate's efforts by retaining as an associate a lawyer who actually meets the partnership standards. By committing itself to fire anyone who is not made a partner, the firm effectively eliminates its incentive to undertake the very opportunistic behaviour that creates the associate's uncertainty. With the up-or-out system in place, the firm cannot manipulate the partnership decision so as to retain in some other capacity the services of an associate whose performance really merits partnership.[21]

In our view, then, the up-or-out system is a structural response to the dual uncertainty confronting the law firm and the associate at the time the associate is hired. It responds to the associates' uncertainty concerning the fairness of the future partnership decision by credibly committing the law firm not to do the only thing that would make later cheating on the initial promise of fair partnership consideration profitable to the firm.[22] And by eliminating the associate's uncertainty about the firm's future conduct, the up-or-out system goes a long way toward making the apprenticeship period a viable solution to the firm's uncertainty about the abilities of the pool of associates it hires.[23]

The remaining problem: associate risk aversion
Although the up-or-out system responds to the major barrier to an apprenticeship solution to the law firm's uncertainty, the firm's commitment itself creates a problem that must be confronted before the structural solution is stable. From the associate's perspective, eliminating the uncertainty concerning the fairness of the partnership decision is costly. In a world without opportunism – that is, if the law firm somehow was incapable of cheating on the partnership decision – the option to remain an associate if partnership standards are not met has the desirable characteristic of reducing the risk of the associate's investment in firm-specific human capital. Rather than making an up-or-out bet, the associate may prefer the potential of a non-partner position as a consolation prize. The variance of the return to the associate's human capital investment in the firm is thereby reduced without reducing the mean, and the associate is better off as a result.

Giving up this risk-reducing option is costly to the associate. To be sure, by assuring the associate that the partnership decision will be made fairly, the up-or-out system does assure that the associate's investment in firm-specific human capital will be a fair game. But because associates are risk averse, the increase in risk that results from the up-or-out system must also be ameliorated for the system to be stable. The next puzzle in explaining the historical dominance of the up-or-out system in corporate law firms is to understand how the system responds to the resulting increase in the risk of the associate's investment.

The traditional analysis of this problem is that the firm offsets the increased risk of an up-or-out system by facilitating outplacement of associates who do not make partner. Because providing an *internal* consolation prize – non-partner employment – to associates undermines the credibility of the partnership decision, the increased risk from the up-or-out system is reduced by providing an *external* consolation prize – for example, a job in the general counsel's office of a client, or a partnership in a less prestigious law firm. For this solution to work, however, it is critical that the law firm minimize the negative implications of an associate not making partner. Put differently, to succeed in outplacement, the firm must overcome the firm-specific character of the associate's human capital investment in revealing her abilities.

The available anecdotal evidence is consistent with this approach – outplacement and minimizing firm specificity – to reducing the associate's risk. For example, Swaine's discussion of the Cravath experience emphasizes the difficulty of the partnership decision and readily concedes that the partnership decision often errs in the direction of denying partnership to qualified associates:

> Obviously not all men competent to be partners can be taken into the firm – for that would make the firm unwieldy. The choice is difficult; factors which control ultimate decisions are intangible; admittedly they are affected by the idiosyncrasies of the existing partners. Mental ability there must be, but in addition, personality, judgement, character. No pretence is made that the ultimate decisions are infallible. Only infrequently have mistakes been made in taking men into the firm; more often, mistakes not so easily remedied have been made in not admitting others. (Swaine, 1948, vol. 2: 8–9)

Moreover, if successful outplacement is critical to supporting the up-or-out policy, we would expect the firm, in effect, to subsidize the process. For example, a firm might make its unsuccessful associates attractive to other firms by offering an implicit promise to send them referral business. Again, Swaine's description of the practice of the Cravath firm is consistent with this prediction:

Almost without exception, the relations between the Cravath partners and the men who have left the office to compete professionally have remained friendly, and often intimate. . . . Business which such men have been doing while with the firm has frequently been encouraged to continue with them; new business is often referred to former associates. (Swaine, 1948, vol. 2: 9)[24]

What happens, however, when outplacement is not available to reduce the increased risk to associates resulting from using the up-or-out system to assure the fairness of the partnership decision?[25] An alternative way to reduce this risk is simply to increase the likelihood of making partner. Understanding how firms choose between outplacement, an external approach, and increased likelihood of making partner, an internal approach, poses an additional puzzle. Compared to outplacement, increasing the likelihood of making partner seems to be a very expensive way to reduce associate risk. And the puzzle is further complicated by the unusual pattern of firms that nonetheless select the more expensive approach.[26]

A useful measure of a firm's success in reducing associate risk by outplacement rather than by an increased likelihood of making partner is its leverage: the ratio of associates to partners. By definition, the higher the ratio, the lower the likelihood of becoming a partner, and the higher the internal risk to the associate's human capital.[27] Therefore, the higher the firm's leverage, the more successful must be the firm's efforts at reducing associate risk by external means.

The puzzling pattern of firm choice between external and internal approaches to reducing associate risk appears when we recognize two empirical patterns. First, firm leverage is directly related to firm profit: the higher the firm's leverage, the higher the firm's per partner profit.[28] When one outlier is eliminated, regression analysis of data concerning the *American Lawyer*'s compilation of the one hundred most successful corporate law firms for 1987 discloses that differences in leverage explain 34.3% of the differences among firms in per partner profit profitability.[29] Second, the degree of firm leverage appears to be geographically determined: the same data indicates that among these one hundred firms, those based in New York City firms had an average associate/partner ratio of 2.55%, while those based outside New York had an average ratio of only 1.66, a difference of some 4%.[30] If an important determinant of per partner profit is leverage, and leverage seems to be predicted by geographical location, what has kept firms outside New York from increasing their partners' profit by increasing their leverage?

One hypothesis for why firms outside New York may appear to voluntarily eschew profits by selecting lower leverage derives from understanding the impact of leverage on the stability of the up-or-out system. Forgoing an internal approach to reducing the risk to associates from an up-or-out system by maintaining high leverage (and a low likelihood of making partner) requires the ability to reduce that risk by an external approach – outplacement. Now suppose that the concentration of corporate activity in New York – for example, the presence of corporate headquarters and, therefore, corporate counsel positions – facilitates outplacement by New York firms as compared to firms located elsewhere. This would allow New York firms to reduce the risk to associates' human capital created by the up-or-out system externally through outplacement, while firms in other geographical areas would be left to reduce the risk of the associates' human capital internally through an increased likelihood of making partner.[31]

The picture painted, then, is of varied responses to associate risk aversion depending on the real alternatives available to the firm. When a firm is successful at outplacement, the leverage maintainable by the firm can be higher than that of other firms, whether in other cities or within the same city, with less successful outplacement.[32] In contrast, when a firm is less successful at outplacement, associate risk must be reduced by increasing the likelihood of partnership and, as a result, decreasing the per partner profitability of the firm.

Why are associate career patterns changing?

The bonding explanation for the historical dominance of the up-or-out system leaves one observed pattern unexplained. Recently there has been a significant increase both in criticism of the system and in the number of firms that, in one fashion or another, have deviated from the practice of firing all associates who are not made partners.[33] To fully understand the up-or-out system, we must also be able to account for the changes in the environment that have caused the movement away from it. And to fully evaluate the bonding explanation for the dominance of the up-or-out system, we also must be able to account for how these changes alter the conditions that required bonding in the first place.

Two different, although not mutually exclusive, types of change can explain this incipient shift in associate career patterns. The first, a change in the nature of the standards that firms use to make the partnership decision, goes directly to the conditions that give rise to the need for a bonding mechanism at all. The second, a substantial increase in the demand for associates, has the same effect, albeit indirectly.

Increased ability to monitor the partnership decision

The linchpin of our explanation for the up-or-out system as a means by which a law firm bonds itself not to cheat on the partnership decision is the associate's inability directly to monitor the fairness of that decision. Suppose the standards for partnership were purely quantitative – for example, hours worked multiplied by fees actually collected. Then the associate could easily monitor the partnership decision; all that would be necessary would be access to the firm's timekeeping and billing records.[34] To be sure, the firm could 'cook' the books to achieve an opportunistic result even with a quantitatively mechanistic formula. But the records involved are central to the firm's operation, so that the management cost to the firm of intentionally inaccurate records would be high, and their very importance makes it unlikely that a separate, accurate, set could be kept secretly for management purposes while the public set was skewed to support opportunistic partnership decisions.[35]

Thus, to the extent that the standards for partnership become more observable, direct associate monitoring can replace the bonding function of the up-or-out system as a means of assuring that the firm makes the partnership decision fairly. The question, then, is what might account for such a shift in the standards used for the partnership decision.[36]

One obvious cause may be a shift that is taking place in the methods by which many law firms divide their profits. An important reason for subjective partnership criteria is a sharing approach to income division (Gilson and Mnookin, 1985: 374–80). A firm that divides its income by a method that emphasizes risk sharing to the virtual exclusion of incentives needs partners who, because of their personal characteristics, will not take advantage of the incentive to grab, shirk or leave that a sharing approach creates.[37]. And the criteria which identify associates that have the desired personal characteristics are unavoidably subjective and, therefore, unobservable by third parties. Thus the firm's method of dividing profits influences what standards govern the partnership decision, the unobservability of which creates the potential for the opportunism to which the up-or-out system is responsive.

Now consider what happens when, as increasingly appears to be the case,[38] the firm changes its method of dividing profits from a sharing model to a productivity approach in which profits are divided based on an effort to measure the actual contribution of each partner. As the formula for measuring productivity becomes more mechanistic – emphasizing, for example, such quantifiable factors as hours worked, amounts billed and clients attracted[39] – the need for subjective partnership standards diminishes because the damage that results from making a 'wrong' partnership decision is reduced. If a partner does not work out in a firm with a productivity approach to dividing profits, the unproductive partner receives only what he has 'earned', an amount presumably substantially lower than more productive partners, rather than receiving the same amount as more productive partners as in a sharing firm. Indeed, at the extreme, a mechanistic approach to income division can eliminate the need for an apprenticeship period and, at the very extreme, even eliminate the concept of partnership. Recall that the apprenticeship period is a response to the firm's uncertainty about the quality of the associates it has hired. An alternative way to eliminate that uncertainty is to eliminate its consequences. If associates' productivity can be measured so that they are never repaid more than they are worth, uncertainty about their ability at the time they are hired is no longer important, and the apprenticeship period that defines the functional distinction between partner and associates is no longer necessary. Then we simply might make all lawyers partners (or associates).[40]

Thus, as the formula for income division becomes more mechanistic, so too can the standards for partnership. And this means that associates can more effectively monitor the fairness of the partnership decision. In this setting, preventing the firm from behaving opportunistically in making the partnership decision no longer requires the up-or-out system. Indeed, in this setting, the up-or-out system would actually present the puzzle with which we started: it would work to neither party's advantage. A movement away from the system, to allow both the firm and its associates to benefit from an option for associates to remain in that capacity, would follow naturally.[41]

Increased demand for associates

There is, however, another explanation for the movement away from the up-or-out system that does not depend on a change in the manner in which the firm divides its profits. The business of major corporate law firms, and hence their demand for associates, appears to be growing so fast that the traditional sources of new associates no longer provide an adequate supply.[42] The least restrictive version of the familiar story told by major law firm recruits is that their firms hire as new associates only law students in the top half of their class at, say, the top twenty law schools.[43] It now appears that this source of associate supply does not meet current firm demand. One commentator recently calculated that in 1986 a total of 6080 students received law degrees from schools comprising his top twenty list, resulting in 3040 graduates in the top half of their classes.[44] He then calculated that 4807 new associates began working for the top 250 law firms that year, a number that exceeded the supply of top-half, top-twenty graduates by some 58%.

The clear implication of this calculation is that major firms have begun to hire a different, in the minds of the firms less capable, category of associate than in the past.[45] And the question for associate career patterns is whether law firms' traditional up-or-out system can accommodate the impact of an influx of higher-risk associates on two of its critical elements: the screening function of the apprenticeship period and successful outplacement of associates who do not become partners. Expanded recruitment, both in the numbers of associates hired and the number of schools from which they are hired, has three effects that may strain the firm's capacity to evaluate during the apprenticeship period all of the associates that it hires. First, the size of the pool of associates whose abilities must be evaluated increases without, even in the medium run, an increase in the number of partners making the evaluations. Increased leverage simply increases the burden on the evaluative process. Second, the decrease in the quality of the pool – a decrease in the mean and an increase in the variance of the abilities of new associates – increases the difficulty of making evaluations. More effort is necessary to screen effectively. Finally, the deterioration in the law firm's screening can affect not only the new lower-quality associates, but also the traditional higher-quality associates. Unless some special accommodation is made, the likely result is that more mistakes are made with respect to *both* groups, thereby decreasing the firm's attraction to traditional associates,[46] and creating the potential for a 'lemons' market.[47]

Just as the increase in the number of associates *entering* the apprenticeship period hampers its ability successfully to screen associates, so the increase in the number of associates *exiting* the apprenticeship period – those who do not make partners – because of increased initial hiring of less talented associates, may hamper the firm's ability to provide outplacement for unsuccessful associates. An increase in the supply and a decrease in quality of associates to be placed unavoidably affects demand.

Outplacement may be hampered further by the increased variance in the quality of the marginal group of associates. Recall that to maximize its capacity to place associates who do not make partner, the firm should give the appearance that the partnership decision is so selective as perhaps to be arbitrary, so that being turned down for partnership is not a negative signal of the unsuccessful associate's ability. To the extent that the change in the pool of associates hired makes this story less believable, outplacement becomes more difficult. And this, in turn, makes less effective the firm's efforts to offset the increased risk to the associate resulting from the up-or-out system's elimination of the permanent associate category. The outcome is a threat to the continued viability of the system.

Moving away somewhat from the up-or-out system responds to the problems caused by increasing the size and the variance, and decreasing the average quality, of the pool of associates hired. But responding to these problems requires a very different kind of move than that suggested by the increased ability to monitor the explanation discussed in the previous section. Now the need is to expand the number of associates, but without diluting the quality of the apprenticeship period's operation – no increase in screening error and no decrease in outplacement success – with respect to the traditional pool of new associates from which, presumably, new partners will come.

This can be accomplished not, as implied by the increased ability to monitor explanation, by treating all associates alike until the partnership decision divides them into new partners and permanent associates, but by dividing associates into two categories from the time they are hired. Those in the category drawn from the traditional pool of associates are treated as associates in an up-or-out system always have been: their performance during the apprenticeship period is carefully evaluated and those who do not meet the partnership standard are placed elsewhere. The category drawn from the new, non-traditional sources are advised from the outset that they will never be considered for partnership, thereby imposing no additional burden on the apprenticeship period's screening function. And because the new category of associates is clearly designated as such from the outset, there is no danger of compromising the firm's ability to place associates from the traditional category.

Variations on this theme – an identifiable group of associates who will not be considered for partnership – are also possible. Contract lawyers, the equivalent of legal temps, serve the same function.[48] Additionally, one can imagine implicit tracking within a firm so that some associates are given work that provides the opportunity to show that one has partnership qualities while others are given work, like document discovery in a large antitrust case, that does not burden the screening function.[49]

Evaluation

Each of the explanations for the observed movement away from the up-or-out system is consistent both with observed changes in the firm's environment and, happily, with a bonding explanation for the historical dominance of the up-or-out system. The two explanations, however, are not mutually exclusive and, indeed, predict different kinds of movements away from the up-or-out system. The increased ability to monitor explanation predicts new categories of non-partner lawyers who are identified only after they complete the apprenticeship period and do not meet partnership standards. The increased demand explanation in contrast, predicts new categories of non-partner lawyers who are so identified from the time they are initially hired. In fact we observe both kinds of movements. A significant number of firms have created new categories of positions for associates who, following completion of the associate period, are not promoted to partner.[50] In contrast, Jones, Day, Reavis & Pogue, one of the largest firms in the US,[51] has created a category of associates, currently numbering forty-three, who are hired with the understanding that they will never be considered for partnership, and the concept is described as 'on lots of law firms' retreat agendas'.[52]

The puzzle that remains is to understand the firm characteristics that lead to one or the other approach. At this juncture, however, we can do no more than identify a number of testable propositions. The increased ability to monitor explanation predicts that firms that create a new category of position for associates who do not make partner will divide their income on a productivity basis and will probably have moved to that method recently from a method concerned more with risk sharing than with incentives. The increased demand explanation, because it contemplates the firm hiring associates of lower mean ability and higher variance than in the past, predicts that such firms will have increasing amounts of legal work of the sort that can be competently accomplished by lower-quality lawyers. Thus, it would be interesting to know whether firms that have gone this route have categories of work, particularly susceptible to being done by such lawyers, that other firms have not attracted.

Conclusion

In this chapter we have attempted two tasks. First we tried to explain the efficiency characteristics of the up-or-out system, the peculiar capital budgeting process by which corporate law firms traditionally have acquired and retained human capital. Second, we tried to identify the changes in the organizational environment that have caused a shift away from the traditional associate career pattern. Our study suggests the central influence of risk sharing and incentives on organizational structure when, as in service industries, the dominant firm input shifts from industrial to human capital. In this respect law firms are interesting organizations. They are, in many ways, the quintessential service firm, one whose only significant input is human capital. It is the dominance of human capital, we believe, that is the major determinant of law firm organization. So, because human capital is difficult to diversify, the need for risk sharing is an important influence on organizational structure. Non-productivity based methods of dividing profit reduce the risk of partners' human capital investment (Gilson amd Mnookin 1985: 341–6). Emphasis on outplacement or, where that is not possible, increased likelihood of becoming a partner, reduce the risk of associates' human capital investment. And because human capital is susceptible to opportunism, the need for incentives is the second major influence on law firm organization. The development of firm-specific capital protects the firms against some partners grabbing, shirking or leaving (Gilson and Mnookin, 1985: 353–71). The up-or-out system protects associates against the firm cheating on its promise of a fair partnership decision at the close of an associate's apprenticeship period.

Notes

Research for this chapter was supported by a bequest from the Claire and Michael Brown Estate and a grant from the John M. Olin Program in Law and Economics. We are grateful for comments by Robert Ellickson, Jeffrey Gordon, Leo Herzl, Reinier Kraakman and Marshall Small on an earlier draft of this chapter. A revised version appears in the *Stanford Law Review*, 46(3), February 1989.

1. A number of the alternatives to the up-or-out system, both in nomenclature and substance, are surveyed in Heintz and Markham-Bugbee (1986). For a discussion of the approaches taken by particular firms, see the sources referred to in note 33.

2. The only historical datum that we have discovered bearing on the origin of the up-or-out system concerns Cravath, Swaine & Moore, one of the oldest, most

successful and most prestigious law firms in the United States. See, for example, Brill, 'What Recession? Why Cravath's Balance Sheet Looks as Good as Ever', *American Lawyer*, March 1983: col. 1. Swaine's history of the firm indicates that the system was in place at least by 1916. Describing the opportunity that is held out to a young lawyer by the firm, Swaine states that: '[e]very lawyer who enters the Cravath office has the right to aspire to find his life career there – but only by attaining partnership' (Swaine, vol. 2: 7).

3. Even law teachers acknowledge that a student's performance in law school is a very noisy signal of long-term performance as a lawyer.

4. Heintz and Markham-Bugbee (1986: 32, 39) set out what are traditionally thought to be relevant partnership criteria, including 'personal qualities', said to be important. For a detailed and thoughtful analysis of 'what you [an associate] should be doing to impress the partners of the firm, so that one day you'll be added to their number', see Freund (1979: 5).

5. This account of the associate's apprenticeship period emphasizes the learning, as opposed to the incentive, aspect of labour contracts. The learning aspect posits that the process by which the employer comes to understand an employee's real productivity dictates the shape of the employee's earning profile. From this perspective, earnings are positively related to performance not because the relationship between pay and performance is designed to provide an incentive, but because performance reveals the employee's actual productivity (Murphy, 1986). Building on a learning approach, Holstrom constructs an interesting model in which new employees work very hard because the greatest uncertainty concerning their actual ability exists early in their career. If working hard is treated by the firm as a favourable signal of their ability, then the marginal impact of their effort is great in the early years of their employment because there is so little other information. As the firm learns more about the employee with the passage of time, additional effort has a smaller impact on the employer's overall assessment of the employee's ability and, as a result, the incentive to provide the effort decreases with time (Holstrom, 1983). It is interesting that Holstrom's extension of the learning model nicely fits familiar aspects of traditional associate career patterns. First, it is generally perceived that new associates work very hard, and that those who work the hardest are seen as the most promising. Second, and more telling especially in the early years of employment, associate salaries are typically not subject to substantial variation based on actual performance. Thus, there is no short-term incentive aspect to the employment contract; the learning aspect seems dominant at this stage of the associate's career, at least with respect to current wages. For young associates in law firms, then, the anecdotal evidence suggests a result consistent with that found by Murphy: learning dominates incentives as an explanation for the character of the labour contract.

6. Becker (1975: 26–37) is the seminal work.

7. The two functions of the law firm apprenticeship period discussed in the text – facilitating the firm's *learning* about the associate's real attributes and providing the associate with an *incentive* to acquire firm-specific capital – in fact blur in the middle, as is often the case when models are applied to the real world. If, as intuitively seems sensible, an associate's successful acquisition of firm-specific human capital is a function not only of incentive, but of the associate's ability as well, then the associate's success in acquiring it also provides information concerning the associate's abilities, a learning function.

8. It is interesting that the apprenticeship period in corporate law firms is quite lengthy, generally no shorter than six years and not uncommonly as long as ten. In contrast, the apprenticeship of medical partnerships that use an up-or-out system is typically much shorter. For example, that of the Permanente Medical Group, the physician component of the largest and oldest health maintenance organization in the United States, is expected to be no more than three years. This discrepancy highlights a third function of the apprenticeship period in law firms. Law schools simply have not fully trained their graduates to be corporate lawyers (Gilson, 1984: 303–6). Thus, in law firms the apprenticeship period must be long enough both to provide this additional training and to evaluate how effectively it has been learned by the associate. Post-medical school training of physicians, however, is provided by internship, residency and specialty programmes, taking from three to five years and generally completed before a physician joins a medical partnership. Thus, all that is left for the medical partnership's apprenticeship period is the learning function. In this regard, it is curious that the apprenticeship period of a medical partnership together with the post-medical school training period is of a length comparable to the apprenticeship period of a law firm.

9. The explanation for the profitability of senior associates is familiar. By this time, the associate has completed his or her training as a corporate lawyer and the firm has learned enough about the associate's abilities and attributes to use them effectively. The associate then provides profit for the firm to the extent that amounts billed and collected for the associate's time exceed the associate's salary plus related overhead. Partners debate vigorously precisely when associates become profitable, and it is critical in evaluating the positions taken to keep in mind whether profitability is being determined on an average or marginal cost basis and to be careful in specifying what costs are marginal and over what period. However, the fact that differences among firms in associate/partner ratios explain a substantial amount of variance among firms in per partner profits (see text accompanying notes 28–30) strongly suggests the importance of associate profitability. For a detailed discussion of the mechanics of non-partner profitability in service firms, see Maister (1982).

10. The presiding partner of Cravath, Swaine & Moore has acknowledged this point: 'The most valuable persons in some ways to use are associates with whom the clients are happy.' 'Getting Rid of the Simple Up-Or-Out Partner–Associate Structure', *American Lawyer*, September 1987: 26, 30 – remarks of Samuel Butler.

11. This does not mean a system that requires retaining all associates passed over for partnership or that gives associates who are retained some form of tenure. The need to attract new associates with the potential to be partners would counsel against retaining too many associates, and the need for flexibility to respond to changes in business conditions by reducing the numbers of 'permanent' associates, rather than decreasing the inflow of new associates with partnership potential, would counsel against providing too much job security. What requires explanation is the up-or-out system's extreme position that, as a general rule, a firm *never* retains an associate who is not promoted.

The presence of some types of permanent associates is not inconsistent with this general rule. Cravath, Swaine & Moore has a group of twenty-four specialist lawyers who will never be considered for partnership. However, these lawyers are generally not regular associates who were passed over for partnership. Rather most 'had been hired laterally with their specialties already in hand'. 'Getting Rid of the Simple Up-Or-Out Partner–Associate Structure', op. cit.: quoting presiding partner Samuel Butler.

12. This insight originates with Kahn and Huberman (1986).

13. Gilson and Mnookin (1985: 356–71) discuss the character of firm-specific capital in a successful law firm.

14. Becker (1975: 27): 'Expenditures on acquiring knowledge of employees' talents would be a specific investment if the knowledge could be kept from other firms, for then productivity would be raised more in firms making the investment than elsewhere.'

15. See Greenwald (1986) (application of 'lemons market' concept to labour market).

16. To be sure, the associate also invests in other forms of firm-specific capital. For example, knowledge of the firm's way of doing things and the particular traits of firm lawyers, and knowledge concerning the firm's clients and working relations with such clients, all have aspects of firm specificity about them. In our analysis, however, the associate's investment in revealing her actual abilities is the most significant.

17. Where disagreement existed, the upshot of an explicit contract would be to transfer the partnership decision from the firm to a court. And because the subjective criteria for partnership would not significantly restrict the court's discretion, the result inevitably would be significant uncertainty for the firm with respect to which associates would become partners.

18. From this perspective, for example, the traditional employment at will doctrine by which an employer can terminate an employee at any time without cause is not a statement of the terms of an explicit contract – that labour is acquired in a spot market – but, rather, a statement that the implicit contract with respect to the complete terms of employment is not *legally* enforceable.

19. Plaut (1986: 257) stresses that the central concern of the implicit contract literature is enforceability: 'The problem is that for any contract to trade labour services, or some other good at some future time, there will always be a motivation for one of the contracting parties to breach the contract whenever the future spot price deviates from the contractual price. In the absence of some formal enforcement mechanism (i.e., courts), or informal mechanism (such as the concern for reputation or front-end loading) contracts would never be fulfilled.'

20. Professor Steven Shavell has suggested to us circumstances in which a reputation model might work in this context even if associates could not monitor the fairness of the partnership decision with respect to any particular associate. So long as new associates are told at the time they are hired the *percentage* of associates who will make partner, all that must be observable at the time of the partnership decision is the number of associates who in fact become partners. Although a particular associate still may not know whether he was cheated, it will be apparent if anyone was, and that is all a reputation model requires to operate.

The difficulty with Professor Shavell's analysis is that the partnership decision is more complicated than we have acknowledged up to now. We have stressed the firm's uncertainty about associate ability and the associates; uncertainty about firm opportunism because we believe this dual uncertainty explains the central characteristic of associate ability and dual uncertainty explains the central characteristic of associate career partners. There is, however, an additional uncertainty present that bears both on the likelihood that a particular associate will become a partner and on the percentage of associates who will become partners: the firm's future success. The implicit contract for associates also reflects some risk sharing concerning the impact of future downturn in legal business generally, or in the fortunes of the particular firm. Opportunism at the time of the partnership decision is also possible with respect to the allocation of these business risks between the firm and the associate. A firm falsely may represent that its needs, for partners generally or within a particular specialty, have changed since the firm made its representation concerning the percentage of associates who would become partners.

Professor Shavell might respond that a reputation model would work for this type of opportunism as well. A fear of the impact on future hiring would deter the firm from making fewer partners than originally promised. We believe this type of reputation model is unrealistic. For such a model to work, the terms of the implicit contract must specify the percentage of associates making partner in all possible future states of the world. In addition, the state of the world that exists at the time the partnership decision is made must be observable so that associates can determine the applicable percentage and then compare it to the percentage of associates who in fact become partners. If, as we believe, the actual state of the market for legal services and the competitive position of a particular firm within that market are not observable without substantial noise, a reputation model should not work. For a similar analysis with respect to wage rates, see note 23.

21. Moreover, the difficulty of monitoring the firm's partnership decision is no longer a problem once the up-or-out system minimizes the firm's incentive to cheat. Because there is no longer a reason to believe that the firm is not making the partnership decision in good faith, the associate should be less concerned about allowing the decision to be made by the party who has both the best information about the appropriate standards for partnership and the best information about the associate's performance during the apprenticeship period.

22. In our analysis, it is associates' investment in firm-specific human capital during the apprenticeship period that limits their ability to respond to the law firm's cheating. Thus, the presence of significant firm-specific human capital is a central element of the necessity for an up-or-out system. In contrast, Baker, Jensen and Murphy (1988: 593) state that '[u]p-or-out systems work better in situations where the required human capital is general . . .'. Although Baker, Jensen and Murphy do not explain their conclusion, their analysis in fact may be largely compatible with our own. If one looks only at the skills associates acquire during apprenticeship, they appear to be general human capital. It is the information asymmetry between the firm and alternative employers in evaluating the quality of the general human capital acquired that, in our analysis, transforms this general human capital into firm-specific human capital.

23. There are other examples of such commitment solutions in the literature. Hart offers one as an alternative to the standard risk-sharing explanation for riding wage rates. Suppose a company needs to cut either wages or employment as a response to bad times. If employees cannot monitor the company's claim of bad times, then its decision to cut wages, like the law firm's partnership decision, is subject to opportunism. But since the level of employment is related to company profitability, a decision to reduce employment is not subject to the same potential for opportunism as a decision to reduce wages because, unlike reducing wages, reducing employment hurts the company as well as the employees.

Lazear uses a commitment approach to deal with employee, rather than employer, opportunism. Employee incentive schemes, whether designed to encourage employees to reveal their abilities or to invest in firm-specific capital, operate by paying the employee less than his marginal product in the period before the employee reveals his ability or completes making an investment in firm-specific capital (or, as in our case, both), and more than his marginal product thereafter. How then does the firm make sure that it does not overpay employees because of the variance in employee career lengths? By accepting mandatory retirement, employees commit themselves to an effective cap on the firm's total obligation for incentive payments.

24. Current anecdote suggests that referral work after departure continues to accompany Cravath outplacement. From this perspective, because of the need to maintain a continual flow of referral work to power the outplacement process, the firm consciously must decide not to expand to the point where it can undertake all the work that comes to it. The opportunity cost incurred is further evidence that responding to the increased risk resulting from the up-or-out system is costly.

Maister (1985: 9) notes that non-legal professional service firms that enforce an up-or-out system also stress outplacement. McKenzie and Company, a management consulting firm, and Arthur Anderson & Co., a Big Eight accounting firm, are said to 'work actively to place their alumni/ae in good positions with favoured clients. . . . In part, due to the "caring" approach taken for the junior staff, one-firm firms are able to achieve a very profitable high-leverage strategy (i.e., high ratio of junior to senior staff) without excessive pressures for growth to provide promotion opportunities.'

25. The pattern in other settings in which an up-or-out system is dominant reinforces our conclusion that the system's stability requires some means of reducing the risk that results from eliminating the consolation prize of continued employment for those who are not promoted. In the military, for example, the viability of early retirement at full pay provides a risk-reducing consolation prize. If the time at which the up-or-out decision is made corresponds to the availability of early retirement, the risk of non-promotion is very significantly hedged.

In academia, reduced informational asymmetry between current and alternative employers concerning the faculty member's ability may make the problem less important. Recall that one barrier to outplacement by a law firm, overcome by techniques like those ascribed to the Cravath firm, is the negative inference drawn by potential employers from the very fact that the associate was not promoted. In the law firm setting, the barrier is particularly high because it is difficult for a potential employer to evaluate independently the associate's abilities; knowledge about the associate's real abilities is a firm-specific asset. Because the principal measure of an academic's abilities – published scholarship – can be more readily evaluated by alternative employers, the additional risk imposed by the up-or-out system, in an academic setting called tenure, is less significant.

26. The need to offset the increased risk resulting from an up-or-out system does not depend on the associates' accurately assessing their likelihood of making partners. Even if they systematically overestimate their chances because of some cognitive bias (Tversky and Kahneman, 1982), the system still increases the risk.

27. This assumes that the ratio remains constant over time. In a period of growth, a firm's overall leverage may increase even though the percentage of each new group of associates who ultimately will become partners remains the same.

28. This would be necessary just to make the return on the associate's investment a fair game: as the likelihood of winning goes down, the size of the prize must go up for even risk-neutral participants to be willing to play.

29. The outlier is Wachtel, Lipton, Rosen & Katz, a firm specializing in hostile take-over work. In 1987, Wachtel was reported to have an average profit per partner of $1,405,000 – the top in the United States – although its ratio of associates per partner was only 1.05. This firm bills for this work on a transaction, rather than a per hour basis, which significantly reduces the importance of leverage. If Wachtel, Lipton is included in the regression, differences in leverage explains 20.9% of the differences among firms in per partner profit.

30. This analysis is consistent with published data that a new associate's likelihood of partnership in a large corporate law firm is lower in New York. Spurr reports that, over the period 1970–7, new associates joining large Chicago firms had a 48.8% chance of making partner, while those joining large New York City firms had only a 22.8% chance of partnership.

31. One approach to testing the hypothesis would be to examine, by large metropolitan area, the ratio of non-corporate law firm sophisticated legal jobs to the number of lawyers in corporate law firms. The hypothesis predicts that this ratio will vary directly with firm leverage.

32. Thus the hypothesis also extends to explaining variance in leverage among firms within a single metropolitan area.

33. See, for example, Blum and Lobaco, 'When Associates Don't Make Partner', *California Lawyer*, 51 (January–February 1988); Singer, 'Senior Attorney Programs: Half a Loaf', *American Lawyer*, January–February 1987: 12; Freeman, 'Alternatives to the Old Up or Out', *California Lawyer*, 44 (December 1987); 'Getting Rid of the Simple Up-or-Out Partner Associate Structure', op. cit., note 26; Carbonara, 'Gaston Snow Reinvents the Two-Tier System', *American Lawyer*, October 1987: 14; Snider, 'Inside the Megafirms', *California Lawyer*, 32 (September 1987); Brill, *American Bar Associates Journal*, 30(1) (April 1984); Graham, 'New "Senior Attorney" Program Draws Attention to Davis Polk', *Legal Times*, 28 February 1983: 3, col. 1; Galante, 'Firms Look Closer at How to Create Lawyer Categories', *L.A. Daily Journal*, 22 August 1983: 1, col. 6; Hallam, 'Big Firms Search for Alternatives to Traditional Form', *L.A. Daily Journal*, 18 March 1983: 1, col. 5; Glasser, 'Firm Explores New Partnership Category', *Legal Times*, 14 February 1983: 12, col. 2; Galante, 'Meet the Permanent Associate', *National Law Journal*, 24 October 1983: 1, col. 5.

34. McChesney documents the pervasive monitoring by law firms of hours worked by individual lawyers.

35. There are other barriers as well. First, the firm does not have exclusive access to the data underlying the records. At least with respect to hours worked, an associate is capable of keeping her own records as a check on the accuracy of the firm's records, a result that is more likely the more important is the data to the associate's future. If this information were shared among associates, the firm's data could be duplicated by the associates. Second, because the firm presumably bases the partnership decision on an associate's performance over a number of years, opportunistic record keeping requires that the firm be able to identify those associates who will be the object of this behaviour a significant time before the partnership decision is to be made. To this extent, however, opportunistic manipulation of the underlying data conflicts with the very point of the apprenticeship period – to allow associates to reveal their true abilities.

36. See, for example, Carbonara, 'Gaston Snow Reinvents the Two-Tier System', op. cit., note 33 (simultaneously with adopting a complex two-tier partnership

structure, Gaston Snow & Ely Bartlett adopted for the first time written partnership standards that emphasized business generation, a more quantitative criterion).

37. Gilson and Mnookin (1985: 321) describe the three problems with a sharing approach to dividing profits. It may lead to: '*shirking*, a partner's failure to do his "fair share" of the work; *grabbing*, a partner's extraction of a larger than previously agreed share of firm profits by threatening to depart; and *leaving*, a partner's departure from the firm with clients and business in tow'.

38. See the sources referred to in Gilson and Mnookin (1985: 315 n. 6). Los Angeles' Tuttle & Taylor is a recent example. See 'Bar Talk', *American Lawyer*, April 1988: 14.

39. These are not as easy to quantify as may at first appear. For example, with respect to client attraction, does a client belong to the partner who brought the client in the door or the partner who, by doing the work, keeps the client from leaving? For a discussion of the difficulty in specifying productivity formulas and the risk of creating perverse incentives, see Gilson and Mnookin (1985: 349–52). There are, however, ways of approaching this issue. If bringing in the client initially works Williamson's fundamental transformation from a competitive market to bilateral monopoly (Williamson, 1985: 61–3), then the importance of attracting the client, as opposed to servicing the client, goes up. In all events, however, an accurate determination is likely to be quite context specific.

40. Just such an approach – abolishing the concept of partner (or, instead, of associate) – was recently suggested by the former managing partner of Morrison & Forester, a large national law firm. See Brill, 'Headnotes', *American Lawyer*, November 1986: 1; Mode and Raven, 'Associate Leverage is Doomed', *American Lawyer*, November 1985: 10. See also Stuart, 'Anderson Russell's Classless Society', *American Lawyer*, December 1986: 10 (description of an 'all partner' firm).
    The ability accurately to measure an associate's productivity does not entirely eliminate the need for some screening by the firm. If there is the potential that some associates in the pool are so bad that they will expose the firm to affirmative loss – for example, through damages for malpractice or loss of clients – then paying even a zero wage does not fully protect the firm. It may be possible, however, to eliminate this risk through very selective criteria for initial hiring.

41. Recognizing that the unobservability of the partnership decision creates the need for the up-or-out system as a binding device suggests another approach to increasing the associates' ability to monitor. If a firm can identify one or more associates who are very likely to be made partners, allowing those associates to participate in the partnership decision process – perhaps by serving on the relevant committee and attending the partnership meeting at which the decision is made – may increase substantially the extent to which associates can directly monitor the decision. To be sure, the solution is not complete because of the possibility that the associate monitors either may be co-opted (by the promise of, or a threat to, their future partnerships) or fooled, but the ability of the firm to behave opportunistically would still be significantly constrained. We are grateful to Marshall Small for calling this point to our attention.

42. See, for example, 'Busy Law Firms' Profits Leap', *New York Times*, 2 July 1987: 25, col. 3; Gray, 'Law Firms' Big Fee Hikes Reflect Higher Pay and Booming Business', *Wall Street Journal*, 19 March 1987: 23, col. 4.

43. Those familiar with the interviewing practices of elite firms as recently as five

years ago will object that typically such firms hired associates from nowhere near as many as twenty schools. As will be apparent, this observation only underscores the explanation offered in the text.

44. Bernstein, 'Does a Hiring Crisis Threaten the Profession?', *The National Law Journal*, 28 December 1987: 20, col. 2. The author had the good sense to decline to identify the composition of his top twenty. Robert Raven, former managing partner of Morrison & Foerster, has a considerably more pessimistic estimate of the supply of desirable associates· 'Depending on how many schools you go to and how deep you go into the class, there's a pool of about 1,200 to 1,400 people out there you would like to confine your offers to.' 'Getting Rid of the Simple Up-or-Out Partner–Associate Structure', op. cit.: note 33.

45. Snider 'Inside the Megafirms', op. cit., note 33 (describing expanded law school recruiting and hiring by major California firms); Jensen, 'Perks: When High Salaries Aren't Enough', *National Law Journal*, 22 June 1987: 1, col. 1 (describing expanded law school recruiting and hiring by Morgan, Lewis & Bockius; Dewey, Ballentine, Bushby & Palmer; and Brown & Wood).

46. From the perspective of traditional associates, the increase in the likelihood of a mistake serves to increase the risk associates with their human capital, and makes working for that firm less desirable.

47. In a lemons market, high-quality producers are unable to distinguish their products from those of low-quality producers. High-quality products therefore command no higher price than low-quality products and, as a result, only low-quality products are produced (Akerlof, 1970).

48. Interestingly, at the same time this phenomenon is growing in importance, see Beckman, 'Temporarily Yours: Associates for Hire', *American Lawyer*, March 1988: 24, col. 1, and 'Contract Associates', *American Bar Association Journal*, 1 February 1987: 24, agencies that provide contract lawyers have come under attack as being engaged in the unauthorized practice of law. See 'Lawyers Warned Against Role in Job Placement Agencies', *New York Law Journal*, 6 April 1988: 1, col. 1; '"Temp" Agencies Up in Arms Over City Bar Ethics Ruling', 8 April 1988: 1, col. 1.

49. To the extent that the implicit tracking system is not observable from outside the firm, outplacement can be extended to some of these associates as well, thereby allowing the firm to attract better-quality second-tier associates.

50. See sources referred to in note 33.

51. As of September 1987, Jones, Day had 727 lawyers. 'Getting Rid of The Simple Up-Or-Out Partnership–Associates Structure', op. cit.: 31, note 26.

52. 'Are Staff Attorneys Catching On?' *National Law Journal*, 2 May 1988: 2, col. 1. Consistent with our analysis, the Jones, Day associates are described as coming from 'second tier' law schools. Paul, Weiss, Rifkind, Wharton & Garrison is also reported to have initiated such a programme. Ibid.

References

Akerlof, George (1970) 'The Market for "Lemons": Quality Uncertainty and the Market Mechanisms', *Quarterly Journal of Economics*, 84: 488.

Baker, George, Michael Jensen and Kevin Murphy (1988) 'Compensation and Incentives: Practice vs. Theory', *Journal of Finance*, 43: 593.

Becker, Gary (1975) *Human Capital*, 2nd edn. Chicago: University of Chicago Press.

Bull, Clive (1983) 'Implicit Contracts in the Absence of Enforcement and Risk Aversion', *American Economic Review*, 73: 658.

Bulow, Jeremy and Myron Scholes (1984) 'Who Owns the Assets in a Defined-Benefit Pension Plan?', in Z. Bodie and J. Shoven (eds) *Financial Aspects of the U.S. Pension System*, p. 17. Chicago: University of Chicago Press.

Freund, James (1979) *Lawyering: a Realistic Approach to Legal Practice*. New York: Law Journal Seminars-Press.

Gilson, Ronald (1984) 'Value Creation by Business Lawyers: Legal Skills and Asset Pricing', *Yale Law Journal*, 94: 239.

Gilson, Ronald and Robert Mnookin (1985) 'Sharing Among the Human Capitalists: an Economic Inquiry into the Corporate Law Firm and How Partners Split Profits', *Stanford Law Review*, 37: 313.

Greenwald, Bruce (1986) 'Adverse Selection in the Labour Market', *Review of Economic Studies*, 53: 325.

Hart, Oliver (1983) 'Optimal Labor Contracts under Asymmetric Information: an Introduction', *Review of Economic Studies*, 50: 3.

Heintz, Bruce and Nancy Markham-Bugbee (1986) *Two-Tier Partnerships and Other Alternatives: Five Approaches*. Chicago: Section of Economics of Law Practice, American Bar Association.

Holstrom, Bengt (1983) *Managerial Incentive Problems: a Dynamic Approach*. New Haven: mimeo.

Jensen, Michael (1983) 'Organizational Theory and Methodology', *Accounting Review*, 53: 319.

Kahn, Charles and Gur Huberman (1986) *Two-Sided Uncertainty and 'Up-Or-Out' Contracts'*. Stanford: Hoover Institution Working Paper in Economics No. E-86-47.

Klein, Benjamin and Keith Leffler (1981) 'The Role of Market Forces in Assuring Contractual Performance', *Journal of Political Economy*, 89: 615.

Leazer, Edward (1979) 'Why is There Mandatory Retirement?', *Journal of Political Economy*, 87: 1261.

Maister, David (1982) 'Balancing the Service Firm', *Sloan Management Review*, 24: 15.

Maister, David (1985) 'The One-Firm Firm: What Makes It Successful', *Sloan Management Review*, 24: 2.

McChesney, Fred (1982) 'Team Production, Monitoring, and Profit Sharing in the Law Firms: an Alternative Hypothesis', *Journal of Legal Studies*, 11: 379.

Murphy, Kevin (1986) 'Incentives, Learning and Compensation: a Theoretical and Empirical Investigation of Managerial Labor Contracts', *Rand Journal of Economics*, 17: 59.

Plaut, Steven (1986) 'Implicit Contracts in the Absence of Enforcement: a Note', *American Economic Review*, 76: 257.

Spurr, Stephen (1987) 'How the Market Solves an Assignment Problem: the Matching of Lawyers with Legal Claims', *Journal of Labor Economics*, 5: 502.

Swaine, Robert (1948) *The Cravath Firm and its Predecessors: 1819-1948*.

Telser, Lester (1980) 'A Theory of Self-Enforcing Agreements', *Journal of Business*, 53: 27.

Tversky, Amos and Daniel Kahneman (1982) 'Judgment Under Uncertainty:

Heuristics and Biases', in D. Kahneman, P. Slovic and A. Tversky (eds) *Judgment Under Uncertainty: Heuristics and Biases*, p. 3. Cambridge: Cambridge University Press.

Williamson, Oliver (1983) 'Credible Commitments: Using Hostages to Support Exchange', *American Economic Review*, 73: 519.

Williamson, Oliver (1985) *The Economic Institutions of Capitalism*. New York: The Free Press.

Williamson, Oliver (1988) 'Corporate Finance and Corporate Governance', *Journal of Finance*, 43: 567.

PART IV

FINANCE AND THE POLITICAL STRUCTURE OF THE FIRM

11

Capital Structure as a Mechanism of Control: a Comparison of Financial Systems

Erik Berglöf

1. Introduction

A firm's capital structure can be viewed as describing the allocation of risk and control among investors. Capital structure here refers not only to the ratio of debt to equity, but also to the relative importance of different debt and equity instruments as well as to the degree of concentration and the homogeneity of holdings of these instruments. Casual observation indicates that capital structure varies substantially across capitalist countries. Yet our understanding of these differences and their implications is limited. Why are creditors (shareholders) in some countries willing to extend (accept) credit far beyond levels considered viable in other countries? Why has ownership of debt and equity become widely dispersed in a few countries, while holdings of these instruments remain much more concentrated in most countries? What effects, if any, do these differences in capital structure have for real decisions?

This chapter compares capital structure in six capitalist economies. These countries are classified into market- and bank-oriented financial systems and the features distinguishing the two types of system are interpreted using the incomplete contracting literature. The comparison shows higher gearing ratios and more concentrated ownership of both debt and equity in bank-oriented financial systems. The higher debt levels indicate a greater likelihood of insolvency, that is, creditors have control and carry risk over a wider range of future states.

The claim here is that these differences are, at least to some extent, related to the absence of strong restrictions on commercial banks in these countries. Since banks can more effectively exercise control, they are willing to extend credit beyond levels observed in market-oriented financial systems. In fact, commercial banks actively utilize higher gearing ratios to initiate financial distress as a means of reorganizing problem firms. This claim is consistent with the observation that creditor reorganization is relatively more common and take-overs not as frequent in bank-oriented financial systems. In general, firms in these systems seem to rely more on internal conflict resolution while market-oriented financial systems are more prone to solutions involving outsiders to the firm, for example, courts and other companies. As a result, ownership structures are more stable in bank-oriented systems.

The theoretical framework chosen for this analysis focuses on the incomplete nature of the firm's contracts, that is, that they do not fully specify the parties' obligations for every conceivable contingency. The interpretation of capital structure put forward by the incomplete contracting literature provides us with both a descriptive model and an analytical tool. This framework allows us to describe the allocation of risk and control and analyse its consequences without initially imposing an informational structure, that is, without making assumptions about the degree and nature of asymmetric distribution of information between the contracting parties. This makes the incomplete contracting approach particularly suitable for international comparisons since such informational asymmetries, to the extent that they can be captured and quantified, are less likely to vary systematically across countries.

The incomplete contracting literature views the standard financial instruments, debt as well as equity, as conferring both control rights and rights to return streams. Furthermore, the literature does not *ex ante* confine the contracting parties to a narrow set of standard instruments, but rather leaves the design to the parties. The conclusions arising from this approach also seem to capture fairly well some of our intuitive understanding of the differences between financial systems. In addition, as a theoretical framework the incomplete contracting literature generates a number of interesting hypotheses which can be analysed in formal models and tested empirically.

Some stylized facts about differences in capital structure are derived by analysing data from six countries – five large capitalist economies (the Federal Republic of Germany, France, Japan, the United Kingdom and the United States) and Sweden. The choice of countries was quite natural considering their size and importance to the world economy. Sweden was included since data for that country was easily accessible. The data has been derived primarily from national accounts and surveys of the corporate sector in the individual countries. The methodological problems involved in using this type of data are immense. The limitations of particular data will be indicated as they are used.

The outline of this chapter is as follows: Section 2 briefly presents the incomplete contracting approach to capital structure. A number of new interpretations of empirical observations on capital structure emerge from this literature. In Section 3 the financial systems of six countries are described and classified as either bank- or market-oriented. A number of features distinguishing the two types of system are identified. These characteristics are interpreted in Section 4, based on the incomplete contracting literature. Particular emphasis is given to the procedures for handling conflicts between investors when firms are in financial distress. The concluding Section 5 discusses the implications of this incomplete contracting interpretation for the functioning of the two systems.

2. The incomplete contracting view of capital structure

The theory of capital structure is concerned with why financial contracts appear in certain patterns and why these patterns differ across industries and across countries (Hart, 1987). Our focus here is on international differences in capital structure. In modern finance literature *à la* Modigliani and Miller (1958) where financial instruments only entitle their holders to return streams and where capital structure does not matter, such differences between countries are merely accidental.[1] At the most, explanations based on different corporate tax schemes could be put forward.[2]

According to the traditional property rights school, capital structure is not a matter of indifference (for a survey see De Alessi, 1983). This approach emphasizes that financial instruments also confer rights of control. Its primary concern has been with the identification of ownership and control rights and with the effects on efficiency as these two types of rights are separated from each other. However, the property rights school has little to say about debt and the relative importance of debt and equity, since ownership rights are by definition vested in the owners of the firm and no distinction is made between control in different states of nature.

The claim here is that the incomplete contracting literature provides a better framework for description and analysis of international differences in capital structure (for two surveys of this literature see Hart and Holmström, 1987, and Holmström and

Tirole, 1989). As in the property rights approach, it is recognized that shares of corporate stock confer both rights to return streams and control rights. But, in contrast to the property rights literature, the incomplete contracting framework also considers the control element of debt contracts and the state-contingent nature of control, that is, that contracts often make the allocation of control dependent on the state of nature. The foundation is that contracts are necessarily incomplete, in that they do not stipulate the parties' obligations for every conceivable eventuality.[3] Incompleteness gives rise to the problem of how to allocate control in situations not covered by the initial contract, the so-called residual control rights. Indeed, control is void of meaning if all future actions and states could be specified *ex ante*. In the incomplete contracting literature financial contracts are defined in terms of how they allocate the residual control rights. In fact, instruments cannot be distinguished based on their return characteristics.

To better understand the incomplete contracting approach to capital structure, it helps to think, as Aghion and Bolton (1988) do, in terms of a simple two-period model with one owner/entrepreneur and one outside investor. The parties *ex ante* have to agree how to allocate control in the second period. They may decide to share control or to let one of the parties have control irrespective of what happens in the first period.[4] Aghion and Bolton demonstrate how both parties can be made better off, if they make the allocation of control in the second period contingent on the first-period outcome. In 'good' states the entrepreneur maintains control, while the outside investor assumes control in 'bad' states. This, according to Aghion and Bolton, is the essence of the debt contract, since contracts in the incomplete contracting literature cannot be distinguished by their return characteristics.

By deciding on the level of debt the parties implicitly determine the point of insolvency. Financial distress is thus endogenous, that is, distressed states are merely those 'bad' states in which the parties *ex ante* agreed to transfer control from shareholders to creditors. The contracting parties, through the debt contract, *ex ante* build in a mechanism of control transfer.

Whereas the agency literature (see, for example, Jensen and Meckling, 1976) takes the standard debt and equity instruments as given and discusses the allocation of control based on the characteristics of these contracts, the incomplete contracting approach asks why these instruments were chosen in the first place. The standard agency conclusion is that owners should have control since they are the residual claimants. This, however, is merely

Liquidator   Entrepreneur

Figure 11.1   Allocation of control across investors and states

tautological in that it is assumed at the outset. The incomplete contracting approach, on the other hand, suggests that the parties first decide who is most suited to control the firm in various situations. Given this allocation of control, returns streams are shared to provide the appropriate incentives to exert effort, that is, the investor holding the residual control rights over a certain range of states should bear the risk associated with the decisions in these states.

In the Aghion and Bolton context, the owner/entrepreneur obtains private benefits from the firm as a going concern, or alternatively he suffers costs if the firm is closed down. Consequently, he is assumed to be less suited as manager when the going concern value of the firm falls below liquidation value (L) (see Figure 11.1). Thus, control should be transferred to the external investor in these states.[5] This is achieved by setting the level of debt (D) equivalent to L.

In the Aghion and Bolton model, the transfer point is set to approximate liquidation value. Thus the outside investor only carries risk to the extent that profits are an imperfect indicator of firm value. In real life, however, we observe that creditors are willing to extend loans far beyond the liquidation value. As a result, creditors' claims are partially secured, partially unsecured.

To illustrate this we assume that there are states above liquidation value (L through R in Figure 11.2) where the parties *ex ante* would prefer control to be transferred. For example, there might be certain investors specializing in reorganizing problem firms. This 'reorganization specialist' normally has a stake in the firm as a going concern. So he should also be relieved of control when the firm value slides below L.

Liquidator   Reorganization specialist   Entrepreneur

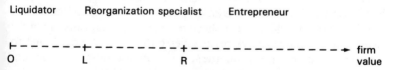

Figure 11.2   *Allocation of control across investors and states (with reorganization specialist)*

Given that this is the desirable allocation of control, each investor should have a contract which makes him the residual claimant in the states where he is in control. Grossly simplified, the liquidator should hold secured debt, the reorganization specialist unsecured debt (or equity), and the entrepreneur equity. Again, the likelihood of financial distress is generated endogenously and not directly related to any particular firm value. The parties might very well decide *ex ante* to let shareholders, potentially an outsider group of shareholders, deal with firm reorganization at low firm values between L and R. They do so by setting the debt level at, or close to, liquidation value.

So far we have only dealt with the immediate conflict arising from the fact that the entrepreneur obtains private benefits from continued operation of the firm whereas the external investor does not.[6] However, once the parties have agreed *ex ante* on the design of the financial contract, a security-based *ex post* conflict emerges. When firm value slides and the likelihood of financial distress rises, the incentives of equity holders become increasingly distorted. The owner–entrepreneur wants to pursue more risky strategies, that is, to gamble with external investors' money. This is the conflict between shareholders and creditors addressed in, for example, Stiglitz (1985).

The potential take-over raider was introduced here somewhat arbitrarily. The determination of capital structure becomes immensely more complicated as we consider the case with more than one external investor, not to speak of the widely held firm. For example, it is hard to argue that shareholders as a collective obtain considerable private benefits from the operation of the firm. Thus an argument for why control in widely held firms should be transferred has to be based on security-related benefits. When the firm is in financial distress, shareholders do not bear the full costs of their decisions, that is, they have an incentive to gamble with creditors' claims.

Furthermore, in the widely held firm the production decision has to be taken by a collective, either by the shareholders when the firm is in non-distressed states or by the creditors when the firm is insolvent. The optimal transfer point will be affected by the relative costs of these two collective choice mechanisms. In most cases creditor interests are more diverse than shareholders' due to differences in maturity, collateral and interest rates (Hansmann, Chapter 8, this volume). Therefore, *ceteris paribus*, the transfer point, and consequently debt levels, should be lower in widely held firms than in the case with only owner/entrepreneur and one external investor. According to the same line of reasoning, we expect lower debt levels when the creditor structure is dispersed than when it is concentrated, assuming that creditors are risk neutral. However, these effects have yet to be modelled carefully.

Another observation from the incomplete contracting literature is that a contracting party cannot be trusted to hand over control voluntarily. Since firm value is assumed not to be verifiable by an external party, transfer is made contingent on profits. However, even accounting figures are imperfectly verifiable and relatively easily manipulated by the firm's management. Consequently we seldom observe real-life contracts where the allocation of control is contingent on profit levels. Rather, transfer is triggered at the point of technical insolvency, that is, when the firm cannot meet its obligations towards creditors. If only failure to fulfil payment obligations is verifiable, the determination of the transfer point is transformed from a valuation problem to a cash-flow issue. In the case of a closely held firm with one investor this distinction might not be so important, but when we analyse the widely held corporation it is of major importance. To ensure that transfer occurs at the appropriate firm value, the outside investor might require to have a non-negligible share of votes also in 'good' states.

The incomplete contracting approach to capital structure also maintains that basically any allocation of control across investors and states of nature can be achieved through the design of the financial instruments. Yet, the theoretical discussion suggested that debt levels are related to the concentration and relative homogeneity of the shareholder and creditor collectives. Furthermore, the debt/equity ratio has implications for the choice of mechanism when a firm is in need of reorganization. In the following section, data on capital structure in the corporate sector of six capitalist economies are used to explore these correlations between different dimensions of capital structure and between capital structure and real decisions.

3. Six financial systems – a statistical overview

Financial systems defined

The *financial system* refers here to the industrial finance system, that is, the institutional arrangements designed to transform savings into investments and to allocate funds among alternative uses within the industrial sector. This allocation is handled by a set of financial markets and a set of financial institutions providing various intermediation services. In the following, we will discuss two types of financial system and identify their main characteristics based on official statistics and secondary material for the six countries in our study.[7]

Bank-oriented and market-oriented systems

The financial systems of the capitalist countries can be classified in two groups – bank-oriented and market-oriented financial systems. The two concepts are frequently used in the literature, but they are rarely clearly defined (for some rudimentary definitions and classifications, see Rybczinski, 1985). It is not our intention to show that the two models are the only existing ones, nor do we claim that the countries covered by our study perfectly match our models.[8] As Zysman (1983) points out, there do seem to be a limited number of feasible arrangements, certainly empirically and perhaps theoretically.

The *bank-oriented systems* are normally characterized as having less developed financial markets, in particular for risk capital. Consequently, the opportunities for diversification and hedging are more limited than in the market-oriented financial system. The savings in the bank-oriented system are primarily transferred in the form of short-term and long-term credits through banks and other savings institutions. Typically, government supports bank lending and actively intervenes to influence the costs of various forms of finance.

In the *market-oriented systems* there exists a wider range of financial instruments and capital markets. Households here invest a larger share of their savings directly into production. Banks primarily meet the short-term financing needs of the corporate sector and are thus less important in the provision of long-term funds. They also receive a larger share of the funds from sources other than households, primarily through borrowing in intermediate markets. The central bank is concerned primarily with the control of monetary aggregates, that is, money supply or interest rates. Government regulates the banking sector but normally refrains from active intervention.

Following this classification scheme, the United States and the United Kingdom are normally referred to as market-oriented, while France, Japan, and West Germany are characterized as bank-oriented.[9] Sweden, the sixth country in our study, is much smaller than the others, making direct comparisons more difficult. Most observers would probably characterize the Swedish financial system as bank-oriented, at least as it appeared in the early 1980s. As is obvious from this crude classification, there are substantial variations within the two categories. Indeed some of the more interesting international differences, from an institutional point of view, are found within the group of bank-oriented systems. Furthermore, due to recent developments in the financial markets, in particular increasing securitization and internationalization, financial systems have converged along some dimensions. Nevertheless, we believe the distinction to be of significant interest for the subsequent analysis. In fact it might help us understand the implications of the ongoing changes in the financial systems.

Financial market and financial institutions
Judging from some standard measures, the six countries are remarkably similar when it comes to the size of the financial sector relative to the economy as a whole or to the real sector (see Goldsmith, 1985; and Berglöf, 1988). In fact, even when we compare the relative importance of primary and secondary security markets for corporate securities it is difficult to identify systematic differences between the two types of system. Traditionally, the United States has had by far the largest (in absolute terms) and most developed secondary markets for stocks and corporate bonds. The security markets in West Germany and France have trailed far behind in most respects. The ranking is less clear-cut for the United Kingdom and Japan. It depends on whether we compare equity or bond markets, primary or secondary markets, and size or activity levels.

The differences between the two types of financial system stand out clearly first when the relative importance of various financial institutions is compared. As expected, banks hold a higher share of total domestic financial assets in the bank-oriented systems covered by our study (Goldsmith, 1985). Furthermore, the lending activity of the banking sector is more directed to corporate financing.[10] Yet another characteristic of the banking sector in the bank-oriented financial systems is the heavy concentration and substantial government ownership.[11]

Capital structure
The differences between the two systems are further highlighted when the capital structure of the corporate sector is analysed. When compared to their counterparts in market-oriented systems, firms under bank-oriented financial systems typically have a capital structure characterized by low degrees of internal funding and high debt/equity ratios (Figure 11.3 and Table 11.1). Accounting procedures differ across countries, distorting international

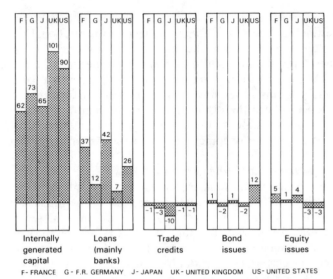

Figure 11.3   *Net sources of finance 1970–85 (a) (per cent (b) of 1985 capital stock (c))*

(a)   A net source of finance is defined as new issues or disposals of a particular type of liability less acquisitions of the same type of liability (e.g. new issues and sales of share less purchases of shares). A negative number therefore implies that non-financial enterprises have made net purchase of an asset from other sectors of the economy over the whole period.

(b)   Shares do not add to 100% because of the omission of capital transfers, short-term securities, trade credit, other sources and statistical discrepancy reported by the OECD.

(c)   The capital stock is calculated as the sum of annual investment since 1970, valued at 1984 prices and assuming straight-line depreciation over 17 years.

Source: OECD *Financial Statistics*, Part 3, various years.
Mayer, Colin (1987) 'New Issues in Corporate Finance', mimeo.
London: City University Business School

comparisons of debt/equity ratios. Table 11.2 shows some attempts to make data on market value gearing ratios comparable across countries. The structure of debt in the bank-oriented financial systems is characterized by a significantly higher share of bank credits (see Table 11.3). Furthermore, the creditor structure in large companies in these systems is heavily concentrated and dominated by main banks. Creditors are considerably more dispersed in the market-oriented systems. This is particularly true for the United States, the only country where bond financing is of any major

Table 11.1   *Debt/equity ratios in six countries*

	Net debt/equity equity ratio[1] 1983	Gross debt/ equity ratio[2] 1983
F.R. Germany	N/A	0.59
France	0.67	0.73
Japan	0.68	0.77
Sweden	0.50	0.65
United Kingdom	0.40	0.55
United States	0.23	0.41

1. Book value of net liabilities in relation to equity excluding holdings of shares in other corporations.
2. Book value of short-term and long-term liabilities relative to total assets.

Source: OECD (1985) *Financial Statistics.*

Table 11.2   *Market value gearing ratios in Japan and the US: 1979–81*

	Japan		United States	
	A	B	C	D
1979	0.59	0.64	0.38	0.36
1980	0.57	0.60	0.35	0.32
1981	0.56	0.62	0.30	0.28

Sources: (A) Wakasugi et al. (1984); (B) Unofficial Bank of Japan estimates (1986); (C) Holland and Myers (1984); (D) Taggart (1985).
   Sources quoted in Jenny Corbett (1988) 'International Perspectives on Financing: Evidence from Japan', *Oxford Review of Economic Policy*, 3 (4).

Table 11.3   *Bank credits as a percentage of total liabilities*

F.R. Germany	N/A
France	0.247
Japan	0.393
Sweden	0.242
United Kingdom	0.103
United States	0.089

Source: OECD (1985) *Financial Statistics*, Part 3.

Table 11.4 *Ownership concentration in individual firms (the largest owner's share of capital)*

Largest owner's share	France 1	United States 2	United States 3	Japan 4	Japan 5	United Kingdom 6	Sweden 7	F.R.G. 8	F.R.G. 9
> 50	55	5	9	17	5	2	42	66	59
30–50				11			31	23	
25–30	42		29			9	12		41
20–25				31	70				
15–20		1				5		12	
10–15		6	10	16			11		
5–10		15	29	25	25	32	4		
> 5	2	73	23			52			

1. Morin (1982). Covers the 500 largest non-financial firms (parent companies) by turnover in 1976. The large public utilities are not included.
2. Herman (1981). Shows distribution according to size of all holdings over 2% in the 200 largest manufacturing corporations by turnover at the end of 1974.
3. Isaksson and Skog (1986). The computations are based on data from the Securities and Exchange Commission from 1980 covering the 500 largest firms by employment according to *Fortune* magazine.
4. Miyazaki (1972). Covers the 466 largest firms by turnover in 1966. Groupholdings merged.
5. Mito (1983). Referred to in Gerlach (1986). Includes the 200 largest firms by turnover in 1976. Groupholdings merged.
6. Collett and Yarrow (1976). Refers to 85 large firms within machine-building, electronics, foodstuffs and textile industry.
7. Isaksson and Skog (1987). Includes 107 public companies in 1985. Based on voting power.
8. Iber (1985). Includes all firms listed on the German stock exchanges in 1983.
9. Monopolkommission (1986). The 100 non-financial largest firms by turnover in 1984.

Source: Berglöf, Erik (1988) *Ägarna och kontrollen över företaget – en järnförande studie av finansiella system.* Stockholm: Statens Offentliga utredningar

Table 11.5 *Ownership of listed stocks according to sectors
(1980 unless indicated otherwise)*

	Households	Non-financial corp.	Government institutions	Financial	Foreign owners
F.R. Germany (a)	17	51	10	15	8
France (b)	38	22	0	24	16
Japan (c)	27	25	0	42	5
Sweden (d)	33 (e)	7	0	56	4
United Kingdom (f)	28	5	3	60	4
United States (g)	51	15	0	28	6

(a) 1983. Includes all public companies with capital over DEM 4.75. The share of non-financial corporations is exaggerated due to double-counting in the statistics.
(b) All listed stocks.
(c) Stocks listed on the Tokyo Stock Exchange 1979.
(d) Stocks listed on the Stockholm Stock Exchange 1981.
(e) Includes mutual funds (*aktiesparfonder*).
(f) Stocks listed on the London Stock Exchange.
(g) All stocks listed on US Stock Exchange.

Sources: F.R. Germany: Iber (1985)
France: Société d'Etudes pour le Développement Economique et Social (SEDES) and Banque de France, Commissiondes Operations de Bourse
Japan: Aoki (1984)
Sweden: *Industri och industripolitik 1983–84*, Industridepartementet 1985.
United Kingdom: The Stock Exchange Survey of Share Ownership (1981)
United States: Securities and Exchange Commission, Monthly Bulletin (1981).

importance to the corporate sector (see Figure 11.3). The bank lenders in these systems are also less co-ordinated, lacking the dominance of the main banks.

The ownership structure in individual firms under bank-oriented systems is, in general, more concentrated (see Table 11.4).[12] The incidence of controlling owners, that is, shareholders abstaining from diversification opportunities in order to control companies, is higher.[13] This is true for individual as well as institutional owners. In particular, bank shareholdings are more important, both as a share of bank portfolios and when seen from the perspective of the company.[14] The shares of interfirm shareholdings are also higher in countries with bank-oriented financial systems (see Table 11.5). The fact that firms in these systems are generally more closely held can be partially attributed to the smaller average firm size, but it also holds for firms with the same market value.

Table 11.6 *Financial systems and capital structure*

General characteristics of financial markets and financial institutions	Type of financial system	
	Bank-oriented	Market-oriented
Level of development of financial markets (i.e. the opportunities for diversification)	Low	High
Ratio of financial assets held by banks to total assets held by financial institutions	Large	Small
Overall capital structure		
Degree of internal finance	Low	High
Debt/equity ratios	High	Low
Creditor structure		
Ratio of bank credits to total liabilities	High	Low
Importance of bond financing	Low	High (not in the UK)
Degree of concentration	High	Low
Turnover of loans	Low	High
Shareholder structure		
Degree of concentration	High	Low
Commercial bank shareholdings	Significant	Insignificant
Interfirm shareholdings	Widespread	Less common
Turnover of controlling blocs	Slow	Faster

Another feature distinguishing the bank-oriented systems in our study from their market-oriented counterparts is their longer-term shareholdings (see Berglöf, 1988). Controlling blocs of shares are relatively seldom transacted. Hostile take-overs as a mechanism of transfer of control from one set of shareholders to another has been much less common. As a result of the higher incidence of control posts and the long-term holdings, owners are generally well known and at least easily identified.

Summary of statistical overview
The results of our statistical comparison of the six financial systems are summarized in Table 11.6. The measures (small-large, high–low etc) should be regarded as characterizations relative to the other type of system. As is obvious from the table, a number of dimensions and aspects of the financial systems have been left out.

4. Bank-oriented and market-oriented financial systems – an incomplete contracting interpretation

In this section the incomplete contracting literature is used to interpret the observed differences in capital structure. The focus is on six stylized facts which stand out when bank-oriented financial systems are compared to their market-oriented counterparts: (1) debt/equity ratios are higher; (2) ownership of debt is more concentrated and more homogeneous; (3) shareholdings are also less dispersed; (4) commercial banks often have large shareholdings in individual firms; (5) ownership of debt and equity is relatively more stable over time; and (6) corporate take-overs are less common.

The differences in capital structure in the six countries covered by this study are larger when it comes to the design and distribution of debt instruments than equity. Much of the previous economics literature on capital structure and control has viewed debt as a non-voting instrument and as such not relevant to the analysis of control. The incomplete contracting approach, however, recognizes that residual control rights are to be transferred to creditors when the firm is in financial distress. This view of debt as also conferring rights of control is important for our understanding of international differences in capital structure.

While recognizing that the stylized facts outlined here can only be fully understood in a much broader historical context, this section concentrates on the effects of government regulation of investors. More specifically, it focuses on the combined effects of three sets of rules pertaining to commercial banks in market-oriented financial systems: those limiting the size of individual institutions, those constraining their portfolio choices, and those preventing them from intervening when client firms are in financial difficulties. In all these respects, bank-oriented financial systems are less regulated.

These restrictions help explain perhaps the most significant difference between the two types of financial system: the role of commercial banks in the corporate sector. In practice, the countries with market-oriented systems through regulation have eliminated one type of investor, that is, a creditor capable of holding considerable shares of both debt and equity in the same firm. The regulations of commercial banks directly affect concentration of the creditor structure. The limits on the size of individual institutions increase the costs of control. Furthermore, the restrictions on bank shareholdings limit commercial banks' opportunities to diversify their portfolios.

The existence of large commercial banks in the bank-oriented financial systems is important in explaining the higher gearing in the corporate sector. The incomplete contracting literature suggests that the higher debt/equity ratios in the bank-oriented financial systems indicate that control is shifted from shareholders 'earlier', that is, creditors have control over a wider set of states of nature. In other words, financial distress or insolvency is a much more common phenomenon in these countries. As we saw in Section 2, distress can be actively used by the contracting parties to reorganize problem firms. The initial contract implies that parties agree *ex ante* to let creditors, more specifically main banks, act as reorganization specialists. In market-oriented systems, this role is normally played by an external group of shareholders. Thus, the higher debt/equity ratios in bank-oriented financial systems could be related to the observation that take-overs are not as common as in countries with market-oriented financial systems.

The commercial bank of the bank-oriented type, as marginal lender and main risk-bearer when the firm is in financial distress, has been willing to accept these higher debt levels because it can exercise control much more freely than its counterpart in the market-oriented systems. In Williamson's (1987) terms, the less restrictive regulations in bank-oriented financial systems reduce the costs of debt as an *ex post* governance mechanism.

The higher debt/equity ratios imply that creditors are carrying larger shares of firm-specific risk in bank-oriented financial systems. Data also suggest that this increased risk exposure is to a large extent absorbed by commercial banks. Because of its higher risk content, bank debt in these countries is sometimes referred to as 'crypto equity' (Hart, 1987). The incomplete contracting approach allows us to characterize the nature of bank control and risk bearing more precisely. Commercial banks carry risk and have full control in a wider set of 'bad' states. To the extent that they have large shareholdings in the same firm, they also share risk and control in 'good' states.

The heavier reliance on debt in bank-oriented financial systems has made it possible for firms to grow without diffusing control in 'good' states to the same extent as in countries with market-oriented systems. The incomplete contracting approach suggests that parties have preferred to give up control in a wider range of states to maintain a more concentrated ownership of equity. Again, the stylized facts seem to be strongly interconnected, that is, the levels of debt are related to the structure of equity.

The domination of commercial banks in corporate finance is likely to have hampered the development of markets for debt instruments in the bank-oriented financial systems. On the one hand, this has resulted in fewer opportunities for investors to diversify their portfolios. On the other hand, the more homogeneous creditor structure has kept the collective choice costs associated with creditor reorganization at a lower level, making this transfer mechanism more attractive relative to take-overs.

The relative underdevelopment of capital markets in bank-oriented financial systems makes control less expensive for investors. The risk cost of holding a control block is determined by the size of individual portfolios and opportunity costs of foregone diversification. In a more shallow market the investor has fewer opportunities to diversify his holdings. Consequently, his costs of holding control, *ceteris paribus*, are lower. This reinforces the effects of the less rigid regulatory constraints on the size of individual institutions. The greater reliance on creditor reorganization is conducive to a more stable ownership structure. Control blocks are transacted less frequently and bank customer relationships are relatively stable over time.

The widespread holdings of control blocks by banks may be interpreted in several ways broadly consistent with the incomplete contracting approach. Large shareholdings allow banks to influence the likelihood of take-overs by outside owners also when control has not been transferred to creditors. An alternative, but not necessarily contradictory, interpretation views bank-held control blocks as arrangements to reduce conflicts between shareholders and creditors when firms are in financial distress and to ensure the transfer of control to creditors. According to this latter explanation, the appropriate contractual arrangement for a reorganization specialist contains both debt and equity instruments. The arrangement entails almost full control and risk bearing in financial distress, and shared control and risk in 'good' states.

The claim here is that the observed differences between financial systems have important implications for how conflicts between shareholders and creditors are mitigated and resolved. We have suggested that conflicts arising from poor performance are handled internally through an earlier transfer of control to creditors in bank-oriented systems. In countries with market-oriented systems, an intervention by an external party – a take-over – is more likely. We suggest that there is also a higher reliance on external solutions in the latter type of system when there are conflicts between creditors once firms are in financial distress. The diffused creditor structure, often in combination with strict restrictions on creditor involvement in individual firms, makes more informal procedures difficult to administer. In bank-oriented systems, the dominating commercial bank normally assumes control in these situations through its large share of claims. The higher degree of repetition in contractual relations should increase the likelihood of successful informal procedures.

5. Two models of financial systems

The six financial systems in this study have maintained their fundamental characteristics from the Second World War well into the 1980s. The two types – bank-oriented and market-oriented systems – have undoubtedly demonstrated survival properties. We cannot rule out that they do indeed represent two model 'equilibria' with different and interconnected structural characteristics. Even if this is true empirically, it is not easy to substantiate based on existing economic theory. This section discusses the two systems as two fundamentally different solutions to the problem of allocating control and risk.

In the market-oriented system the emphasis is on specialization of management and risk bearing through diversification of risk among shareholders and creditors. To deal with the collective choice problems arising as a firm's securities become widely held, control is delegated to management. External control mechanisms, such as markets for corporate control and managerial labour controls, are assumed to reduce the agency costs associated with the separation of ownership and control. The bank-oriented system, on the other hand, stresses risk shifting from shareholders to creditors in intermediate states. The emphasis is on reducing collective choice costs and providing investors with adequate incentives to monitor firms and engage in entrepreneurial activities. In evaluating the properties of the two systems, the costs of delegating strategic decisions from shareholders to managers and the potential under-production of monitoring services due to free-riding among investors should be compared to the gains from risk spreading.

Many previous international comparisons have emphasized that financial systems differ markedly in how they handle problem firms (Rybczinski, 1985; and Zysman, 1983). Our analysis supports this observation. In the bank-oriented system, creditor reorganization dominates, while take-over by an external group of shareholders is the predominant mechanism in market-oriented financial systems. The relative merits of these two mechanisms are difficult to establish since their effectiveness is conditioned by the institutional constraints under which they operate.

Creditor reorganization, however, is likely to reinforce reputation effects in contractual relations since it relies on internal conflict resolution. The less developed markets for financial instruments in bank-oriented financial systems reduce incentives for investors to leave established relationships. These lock-in effects should also facilitate internal conflict resolution. In market-oriented financial systems these relationships are more flexible and change over time. The more frequent emergence of new combinations might be more conducive to innovation, while it is likely to promote short-sightedness in the strategic interaction between investors.

In addition, there seems to be a difference between investors in bank-oriented and market-oriented systems in terms of their relative propensity for exit and voice behaviour (Hirschman, 1970). When an organization is in decline, its members can either decide to leave (exit) or to try to improve it (voice). The mentioned lock-in effects in bank-oriented systems induce voice behaviour by making exit more costly. Again, the relative effectiveness of the two systems is likely to depend on characteristics of the individual firm – in which phase of the life cycle it is and in which activities it is involved (for an application of Hirschman's approach to shareholders see Hedlund et al., 1985).

The earlier discussion suggested that incumbent management or owners are unlikely to give up control without resistance. For this reason it is important to evaluate the two systems and their chief reorganization mechanisms in terms of how they ensure that a transfer of control really takes place. To trigger a transfer of control when widely held firms are in financial distress, appears to be much more difficult in the market-oriented systems. The creditors often have to rely on the expensive court-administered bankruptcy solution. In a bank-oriented system, the commercial banks normally initiate an informal, less costly reorganization procedure. This latter type of system also appears better equipped to handle the incentive distortions that arise as the firm approaches financial distress. However, market-oriented systems seem to be relatively superior when a transfer from one group of shareholders to another is called for. A number of results indicate that take-overs are less likely to succeed when the ownership of equity is concentrated (Stulz, 1988; Harris and Raviv, 1988).

The more diffused and less stable ownership structure in the market-oriented systems makes investors more anonymous. The relative anonymity of shareholders and creditors in these systems should have implications for the relative role of management. Furthermore, it is likely to make it more difficult to hold investors accountable for firm decisions. In the bank-oriented system, where the separation of ownership from control has not gone as far, ownership contracts are less standardized, that is, shareholders are expected to intervene actively in the strategic decisions of the firm.

Even though the financial systems of the countries in this study have maintained their principal features over most of the post-Second World War period, we observe tendencies towards convergence along some important dimensions during the last decade. For example, longitudinal studies in the United States indicate that debt/equity ratios have been increasing in recent years. In particular, leveraged buyouts have many of the features associated with firms in bank-oriented financial systems, for example, high gearing and strip financing (combined debt and equity holdings). Venture capitalists also share some characteristics of main banks in these systems. Control is shared in good states, while it is transferred to creditors when the firm's performance deteriorates.

The capital markets in most of the bank-oriented systems, on the other hand, have developed rapidly in recent years. A range of new instruments have been introduced and rules stifling foreign competition in capital markets liberalized. All this has contributed to the convergence of the two financial systems.

I suggested earlier that the market-oriented system is an outcome of government regulation. This less than intuitive and, at least at first glance, implausible proposition warrants two remarks. First, I do not want to overemphasize a strong, causal correlation between the observed patterns of capital structure and government regulation. Legislation clearly to some extent developed in response to existing institutional arrangements. In any case, the laws constraining commercial banks in market-oriented systems have certainly re-enforced these arrangements. Secondly, there have certainly been other, and more direct, forms of government intervention in the design of the bank-oriented financial systems. Here only the effects of regulation of commercial banks have been discussed.

If government regulation is related to capital structure in the ways suggested, the current liberalization of capital markets on the European continent and in Japan might have a number of less than immediately intuitive consequences for the financial systems involved. Because of the strength of the underlying technological changes in the financial markets the degree of market orientation, on the whole, is generally predicted to increase. However, if regulation of commercial banks is relaxed, we could expect an increase in bank holdings of control blocks in non-financial corporations. Furthermore, leverage ratios are likely to rise. We might also see an increase rather than a decrease in the concentration of debt and equity ownership. The predicted surge in take-over activity could well be accompanied by increased bank participation in the reorganization of troubled firms.

There could also be important transitional problems in moving from one type of system to another. The market-oriented financial systems rely on a number of external control mechanisms. As the bank-oriented financial systems become increasingly market-oriented, they risk being 'stuck in the middle' or at least caught in a costly change process. These external control mechanisms need time to develop. In the transition period there could be considerable scope for managerial excess. Similarly, if market-oriented systems move in the direction of bank-orientation, creditors capable of reorganizing firms do not emerge overnight.

6. Summary

This chapter set out to identify differences in capital structure between countries and relate these differences to properties of the financial systems. Furthermore, the intention has been to suggest some interpretations based on the incomplete contracting literature, and to demonstrate how the different dimensions of capital structure are interconnected.

The statistical overview of the six countries showed considerable variations in capital structure. The ratio of debt to equity, the concentration of debt and equity, and the turnover of holdings were all found to be markedly different. These differences are clearly related to the role of commercial banks in the corporate sector of the economy. Two fundamentally different financial systems were identified – bank-oriented and market-oriented financial systems. Countries with the former type of system generally have higher debt/equity ratios, higher shares of bank credits in their liabilities, more concentrated holdings of both debt and equity, and a lower turnover of these holdings.

The incomplete contracting literature submits that these differences in capital structure could be interpreted as reflecting differences in the allocation of risk and control across investors and states of nature. In the bank-oriented financial systems the creditors carry risk and have control in a wider range of future states. In many cases, commercial banks hold controlling blocks of shares in addition to large debt claims, that is, they bear risk and have some control across all states of nature. The theoretical analysis suggested that such joint combined holdings could alleviate conflicts inherent in equity and debt contracts. This could be particularly important when the firm is in need of reorganization.

The bank-oriented financial systems have more stable ownership of debt and equity. Investors are locked into contractual arrangements over long periods of time. Consequently, they are more prone to internal conflict resolution. While these long-term relationships foster continuity and reputational enforcement of contracts, they could discourage innovation.

Finally, the analysis suggested that government regulation of commercial banks could be important in explaining the observed differences in capital structure. Where banks are allowed to hold shares and intervene in troubled firms, they are also willing to extend more credit. This claim could lead to some unforeseen consequences as the liberalization of the capital markets in Europe and Japan proceeds. To the extent that the regulation of commercial banks is relaxed as a result, we might see a surge in commercial bank shareholdings, higher leverage ratios in the corporate sector and more concentrated holdings of debt and equity.

Notes

This chapter has benefited from comments on earlier versions from Masahiko Aoki, Patrick Bolton, Ingemund Hägg, Reinier Kraakman, Göran Skogh, Joakim Stymne and Stavros Thomadakis. I am particularly indebted to Gunnar Hedlund and Colin Mayer for continued advice and encouragement. I gratefully acknowledge financial support from Humanistisk-samhällsvetenskapliga forskningsrådet (HSFR F 560/87). Thanks to Scandinavia Foundation, Fulbright Commission, and the Harvard Law School Program in Law and Economics, which is funded by the John M. Olin Foundation.

1. In fact it is widely held that 'there is no difference between debt and equity from an economic perspective' (Easterbrook and Fischel, 1986).

2. Studies of the relationship between taxation and capital structure find no systematic support for this conjecture (see, for example, King and Fullerton, 1985; Ando and Auerbach, 1985).

3. A complete contract specifies each party's obligation in every conceivable eventuality; that is, both states and actions are stipulated in the contract (Hart and Holmström, 1987). This should be distinguished from a contract that is fully contingent in the Arrow–Debreu sense.

4. Control is here understood as the right to determine the action to be taken in a certain state. It is depicted as a dichotomous variable – an investor or a collective of investors have either full control or no control at all. In real life, of course, control is transferred gradually from one party to another.

5. Aghion and Bolton (1988) assume that firm value is not verifiable by a third party while profits are. Thus, contracts are made contingent on profit realizations rather than value. Hart and Moore (1989) discuss the case where not even revenues are verifiable.

6. Alternatively, the owner/entrepreneur suffers private costs, such as loss of reputation, if the firm is shut down.

7. The methodological problems involved in this type of cross-country comparison are tremendous. The most important data sources for the study of financial systems are national accounts and surveys of company financial statements. The comparability of data is reduced because of differences in accounting principles and coverage of surveys. Recent improvements in data collection have been offset by the increasing pace of change in the financial systems. This study uses primarily OECD *Financial Statistics*, Parts I–III. The pioneering work by Goldsmith (1985) as well as the work within the CEPR project (Bray et al., 1987) have been helpful in developing comparable measures with interesting content. The statistics used here only cover the period up to 1983, and in some cases 1984. The major changes in the financial markets during the second half of the 1980s are not covered by the study.

8. Zysman (1983) uses the term credit-based instead of bank-oriented. For these financial systems, he also distinguishes between those with administered prices and those where price formation is dominated by banks. This distinction is particularly important for Zysman's analysis of the role of government intervention in the economy.

9. This classification follows Rybczinski (1985), but is also identical to that used by Bray et al. (1987) even though they do not use the terms bank-oriented and market-oriented. The most questionable characterization probably concerns the British financial systems. After the Second World War the financial systems of the United States and the United Kingdom were relatively intact and well developed. However, during the postwar period the two systems developed quite differently, in particular during the 1970s. While bond markets have grown in importance in the United States, the British corporations have increasingly been seeking other forms of debt finance. The recent liberalization of the financial markets has again strengthened the market orientation of the financial system in the United Kingdom. As stated earlier, Zysman (1983) distinguishes between two types of bank-oriented (or in his terminology credit-based) systems: those with administered prices (Japan and France) and those where price formation is dominated by banks (West Germany).

10. During the 1970s on average 80–90% of the commercial bank lending went to the corporate sector. The corresponding figure for the United States was approximately 40%.

11. In France, for example, seven of the ten largest banks are government controlled. The three largest banks accounted for close to 50% of total bank lending in 1986. The Japanese government does not have a major ownership interest in any of the major commercial banks, but it exercises control over the influential Industrial Bank of Japan and the banks specializing in long-term lending to industry. In addition, the government-owned Postal Savings System plays a major role in channelling funds from savers to the corporate sector. The postal system alone accounted for 20% of the total assets of the financial sector in 1986. In West Germany, the publicly owned special giro institutions and the savings and loans associations handled slightly more than half of the commercial banking activities. Westdeutsche Landesbank with public ownership now belongs to the three largest commercial banks in terms both of total assets and of total lending. The degree of concentration is substantially lower and government ownership in the commercial banking sector virtually non-existent in the United States and the United Kingdom.

12. The statistics on ownership structure in industry are often of poor quality. Furthermore, data are rarely directly comparable across countries owing to differences in methods of collection and in institutional arrangements. For this report a number of independent studies have been used. They differ primarily in terms of sample size and measures of concentration. Sample sizes range from the 100 largest companies to slightly below the 600 largest according to turnover or employment. (For our purposes, market value would have been the best measure, since it provides an estimate of the cost of control.) Because of the limited comparability of the results only preliminary conclusions can be drawn. In particular, the difference in firm size across countries is critical. Despite these short-comings, a clear pattern emerges. The results appear remarkably robust to various tests of sensitivity (Berglöf, 1988).

13. The statistics on ownership concentration conceal important differences in shareholding patterns within the group of bank-oriented financial systems. In France and West Germany, family control is still important even in large firms. The role of family ownership in large Japanese companies was effectively eliminated after the Second World War, when the occupation forces dismantled the family-controlled holding companies. Controlling shareholders are mainly industrial corporations and financial institutions. Furthermore, the aggregation of shareholdings in Japan according the corporate groupings (financial *keiretsu*) might give a misleading picture. The co-ordination within these groups is limited and varies from group to group (see Sheard, 1986), and Aoki, 1988, for a discussion of these groupings and the role of commercial banks). Nevertheless, since one of our primary concerns is with the effects of ownership concentration on the likelihood of take-overs, we have chosen to combine holdings.

14. In the United States and Sweden, where commercial banks are, in principle, not allowed to hold shares, bank shareholdings were negligible according to OECD *Financial Statistics*, (Parts 1 and 2, 1986). For British banks the importance of shareholdings in their portfolios has decreased markedly during the last decade. If viewed from the perspective of ownership structure in industry, banks held about 4% of outstanding stock value on the Paris Exchange in 1979. In Germany, the corresponding figure was 8% (1983) and in Japan as high as 20% (1982). In the United Kingdom bank ownership was of little significance as measured by its share of total listed stocks.

References

Aghion, Philippe and Patrick Bolton (1988) 'An "Incomplete Contract" Approach to Bankruptcy and the Financial Structure of the Firm', MIT Department of Economics: Working Paper, No. 484, March.

Alchian, Armen and Harold Demsetz (1972) 'Production, Information Costs and Economic Organization', *American Economic Review*, December.

Ando, Albert and Alan Auerbach (1985) 'The Corporate Cost of Capital in Japan and the US: a Comparison', National Bureau of Economic Research: Working Paper No. 1762.

Aoki, Masahiko (1984) *The Economic Analysis of the Japanese Firm*. Amsterdam: North-Holland.

Aoki, Masahiko (1988) *Information, Incentives, and Bargaining in the Japanese Economy*. Cambridge: Cambridge University Press.

Berglöf, Erik (1988) *Ägarna och kontrollen över företaget – en jämförande studie av finansiella system*. Stockholm: Statens offentliga utredningar Industridepartementet.

Bray, Margaret, Jeremy Edwards and Colin Mayer (1987) 'An International Study of Corporate Financing', Centre for Economic Policy Research: research proposal.

Caves, Richard and M. Uekusa (1976) *Industrial Organization in Japan*. Washington, DC: Brookings Institution.

Corbett, Jenny (1988) 'International Perspectives on Financing: Evidence from Japan', *Oxford Review of Economic Policy*, 3 (4).

Cubbin, John and Dennis Leech (1983) 'The Effect of Shareholding Dispersion on the Degree of Control in British Companies: Theory and Measurement', *The Economic Journal*, 93 (June).

De Alessi, L. (1983) 'Property Rights, Transaction Costs, and X-inefficiency', *American Economic Review*, 73.

Easterbrook, Frank H. and Daniel R. Fischel (1986) 'Close Corporations and Agency Costs', *Stanford Law Review*, 38.

Gerlach, Michael (1986) 'Institutional Markets: Corporate Control and Large-Firm Organization in Japan', Yale University: unpublished working paper.

Goldsmith, Raymond (1969) *Financial Structure and Development*. New Haven: Yale University Press.

Goldsmith, Raymond (1985) *National Balance Sheets for 20 Countries*, National Bureau of Economic Research, New Haven: Yale University Press.

Hägg, Ingemund (1987) 'Ägande och kontroll i Frankrikes näringsliv', unpublished paper.

Hägg, Ingemund and Erik Hörnell (1987) 'Ägande och kontroll i Storbritanniens näringsliv', Studie förbundet Näringsliv och Samhälle: SNS Occasional Papers.

Hansmann, Henry (1986) 'A General Theory of Corporate Ownership', Program in Law and Economics, Harvard Law School: Discussion Paper No. 33.

Harris, Milton and Arthur Raviv (1988) 'Corporate Control Contests and Capital Structure', *Journal of Financial Economics*, 20.

Hart, Oliver (1987) 'Capital Structure as a Control Mechanism in Corporations', MIT Department of Economics: Working Paper (January).

Hart, Oliver and Sanford Grossman (1988) 'One Share–One Vote and the Market for Corporate Control', *Journal of Financial Economics*, 20.

Hart, Oliver and Bengt Holmström (1987) 'The Theory of Contracts', in Truman E. Bewley, *Advances in Economic Theory, Fifth World Congress*. New York: Cambridge University Press.

Hart, Oliver and John Moore (1989) 'Default and Renegotiation: A Dynamic Model of Debt'. Harvard Business School: Working Paper.

Hedlund, Gunnar et al. (1985) *Institutioner som aktieägare*. Stockholm: SNS Förlag.

Herman, Edward S. (1981) *Corporate Control, Corporate Power*. Cambridge: Cambridge University Press.

Hirschman, Albert (1970) *Exit, Voice, and Loyalty*. Cambridge: Harvard University Press.

Holmström, Bengt and Jean Tirole (1989) 'The Theory of the Firm', in R. Schmalensee and R. Willig (eds), *Handbook of Industrial Organization*. Amsterdam: North-Holland.

Iber, Bernhard (1985) 'Zur Entwicklung der Aktionärsstruktur in der

Bundesrepublik Deutschland (1963–1983)', *Zeitschrift für Betriebswirtschaft*, 55.

Isaksson, Mats and Rolf Skog (1986) 'PM ang ägarkoncentration i Förenta staterna', unpublished paper.

Isaksson, Mats and Rolf Skog (1987) 'Ägandekoncentration i privatägda aktiebolag pa den svenska aktiemarknaden 1975–1985', unpublished paper.

Jensen, Michael C. (1986) 'Agency Costs of Free Cash Flow, Corporate Finance and Takeovers', *American Economic Review*, 76.

Jensen, Michael C. and William H. Meckling (1976) 'Theory of the Firm: Managerial Behavior, Agency Costs, and Capital Structure', *Journal of Financial Economics*, 3.

King, Mervyn and Don Fullerton (eds) (1985) *The Taxation of Income from Capital*. Chicago: University of Chicago Press.

Leland, Hayne and David Pyle (1977) 'Information Asymmetries, Financial Structure, and Financial Intermediaries', *Journal of Finance*, 32.

Mayer, Colin P. (1987) 'New Issues in Corporate Finance', inaugural lecture given at the City University Business School, London.

Modigliani, Franco and Merton Miller (1958) 'The Costs of Capital, Corporation Finance, and the Theory of Investment', *American Economic Review*, 48.

Monopolkommission, *Hauptgutsachten*, 1973–4, 1975–6, 1977–8, 1980–1, 1983–4 and 1985–6.

Myers, Stewart C. (1984) 'The Capital Structure Puzzle', *The Journal of Finance*, (July).

OECD (1972–84) *Financial Accounts*.

OECD (1985) *Financial Statistics*.

Rybczinski, Tad M. (1985) 'Industrial Finance Systems in Europe, United States and Japan', *Journal of Economic Behavior and Organization*.

Sakakibara, Eisuke and Yoriuki Nagao (eds) (1985) *Study on Tokyo Capital Markets*, Japan Centre for International Finance: JCIF Policy Study Series, No. 2.

Sheard, Paul (1986) 'Corporate Organization and Structural Adjustment in Japan', unpublished paper.

Stiglitz, Joseph E. (1985) 'Credit Markets and the Control of Capital', *Journal of Money, Credit, and Banking*, May.

Stulz, René (1988) 'Managerial Control of Voting Rights: Financing Policies and the Market of Corporate Control', *Journal of Financial Economics*, 20.

Tirole, Jean (1988) *The Theory of Industrial Organization*. Cambridge: MIT Press.

Williamson, Oliver (1975) *Market and Hierarchies: Analysis and Antitrust Implications*. New York: The Free Press.

Williamson, Oliver (1985) *The Economic Institutions of Capitalism*. New York: The Free Press.

Williamson, Oliver (1987) 'Corporate Finance and Corporate Governance, Economic Analysis & Policy', Working Paper No. EAP-26. Berkeley CA: University of California.

Zysman, John (1983) *Governments, Markets and Growth*. Ithaca, NY: Cornell University Press.

12

Long-term Contracts in Financial Markets: Bank-Industry Connections in Sweden, Illustrated by the Operations of Stockholms Enskilda Bank, 1900–70

Håkan Lindgren

Research on the theory of the modern firm has increasingly made clear that the categories of conventional neoclassical analysis are manifestly insufficient in accounting for the structure and behaviour of the firm. Neoclassical theory has thus been supplemented by a succession of new concepts and theories focusing on bargaining, hierarchies, information, contracts, networks, treaties and so on. It may still be too early to pass judgement on the outcome of these new trends. However, this much seems to be clear: a more realistic understanding of the modern firm forces us to enlarge the conceptual tool-box over and above what is to be found in existing theory. In this new trend historical investigations should also be allowed to play a larger role. History – and especially comparative history – can show us how identical objectives may be reached by different means, and also how differences in social structure and institutional arrangements may decisively influence the choice of methods to reach given objectives and even the choice of the objectives themselves.

One neglected area of historical research in economics of vital importance to the understanding of firm behaviour concerns the relationship between banks and industry. The simple reason for this neglect is that few researchers have had access to the archives of the commercial banks. Sweden is an exception, at least concerning the period up to the beginning of the 1970s. Thus bank-industry connections may be illuminated and given a firm empirical footing, thereby increasing our understanding of the modern firm.

The object of this chapter is to survey the structure and quality of the relationships between Swedish commercial banks and their industrial clients in a long-term, historical perspective, with one important limitation. The credit stipulations, as are expressed in the actual loan contracts, are not dealt with here.[1] Rather, it is the qualitative relationships between bank and client which are analysed. These relationships could be short term and transitory, but it is more usual for bank–client relationships to take the form of long-term connections or even bonds. Above all, my intention is to demonstrate the existence of formal and informal contracts that regulated – and even allocated – the business relations of industrial firms with banks. Furthermore, my purpose is to show how, and on what conditions, the commercial banks replaced market relations to their industrial clients with co-ordination, monitoring and hierarchical control.

This qualitative approach is hardly ever used. Research on bank–industry relations often comes to a halt outside the company archives, where business history starts. Research in this field has focused primarily on the control aspect, and a lot of energy has been applied to measure stockholdings, creditor dependence and interlocking directorates on both the firm and industry levels. New sophisticated statistical methods to measure and identify networks of interlocking directorates have been developed, introducing concepts like intensity and centrality, which have added new, interesting dimensions to the old debate on influence and control. However, the refined methods still mean a measurement of *potential* power only, while the empirical content or actual use of this power is not examined. If, and how, different financial institutions actually used their potential influence may be important to understand *why* certain bank–industry relationships developed.[2]

In this chapter the qualitative aspects of the relationships between banks and their clients are exemplified by a case study of Stockholms Enskilda Bank (SEB) and its client connections. In comparison to the other large Swedish banks, the operations of Stockholms Enskilda Bank were distinctive in some important respects. It was a family-owned bank, which from its foundation in 1856 up to its merger into Skandinaviska Enskilda Banken in 1972 was led by four generations of the Wallenberg family. The activities of Stockholms Enskilda Bank were concentrated on a more active financial support, and even a direct management of its industrial companies, compared to other big banks.

Despite the unique characteristics of Stockholms Enskilda Bank, it is not difficult to draw general conclusions from a case study such as this one. The first and very obvious reason for this is that contracts allocating the business relations of industrial firms with banks involved more than one, and sometimes up to four, of the major Swedish banks. The second and more important reason is that the basic source material used for this study is extremely good, providing information not only on the relationships between

Stockholms Enskilda Bank and its clients, but also on the competitive behaviour of other banks vis-a-vis the industrial clients (see pp. 270–1). It is also clear that the conclusions drawn from this case study are not only representative of Sweden; they also reflect conditions which have characterized Central Europe during the twentieth century.[3]

The stable, long-term relationships that developed between banks and industry in some countries were determined by the way in which the financial system as a whole developed and was organized. Like other late-comers on the industrial scene with ambitions to keep up with those who seemed to be ahead, the need was felt in Sweden to use bank capital as venture capital and as a spearhead in the industrialization process. However, the mobilization of bank capital as venture capital had to be balanced with the need for deposit protection and financial stability in general. In order to explain why the Swedish financial system came to be so very dominated by the commercial banks, it is necessary to look briefly at the origins of the banking system and how it gradually changed, against the background of developments in the more important and influential European economies of that time.

This study is written within a theoretical framework that is, in a broad sense, institutional. According to institutional theory, supply and demand conditions are not seen as sufficient or even decisive forces behind the *transformation* of the economy. While the mechanism of supply and demand has been applied successfully by neoclassical economists to explain price formation, it is less adequate for understanding the process of historical development. For this, we must look at what happens in economic and social 'institutions'.

In every society, different kinds of regulating mechanisms and sets of rules are established to support the allocation of productive resources and the distribution of the results of production. The rules and organizations developed to maintain these regulating mechanisms are termed *institutions*. In the area of finances, we need only point to the important role played by the state, the central bank and banking legislation. It is in the intersection between the purely supply and demand relationships on the one hand and institutions, either limiting or supporting the function of the markets, on the other that we can explain existing systems of allocation.

An operational problem in the present study has been to choose a concept that satisfactorily describes the business relationships between the commercial banks and their industrial customers. The application of a contractual approach is clearly motivated by the fact that these relationships sometimes took the form of written contracts which regulated the ties between bank and company. However, the term 'contracts', used as an economic concept, covers much more than just formal agreements of this kind. Contracts are also instruments for private ordering (treaties) characterized by the absence of legal sanctions to be taken.

The term 'contract', as it is used here, refers to any form of organized exchange relations between two or more parties, that is exchange relations conditioned and regulated by some consciously made arrangement between the parties. The nature of these relations can vary, as can their appearance. They can be legally binding contracts, but they can also be what has been termed 'implicit contracts', that is different kinds of informal agreements and arrangements. However, the requirement that these relations must be *organized* precludes norms and conventions from being defined as contracts. Our attitudes, it is true, bear on the actions of man, but attitudes can hardly include consciously made arrangements. The contracting parties can be individuals (actors) or institutions (organizations), and the contracts can – but do not necessarily have to – be part of a larger network of relations.

The growth of a bank–oriented financial system in Sweden

During the 1830s and 1840s a number of commercial banks or so-called 'enskilda' ('private') banks were founded in Sweden. These were small, regional banks, totally dependent for their operations on the right to issue notes. Not until the late 1850s did any dramatic changes occur. The establishment of Stockholms Enskilda Bank in 1856 proved that a Swedish commercial bank could base its activities primarily on deposits. The most important reason for considering the 1850s as the breakthrough period for modern banking in Sweden, however, is that the existing banks then began to co-operate in a national system for clearing and payments service.

The prototype for the Swedish banking system was the Scottish system, internationally renowned at this time for its stability and nationwide clearing.[4] Scottish banks dominated the entire credit market, and they did this in a financial system characterized by extensive co-operation and unification. The right to establish banks was free. Despite the large number of banks and intense competition, the banks accepted each others' notes and payments were made through a system of clearing between banks.

The Swedish commercial banks, like the Scottish, concentrated on bill discounting and short-term lending, attracting mainly liquid and short-term deposits. However, the credit market in Sweden at the middle of the nineteenth century was still quite undeveloped, making a direct importation of the Scottish model in its entirety impossible. Owing to a less developed deposits market, for example, note issuing became much more important for the Swedish 'enskilda' banks than for their Scottish counterparts. It was not until 1903 that the Central Bank became the sole legal issuer of bank notes in Sweden. Moreover, during a long period the Swedish credit market was dominated by moneylenders, private merchant houses, and trading houses, and only gradually, in the 1890s, did the commercial banks take over their role in financing industry.

In contrast to the British system of deposit banks, another system developed in continental Europe during the latter part of the nineteenth century. The German banks in particular provided an example of a mixed banking system, combining regular retail banking with corporate finance, including share acquisitions and issuing activities. These so-called universal banks became known as initiators and promoters of industrial change, co-operating quite intimately with industry, initiating mergers and collaborating with each other in the creation of cartels and syndicates.[5]

In Germany it was the banks that promoted the development of the financial market. There was a marked scarcity of capital, particularly venture capital, and the market was undeveloped. The commercial banks that were established in Germany after 1870 thus came to perform functions that in Great Britain were carried out by other institutions, such as private investment companies and the so-called merchant bankers.

The rapid process of industrialization in Germany, and the participation of German banks in that process, became an ideal for influential groups in Sweden and other countries on the periphery of Europe. By the end of the nineteenth century the commercial banks had begun to play an increasingly important role in providing capital for Swedish firms. The boundaries between short-term deposit banking and long-term involvement in industry became increasingly difficult to uphold, as the growing industrial sector required first and foremost credits for investments.

This problem was solved by the regular prolongation and renewal of what were formally short-term loans which in reality became long-term credits. The commercial banks also became more involved in industrial long-term finance by underwriting industrial bond issues, which were normally intended for subsequent public offer. Trading in shares and new share issues became much more common in Sweden during the 1890s, which necessitated the reorganization of the Stockholm Stock Exchange in 1901. A discussion arose over whether bank capital could not be used, at least in a limited fashion, as venture capital and as a spearhead in the industrialization process.

While this question was being discussed and publicly investigated, the commercial banks were by no means idle. Against the spirit of existing legislation, with its ban on the owning of shares by banks, embryonic forms of modern financial concerns developed. Leading managers of the larger banks organized themselves into consortia or syndicates, eagerly looking for opportunities to engage in share underwriting and structural reorganization operations. Investment and issuing companies were formed, juridically separated from, but totally financed by and working in close collaboration with, different commercial banks. Thus more permanent banking groups were established, offering a complete programme of investment banking to industry, and close contacts developed between the larger commercial banks and their industrial clients.

In this way the banks had become active in supplying venture capital to industry long before share acquisitions on the banks' own accounts were to some degree permitted by the 1911 Banking Law. Moreover, the limitations laid down by the new Banking Law were not crucial impediments to the large-scale involvement of larger banks in venture capital provisions, and their operations developed along the lines of the German universal banks. Nothing prevented a commercial bank from legally establishing a subsidiary company, with a relatively small equity, which did extensive business with funds borrowed from the parent bank.[6]

During the hectic boom of the First World War, the banks' operations in share issuing exacerbated the violent credit expansion, financial over-speculation and inflation. A variety of investment and issuing companies were established. Many were directly connected to the parent bank through ownership, while others could be 'affiliated' to a bank, although there were no clear ownership links. The activities of the issuing companies were to a large extent financed by the banks, with shares in the companies' portfolios as collateral for loans. When the deflationary crisis occurred in 1920–1, bringing in its wake a suspension of dividend payments and falling share prices, the issuing companies were hit severely, and within a few years most of them had been liquidated. The commercial banks were forced to take over collateral shares en masse in order to protect their claims, and suddenly the banks found themselves owners of a substantial portion of Swedish large industry. In this way, the interdependence of banks and industry further deepened.

A considerable portion of the stocks held by the banks were sold during the subsequent boom years, forming the base for the rapid build-up of Ivar Kreuger's empire in the late 1920s. The Kreuger collapse of 1932 returned these stocks to the banks, also producing a redistribution of industrial ownership between the leading commercial banks. For Swedish banking practices, however, the most important effect of the Kreuger crash was a new Government Bill in 1933, prohibiting bank ownership of shares. The intention was to prevent the commercial banks from mixing credit and entre-preneurial functions, the risks associated with loan operations being so substantial 'that the banks should not assume the addi-tional risks of entrepreneurship'.[7] The swing of the pendulum was now back where it started. The long-run significance of the 1933 bill was to give priority to retail banking, careful credit examina-tion and the safety of deposits, thereby deliberately excluding corporate finance from the functions of commercial banks.

These developments, however, did not essentially affect the close connections between banks and industry built up during earlier decades. As I have shown elsewhere, the larger banks did not actually dispose of their shareholdings, but transferred them in the 1930s and the 1940s to affiliated investment companies, indirectly controlled by the banks. Competition between the banks and a fear of losing important industrial clients were clearly important factors behind the decision of the banks not to wholly release control over companies in which they had gained ownership rights.[8]

In the very long-run perspective, the firm structure of both large industry and large banking in Sweden shows an amazing continuity and stability during the twentieth century. Firms that became large and international at the beginning of the century continue even today to form the backbone of Swedish industry, dominating their industrial environment still more. Despite important changes within the top group of commercial banks, the banking structure that developed during the First World War can still be observed very clearly. And even if the relations between big banks and big industry in many ways have changed during the 1970s and the 1980s, involving greater industrial independence and greater mobility in bank connections, it is still easy to trace existing bank–industry relationships far back into history.

Many of these client relationships were established before the

First World War, when Swedish industry made its breakthrough on a broader front. One effect of the crisis of the early 1920s was to tighten bonds between banks and industry. In this longer-term perspective, the Kreuger debacle only meant some turbulence within the established financial–industrial network. After the Kreuger crash, when the commercial banks were forbidden to own shares, they were still able to keep some indirect ownership–control in their spheres of industrial interests by disposing of their share-holdings to affiliated investment companies. This suggests that the Swedish financial system up to the 1970s was typically bank-oriented, characterized by compact and stable long-term relation-ships between banks and industry.

Stockholms Enskilda Bank

Originally founded in 1856 as a commercial bank of the Scottish model, Stockholms Enskilda Bank (SEB) followed the general trend, developing into a true banking concern, bringing together normal commercial banking service with merchant banking/inter-national business and investment banking/industrial promotion. In its corporate finance policy SEB was not seriously impeded by the restraints on share dealing and share owning placed upon it before 1912 by the law. Like the Stockholms Handelsbank, later called Svenska Handelsbanken, SEB was considered an industrial bank *par préférence* at the eve of the First World War.[9]

In 1910 a merger movement began, which during the next decade transformed the whole firm structure of Swedish commercial bank-ing.[10] Stockholms Enskilda Bank was not involved in these mergers and succeeded in defending or even strengthening its posi-tion without having to incorporate any other bank. SEB did business nationwide, but remained, in terms of its location, a typical Stockholm bank, only occasionally establishing branches outside the capital. Its relative size, as measured by total assets, grew slightly, from 6% in 1907 to 8% by the mid-1920s, thereafter oscillating around the 8% figure right up to the merger with Skan-dinaviska Banken in 1972.

One effect of the intensive merger activities of the 1910s was that two of the commercial banks, Svenska Handelsbanken and Skan-dinaviska Banken, became the largest banks in Sweden. In the mid-1920s they ranked in a class of their own, accounting for more than one fifth each of total Swedish banking business. Despite its moderate size, SEB was considered one of the major commercial banks, a position which was also attributed to Göteborgs Bank and

– since 1951 – to the state-owned Sveriges Kreditbank (today PK Bank, PKB). The importance of SEB could, however, easily be compared with that of the two largest banks, thanks to the distinct character of the bank. In reality, Stockholms Enskilda Bank managed to maintain its character as a universal bank for a long time, including investment banking operations in its business by working within a network of closely related financial and investment companies.

In this way SEB emerged as the leading institution in a group of companies, which ultimately were associated with the Wallenberg family (or rather that part of the family constituting the bank's management). The organization of a solid and viable Wallenberg group made it possible to use the resources of the bank in structuring operations and in promoting large industrial development schemes.

The Wallenbergs' interest in Swedish industry has grown steadily during this century. In 1924 the number of employees in industrial firms linked to the Wallenberg group has been estimated as only 4%. At the end of the Second World War, this figure had increased to 11% and at the end of the 1960s the percentage had doubled once more. In 1969 almost 23% of the industrial labour force were employed in companies tied in one way or another to the Wallenbergs' sphere of interest.[11]

In a programmatic way the SEB management actively combined ownership, entrepreneurial and creditor functions. In all probability the Wallenberg group was unique when it comes to the consistent vigour with which this programme was realized. Nevertheless neither industrial finance nor the organizing of banking groups were unfamiliar to the other major banks. Without having such extensive ambitions as SEB it is quite clear that both Svenska Handelsbanken and Skandinaviska Banken established 'spheres of interest', actively enforcing and defending their client relationships and making important contributions to industrial development by corporate finance operations.

The SEB clients: a classification

As the first commercial bank in Sweden, Stockholms Enskilda Bank created a separate department for credit information in 1900. The prototype was to be found in the organization of Crédit Lyonnais, SEB's correspondent bank in Paris. At this time it was a delicate business to make credit-ranking investigations, and the new SEB division was neutrally called the statistical department.

All information on clients, and on other firms of interest, was accumulated in this department, which supplied the base material for credit decisions made by the credits department or by the managing directors. Thanks to a careful control of credit balances and to an elaborate keeping of diaries for each client, showing all contacts made and each decision taken, the statistical department has given posterity unique material for analysing bank–client relationships.

The top managers of Stockholms Enskilda Bank often surprised inspectors from the governmental banking authorities by having detailed information on individual credit arrangements. Contributing to this, of course, was the extensive work on credit rating and credit control done by the statistical department. Another prerequisite was, however, the very concentration of the SEB business. The number of regular clients was relatively few, and the bank's lending was very concentrated: up to 1945, some hundreds of clients each year accounted for 90 to 95% of all credits. This concentration can be explained by the fact that the major objective of the bank was to support those companies connected to the Wallenberg group. The combination of business concentration and unique records makes it possible to reconstruct and systematize all contacts, whether made in person, by phone or by letter, between the clients and the bank from as early as before the First World War to the end of the 1960s.

Among the clients, there was first of all a group of individuals (members of the family, bank managers and so on) and finance, holding and investment companies, owned and controlled by the Wallenbergs, that worked intimately with the bank, being the tools of the family business (Group 1). Together with the SEB, these companies constituted a true banking group, the Wallenberg group. The bank–client relationships within this group are 'unproblematic' from a contractual point of view, and will not be dealt with here. Stockholms Enskilda Bank was responsible for creditor, ownership and managerial functions. The two contracting bodies, the bank and its client, were operating within the same governance structure, being subordinated to one and the same decision-making centre.

The remaining clients of the bank divide into two other specific clusters:

Group 2: Clients that were *independent* of the Wallenberg group with respect to ownership. In relation to these clients, SEB fulfilled creditor functions only, and under normal circumstances these firms remained autonomous in other respects as well.

However, if the instalments or interest payments were mismanaged, the bank could begin to exert pressure on its client. The bank could for example appoint an accountant or even a representative to the board of the firm in order to supervise the management of the loan. In this way, a temporary credit dependence was created.

Group 3: Client companies, mainly in industry, in which the SEB management had a distinct influence. As a basic principle for classification, such 'influence' is said to be exercised when two conditions are jointly fulfilled. First, the banking group should own a minority interest of at least 5% of share votes, and secondly, the bank should be represented on the board of the company. Vis-a-vis the clients in this group, SEB mixed to a varying degree creditor, ownership, managerial and even entrepreneurial functions.

The credits granted by Stockholms Enskilda Bank during the interwar years can be divided, roughly speaking, into three equal portions. This means that as much as one-third of total credits were used by affiliated finance, holding and investment companies, working intimately with the bank (Group 1). On average, only 37% of credits were granted to clients independent of the Wallenbergs (Group 2), about 30% being destined for the industrial companies in which the SEB management had a decisive influence (Group 3). During the 1940s and 1950s, credits to affiliated finance and investment companies within the banking group decreased, in that increased governmental regulation of the operations of the commercial banks after the war made it more difficult to operate through affiliated companies. Most striking, however, during the period after the Second World War, is the increase of credits granted to the industrial concerns tied to the Wallenbergs (Group 3). The major reason for this was a growing demand for credit after the war among the swiftly expanding industrial firms that were dominated in one way or another by the bank management.

Contractual relations to independent clients

In relation to clients without ownership bonds to the banking group, (Group 2), SEB mainly performed credit functions. In this category some of the most well-known financial and industrial groups of Sweden, such as the Bonnier, the Johnson and the Söderberg groups of companies, are to be found. These groups operated quite independently of the bank, and the contractual relations – besides the explicit credit contracts – were based on common business interests. It was from among the leading figures of these groups that prestigious members of the Stockholms Enskilda Bank board of directors were recruited, duly qualifying when being among the permanent customers of the bank and 'owning their own firm'.[12] This meant, no doubt, that one should combine – as did the Wallenbergs themselves – ownership and governance, being independent of other capitalist groups. Some of these men also were or became associated with the Wallenberg group through friendship and family ties, something that further strengthened their common network of business and credit relations.

The relations between SEB and the important family capitalist groups were characterized by stability and balance. One of the later presidents of the bank expressed this balance indirectly when he noted that the SEB management 'had been extremely tactful in their treatment of Axel Ax:son Johnson'. The long-term balance of the relationships between the most important clients and Stockholms Enskilda Bank could nonetheless temporarily be disturbed. An example illustrative of this is that when Nordiska Kompaniet (NK, the cornerstone of the Sachs' group) ran into difficulties in the 1920s and 1930s, the Wallenbergs mobilized venture capital to support the position of the Sachs family in NK. By 1934 the Wallenberg group was the largest shareholder of NK, controlling 11% of the stock measured by voting power. At this time the Sachs family was forced to give an account of its total financial position to Stockholms Enskilda Bank, a most exceptional move to take in connection with clients of the Sachs' category.[13]

The contractual relations between SEB and its clients were much more asymmetrical when it comes to the numerous small and medium-sized firms having an independent managerial and ownership position with regard to the bank. These firms were located mainly in Stockholm and its suburbs and secured to SEB by active recruitment work. They were reckoned an important field for acquisition work, and the statistical department energetically traced small firms with growth potentials that could be secured as clients. The reason why competition between banks was intense in this field was, as will be shown, that big business was firmly tied to its banks by tradition and long-term contracts. One possible way for banks to enlarge their markets was to invest in new client connections or networks, which might be maintained and developed into important long-term contracts as the firm grew.

The credit balances and the entire economic situation of those small firms were exposed to close examination by the credits department. Before accepting a new client, a formal visit was paid to the firm. A visit of this kind was to be compared to an inspection, including examination of books and book-keeping practices. The impressions of the visiting bank manager were compiled into a detailed and comprehensive report. Current credit balances were controlled regularly, and all parties to bills were examined every one to three years. If the bill holdings were unsatisfactory, the examination was followed up by correspondence or private interviews, in which uncreditworthy names were rejected.

It is an interesting question why independent, small-sized firms without shaky finances accepted a close examination of balances, showing their total financial situation, when competition between banks for new clients demonstrably was intense. It is obvious that the client firms also had some advantages of contracting on these terms. These benefits can be summarized as long-term financial support and security. Being 'reliable' and 'co-operative', accepting some bank control in one's business – 'mutual confidence' were the prestige words used in this context – one had, as a matter of fact, bought insurance to be helped by Stockholms Enskilda Bank in both growth and crises. Another condition of reliable bank support was to stick to one bank only. A consistent SEB ambition was, if possible, to be recognized the sole bank connection of a firm. In practice, however, Stockholms Enskilda Bank often had to give up this ambition.

When the finances of these independent clients got into a muddle, the SEB's demands for information became more insistent. Yearly final accounts were requested, plans for amortization were approved, and the bank gave more or less detailed instructions on how to run the business. In these cases the Stockholms Enskilda Bank often nominated one of the accountants or, as an indication of tighter control, even a member of the board of directors. Somewhere on this sliding scale, independence was transferred into what can be termed *credit dependence*, which was not necessarily combined with ownership on the part of the bank. My empirical research supports the idea that a convenient criterion for determining this boundary is when business was continuously supervised by a bank representative on the board of the client company.

Combinations of ownership and credit contracts

The qualitative relationships between SEB and its clients are most varied, and thus hardest to grasp, when it comes to the group of companies in which the bank combined ownership and creditor functions, often mixed with managerial or entrepreneurial functions to a varying degree (Group 3). To exert influence in a company, the SEB management supplemented minority ownership with board membership. It is quite obvious, however, that the basic function of the bank representative on the board of directors of an industrial company was to be an observer and informant, and, not least, to secure the company as a client of the bank.

In order for the bank to be able to exercise any form of actual monitoring, it had to be represented on the board of the firm. However, the amount of influence wielded by the bank could vary quite dramatically. In several cases it was clear that the bank did not engage itself in the firm to any great extent even though a position on the board was earmarked for a representative of the bank. The most fundamental and important task for this board member seems to have been to guarantee that the firm used the SEB as its bank connection. Representation on the board can thus be seen as a necessary prerequisite for the development of some form of hierarchical decision-making structure in the relation between the bank and its client, but it does not necessarily imply any extensive co-ordination of operations.

The decisive factor for the development of far-reaching hierarchical relations between the bank and a firm was the size of the ownership interest. In firms in which the bank owned a majority interest, its influence was extensive and included both strategic decision making and intervention in routine, daily business. This was the case for example in firms such as Scania-Vabis, in which the bank owned the entire share capital up until 1946, and Atlas Diesel. In the latter case, the bank group owned almost 54% of the share capital even though the firm was listed at the Stock Exchange.

In the case of a number of large industrial concerns in which the bank group owned a clearly dominating minority interest while there were no other important ownership groups, we also find relations characterized by an extensive co-ordination between the bank and the firm. This applied to Papyrus (45% ownership 1945), Kopparfors (barely 18%) and Wifstavarv (25%) for example. In all these cases, bank–client relations involved co-ordinated efforts to reach certain goals, with the bank placing its resources, contacts and knowledge of the market at the disposal of the firm in order to achieve these goals.

On the other hand there were minority-owned companies, with clear Wallenberg ownership dominance, in which the position of local management by tradition or by coincidence, was very strong. In ASEA and in Stora Kopparberg (today STORA) during the 1930s and 1940s, for example, the relationships between bank and client can hardly be described as a principal–agent relation. Despite a considerable minority interest, established by SEB in 1929, and despite bank representatives as board members of both ASEA and STORA, conflicts between local management and SEB were by no means settled by instructions or orders, but rather by negotiations and compromises between the contracting parties. The managing directors of big business, traditionally having strong positions in 'their' companies, were often very eager to emphasize their independence with respect to different groups of owners.

Other examples can be given, showing how communities of interest were the sole basis for extensive co-operation, including both interlocking directorships and mutual minority shareholdings. The relationships between Stockholms Enskilda Bank and some of the larger Swedish insurance companies are typical examples of these bases for contracting. Skandia had long been a client of SEB, having both large deposits and, occasionally, large short-term loans. For a large insurance company, however, it was very important to have more than one banking connection, and Skandia also had close contacts with both Svenska Handelsbanken and Skandinaviska Banken. From the SEB point of view it could be justified to include the Skandia company in a Wallenberg sphere of interest. But, as a matter of fact, from the Skandia point of view it was as justified to include Stockholms Enskilda Bank in a Skandia sphere.

The importance of Skandia to SEB – and of SEB to Skandia – was in mutual business. The bank could place underwritten bond issues and long-term loans in the portfolio of Skandia, and the international contacts of the bank were often used by Skandia as a source of information when investing in foreign securities. Moreover, through Stockholms Enskilda Bank, Skandia acquired industrial insurance, in particular fire insurance for industrial plant, which for a long time served as a 'golden egg' in the insurance business.

Clearly, the appointment of bank representatives to the board of directors was an important step in the transition from impersonal market relations to more hierarchical decision-making relationships between bank and client. However, majority ownership or a strong minority influence were decisive in giving the bank active influence over its client. Between the two poles of appointing a representative to the board for information purposes only and 100 per cent ownership, there existed a variety of intermediate forms of bank influence. A rough measurement of the degree of influence is whether SEB was made the sole banking connection or not.

Client contracts as a substitute for ownership

A permanent goal for Stockholms Enskilda Bank was to be chosen as the only bank connection for its clients. The Wallenberg group aimed at a variety of things with its ownership interests, but one very fundamental purpose was to link the company closer to the bank. A minority interest that was large enough to give the bank influence over a company's choice of bank connection was a rational investment in order to reduce the insecurities of the market and secure a demand for the services of the bank.

Whenever changes in the Wallenberg group's ownership interests were discussed, the bank management considered very carefully how the SEB contacts with the client companies would be affected by the changes. The possibility of tying a company to the bank through hierarchical co-ordination was lost upon the liquidation of an ownership interest. If the sale of an ownership interest was decided upon, agreements with the buyer were made regularly so that the company would remain a client of SEB.

Sometimes these contracts were purely oral agreements. When the Wallenberg family sold its block of shares, one-third of the capital, in Köpings Mekaniska Verkstad to AB Volvo in Autumn 1942, Managing Director of Volvo, Assar Gabrielsson, promised by word of mouth, and with some solemnity, that change in the business relations of the acquired company with SEB would take place, 'neither directly, nor indirectly'. This promise was expressly renewed in December 1942, 'at lunch after the extra shareholders meeting', after SEB's representative Richard Julin took up the question of whether Volvo, the new parent company (and client of Skandinaviska Banken) would finance the planned expansion of Köping by borrowing from Skandinaviska.

Normally, however, agreements of this kind were written and either included as a special clause in the sales contract itself or as a separate clause added to the contract. Even in these cases, the contracts were highly incomplete, despite their referring to future commitments that were without explicit time limits. Specifications as to how these generally formulated commitments were to be interpreted and operationalized were only exceptionally included in the contract. One such exception was a contract made with Torsten Kreuger in 1928 when he bought the Wallenberg group's stock interests in Stockholms Rederi AB Svea. Svea was a large shipping company with extensive traffic in the Baltic Sea, among other things between Finland and Sweden. Torsten Kreuger promised that the SEB would in the future receive 60% of the company's bank business, while the other 40% would go to Sydsvenska Banken in Malmö, a bank recently acquired by Kreuger. However the promise was valid only as long as Stockholms Enskilda Bank gave 'Svea the same advantages as Svea at any point could obtain at any other bank affiliated with the Swedish Federation of Commercial Banks'. For Svea subsidiary Finnboda Varv, it was agreed that 50% of the company's business would go to SEB.

Moreover, there was rarely a time limit on the contracts. If one did exist, it was usually tied to the special lending arrangements that were part of the purchase. Stockholms Transport- och Bogserings AB was, during the interwar period, a large enterprise, dealing in shipbuilding, as well as towing and barge transports in Lake Mälaren and the Baltic Sea. The company had been restructured and taken over by SEB during the crisis of the 1920s, but was sold in 1938 to its competitor Kran- och Bogserings AB. In the sales contract, it was stipulated that 'for a period of at least 5 years, the Transportbolag is to conduct bank business solely with SEB'. The time limit can be explained by the fact that the bank promised the buyer a loan without amortization for the same period of time. After the loan had matured, the Transportbolag was free to choose the bank it wished to do business with.

The generally vague wording of these contracts is attributable to the fact that there were practically no legal sanctions in Sweden for this type of agreement. Technically and formally there was nothing to prevent an injured party from taking legal action upon a breach of contract, but in fact, because of the negative publicity such an action would engender, this was an impossibility. It is significant that there were no stipulations whatsoever regarding sanctions included in the contracts. The contract procedure should be seen as a way of codifying the will of the contracting parties to engage in future business co-operation. To what extent the contract was observed depended entirely on how the contracting parties assessed the advantages of continued co-operation. As soon as one of the parties felt that the disadvantages of continuing a business relationship outweighed the advantages, the contract could be broken without the risk of official sanctions. Nor did private or informal sanctions, in the form of some sort of social reprisal for example, seem to have been contemplated upon a breach of contract. It would seem that when a company changed its bank connection, it also in some respects entered into the social and financial sphere of the new bank, which could provide the company with a form of 'protective net'.

Once the bank had lost its control over a company through shareholding, it proved difficult to maintain contracts that secured a client relationship to the SEB for any longer period of time. In many cases, the company left the SEB after a while, either precipitously after a conflict of interest or slowly through a successive termination of its contacts with its former bank. In the case of Köpings Mekaniska Verkstad, for example, Volvo and Skandinavbanken did eventually take over the company's financing, much as the SEB bank management had feared. When Volvo, after the Second World War, made renewed enquiries regarding credit for Köpings Mekaniska Verkstad, they were made as invitations for open tender between SEB and Skandinaviska Banken, a competitive method which SEB considered to be a provocation and which soon made it give up bidding.

In 1936 the Wedevåg Ironworks was sold to a holding company, AB Svea-export, which was independent of the Wallenberg group. A clause, stipulating that Stockholms Enskilda Bank in future was to be the major bank connection of the Wedevåg company was included in the contract of sale. In an unpleasant surprise to the SEB management in 1950, all advances and loans which Wedevåg had raised in SEB were paid by Svenska Handelsbanken. The head of the credits department of SEB immediately called the former client, reminding him of the clause, but nothing could actually be done. Wedevåg had left SEB for Svenska Handelsbanken.

Despite the fact these these contracts – which were meant to maintain bank–company connections even after Stockholms Enskilda Bank no longer owned shares in the company or was represented on the board – were for the most part explicit and included in the sales contract, they turned out to be difficult to enforce in practice. There were no sanctions, either formal or informal, and these contracts must therefore be considered to be a less effective means of linking clients to the bank than the hierarchical co-ordination that could be achieved through ownership and board representation.

The allocation of big industry's business with banks

When scrutinizing the relationships between Stockholms Enskilda Bank and its more important industrial clients, it is striking to note that SEB often shared business with other major banks. A number of the SEB's large industrial clients were located far away from

Stockholm, and for daily business the company was dependent on a local bank contact as well, where documentary credits, foreign exchange business, and occasional overdrafts could easily be taken care of.

From the point of view of the SEB, it was important in such a case to co-operate with a regional commercial bank that could provide service in the community in which the company's head office and operations were located. Stockholms Enskilda Bank was the major bank connection of the company and the regional bank the secondary connection. For the regional bank, the reason for contracting with one of the major commercial banks could be related to a problem of scale: the desire of the regional bank to support a growing client without, however, having the financial resources to maintain its position as the sole supplier of credits and other banking services.

Allotments between a major and a regional commercial bank were made, for example, between SEB and the regional Sundsvalls Enskilda Bank concerning the contractual relation with banks of Wifstavarf. Wifstavarf was a large forest group (pulp-, saw- and boardmills) near Sundsvall, closely related by ownership interests to the Wallenberg group. All of Wifstavarf's business, including credit, was divided between the SEB and Sundsvalls Enskilda Bank according to a special agreement, with one-third going to the latter bank and two-thirds to the SEB.

It was moreover not uncommon for even the large commercial banks to allot the bank business of the larger industrial companies between themselves. ASEA and LM Ericsson will be used here as illustrative examples, but in fact the evidence could easily be multiplied. These examples have been chosen in order to bring out certain general characteristics in the development of bank–industry relations.

At the turn of the century, Stockholms Enskilda Bank was deeply involved in ASEA. SEB reconstructed the business, provided new venture capital and piloted the company through the difficult crises of 1900 to 1903. Gradually SEB sold its ASEA shares but, the relationship being strengthened by personal bonds between the managing directors, ASEA remained a faithful client to the bank.

In 1916 ASEA acquired the largest Swedish competitor, NFEA (Nya Förenade Elektriska AB), which had Skandinaviska Banken as its bank connection. As a condition of the merger, it was stated that Skandinaviska Banken would have one-third of ASEA's business with banks in the future. This portion was diminished to one-sixth in 1932, when the position of Skandinaviska Banken was weakened following the Kreuger crash. As a third bank connection Svenska Handelsbanken now entered the scene, taking over the share lost by Skandinaviska Banken. In return for the portion allotted, Svenska Handelsbanken promised to stimulate companies in its sphere of interest to buy electrical equipment from the ASEA group.[14]

In 1918 the business with banks of LM Ericsson – the telephone company – was divided between Svenska Handelsbanken (75%) and SEB (25%). As in the case of ASEA, the division was a result of a merger, the portions roughly corresponding to the two banks' business with the merging companies. When Ivar Kreuger for a period in 1930–1 acquired a controlling interest in LM Ericsson, Kreuger's major bank connection Skandinaviska Banken also got a share of the LM Ericsson business with banks and was even allowed to nominate a member of the board of directors. As a consequence of the Kreuger débâcle however, Skandinaviska Banken was removed. Svenska Handelsbanken and SEB engaged heavily in the reconstruction of LM Ericsson. In 1936 these two banks decided to participate fairly in the telephone company's contractual relations with banks, a state of affairs which still prevailed when Stockholms Enskilda Bank merged in 1972.[15]

As these examples show, the relationships between the major Swedish commercial banks and their large industrial clients were surprisingly stable for a long time. The allocation of the banking business of large companies between different banks can to a great extent be traced back to the extensive merger movement in Swedish industry during the First World War, when the commercial banks actively participated in the process of structural change as issuing and industrial banks. Mergers and other changes in the ownership structure of the companies also later affected the allocation of bank business, as was clearly illustrated by events during and after the Kreuger epoch.

That the origins of business quotas are to be found in the merger movement is quite natural. It was the end of the turbulent *Gründerzeit* of Swedish industry, when the initial structure of firms changed. But, as Ragnhild Lundström has stressed, during the period before the First World War, the intermediating foreign loan business was the main source of revenue – and an important basis for deposits – for the commercial banks. When capital imports ceased, Swedish industry grew more important as clients of the banks.[16] This growing importance is clearly demonstrated by bank behaviour in industrial mergers, and banks were very active in defending their networks of client relationships when taking part in structuralizing operations.

When the allotment of bank business was the result of a merger, stipulations on how to share the business of the new company between the banks can often be found as an article in the formal merger agreement, and it was these banks which, by their financing, made the creation of the new company possible. Changes in the quotas were often discussed and agreed upon in a personal meeting, of which the diary records of SEB bear testimony, and were later confirmed by phone or letter.

It is an interesting question why these agreements allotting the business of the large industrial companies between different banks have shown such an extraordinary stability and vitality. The question becomes of particular interest if these agreements are compared to the less stable bank–client contracts that were meant to retain a company as a client even after ownership ties had disappeared.

Superficially, these two types of agreement resembled one another. They were usually written, but they were very general and fragmentary and without any legal sanctions. Both had the form of gentlemen's agreements, and their observance was dependent upon the goodwill of the contracting parties. They differed, however, in one decisive way. The contracts allotting the bank business of the large industrial companies were made between two or more large banks, with the industrial company entering into the contract as a secondary party. Together the large banks and large industry formed a limited and manageable network of mutual relations that were difficult to escape from without great social costs.

Conclusions

The Swedish banking system was originally organized as a system of deposit banks, giving priority to retail banking and preventing venture capital provisions to industry through regulation. Despite this, and owing to a less developed capital market, the Swedish banks in reality also practised corporate finance. The commercial banks in Sweden, as in Germany, thus promoted the development of national financial markets.

When capital imports ceased at the eve of the First World War, and the intermediating foreign loan business was no longer an important source of revenue for Swedish banks, the fast-growing industrial companies became clients of vital importance to the banks. During the turbulent merger movement in the 1910s, the larger Swedish commercial banks and big industry clustered together in close networks of reciprocal relationships and ties. It is quite remarkable that the contractual structure of industry and banking business which was established in Sweden in this period can still be observed today.

The stable bank–industry relations were sometimes expressed in formal contracts, in which two or even three banks were the main contracting parties, allotting the business relation of industrial firms with banks between themselves. The quotas were settled as a clause in contracts regarding mergers, which were financed by the banks. The business of large firms could also be allotted between the large banks by means of more unconventional contracts that were essentially agreements made at informal meetings and sometimes later confirmed by letter or telephone.

Even the written contracts were actually 'gentlemen's agreements', which were based on confidence and enforced by moral standards only. Formally there was nothing to prevent an injured party from taking legal action upon a breach of contract, but because of the negative publicity that would follow, this was never done. No stipulations regarding sanctions were included in the contracts, and neither were there any time-limit conditions. Despite their imprecise nature and the lack of legal sanctions, these types of contract endured. Up until the 1970s, when an increasing mobility in bank–industry connections was observed, large Swedish firms still dealt with the same banks as at the turn of the century. The stability of the system of quotas and relations was made possible by the fact that the large banks and large firms were part of an enduring network of social relations and ownership ties. The compactness of the network made it possible to maintain a firm set of rules for a 'decent' market behaviour.

There were also other types of contract, agreed upon between a bank and a client when a company within the bank's sphere of ownership interest was sold off to outsiders. These contracts mostly had a formal character, constituting a clause of the selling contract, or being explicitly formulated as an additional stipulation. In many respects these contracts were similar to the quota agreements sharing the business with banks of big companies. Although written and formal, there were as imprecise as the others. Their enforcement also depended on the will of the contracting parties, and it was more or less impossible to bring legal action for breach of contract because of the negative publicity such a lawsuit would generate. But an important difference was that these contracts were much less stable than the allotment contracts, despite their being based on the same premises. The reason for this relative instability was that the contracting parties, the bank and the firm, were not as tightly bound to one another, socially or economically, as were the large banks and large industrial firms. If the firm changed its bank connection it became part of a new network – which could function as a 'protective net' – revolving around the new bank.

Through informal and formal contracts and through ownership and board representation, the Swedish commercial banks have striven to replace impersonal market relations with co-ordination and hierarchical monitoring and control. Contracts which allotted the bank business of the large firms and secured companies that had been sold off as clients to the bank were steps to make hierarchical co-ordination possible. The extent of bank monitoring has varied, both between different bank groups and over time. During the 1970s and 1980s the old stable network of relationships between bank and industry has started to dissolve. To a large extent this is explained by the establishment of large financial departments within the big industrial concerns, taking up more intense cash management business. Changes in industry's bank connections have been more frequent. Thus no long-term, one-way movement from market relationships to co-ordination and control can be observed.

The behaviour of the commercial banks, in relation to their industrial clients, to replace markets with co-ordination and hierarchical control can be analysed as forming two steps. Contracts, both implicit and explicit, can be termed step one. Allotment contracts, in which two or more big banks were involved, sharing the business with banks of large industrial companies, seem to have produced the desired result, while contracts between one bank and its client were less efficient. But it was only through board representation and ownership, being the second and more decisive step, that a more thorough hierarchical co-ordination of operations could in fact be guaranteed for a longer period of time. The size of the ownership interest had great significance in the development of far-reaching hierarchical relations. In firms in which a banking group owned a majority interest, its influence was extensive and included both strategic decision-making, and intervention in routine, daily business. Minority ownership, supplemented with board membership, was often a way of supporting both written and oral contracts.

The fundamental motive for bank behaviour was to achieve closer ties to their large industrial clients, and the contracts discussed in this chapter are an illustration of this. Ownership in the form of a minority interest large enough to influence the company's choice of financial arrangements was, however, a more effective means of control than both informal and formal contracts. The Swedish credit market can clearly be characterized as oligopolistic, and in certain areas competition was very intense. However, price competition was avoided, and the banks competed mainly by renewing their package of products and developing qualitatively high competence in areas deemed important for their clients. The ownership interests of the commercial banks in industry can be considered to be one way for the banks to reduce market insecurities in an oligopolistic market situation, which of course also opened up possibilities for co-ordination and co-operation between the banks.

Notes

An earlier draft of this chapter has been discussed in a seminar with the Banking History Unit at Uppsala University, Department of Economic History, and I would like to thank all the participants of the seminar for their helpful comments and suggestions. I am also indebted to Docent Kersti Ullenhag and Professor Bo Gustafsson for their constructive criticism, which has affected both the disposition of and analysis in this chapter.

1. An investigation of the terms of credit and how these have changed over time (the degree of standardization in the loan contracts, the actual maturity of the loans, the loan value for different types of collateral) would of course be of great interest, especially as a measurement of how intense competition in the credit market has been during different periods. Such a study is now being planned within the research project, supported by the Bank of Sweden Tercentenary Foundation, 'The Role of Commercial Banks in the Industrial Transformation during the 20th Century' at the Department of Economic History, Uppsala University.

2. The traditional approach, measuring potentials of influence and control in business, may be illustrated by two impressive investigations on American power relations, D.M. Kotz, *Bank Control of Large Corporations in the United States*, University of California Press, 1978, and B. Mintz and M. Schwartz, *The Power Structure of American Business*, University of Chicago Press, 1985. For an interesting application of centrality analysis to historical records, see W. Roy and Ph. Bonacich, 'Interlocking Directorates and Communities of Interest among American Railroad Companies, 1905', *American Sociological Review*, 53 (June 1988): 368–79.

3. This conclusion is based mainly on the period up to the Second World War. As important bank archives gradually open to scientific business history research, it will also be possible to do more international comparative investigations on qualitative bank–industry relationships for the 1950s and 1960s. For Central European examples, see A. Teichova, 'Rivals and Partners: Banking and Industry in Europe in the First Decades of the 20th Century', *Uppsala Papers in Economic History*.

Working Papers No. 1, 1988. When no special reference is made in this chapter, the conclusions refer to my study *Bank, investmentbolag, bankirfirma. Stockholms Enskilda Bank 1924–1945 (Bank, investment company, banking firm. Stockholms Enskilda Bank 1924–1945)*, Norstedts, 1987: 266–80. For an English summary see pp. 482–505.

4. The rise of the modern Swedish banking system during the 1850s has been analysed and placed in its economic policy context by G.B. Nilsson in *Banker i brytningstid (Banking in Pioneer Times)*, Norstedts, 1981. For an English summary, see pp. 369–84.

5. The German mixed banking programme was deeply rooted in the private banking traditions of the country, as has been shown by Richard Tilly in his *Financial Institutions and Industrialization in the Rhineland, 1815–1870*, University of Wisconsin Press, 1966: 81–109. On the continent, investment and share-issuing banks modelled on the well-known Crédit Mobilier de Paris (1852–67) were also established quite early. These types of bank, originally established in Belgium during the 1830s, attempted to finance industrial development by raising venture capital through bond issues. See B. Gille, 'Banking and Industrialisation in Europe 1730–1914', *The Fontana Economic History of Europe 3* (1978): 255–74.

6. The movement during the decades prior to the First World War towards a more bank-dominated financial system in Sweden, characterized by closer relations between banking and industry, has interesting similarities with what took place in the Austro–Hungarian Empire. In the latter part of the nineteenth century, the Austrian banks were clearly averse to taking risks and did not get involved in providing venture capital. After the turn of the century, however, there was a marked change of attitude in this respect. See Richard Rudolph, *Banking and Industrialization in Austro–Hungary. The Role of the Banks in the Industrialization of the Czech Crownlands, 1873–1914*, Cambridge: CUP 1976: 184–200.

There is a voluminous but somewhat diverse literature on Swedish banking developments 1860–1913. In English there is a well-balanced survey by Ingemar Nygren, 'Transformation of Bank Structures in the Industrial Period. The Case of Sweden 1820–1913', *The Journal of European Economic History*, 12 (1983): 29–68. Moreover, there are some very interesting contributions by Lars Sandberg, the most important being 'Banking and Economic Growth in Sweden before World War I', *Journal of Economic History*, (1978): 650–80. The role of the commercial banks in the early internationalization of Swedish firms is analysed by Ragnhild Lundström in her thought-provoking 'Banks and early Swedish Multinationals', in *Multinational Enterprise in Historical Perspective*, A. Teichova, M. Lévy-Leboyer and H. Nussbaum (eds), Cambridge: CUP, 1986: 200–17. Still unsurpassed in penetration and analysis is the Olle Gasslander study on the *History of Stockholms Enskilda Bank to 1914* (643 pp., 1962), in which the active role of banks in the Swedish process of industrialization is clearly demonstrated.

7. Quoted from *SOU Parliamentary Report 1932:30*: 49.

8. That the oligopolistic structure of the Swedish credit market is sufficient reason for banks to become actively involved in industry through ownership – at least to such a degree that it becomes possible to influence the industrial firm's choice of banking connection – is a thesis discussed in more detail in H. Lindgren, 'Banking Group Investments in Swedish Industry', *Uppsala Papers in Economic History*, Research Report No. 15, 1987.

9. K.G. Hildebrand, *Banking in a Growing Economy. Svenska Handelsbanken*

since 1871, Svenska Handelsbanken, 1971: 14–29. Cf. J. Potter, 'The Role of a Swedish Bank in the Process of Industrialization', review article of O. Gasslander's *History of Stockholms Enskilda Bank to 1914*, in *The Scandinavian Economic History Review*, 11 (1), 1963.

10. The number of commercial banks, 83 in 1908, declined quickly, though the number of branch offices increased at the same time. There were only 32 banks left in 1924, by 1945 the number had declined to 22, and by the end of the 1960s there were only 16 commercial banks active in Sweden. During recent years, however, the whole competitive situation in Swedish banking has changed. Savings banks and rural credit societies ('farmers' banks') have acquired commercial bank functions, and during the 1980s a number of financial firms have been formed, many of them completely independent of the established commercial banks. Moreover, after 1 January 1986 foreign establishments were allowed in the Swedish banking sector, and during 1986 the number of commercial banks suddenly increased from 14 to 26 (*Den svenska kreditmarknaden*, Svenska Bankföreningen, 1987).

11. U. Olsson, *Bank, familj och företagande. Stockholms Enskilda Bank 1946–1971*, Norstedts, 1976: 239; H. Lindgren, *op. cit.*: 407.

12. Quoted from Marcus Wallenberg, Sr.

13. The statement regarding Johnson was made by Göte Engfors, Vice-president of SEB 1946–63. The Sachs–NK example is described in detail in H. Lindgren, *op. cit.*: 54–5.

14. J. Glete, *ASEA under hundra år 1883–1983*, ASEA, 1983: 42–8; ibid., *Storföretag i starkström*, ASEA 1984: 61.

15. A. Attman, 'From the Kreuger Crash to Stabilization 1932–1940', in *LM Ericsson 100 Years*, Vol. 1, 1977: 22–8.

16. R. Lundström, *op. cit.*, 1986: 209.

13
The Principle of External Accountability in Competitive Markets

Herbert Gintis

Consider a firm funding its operations by borrowing or issuing securities. Since the firm cannot offer an enforceable contract specifying all relevant aspects of the return to the lender[1] – rate of return, probability of default, and level of risk – it is in the lender's interest to offer incentives to influence the firm's strategic choices. The 'principle of external accountability' asserts that the lender will then prefer that the firm have a political structure in which decision-making power lies in the hands of a small group unaccountable to the firm's employees. This chapter develops a set of sufficient conditions under which the principle of external accountability holds.

The intuition behind the principle of external accountability is straightforward. Lenders can increase the expected return on their investments by (a) controlling the job tenure of managers, maintaining their salaries sufficiently high to render the threat of dismissal credible; and/or (b) offering managers stock options and other residual claimant incentives. Such inducements are 'enforcement rents', the threatened withdrawal of which promotes managerial compliance. If the firm is democratically accountable, owners will be compelled to offer similar enforcement rents to all firm members. Such firms will thus be shunned by financial investors in favour of firms whose leadership is unaccountable to the firm's employees.

This analysis suggests an explanation of the paucity of democratically organized enterprises in competitive market economies: it is less costly to offer incentives to a few key decision-makers than to extend such incentives to all members of the firm. In contrast to some recent contributions to the economic theory of organizations,[2] the principle of external accountability suggests that, while efficiency considerations may dictate the organizational structure of the firm, distributional issues are of central relevance to the choice of the firm's structure of political accountability.

The political structure of the enterprise

An economic enterprise must have rules for determining which members have decision-making authority, and upon whose will their tenure depends. We may generally refer to these rules as the political structure of the enterprise.

A key element of the political structure of the enterprise is the pattern of accountability of its managerial leadership. We say the firm is *democratically accountable* if individuals in positions of authority serve at the will of those involved in the firm's day-to-day operation as a system of production; otherwise we say the firm is *externally accountable*. Firms in contemporary capitalist economies exhibit mainly external accountability, in that their leadership is beholden to stockholders rather than employees. Is this a market failure of some sort, or is there some defect in the democratically accountable enterprise which competitive markets recognize and penalize?

The possibility of market failure is often dismissed. It is widely argued that competitive markets impartially favour allocationally efficient organizational structures. For instance, Eugene Fama argues that competition 'forces the evolution of devices for efficiently monitoring the performance of the entire team and of its individual members' (Fama, 1980: 289).

Thus for Fama, the prevalence of the stockholder-controlled firm provides a quasi-Darwinian 'proof' of its superior efficiency. Similarly, Oliver Williamson argues in the following terms: 'Contrary to earlier conceptions – where the economic institutions of capitalism are explained by reference to class interests, technology, and/or monopoly power – the transaction cost approach maintains that these institutions have the main purpose and effect of economizing on transaction costs' (Williamson, 1985: 1).

Such arguments appear *prima facie* reasonable, since the Fundamental Theorem of Welfare Economics (Arrow, 1951) shows that, under proper conditions, competitive markets promote efficient allocations. But the Fundamental Theorem assumes that contracts are exogenously enforceable, while monitoring and incentive systems arise precisely when exogenous enforcement is not available.[3] Hence the claim that competitive markets favour efficient incentive structures is not rendered plausible by the Fundamental Theorem. In particular, lenders may enjoy higher expected rates of return by directing their assets to externally accountable firms; but this does not prove the superior efficiency of such firms over others with different political structures.

The lender preference for external accountability does not promote efficiency for the following reason: incentives and other enforcement rents represent pure wealth transfers among agents, and hence involve no consumption of real resources. Thus organizational choices based on 'economizing' such transactions do not entail an efficient allocation of resources.

A model of the firm's political structure

Consider a firm consisting of members $i = 1$ to n. We assume the available personal financial resources of firm members is insufficient to fund the firm's operations. The firm must thus contract with a lender, who receives a benefit r as a result of the firm's activities. We may think of the return r as the *ex post* return to equity capital, or as the real return on a loan having a positive default probability.[4]

To maximize the return r, the lender will in general monitor the behaviour of the firm, creating an exchange situation in which rewards and sanctions (including renewal and non-renewal of contract, the payment of incentive bonuses, and applying pressure towards the promotion or removal of key personnel) can be effectively imposed upon decision-makers in the firm.[5]

Suppose that the return r is a function of a vector $\alpha = (\alpha_1,...,\alpha_m)$ of choice dimensions, where the $(\alpha_j \epsilon A_j | j = 1$ to $m)$ are real numbers. If r represents a real rate of return, for instance, α will reflect factors affecting the probability of default, such as the degree of product diversification, the level and type of research and development, the pattern of insurance coverage, the degree of commitment to risky ventures, the strategic response to financial distress, and the riskiness of the firm's portfolio.

We shall assume that α is chosen by members of the firm, and investigate the effect of the political structure of the firm on this choice. We call

$$\Pi = (\nu = (\nu_1,....,\nu_n) \geq 0 \mid \Sigma_i \nu_i = 1)$$

the set of participation vectors of the firm, where ν_i is the relative power of member i in the decision process. We say that member i participates if $\nu_i > 0$.

We represent the choice of α by member i as the vector $\alpha^i = (\alpha_1^i,...,\alpha_m^i)$. We assume α^i is an argument in the objective function of member i, and hence is determined by constrained optimization. Both the objective function and the constraints will

in general depend upon the member's location in the political structure of the enterprise, as well as upon any incentive systems
instituted by the firm and/or the lender.

A firm *decision mechanism* is a mapping $\alpha = \psi(\alpha^1,...,\alpha^n,\nu)$
which translates member choices (α^i) and a participation vector ν
into a final decision α. We may think of ψ as a game, and the α^i
as player strategies. We shall assume that all decision mechanisms
have the following property: when $\nu_i = 0$, α does not depend
upon α^i. In other words, a member must have the right to
participate in a decision in order to affect the outcome. Examples
of decision mechanisms in which the α^i represent 'voting' are
unanimity, proportional representation, majority rule and weighted
averaging.

We shall take ψ as chosen from a set of *admissible decision
mechanisms* Ψ from $A \times \Pi$ to A, and assume that Ψ is determined
by legal admissibility and incentive compatibility. For instance laws
governing personal rights may exclude some forms of surveillance
and negative reward. Similarly, incentive compatibility may require
that the choice of work intensity be dictatorial; that is, individual
work intensity may, for any firm member, necessarily be a decision
variable rather than a parameter.

The *political structure* of the firm is a pair (ψ,ν) consisting of an
admissible decision mechanism and a participation vector. The
issue of the interaction of market competition and political structure can then be posed in the form of three questions. First, what
is the nature of the preference ordering of lenders over political
structures of firms with which they deal? Second, what are the
conditions determining the relative supply of firms with different
political structures? Third, what are the dynamics of excess supply,
and in what manner is the array of distinctly constituted firms
adjusted to the needs of trading partners, and vice versa? I deal
here only with the first of these questions.

We shall think of the lender's return $r(\alpha)$ as net of the cost of
acquiring the firm's services, but we will explicitly entertain the
possibility that the lender can expend resources to influence
individual decision-makers within the enterprise to modify their
choice of α. For instance, the lender may offer firm members stock
options or a share of profits, or threaten them with dismissal, to
induce lender-favourable choices. Similarly, the lender may be able
to impose collective sanctions, such as the threat to switch to
another supplier, to induce the proper behaviour of decision-
makers.

Without enquiring into the specific mechanisms which the lender can employ to influence a member's choices, let us assume that for an expenditure c^i, the lender can induce member i to choose α^i.[6] We write $c^i = f^i(\alpha^i, \nu)$, recognizing explicitly that the cost of eliciting α^i in general depends upon the participation vector.[7]

We may now characterize the lender's optimal choice of political structure. For any political structure $(\psi, \nu) \in \Psi \times \Pi$ there is a vector $\hat{\alpha} = (\hat{\alpha}^1, ..., \hat{\alpha}^n)$ which maximizes the lender return

$$U(\psi, \nu) = r(\hat{\alpha}) - \Sigma_i f^i(\hat{\alpha}, \nu) \qquad (13.1)$$

The lender then determined the optimal political structure by

$$\max_{(\psi, \nu) \in \Psi \times \Pi} U(\psi, \nu). \qquad (13.2)$$

The principle of external accountability

In general the cost of eliciting behaviour from a decision-maker will depend on that decision-maker's political power. For instance, a firm member may be able to exploit a conflict of interest by influencing a decision in one area which leads to gain in another. Similarly, a member with exclusive jurisdiction over a certain decision may be able to use this privilege to extort the lender. The following property rules out this complexity:

Non-strategic incentives: We call the incentives $\{f^i(\alpha^i, \nu)\}$ non-strategic if each f^i is independent from the participation vector ν.

The principle of external accountability can be expected to hold only when the decision dimensions α are amenable to 'political' determination, in the sense that the outcome involves some sort of weighted average of participating members. We formalize this in the property:

Convex decision mechanisms: The decision mechanism ψ is termed convex if, for $\alpha^i \in A^i$, $i = 1$ to n, $\psi(\alpha^1, ..., \alpha^n, \nu)$ lies in the convex hull of $\{\alpha^i \mid \nu_i > 0\}$.

The assumption of convexity is not strong; it is difficult to conceive of a decision mechanism concerning which political criteria might be applied which is not convex. On the other hand, many other aggregations of preferences into global outcomes are not convex. We might cite, for instance, two alternative aggregation types: cumulative and co-ordinating. A *cumulative decision mechanism* is one in which ψ is an increasing function of the $\{\alpha^i\}$; for instance, total output may be the sum of the output of each worker, or total accidents may be an exponential function of the accident rate of each employee. A *co-ordinating decision mechanism* is one in which a particular α_j depends upon the number of members choosing various α_k^i in various ranges. For instance, some group of $\{\alpha_k\}$ may represent tasks which, if performed by too few or too many, lower the level of some α_j. Clearly co-ordinating decisions are not in general convex.

We shall also require a partial converse of the convexity property, in that any weighted average of member preferences must be attainable by some participatory structure in which only parties to the compromise participate positively. Formally:

Spanning decision mechanisms: We say decision mechanism ψ has the spanning property if the following holds: for every set of member choices $\{\alpha^i\}$, for every subset $I \subset \{1,...,n\}$ of firm members, and for every α in the convex hull of $\{\alpha^i | i \in I\}$, we have $\alpha = \psi(\alpha^1,...,\alpha^n,\nu\}$ for some participation vector ν in which $\nu_i = 0$ for i not in I.

The final criterion needed for our main theorem is a notion of divergence of interests between lender and potential decision-makers in the enterprise:

Divergent interests: We say that the interests of the lender diverge from those of the firm if the solution to the equations (13.1) and (13.2) are such that every participating decision-maker receives positive compensation (i.e., $\nu_i > 0$ implies $c^i > 0$).

Given these preliminary definitions, we have the following principle of external accountability:

Theorem 1:   Suppose there are m choice dimensions, incentives are non-strategic, all admissible decision mechanisms are convex and satisfy the spanning property. Then if the lender's interests diverge from the firm's, any solution to the equations (13.1) and (13.2) involves at most m + 1 participating decision-makers, however large the membership of the firm.

It is in general reasonable to expect lenders to be concerned with relatively few choice dimensions: expected return, risk, and covariance with market risk probably exhaust the factors relevant to the firm's creditors and residual claimants. Thus Theorem 1 suggests that the lender-optimal size of the firm's leadership is likely to be quite small.

The proof of Theorem 1 is straightforward. Let (ψ,ν) be the optimal political structure, with costs $\{c^i\}$, member choices $\{\alpha^i\}$, and outcome α. Suppose there are s participating decision-makers, whom we may assume are members $i = 1$ to s. Then by the convexity of ψ, we know α lies in the convex hull of $\alpha^1,...,\alpha^s$. If $s \leq m+1$, we are done. If $s > m+1$, then since the $\{\alpha^i\}$ all lie in a m dimensional vector space, Caratheodory's theorem[8] implies that α is a linear combination of at most $m+1$ of the $\{\alpha^i\}$. By re-ordering the indices, we may assume α is a linear combination of $\alpha^1,...,\alpha^{m+1}$. By the spanning property, α can be achieved by a political structure in which only members 1 to $m+1$ participate. By the assumption of non-strategic incentives, costs c^i do not change when the participation structure is altered. Hence the cost of achieving α remains $\sum_{i=1}^{m+1} c^i$. Since $c^i > 0$ for $i = 1...s$, by the assumption of divergent interests, the cost of implementing this political structure is strictly less than the cost $\sum_{i=1}^{s} c^i$ of implementing the lender's optimal political structure. This is a contradiction. Thus $s \leq m+1$, which proves Theorem 1.

It is easy to show that none of the assumptions in the principle of external accountability can be dropped without voiding the conclusion. The role of the convexity assumption is of course clear, and we have already noted that if incentives are strategic (for example, if a small number of decision-makers can collude, or can extort the lender) diverse participation may be in the lender's interest. The spanning property is needed not only to exclude clearly degenerate cases of convexity (such as dictatorship), but also to rule out certain potential anomalies of preference aggregation. For instance, in a one-dimensional choice, Theorem 1 suggests that at most two decision-makers will participate in the lender's optimal choice for the political structure of the enterprise. But suppose the optimal weight of one decision-maker is 10% and the other 90%. The presence of indivisibilities might require that a minimum of ten individuals participate. This is ruled out by the spanning property. Finally, it is clear that where there is no divergence of interests, the lender is perfectly happy to have large numbers of members participate.

The Pareto-inefficiency of external accountability

This section develops a stylized economy which exhibits clearly the political bias of competitive credit markets, shows that the market equilibrium need not be Pareto-efficient, and suggests a stylized governmental policy which, if implemented, would allow the market solution to achieve a social optimum within the context of democratic accountability.

Consider a repeated game between a risk-neutral lender and a firm composed of a number n of homogeneous risk-neutral members. We suppose the firm has a one-period investment opportunity which requires a capital outlay of unity, returning either 0 or $\phi \geq 1$ with probabilities p and $(1 - p)$ respectively. In the former case the firm goes bankrupt and the game ends, while in the case where the investment is successful, the game continues. The investment must be financed by borrowing from the lender at competitive interest rate r.

We assume both the probability of bankruptcy and the expected return in case of success are functions of the level of risk α chosen by the firm: $p = p(\alpha)$, with $p' > 0$, and $\phi = \phi(\alpha)$ with $\phi' > 0$, $\phi'' < 0$. For ease of exposition, we normalize the measure of risk by specifying $p(\alpha) \equiv \alpha$,[9] and we assume that $\phi(0) > 1 + r$, so all successful investments are sufficiently profitable to repay the lender.[10]

The lender then receives a gross return $(1 + r)$ if the firm is successful, and $(1 - \hat{f})$ in the case of bankruptcy, where r is the competitively determined interest rate (and may depend upon p) and $\hat{f}$ represents the deadweight loss of reorganization. The lender's expected present value v_1 is given by

$$v_1 = [(1 + r)(1 - p) + (1 - \hat{f})p]/(1 + \varrho) - 1 \qquad (13.3)$$
$$= [(r - \varrho) - p(r + \hat{f})]/(1 + \varrho)$$

where ϱ is the inter-temporal discount rate.

Bankruptcy relieves members of responsibility for the debt and the deadweight loss $\hat{f}$, and each assumes a fallback position with present value $\hat{v}$. Here $\hat{v}$ depends upon such factors as the expected income from alternative employment, the expected search duration for such employment, and the social benefits provided during the search process. The present value v_f of being a member of an active firm then satisfies

$$v_f = [(1 - p)(\phi - \delta)/n + p\hat{v} + (1 - p)v_f]/(1 + \varrho) \qquad (13.4)$$
$$= [(1 - p)(\phi - \delta)/n + p\hat{v}]/(p + \varrho),$$

where the debt burden δ is defined as $\delta = 1 + r$. The firm will attract no members if $v_f < \hat{v}$, so we must have

$$(1 - p)(\phi - \delta) \geq \varrho n \hat{v} \tag{13.5}$$

The optimum level of risk for a firm member is given by the first-order condition

$$\frac{d\phi}{dp} = \frac{(1 + \varrho)(\phi - \delta) - \varrho n \hat{v}}{(1 - p)(p + \varrho)}, \tag{13.6}$$

which maximizes v_f.[11] The lender, by contrast, always prefers lower to higher risk.

While not able directly to choose p, the lender is capable of influencing the firm's choice of p. Suppose the political structure of the firm is such that any coalition of $m \leq n$ members can impose a particular choice of p on the group. Consider then a lender strategy involving the choice of m members of the firm, each being offered a bonus c if the loan is repaid. For these m members, (13.4) becomes

$$v_f = \{(1 - p)[c + (\phi - \delta)/n] + p\hat{v}\}/(p + \varrho), \tag{13.4}$$

giving rise to the first-order condition

$$\frac{d\phi}{dp} = \frac{(1 + \varrho)(nc + \phi - \delta) - n\varrho \hat{v}}{(1 - p)(p + \varrho)}. \tag{13.7}$$

Since these m members can enforce a choice of risk level, (13.7) then determines the firm's equilibrium.

Is it profitable for the lender to choose $c > 0$? In this case (13.3) becomes

$$v_1 = [(r - mc - \varrho)(1 - p) - p(r + \hat{f})]/(1 + \varrho),$$

so at $c = 0$,

$$\frac{dv_1}{dc} = -\left[(r + \hat{f})\frac{dp}{dc} + m(1 - p)\right]/(1 + \varrho). \tag{13.8}$$

It is easy to show that at $c = 0$, we have

$$\frac{dp}{dc} = \frac{-(1 + \varrho)}{(2\phi' - (1 - p)\phi'')(\varrho + p)} < 0,$$

so a positive bonus induces decision-makers to lower the level of risk. Hence $dv_1/dc > 0$ for $c = 0$ and sufficiently large p. Thus if the firm autonomously chooses a sufficiently high level of risk, it is profitable for the lender to offer a positive bonus.

It is clear from (13.3) and (13.8) that the smaller m, the greater the range of p over which it is profitable for the lender to offer a bonus, and the greater the lender's gain from such an offer. Thus the lender's preferred situation is $m = 1$, and this may be strictly preferred to $m > 1$. Thus this model is a special case of Theorem 1, since it is optimal for the lender to restrict loans to firms in which one member is singled out to hold total decision-making power. This member receives $v_f + (1 - p)c/(p + \varrho)$, where v_f is the present value of other firm members. In this case the bonus c can be thought of as a supplementary 'enforcement rent' paid to the decision-maker contingent upon non-default.[12] The firm's first-order condition in this case is

$$\frac{d\phi}{dp} = \frac{(1 + \varrho)(nc + (\phi - \delta)) - \varrho n\hat{v}}{(1 - p)(p + \varrho)}. \tag{13.9}$$

Of course the lender might not be satisfied with this set of admissible decision mechanisms. If it were admissible to have a decision-maker who is not a residual claimant, and who is otherwise not accountable to firm members, it is easy to see that for any c greater than his/her fallback position, such a decision-maker will minimize p subject to $v_f \geq \hat{v}$; that is, a lender optimum will be achieved.

The social optimum level of risk is given by maximizing

$$v^* = [(1 - p)\phi(p) + p(1 - \hat{f})]/(1 + \varrho) \tag{13.10}$$

with respect to p, since $\hat{f}$ represents a real resource cost to society. The asset loss $v_f - \hat{v}$ incurred by firm members upon bankruptcy is not a social cost, since in equilibrium each defunct firm will be replaced by a new entrant, whose members enjoy an equivalent asset again. The first-order condition corresponding to (13.10) is

$$\frac{d\phi}{dp} = \frac{\phi - (1 - \hat{f})}{1 - p}, \tag{13.11}$$

which says that the expected marginal gain from a small increase in risk, $(1 - p)d\phi/dp$, is equal to the real resources loss arising from bankruptcy, $\phi - (1 - \hat{f})$.

A comparison among the three alternative first-order conditions indicates that in general the social optimum (13.11) differs from the 'universal suffrage' optimum (13.6) and the 'autocratic' lender optimum (13.9). This divergence can be explained as follows. The social optimum depends neither on the rate of time preference ϱ, since both gains and losses accrue to society in the same period, nor the fallback position $\hat{v}$, since bankruptcy provides an asset gain for the new firm members equal to the loss for the old. The firm decision-makers, however, are concerned with both ϱ, which affects their valuation of bankruptcy in a future period, and $\hat{v}$, which affects their personal net wealth. Finally, limited liability in the context of a non-contractual p in general implies that firm members have no incentive to internalize the full welfare losses associated with bankruptcy.

Suppose $\hat{v}$ is an instrument of economic policy (for instance, firm members may receive unemployment compensation for a period of time after bankruptcy), and business law is altered to require each firm to choose p through a democratic ballot of firm members. If n is large, it will not be profitable for lenders to 'bribe' decision-makers in this situation, so first order conditions (13.6) would apply. To achieve an optimal level of risk, $\hat{v}$ could be chosen to ensure that (13.11) holds as well. We then have

$$r + \hat{f} = n(v_f - \hat{v}).$$

Note that if n is large, and if the deadweight loss $\hat{f}$ is small, this solution will approximate the unattainable lender's optimum $v_f = \hat{v}$. On the other hand, if deadweight loss increases proportionately with firm size, so $\hat{f}$ is of the same order of magnitude as n, we will generally have $v_f >> \hat{v}$ and a Pareto-optimal equilibrium involves credit rationing.

Concluding remarks

The principle of external accountability is a strikingly simple proposition linking competitive markets to an equilibrium political structure of the firm, and suggests that there may be deep economic principles which can be formulated and analysed only when the notion of a political structure is integrated into a microeconomic model.

But this principle has normative implications as well. Political institutions in a democratic society are commonly evaluated according to the principles of liberty and internal accountability, while economic institutions are judged by their allocational and distributional properties. The principle of external accountability suggests that this compartmentalization of values is untenable.

It is widely recognized that individuals have certain 'personal liberties' which can be enjoyed, but which cannot be bought and sold in the marketplace without destroying them.[13] If my argument is correct, the same may be true of 'democratic rights'. Some form of social intervention redefining the 'rules of the game' under which competitive markets operate may entail the emergence of democratic economic institutions with no loss of allocative efficiency.

Notes

This chapter is part of a larger project with Samuel Bowles on the microfoundations of political economy. I would like to thank Masahiko Aoki for helpful comments.

1. The term 'lender' will be used to cover all financial claimants against the firm, including banks, stockholders and bondholders.

2. See, for instance, Furubotn and Pejovich (1970); Alchian and Demsetz (1972); Jensen and Meckling (1979); Fama (1980); Fama and Jensen (1983a, 1983b); Williamson (1985).

3. For a demonstration of the general Pareto-inefficiency of monitoring under competitive conditions, see Bowles and Gintis (1988).

4. The range of application of the model is in fact considerably wider, and applies to many exchanges between an economic actor and a firm having an uncontractable aspect in that writing a contract for a specific service delivered is excessively costly or unenforceable.

5. In special cases, of course, the optimal level of monitoring will be zero. Such cases still do not necessarily exhibit Walrasian behaviour. See Gintis (1989a, 1989b).

6. For instance, if α_j represents the work intensity of a group of workers, the cost of eliciting a particular level may depend on whether workers participate in choosing their supervisors or not.

7. We will consider $\{f^i\}$ as exogenously given to the lender, though little increase in complexity results from assuming the lender optimizes over $\{f^i\}$, given some family of admissible incentives. The $\{f^i\}$ are in a sense 'supply prices', and hence may reflect the conditions of supply of individuals willing to participate within a given political structure. For instance, it may be less costly to elicit worker performance when there is high unemployment.

8. Caratheodory's theorem states that any point in the convex hull of n points in m dimensional space lies in the convex hull of at most $m+1$ of the n points (Border, 1985: 10).

9. This is possible since any strictly increasing function of a risk measure conforming to the Rothschild–Stiglitz (1970) criterion of increasing risk conforms as well.

10. For a more general treatment of this model, see Gintis (1989b).

11. It is easy to check that the shape of $\phi(p)$ ensures that the second-order condition for a maximum is satisfied.

12. In effect, the firm's manager is subjected to efficiency–wage disciplining of the type discussed in Gintis (1976), Shapiro and Stiglitz (1984), Bowles (1985), and Gintis and Ishikawa (1987).

13. For instance, one cannot voluntarily transfer one's right to vote to another, nor can one contract oneself into servitude. Moreover, such restrictions (and there are many more) are preconditions of rather than constraints upon personal freedom. For an extensive discussion of this issue, see Bowles and Gintis (1986).

References

Alchian, Armen and Harold Demsetz (1972) 'Production, Information Costs, and Economic Organization', *American Economic Review*, 62 (December): 777-95.

Arrow, Kenneth J. (1951) 'An Extension of the Basic Theorems of Classical Welfare Economics', in J. Neyman (ed.) *Proceedings of the Second Berkeley Symposium on Mathematical Statistics and Probability*, pp. 507-32. Berkeley: University of California Press.

Border, Kim C. (1985) *Fixed Point Theorems with Applications to Economics and Game Theory*. Cambridge: Cambridge University Press.

Bowles, Samuel (1985) 'The Production Process in a Competitive Economy: Walrasian, Neo-Hobbesian, and Marxian Models', *American Economic Review*, 75 (1) (March): 16-36.

Bowles, Samuel and Herbert Gintis (1986) *Democracy and Capitalism: Property, Community, and the Contradictions of Modern Social Thought*. New York: Basic Books.

Bowles, Samuel and Herbert Gintis (1988) 'Contested Exchange: Political Economy and Modern Economic Theory', *American Economic Review*, 78 (2) (May): 145-50.

Fama, Eugene F. (1980) 'Agency Problems and the Theory of the Firm', *Journal of Political Economy*, 88 (2): 288-307.

Fama, Eugene F. and Michael Jensen (1983a) 'Separation of Ownership and Control', *Journal of Law and Economics*, 26: 301-26.

Fama, Eugene F. and Michael Jensen (1983b) 'Agency Problems and Residual Claims', *Journal of Law and Economics*, 26: 327-39.

Furubotn Eirik G. and Svetozar Pejovich (1970) 'Property Rights and the Behavior of the Firm in a Socialist State: the Example of Yugoslavia', *Zeitschrift für Nationalökonomie*, 30 (3-4): 431-54.

Gintis, Herbert (1976) 'The Nature of the Labor Exchange and the Theory of Capitalist Production', *Review of Radical Political Economics*, 8: 36-54.

Gintis, Herbert (1989a) 'The Power to Switch: On the Political Economy of Consumer Sovereignty', in Samuel Bowles, Richard C. Edwards and William G. Shepherd (eds) *Unconventional Wisdom*.

Gintis, Herbert (1989b) 'Financial Markets and the Political Structure of the Enterprise', *Journal of Economic Behavior and Organization*,

Gintis, Herbert and Tsuneo Ishikawa (1987) 'Wages, Work Discipline, and Macroeconomic Equilibrium', *Journal of Japanese and International Economies*, 1.

Jensen, Michael C. and William H. Meckling (1976) 'Theory of the Firm: Managerial Behavior, Agency Costs and Ownership Structure', *Journal of Financial Economics*, 3: 305–60.

Jensen, Michael C. and William H. Meckling (1979) 'Rights and Production Functions: an Application to Labor-Managed Firms and Codetermination', *Journal of Business*, 52: 469–506.

Rothschild, Michael and Joseph Stiglitz (1970) 'Increasing Risk I: A Definition', *Journal of Economic Theory*, 2: 225–43.

Shapiro, Carl and Joseph E. Stiglitz (1984) 'Unemployment as a Worker Discipline Device', *American Economic Review*, 74 (3) (June): 433–44.

Williamson, Oliver E. (1985) *The Economic Institutions of Capitalism*. New York: The Free Press.

14
Union Militancy and Plant Designs

Karl Ove Moene

1. Introduction

When firms are faced with militant unions, innovations and plant designs may be inspired by distributional rather than technological considerations. Production techniques can be introduced not because they are efficient but because they allow more control over workers' strategic bargaining position with respect to wages.

These are the kinds of problem addressed in the following. By so doing we take up an old strand of thought. Marx, for instance, believed that employers had strong incentives to partially replace strike-prone workers by machinery. He claimed that 'strikes have regularly given rise to the invention and application of new machines' (cited in Rosenberg, 1976). His reasoning is further developed by Rosenberg (1976: 117–20) who considers fear of strikes to be an important inducement mechanism for labour-saving techniques.

In a similar spirit Offe and Wiesenthal argue that 'by introducing [labour-saving] technical change, capital can release itself partially from its dependence upon the supply of labour, thereby depressing the wage rate' (cited in Elster, 1989: 190). Related points of view are included in the so-called labour process literature (see, for example Braverman, 1974; Marglin, 1974; and Gordon, 1976).

The approach taken in the present chapter pays more attention to the strategic elements in the conflict between labour and capital at the firm level, and the answers differ from those just indicated. The present analysis simplifies and extends some of my earlier work on the subject (see Moene, 1983a; 1983b) by drawing on recent developments in bargaining theory. The approach is also related to Grout (1984) who studies firms' investment policies in the absence of binding wage contracts at the stage when investments are made, and to Hoel (1988) who compares investment incentives in systems with local and central wage bargaining respectively. Compared to this literature I consider more closely the bargaining situation and the conflict weapons at unions' disposal.

In particular I study possible effects of different kinds of industrial action that unions can take.

At least two different ways of obtaining influence in the work place are open to employees. One, which is the topic of the present chapter, is via strong unions forcing concessions by management, the other is by buying (majority) shares which give legal rights to employees to participate in the decision making of the firm. To study possible impacts of union militancy on plant designs is important enough in its own right. Moreover, a better understanding of the behaviour of firms with conflicting interests between labour and capital is important as a contrast to understanding firms with worker ownership. Usually, economists compare worker ownership with a hypothetical competitive firm with a capitalist as chief and workers without a voice in the management. A more interesting procedure is to compare the behaviour of firms with different types of worker influence. This is especially relevant to the Scandinavian bargaining societies where the employees normally pay much more in union fees over their life span than it would have cost them to buy majority positions of the firms where they are employed. (Some tentative calculations for Norway are reported in Moene and Ognedal, 1987.)

One may ask whether there is a continuity in social organization such that a sufficiently high degree of union militancy would force the firm to behave like a labour-managed firm? This question is considered in Section 3. First, however, I discuss, in Section 2, wage bargaining as a non-cooperative game between the firms and the local union. Section 3 then compares the optimal capital–labour ratio of firms with different types of worker influence. Strike-threat and go-slow regimes are compared to worker controlled partnerships. Section 4 provides some generalizations for the capitalist firm faced with unionized workers. We consider the presence of outside wage options and different types workers with respect to internal bargaining positions. Section 5 concludes the chapter.

2. Wage bargaining

The focus is on firm-specific wage bargaining. When the bargaining takes place investments are sunk costs and the bargaining is over the firm's revenues which are denoted by R per period. L is employment which at the stage when the wage bargaining takes place is given by the manning requirements of the chosen production technique. In the bargaining process the union therefore cares about wage level W only.

The model builds on recent advances in bargaining theory (see for example Rubinstein, 1982, and Binmore et al., 1986) where the outcome is a perfect equilibrium of a strategic game. The opposing sides make offers and counter-offers within a stylized environment.

In the present version of the game it is assumed that the bargaining tactic of the union is to commit itself to a conflict of a certain length when it puts forward its wage demand. The intention is of course to convince the opponent that his best choice is to concede.

The unit period length is equal to the short interval between two bargaining rounds. The union moves first and commits itself to a conflict of s periods if the firm does not yield to the initial wage demand. If there is a conflict we assume that the firm earns π per period and the workers w. These conflict payoffs depend on the type of industrial action taken and they will be interpreted differently later. For the moment we shall think of π and w as fixed parameters.

If the threat is carried out no negotiations between the two take place for s periods. The concession process after a conflict is modelled as an ordinary bargaining game where the opposing sides make alternating offers and counter-offers, one in each bargaining round. Accordingly, a picture of the stylized bargaining environment can be drawn as shown in Figure 14.1.

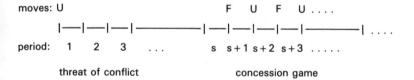

Figure 14.1 Stylized bargaining environment

Here U indicates that the union put forward a wage demand and F indicates that the firm is in position to make a counter-proposal.

The logic of the game is that each player will propose an outcome as beneficial to him as possible, but not so good that the opposing side will turn it down. Hence, if both sides have complete information the threats are not carried out. The equilibrium agreement is reached in the initial period, but the outcome depends on what would have happened if they did not agree.

As usual we must start backwards. First we consider the concession game starting in period $(s+1)$. For simplicity we assume that the time interval between two moves is so short that the length of the wage contract can be considered to be infinite. Let the discount factor of the union be $\delta < 1$ and that of the firm $\beta < 1$. The lowest wage that the union will accept in period $(s+1)$ is W_{s+1} defined by

$$\frac{W_{s+1}}{1 - \delta} = w + \delta \frac{W_{s+2}}{1 - \delta} \tag{14.1}$$

Here W_{s+2} is the highest wage that the firm will accept in bargaining round $(s+2)$ defined by

$$\frac{(R - W_{s+2}L)}{1 - \beta} = \pi + \beta \frac{(R - W_{s+3}L)}{1 - \beta} \tag{14.2}$$

W_{s+3} is the optimal wage demand of the union in bargaining round $(s+3)$. However, since the union then is in exactly the same position as in bargaining round $(s+1)$ we have

$$W_{s+1} = W_{s+3} \tag{14.3}$$

Equations (14.1) to (14.3) define the outcome W_{s+1} of the concession game. The optimal wage demand of the union in the initial period is denoted by W and is implicitly defined by

$$\frac{(R - WL)}{1 - \beta} = \sum_{i=0}^{s-1} \beta^i \pi + \beta^s \frac{(R - W_{s+1}L)}{1 - \beta} \tag{14.4}$$

From the four equations (14.1) to (14.4) we find the equilibrium outcomes of the game which can be written as

$$W = a \left(\frac{R - \pi - wL}{L} \right) + w \tag{14.5}$$

$$R - WL = (1 - a)(R - \pi - wL) + \pi \tag{14.6}$$

where

$$a = 1 - \beta^s \frac{(1 - \delta)}{(1 - \delta\beta)} \tag{14.7}$$

Observe that $0 < a < 1$ and that a is

— increasing in s,

— decreasing in β,
— increasing in δ.

In (14.5) and (14.6), $(R - \pi - wL)$ is the surplus per period which can be obtained by the union and the firm taken together, by not having a conflict. Hence, in the equilibrium solution of the game both sides obtain a certain share of this surplus in addition to their conflict payoff. The parameter a will be called the bargaining power of the union. As shown above this bargaining power is higher the longer the union can precommit itself to a conflict (i.e. the higher is s), the more impatient the firm is (i.e. the lower is β) and the less impatient the union is (i.e. the higher is δ).

The stylized bargaining environment assumed above may seem very restrictive. Most wage negotiations are not so well structured. However, as shown in Moene (1988) the *structure* of the solution in (14.5) and (14.6) is robust for a variety of alternative descriptions including those with a random sequence of bargaining moves. (See also Hoel, 1987.)

3. Capital intensity and types of worker influence

In this section we first study how investment plans are affected by the types of feasible threat used in wage bargaining. The set-up is made as simple as possible to highlight the main points.

Revenues per period R are considered to be a function of employment L and capital K, i.e. $R = R(L,K)$. This function can be interpreted as a choice of technique function with substitution possibilities *ex ante* but fixed coefficients *ex post* (see Johansen, 1972). Further, $R(L,K)$ is assumed to be concave, increasing in both arguments and homothetic. Accordingly we can write $R = \Phi(Lg(k))$ where $k = K/L$ is the capital intensity and $\Phi(.)$ and $g(.)$ are both increasing and concave functions.

The investment decision of the firm is to choose L and k which then remain constant over the economic lifetime of the equipment. Furthermore, as long as quasi rents, $R\text{-}WL$, are positive and no sales constraints prevail the employment level is equal to L in all periods where the equipment is in use. (For a discussion of plant designs with varying capacity utilization and uncertainty see Moene, 1985.)

By assuming that all future periods are alike and neglecting discounting, the profits to be maximized can be written

$$P = (1 - a) (R - wL) + a\pi - qK$$
$$= (1 - a) (\Phi(Lg(k)) - wL) + a\pi - qkL \qquad (14.8)$$

where qkL is the costs of investment. In (14.8) we have inserted the outcome of the wage bargaining from (14.5) and (14.6). Hence, by maximizing P with respect to k and L the firm takes into account how the plant design affects the outcome of future wage bargaining.

Strike threats
When strikes are used as threats the conflict payoffs are

$$w = z \text{ and } \pi = 0 \qquad (14.9)$$

In (14.9) z is the expected support to workers on strike while it is assumed that the firm earns nothing during a work stoppage. Inserting (14.9) in (14.8) we obtain

$$P = (1 - a) (\Phi(Lg(k)) - zL) - qkL \qquad (14.10)$$

The first-order conditions for max P *w.r.t* L and k are

$$(1 - a) \Phi'g(k) - qk = (1 - a)z \qquad (14.11)$$

$$(1 - a) \Phi'g'(k) = q \qquad (14.12)$$

Combining the two we have

$$H(k) = \frac{(1 - a)z}{q} \qquad (14.13)$$

where $H(k)$ is the marginal rate of substitution between L and K which in our case is equal to

$$H(k) = (g(k)/g'(k)) - k \qquad (14.14)$$

$H(k)$ is increasing in k due to the concavity of $g(.)$, that is $H'(k) = -gg''/g'^2 > 0$.

Equation (14.13) determines the optimal capital–labour ratio. The right-hand side of (14.13) is equal to the ratio of the relevant marginal costs of L and K. If the workers were paid an exogenously fixed wage W_f the optimal capital–labour ratio would have been determined by

$$H(k) = W_f/q \qquad (14.15)$$

Let us now consider the impact of internal wage bargaining. Observe first that if instead of bargaining the workers had obtained an exogenously fixed wage W_f equal to their bargaining outcome, W_f would have been strictly higher than z according to (14.5) and (14.9). From (14.13) and (14.15) we then see that the capital–labour ratio is lower with endogenous wages.

Next, increasing union militancy, by being able to commit itself to a longer strike, increases a and lowers the optimal capital–labour ratio according to (14.13).

The above conclusions differ from those of Marx and others. According to our model, strike threats do not induce capital-intensive methods. On the contrary capital-intensive methods make strike threats more efficient for unions because firms will be willing to yield to higher wage demands the higher the value of the labour productivity. As a consequence it is most profitable for firms to let the employees work with labour-intensive methods to prevent the union from obtaining a strong bargaining position.

One might believe that these results hinge on the assumption that the firm is not threatening to sell the equipment in the case of a disagreement in bargaining (since $\pi = 0$ in (14.9)). Firstly, in most cases it is not a credible threat to withdraw from co-operation for ever. Secondly, if it were credible, we would qualitatively have obtained the same results as long as the resale price of the equipment is lower than the price for new equipment q. (Letting the resale price be q_r, this can be seen by inserting $\pi = q_r K < qK$ in (14.8).)

The effect of an increase in a on the employment level L is ambiguous. Intuitively the indeterminacy can be explained as follows: a higher bargaining power of the union induces a more labour-intensive production technique which for a given production capacity of the plant would increase L. The production capacity, however, is not given. The reduction in the profitability of the plant which accompanies increasing union militancy *reduces* the optimal capacity which again means a lower L for a given production technique. In general we cannot tell which of these forces is the strongest.

Go slow or work to rule
Strike threats may sometimes be non-feasible because they are illegal according to higher-level negotiations between employers' and employees' associations or due to governmental legislation. Go

slow or work to rule may then be relevant. Moreover these kinds of industrial action may also be sub-game perfect equilibrium outcomes when both work stoppages and slow-downs are illegal. This is so when the conflict payoffs are highest to both sides with slow-downs. (See Moene, 1988.)

When the intensity of work is slowed down in a wage dispute, the value added of the firm goes down. It may, however, be technically and socially difficult for the firm immediately to economize with other variable factors, and the firm may have to compensate customers for late delivery. All this can lead to a more than proportional reduction in value added caused by a slow-down.

In the following we simply assume that the conflict payoffs in slow-downs are

$$\pi = \Theta R - \alpha \overline{W} L \text{ and } w = \alpha \overline{W}. \tag{14.16}$$

Here $\Theta < 1$ indicates the reduction in value added, $\overline{W}$ is the going wage and $0 \leq \alpha \leq 1$ indicates to what extent it is possible to reduce the going pay during a go-slow action. It should be observed that it is not credible to threaten with such a low Θ that π in (14.16) becomes negative, since the firm will then go temporarily out of operation.

The collaborative work relationships in Scandinavia are very sensitive to work-to-rule threats. The workers have obtained discretionary power over daily operations in the plants. They can therefore credibly threaten to withdraw from co-operation in the case of conflict, which may become very costly to the firm.

Inserting (14.6) in (14.8) gives us

$$P = (1 - a(1 - \Theta))\Phi(Lg(k)) - \alpha \overline{W} L - qkL \tag{14.17}$$

The first-order conditions for max P w.r.t L and k are

$$(1 - a(1 - \Theta)) \, \Phi' g(k) - qk = \alpha \overline{W} \tag{14.18}$$

$$(1 - a(1 - \Theta)) \, \Phi' g'(k) = q \tag{14.19}$$

Combining the two we obtain

$$H(k) = \frac{\alpha \overline{W}}{q} \tag{14.20}$$

where $H(k)$ is the marginal rate of substitution between L and K as defined by (14.14).

Comparing (14.20) with (14.13) we immediately see that as long as $\alpha \overline{W} \geq (1 - a)z$, the optimal capital–labour ratio is higher in the slow-down case. This inequality is always fulfilled as long as the structure of conflict payoffs is such that the compensation for doing some work (when they go slow) is higher than the pay to workers on strike. One might consider threats of go-slow actions and of work to rule as a sign of more collaborative capital–labour relations than strikes. If this is so, the most collaborative regime induces the highest capital–labour ratio.

Further, from (14.5) and (14.15) we find that the equilibrium wage in the slow-down case is

$$W = a(1 - \Theta)R/L + \alpha\overline{W} \tag{14.21}$$

Consider for a moment the bench-mark where the workers obtained the same income as in (14.21) as an exogenously fixed wage W_f. The wage rate W_f would then have been strictly higher than $\alpha\overline{W}$ implying that (as in the case with strike threats) k is lower with endogenous wages according to (14.15) and (14.20).

Contrary to the strike threat case, however, the degree of union militancy in the slow-down regime does not affect the chosen capital–labour ratio since the bargaining power a of the union does not enter in (14.20). For all homothetic choice of technique functions the optimal capital–labour ratio only depends on the relative marginal costs of the factors of production. In the slow-down case these relative costs turn out to be independent of the bargaining power of the union, which is always the case as long as the conflict payoff to the union is paid by the firm and therefore subtracted from its conflict payoff.

A higher bargaining power a has only employment effects. Since k is independent of a we have from (14.18) that

$$\frac{dL}{da} = \frac{(1 - \Theta)\,\Phi'}{(1 - a(1 - \Theta))\,\Phi''g} < 0 \tag{14.22}$$

which shows that employment is lower the higher the union militancy.

The strength of the union may, however, also be reflected in the parameter α. A strong union may be in position to prevent substantial cuts in the going wage during a slow-down. From (14.20) we see that a higher α induces a more capital-intensive production technique. Hence, the stronger the union is (with respect to α), the more capital intensive is the optimal plant design.

Worker-controlled partnership

I end this section by considering a construction where the workers have majority control of the firm but where some other group of factor owners, who are not members of the co-op, have internal bargaining power over the rents created. One may think of managers who are able to withdraw some necessary fixed input in the production process if the two sides do not reach an agreement in the negotiations. It is reasonable to assume that the conflict payoffs are equal to zero for both sides, that is, $\pi = w = 0$, (but the results are qualitatively the same when the managers obtain strike support). When a as before indicates the bargaining power of the (co-op) workers, the managers as a group obtain $(1 - a)R$, and the workers share the residual

$$y = \frac{aR - qkL}{L} \tag{14.23}$$

Since plant design decisions are related to the long run it is reasonable to consider y as the workers maximand. The first-order conditions for max y w.r.t L and k are then

$$a\Phi'g - qk = y \tag{14.24}$$

$$a\Phi'g' = q \tag{14.25}$$

Combining the two we obtain

$$H(k) = y/q \tag{14.26}$$

where $H(k)$ is the marginal rate of substitution as defined by (14.14).

Observe in (14.26) that the marginal costs of L are equal to the total pay y to each worker. In the former two cases the relevant marginal costs of L were less than the pay to each worker. If the pay per worker were the same in the three cases, it then follows that the worker-controlled partnership would have chosen the highest capital–labour ratio.

From (14.23) and (14.26) it follows that the optimal capital–labour ratio is higher the higher the workers' bargaining power versus managers. This is obviously so, since the higher a is, the higher is the maximum value of y in (14.23) (and in (14.26)), and since the plant design is now chosen to maximize y, the optimal k in (14.26) increases with a. Observe also that the highest capital-labour ratio is obtained for the pure labour-managed firm where a is equal to 1.

It should be noticed that the implications of an increase in the bargaining power of workers are just opposite to those of the capitalist firm with strike threats. So in our model it does matter whether capital hires workers or workers hire capital.

4. Outside options and types of workers

In this section we return to the capitalist firm and study the partial implications of outside options and different types of labour power.

Outside options

In the preceding analysis the outcome of wage bargaining depends only on internal factors. In particular I have neglected outside wage options. Such options function as constraints in wage bargaining in the sense that workers can credibly threaten to leave the firm if the outcome from wage bargaining yields a lower wage than the best option outside the firm (see, for example, Binmore, 1987, and Binmore et al., 1986). Hence, if the outside option is W_b the relevant outcome of wage bargaining would be

$$W = \max \, [W_b, \, a \, \frac{R}{L} + (1 - a)w] \tag{14.27}$$

One way to formalize the maximization problem (in the strike threat case, i.e. where $w = z$) is as follows

$$\max_{L,k,W} \, (R - WL - Kq) \tag{14.28}$$

subject to

$$a \, R/L + (1 - a)z - W \leq 0 \tag{14.29}$$

$$W_b - W \leq 0 \tag{14.30}$$

where at least one of the constraints must hold with equality since we are optimizing with respect to W as well. The optimality conditions can be written as

$$\Phi' g(k) - qk - W = \Omega_1 A \tag{14.31}$$

$$\Phi' g'(k) = q + \Omega_1 D \tag{14.32}$$

$$L = \Omega_1 + \Omega_2 \tag{14.33}$$

where

$$A = [\Phi' - \frac{\Phi}{Lg}] \frac{ag}{L} < 0 \tag{14.34}$$

due to the concavity of $\Phi(.)$, and where

$$D = a \, \Phi' g'(k)/L > 0. \tag{14.35}$$

Further, Ω_1 and Ω_2 are both non-negative Kuhn–Tucker multipliers associated with the constraints (14.29) and (14.30) respectively.

It is easily checked that if the constraint in (14.30) is not binding (14.31) to (14.33) are reduced to (14.11) and (14.12). Consider then the case where (14.30) is binding, but (14.29) is not, implying $\Omega_1 = 0$ and $\Omega_2 > 0$. This case follows when the bargaining power of the workers is sufficiently low. The optimal capital intensity is determined by

$$H(k) = W_b/q \tag{14.36}$$

where we have used (14.30) - (14.33) and $\Omega_1 = 0$.

A higher bargaining power of the workers implies that the constraint in (14.29) is binding as well. The optimal capital intensity is then determined by

$$H(k) = \frac{W_b + \Omega_1 A}{q + \Omega_1 D} < \frac{W_b}{q} \tag{14.37}$$

The value of k determined by (14.37) is lower than the one determined by (14.36) since in (14.37) $\Omega_1 > 0$, $A < 0$ and $D > 0$.

In the presence of binding outside options the firm may still have to pay attention to the internal bargaining power of its workers. Two identical firms who have equal wage rates due to the same outside options, may have different optimal capital intensities because of differences in the bargaining power of their local unions. Moreover, even though workers are not paid more than their best outside options the profit of the firm depends on the internal bargaining power of the union. This is so since the stronger the union the more careful the firm must be in its investment policy to avoid ending up paying a higher wage than W_b.

Two types of worker

We now consider two types of worker who perform different tasks in the firm. They also differ with respect to wage determination. Type 1 bargains endogenously with managers over wage rates, while type 2 does not. One might think of type 1 as unionized workers and type 2 as non-union.

Type 1's skill may for instance be regarded as a firm-specific asset and these workers can therefore obtain internal bargaining power giving them higher wages than the best outside options. For that purpose they have formed a local union.

Type 2's skills can be utilized elsewhere with equal efficiency and therefore the firm has to pay them a wage at least equal to their best outside option. It is assumed that they can obtain no more than this wage by internal bargaining at the firm level. Therefore they do not form a *local* union, or they are members of a union which bargains over wages at the sector level. Hence, the wage level for type 2 workers is exogenously fixed (equal to W_b).

This description may in some cases fit for skilled workers (type 1) and unskilled workers (type 2). Other cases may be best described by blue-collar workers as type 1 and white-collar workers as type 2. Be this as it may. We are going to analyse the firm's optimal mixture of fixed capital and the two types of worker, denoted by L_1 and L_2 respectively. Type 1 workers use strike threats and the conflict payoffs are

$$\pi = -(1 - c)W_b L_2, \qquad w = z \qquad (14.38)$$

where the parameter $0 \le c \le 1$ indicates to what extent the firm can lay off type 2 workers in the case of a strike. If the firm can lay off these workers without costs immediately after a strike is called, c is equal to 1. If this cannot be done at all, c is equal to 0. Intermediate cases where $o < c < 1$ are perhaps most likely. The rents which the firm and the union now bargain over are equal to

$$R = \Phi - W_b L_2 \qquad (14.39)$$

where $\Phi = \Phi(L_1, L_2, K)$ now is the choice of technique function. Inserting (14.38) and (14.39) in the profit function $P = (1 - a)(R - wL_1) + a\pi - qK$ (cf. (3.1)) we obtain

$$P = (1 - a)(\Phi - zL_1) - (1 - ac)W_bL_2 - qK$$
$$= (1 - a)[\Phi - zL_1 - \frac{(1 - ac)}{(1 - a)}W_bL_2 - \frac{q}{(1 - a)}K] \qquad (14.40)$$

which the firm wants to maximize. In (14.40) the relevant marginal costs of L_1, L_2 and K are z, $W_b(1 - ac)/(1 - a)$ and $q/(1 - a)$ respectively. We immediately see that, as long as $0 < c < 1$, the relevant marginal costs of L_2 and K are both increasing in a. An increase in the militancy of type 1 workers will therefore bias the choice of technique in an L_1 intensive direction. Accordingly, our model does not support the view that militant workers are likely to be replaced either by machinery or by workers with no bargaining power. On the contrary, as long as it is optimal to have some militant workers it is profitable to have relatively many to prevent them from reaping most of the rent because of high average productivity Φ/L_1. In the extreme case where $c = 1$ the firm can costlessly lay off all type 2 workers during a strike. From (14.40) we then see that the marginal costs of L_2 is their full wage, while the relevant marginal cost of L_1 is z which is less than their full wage. For lower values of c the marginal costs of L_2 are higher than the wage rate W_b.

In passing, observe that there are at least two different reasons for type 1 workers to insist on type 2 workers not being laid off during a strike (that is, a low c).

1. A low value of c reduces the conflict of interests between the two groups with respect to the consequences of a strike.
2. The bargaining outcome yields a higher wage to type 1 the lower is c.

The latter can be seen by writing out the bargaining outcome to type 1 workers as

$$W = a\left(\frac{R - \pi}{L_1}\right) + (1 - a)w = a\left(\frac{\Phi - cW_bL_2}{L_1}\right) +$$

$$(1 - a)z \qquad (14.41)$$

where we have used (14.5) and (14.38). As seen, W is higher the lower is c. If $c = 0$, all wage costs related to type 2 workers are sunk costs at the stage when bargaining takes place. Moreover, when $c > 0$ an increase in the wage of type 2 workers would reduce the bargaining outcome of type 1, while there would be no such effect (except long-run effects via changes in plant designs) of a higher W_b, when $c = 0$.

5. Conclusions

Grout (1984), among others, has shown that collective bargaining might reduce investment. My focus is on the choice of production technique. Collective bargaining within this set-up is likely to reduce firms' optimal capital–labour ratio. Some empirical support for this can be found in Clark (1984), who compares the capital–labour ratios in comparable union and non-union firms in the US economy. She finds a slightly higher capital–labour ratio in the firms with non-union workers.

Section 3 of this chapter demonstrates how the optimal capital–labour ratio depends on *the way* workers obtain influence at the work place. The main distinctions are due to ownership rights and types of industrial action. When workers own their firm, they will choose a capital–labour ratio which is *higher* the higher the share of total rents that the workers can retain. This is in sharp contrast to the capitalist firm with strike-prone workers. In that case the optimal capital–labour ratio is *lower* the higher the share of rents obtained by workers. Hence, there is no support for the view that capitalist firms would choose capital-intensive production techniques as a response to possible strike threats in the future. Moreover, there is no support for the view that the stronger the union the more a capitalist firm resembles a worker co-op. There is a discontinuity of social organization which relates to the ownership structure and which is reflected in the relevant maximand of the plant design decision. A high bargaining power over wages in a capitalist firm cannot be substituted for workers' rights to make the plant design decisions themselves if one wants to obtain similar results.

The main proposition of this chapter is that the choice of technique in a capitalist firm easily becomes biased in favour of inputs that have become more expensive because of higher bargaining power.

Note

This chapter is based on research project 'Wage Formation and Unemployment' at the SAF Centre for Applied Research, Department of Economics, University of Oslo.

I wish to thank Erling Barth, Steinar Holden, Michael Riorden and Michael Wallerstein for helpful comments on an earlier draft.

References

Binmore, K. (1987) 'Bargaining Models', in R. Golombek, M. Hoel and J. Vislie (eds) *Natural Gas Markets and Contracts*. Amsterdam: North-Holland.

Binmore, K., A. Rubinstein and A. Wolinsky (1986) 'The Nash Bargain Solution in Economic Modelling', *Rand Journal of Economics*, 17: 176–88.

Braverman, H. (1974) *Labor and Monopoly Capital*. New York: Monthly Review Press.

Clark, K. (1984) 'Unionization and Firm Performance: the Impact on Profits, Growth, and Productivity', *American Economic Review*, 74: 893–919.

Elster, J. (1989) *The Cement of Society*. Cambridge: Cambridge University Press.

Gordon, D. (1976) 'Capitalist Efficiency and Socialist Efficiency', *Monthly Review*, 28 (3): July–August.

Grout, P. (1984) 'Investment and Wages in the Absence of Binding Contracts – a Nash Bargaining Approach', *Econometrica*, 52: 449–60.

Johansen, L. (1972) '*Production Functions*'. Amsterdam: North-Holland.

Hoel, M. (1987) 'Bargaining Games with a Random Sequence of Who Makes the Offers', *Economics Letters*, 24: 5–9.

Hoel, M. (1988) 'Local Versus Central Wage Bargaining with Endogenous Investments', mimeo. Department of Economics, University of Oslo.

Marglin, S. (1974) 'What Do Bosses Do?', *Review of Radical Political Economics*, 6 (2).

Moene, K. O. (1983a) 'Do Workers' Strike Threats Lead to Machine Intensive Production Techniques?', *Working Papers in Economics of Factor Markets*, No. 45, Stanford University.

Moene, K. O. (1983b) 'Strike Threats and the Choice of Production Techniques', *Memorandum*, Department of Economics, University of Oslo, 25/83.

Moene, K. O. (1985) 'Fluctuations and Factor Proportions: Putty Clay Investments Under Uncertainty', in F. Førsund, M. Hoel and S. Longva (eds) *Production, Multisectoral Growth and Planning*. Amsterdam: North-Holland.

Moene, K. O. (1988) 'Union Threats and Wage Determination', *Economic Journal*, 98: 471–83.

Moene, K. O. and T. Ognedal (1987) 'Profit Sharing and Employee Ownership. Economic Consequences of Alternative Remuneration Schemes and Ownership Structures', (written in Norwegian: 'Utbyttedeling og medarbeidereie: Økonomiske konsekvenser av alternative avlønnings- og eieformer'). Ministry of Finance, Oslo.

Rosenberg, N. (1976) *Perspectives on Technology*. Cambridge: Cambridge University Press.

Rubinstein, A. (1982) 'Perfect Equilibrium in a Bargaining Model', *Econometrica*, 50: 97–109.

15
Can Transaction Cost Economics Explain Trade Associations?

Marc Schneiberg and J. Rogers Hollingsworth

Oliver Williamson's transaction cost economics (TCE) has sparked renewed interest in how economic activity is governed in capitalist societies. Focusing on the transaction, and insisting that economic institutions can and must be explained in terms of their capacities to regulate exchange relations in an efficient and economic manner, Williamson's work rejects technological, legal and class analytic approaches and constructs an alternative theory of economic governance via a logic that dimensionalizes transactions, that identifies the mechanisms and institutional arrangements which 'harmonize the interfaces' between economic actors, and that uses a comparative assessment of the cost and performance attributes of these arrangements to specify the conditions under which various governance structures form and develop (Williamson, 1975, 1981, 1985; Williamson and Ouchi, 1981a). What has emerged from Williamson's logic is a refined and sophisticated theory of why, where and when the 'visible hand' of informal or formal–bureaucratic modes of governance supplement and/or replace the 'invisible hand' of autonomous contracting and the market.

Despite the widespread attention TCE has received, its generality remains substantially unassessed. Facing problems with operationalizing core concepts, and struggling to develop the kinds of data which directly test core propositions, scholarship that empirically examines TCE's capacity to explain the transition from markets to hierarchies is just getting under way. In addition, recent research on the governance of capitalist economies has shown that our analyses must extend beyond markets and hierarchies to consider other governance structures such as various forms of networks and the trade association (for example, Hollingsworth and Lindberg, 1985; Streeck and Schmitter, 1985). Neither markets nor hierarchies, these forms have not yet been adequately examined in transaction cost terms. Thus, serious questions persist regarding the scope and applicability of TCE.

In an effort to explore and define the limits of TCE, this study focuses on the trade association – one of the important economic institutions of capitalism. Using comparative and historical evidence regarding the rise and development of one form of trade association – the price and production association – we assess five basic features of the transaction cost approach:

1 Its claim that the transaction is the basic unit in analysis of economic governance (Williamson, 1985: 41);
2 Its assertion that transaction cost economizing is the central force driving governance transformations (Williamson, 1985: 17);
3 Its argument that non-market governance forms emerge, develop and/or persist when transactions are characterized by uncertainty, frequency and asset specificity (Williamson, 1985: 52–63);
4 Its heavy reliance on intra-industry competition as the basis upon which governance forms are selected (Williamson, 1985: 22–3);
5 Its relegation of power to 'a secondary role in the scheme of things' and insistence on a radical separation between the economic and the political (Williamson, 1985: 123–4).

We do *not* present either a comprehensive account of trade associations or a general theory of governance. However, our analysis shows that TCE can explain only certain aspects of the 'life history' of price and production associations. As we shall see, TCE provides considerable insight into the organizational development of associations. Yet it does not offer much leverage for understanding how, why and under what conditions price and production emerge in the first place, and persist over time.

Economic governance and the trade association

Despite its frequent use, little work has been devoted to specifying precisely what is meant by the term 'governance'. As a first approximation, we define economic governance as the set of practices whereby interdependent economic actors (producers, suppliers, distributors, labour and state agencies) voluntarily co-ordinate and/or hierarchically control their activities and interactions. Such practices include – but are not restricted to – negotiating terms of trade and constructing agreements; representing interests; allocating resources and tasks; setting standards; organizing information flows and monitoring compliance; structuring incentives and mobilizing sanctions; resolving conflict; distributing costs and benefits; and managing adaptation to uncertain and changing conditions (for example, Williamson, 1975, and 1985; Chandler, 1977; Pfeffer and Salancik, 1978; Ouchi, 1980; Daems, 1980; Streeck and Schmitter, 1985). 'Governance structures' are the institutional devices through which economic actors organize these practices and manage inter-organizational relations. The study of governance represents an attempt to understand the motives, dynamics and conditions that lead to the 'choice' of a particular governance structure from a range of possible institutional forms (Williamson and Ouchi, 1981a; Daems, 1983; Williamson, 1985). Thus far, most research on governance has focused on markets and hierarchies, but the trade association is also an important governance form.

Trade associations are a form of regulation in which firms in an industry join together and delegate to a central body the rights and powers to promote common interests, regulate relations within the industry, and order relations between industry members and those whose strategies and activities can decisively affect the industry's fortunes (NICB, 1925; Whitney, 1934; NAM, 1942; Pfeffer and Salancik, 1978; Schmitter and Streeck, 1981; Staber and Aldrich, 1983; Grant and Coleman, 1987). While sharing features with other types of business organization, trade associations generally draw their members from those engaged in the same line of business and address a wide variety of member concerns.

In terms of structure and process, the trade association is neither a market nor a corporate hierarchy. Unlike markets, associations subject economic activity to a form of conscious co-ordination and central regulation. While the organizational form through which they operate varies, trade associations 'internalize' the interactions among previously autonomous firms within deliberately constructed institutional arrangements, and encompass members under some form of inclusive decision-making and authority structure (Streeck and Schmitter, 1985).

However, associational governance is *not* based on property rights, common ownership and the employment relation. Trade associations neither consolidate ownership nor hire their members. Moreover, associations in most countries are rarely able to intervene directly in firms' internal affairs, dictate firm policies, disband members, or resolve interfirm disputes via fiat. Instead, the trade association is a more or less voluntary form of *collective self-regulation* which is based on members' common positions and concerns, and which operates through a process of 'structured bargaining' among members, association officers and important social actors in the external environment (see, for example, Foth,

1930; Galambos, 1965; Streeck, 1983; Streeck and Schmitter, 1985; Schmitter, 1986).

Nevertheless, trade associations have emerged in a wide variety of sectors, and have played (and continue to play) an important role in governing economic activity throughout the capitalist world.[1] For example:

1 By developing standard contracts, instituting price-fixing schemes, organizing joint purchases and sales, and by administering and participating in collective bargaining arrangements with labour, trade associations have structured the processes whereby actors construct agreements and establish terms of trade.

2 By creating licensing schemes, and setting standards regarding safety, quality and competition, they have established norms governing market behaviour.

3 By operating inspection and testing services, conducting surveys, and disseminating information about inventories, costs, prices, economic trends and political developments; by forming consumer complaint bureaus, instituting arbitration, and routinizing bargaining; and by imposing fines, organizing boycotts, and selectively providing access to markets, political representation and other 'categoric goods' (Streeck and Schmitter, 1985), associations have played a role in monitoring and enforcing compliance, reducing conflict, and in enhancing members' adaptive capacities.

4 And by apportioning territories and market shares, matching buyers and sellers, and operating exchanges in which members pool and distribute profits, research, patents, labour and surplus output, they have also assumed numerous allocative functions.

Further, associations have engaged in lobbying, joined with state managers in making and administering policy, and have served as vehicles whereby states regulate economies and mobilize support.

It is, of course, rare that any given trade association performs all of these tasks, for the extent to which associations assume governance functions depends on their structural features and administrative capacities which in turn vary considerably across nations, across sectors and over time (for example, Galambos, 1965; Schmitter and Streeck, 1981; Coleman and Grant, 1984; Grant and Streeck, 1985; Jacek, 1987). Generally, trade associations are most developed in Western Europe – particularly in Austria and Sweden – where professional staffs, compulsory membership, quasi-public status, multiple funding sources, rights to levy fines and regulate access to markets and political bodies, and formal inter-associational linkages provide associations and their leaders with the autonomy and capacity to set industry targets, shape investment, assign territories, fix prices, punish violators, and thereby displace market governance (Traxler, 1985, 1987; Pestoff, 1982; Grant, 1987). At the other extreme lie US and Canadian associations – competing voluntary organizations which depend on members for support, resources and staff, which abstain from monopolizing or selectively allocating much of anything, which enjoy little formal authority and which are thus far less able to displace markets with associational control (Galambos, 1985; Schmitter and Brand, 1979; Coleman and Grant, 1984; Staber and Aldrich, 1983; Coleman, 1985). Note, however, that national differences do not exhaust the full range of variation as there are important sectoral and over-time differences. Nevertheless, the trade association is a significant and widely used governance form, and qualifies with the market and the corporate hierarchy as one of the most important economic institutions of capitalism.

Transaction costs economics and the trade association

The transaction cost approach to economic institutions has been presented as a general theory of why, when and where non-market structures supplement and/or displace the market as the means by which economic activities and interactions are co-ordinated and governed. Since trade associations represent an important instance of 'non-market governance forms', empirical generalizations regarding their life histories can be used to assess the scope and explanatory power of TCE.

Prior research (for example, Chandler, 1977; Schmitter and Brand, 1979; Hawley, 1981; Grant and Coleman, 1987; van Waarden, 1987; Pierenkemper, 1988) has found firms turn to trade associations

1 in response to intra-industry competition;
2 as a reaction to the market power or organizational efforts of an industry's transaction partners;
3 in anticipation of, in conjunction with and/or in response to state regulation of the industry.

As space is limited, and as we seek to engage fully the empirical and theoretical material, we focus on the first set of processes – the rise and development of the price and production association.

'Ruinous competition' and the trade association

Chronic or sudden overcapacity, particularly in conjunction with high fixed costs and low to medium levels of industrial concentration constitute the principal set of conditions under which firms in an industry find it in their interest to form and reform price and production associations (for example, Whitney, 1934; Galambos, 1965; Chandler, 1977; Feldman and Nocken, 1975; Hawley, 1981; Lamoreaux, 1985; van Waarden, 1987; Daviet, 1988; Davenport-Hines, 1988; Turner, 1988). Resulting from postwar demobilization, depression, or foreign competition, overcapacity confronts firms with idle plants, accumulating inventory, and through these the real and/or anticipated threats of sustained price warfare, severe price declines and business failure. In response to these threats, firms which lack the protection provided by an oligopolistic industry structure frequently seek to control prices, production and investment by forming trade associations.

The use of the price and production association to manage cartel arrangements has occurred in a wide variety of sectors throughout the capitalist world. In the US, the railroads were among the first to resort to this measure, but the strategy quickly spread, and by the 1880s, associations 'became part of the normal way of doing business in most American industries' (Chandler, 1977: 316–17; Galambos, 1965; Becker, 1971). Like their counterparts in the railroad industry, manufacturing and commercial associations sought to avoid price warfare and mitigate the effects of overcapacity by organizing industry-wide price-fixing; by setting production quotas and arranging for members to produce at some fraction of capacity; and by assigning firms the exclusive right to sell their output in a particular locale (Jones, 1922; NICB, 1925; Whitney, 1934; Galambos, 1965; Chandler, 1977; Becker, 1971; Lamoreaux, 1985).

Similar associational strategies were pursued in other nations. Beginning in 1880, firms in Japanese industries as diverse as cotton, flour, electrical equipment, paper, cement, pig iron, and coal sought to control price, production and investment through their associations, many of which were born or reorganized during depressions and which 'spread in earnest during the Showa panic' (Kikkawa, 1988: 7, 21–32). Likewise suffering from the worldwide depressions in the last quarter of the nineteenth century, firms in a number of German industries – notably iron and steel, chemicals and coal – whole-heartedly embraced this associational strategy: by 1907 almost 25%, and by 1938 nearly 50% of Germany's industrial output was subject to price and production controls that were devised and managed by trade associations (Kocka, 1980: 88–9; Feldman and Nocken, 1975). The same forces evoked comparable responses in Britain (Hannah, 1980; Davenport-Hines, 1988; Turner, 1988) and in France (Levy-Leboyer, 1980; Daviet, 1988).

While price and production associations generally emerge as the result of firms' independent efforts, state agencies and state managers have sometimes taken the lead in the construction and development of this institutional form. During the First World War, for example, the American state promoted the formation of associations in a number of industries as a part of the war effort (NICB, 1925; Foth, 1930; Cuff, 1973); and during the early New Deal, comparable actions were undertaken in an attempt to facilitate economic recovery (Whitney, 1934; Hawley, 1966; Himmelberg, 1976; Skocpol and Finegold, 1982). Similar policies have been pursued by other states, particularly in 'late developing' nations such as Japan and Germany, where state actors routinely fostered the construction of associations as an integral component of their war-making and economic development programmes (Marburg, 1964; Feldman and Nocken, 1975; Caves and Uekusa, 1976; Magaziner and Hout, 1980; Miyamoto, 1988).

In all of these countries, industry members and/or state agencies became convinced that their interests were no longer served by the unqualified operation of the market, and sought to supplement and even displace the market governance of competitive relations with associational modes of control. As noted earlier, the historical record of the use of these non-market forms constitutes a basis upon which TCE can be empirically assessed.

The applicability of transaction cost economics

Price and production associations typically develop in three stages: initial emergence, organizational development, and ongoing reproduction or death. Initial emergence refers to the shift from market (or hierarchical) governance to collective self-regulation, and often involves the rise of 'dinner-clubs' and the formation of 'gentlemen's agreements'. Organizational development refers to the fortification of the association's governance capacities in response to problems of cheating, entry and defection, and involves firms' efforts to make the association capable of enforcing price, production and/or investment agreements. These efforts can produce substantial changes in the organizational form through which self-regulation occurs. Ongoing reproduction or death refers to the association's ultimate prospects, and includes the extent to which the association displaces – or is displaced by – alternative governance forms in the longer term.

The correspondence between this analytic scheme and the actual trajectory of associational development is, of course, variable. Well developed forms sometimes emerge from the outset, and some associations disband or persist without a great deal of organizational development. Nevertheless, many associations do exhibit three empirically distinct developmental stages, and all confront problems of controlling markets, containing defection and ensuring the ongoing maintenance of operations. More importantly, this scheme allows us to consider separately the different forces at work at different points in an association's development, and thus permits a more nuanced assessment of TCE.

Initial emergence Explaining the rise of non-market governance forms first requires a theory of genesis or, at the very least, some specification of the motives which lead actors to transform institutional arrangements. While TCE is largely functionalist in character, it does suggest that economic actors are motivated by interests in transaction cost economizing. Moreover, competition looms large in the model, and while TCE is not a theory of strategic choice, it implies that actors turn to non-market forms in order to gain competitive advantage.

The formation of price and production associations does represent a competitive strategy. However, the motives involved here have little to do with enhancing efficiency or with reducing the costs of establishing, monitoring and governing exchange relations. Instead, the main purpose and intended effects of these forms are to fix prices, limit output and more generally facilitate conscious, co-ordinated efforts to control competition, stabilize profits, and shield members from the adverse consequences of untrammelled market competition. In essence, price and production associations are created for strategic and distributional purposes: they are formed in an attempt by firms to protect and enhance their market positions, shift the burden of adjustment on to their transaction partners, and extract from these partners a form of rent. By rejecting 'monopoly' in favour of efficiency purposes, and by putting aside the possibility that some governance transformations are driven by purely distributional concerns, TCE leaves us without an account of the motives which prompt firms to abandon markets in favour of associational control.

Explaining governance transformations also presupposes a specification of the 'object' of governance, that is, an account of the types of activity and relationship that are co-ordinated and regulated by governance structures. In this respect, TCE is quite clear: the transaction is the basic unit of analysis. Vertical integration, internal labour markets and so on all represent alternatives to the market governance of the transfer of goods and services between suppliers and consumers, managers and workers, and investors and firms. Further, such explanations require an enumeration of the conditions under which non-market governance forms emerge. Here again, TCE is very clear: they emerge when transactions are characterized by uncertainty, frequency and asset-specificity. Under these conditions, managing transactions by market contracts becomes costly, and actors face powerful incentives to supplement or displace market governance with non-market institutions.

The rise of price and production associations poses problems for both of these claims. First, the construction of these associations represents a process in which similarly placed firms create agreements amongst themselves in order to organize, stabilize and govern relations *within* the industry, that is, *horizontal relations among non-transacting competitors*. To be sure, these agreements are designed to influence the terms of trade between industry members and their transaction partners. Yet unlike vertically integrated firms, internal labour markets, or other forms of associational governance, price and production associations do not subject the behaviour of the industry's transaction partners to administrative controls, co-ordinate the activities of the transacting parties, or regulate directly the transfer of resources between industry members and their exchange partners. Instead they are concerned with intra-industry competition, confine their efforts to one side of the market – generally the selling side, and are principally designed to stabilize terms of trade *indirectly* by co-ordinating the activities of, regulating relations between, and forging a united front among firms located in *identical positions* within the economic division of labour. Put simply, the rise of price and production associations involves the construction of agreements which regulate non-contractual – competitive – relations, and which are the outcome, not the principle object, of the associations' initial governance practices. Theorizing governance structures and their transformations strictly in terms of how transactions are regulated and agreements enforced thus constitutes too narrow a basis upon which to describe fully the object and operations involved in the emergence of this associational form.

Furthermore, since price and production associations are principally concerned with governing horizontal relations, TCE's focus on transactional dimensions to explain the rise of non-market forms leaves it poorly placed to specify the conditions under which these types of trade association actually emerge and develop. It is certainly true that such associations form in response to deteriorating terms of trade. Moreover, factors such as frequency, uncertainty and asset specificity *may* contribute to this process indirectly: firms rarely form associations where one-time transactions are involved, and associational strategies are more likely to emerge when actors are unable to redeploy assets across markets and thereby exit from unprofitable situations.

Yet the historical record indicates that the factors which generate declining terms of trade and thus the condition under which price and production associations emerge have less to do with characteristics of transactions than with the characteristics of the industry, that is, with features which render horizontal relations sufficiently problematic for industry members to seek relief from competitive pressures. As already seen, it is industry-level factors – overcapacity, high fixed costs, and low to medium levels of concentration – that engender acute competitive difficulties and produce efforts to manage competitive interdependence via associations. Overcapacity, particularly in conjunction with high fixed costs, creates powerful incentives for price cutting; and unlike firms in oligopolistic industries, firms in relatively unconcentrated industries cannot achieve stability through price leadership and discipline, but must rely instead on price, production and investment agreements organized through trade associations (Galambos, 1965; Feldman and Nocken, 1975; Chandler, 1977; Lamoreaux, 1985; van Waarden, 1987). None of these factors is systematically invoked by TCE.

Finally, theories of governance inevitably make a set of assumptions regarding how broader social, political and cultural factors shape governance transformations. To its credit, TCE has been quite clear in this regard: it argues that there is a fundamental distinction between the 'economic' and the 'political' arena – that the two domains are organized according to very different principles – and proceeds as if 'economic' phenomena can be adequately described and explained in isolation from their socio-political context (Williamson, 1985: 124–5; Granovetter, 1985). Derived from neoclassical economics, this stance further compromises TCE's ability to explain the rise of price and production associations. For comparative analysis indicates that these processes are profoundly shaped by state strategies and policies, that is, on factors which TCE brackets as unimportant.[2]

In Japan and in European nations such as Austria, Germany, Sweden, Switzerland and the Netherlands, states have created a legal and political environment which facilitated the creation of price and production associations (for example, Marburg, 1964; Feldman and Nocken, 1975; Caves and Uekusa, 1976; Keller, 1980, 1981; Kocka, 1980; Pestoff, 1982; Magaziner and Hout, 1980; Traxler, 1985; Farago, 1987; Jacek, 1987; van Waarden, 1987; Kikkawa, 1988; Miyamoto, 1988). All of these countries have passed laws which make legal at least some forms of interfirm agreement regarding prices, production, and/or investment. For example, amendments to Japan's Anti-Monopoly Law allow Japanese associations to form cartels which, among other things, regulate investment and capacity, set export price floors and allocate production among member firms (Magaziner and Hout, 1980). Moreover, states in many of these countries have promoted the formation of associations in 'strategic' sectors, and have provided firms in these industries with powerful incentives for undertaking these efforts. The Swedish state, for example, funded organizational efforts among agricultural firms throughout the 1930s and 1940s as a part of its attempt to establish a system of quasi-public price regulation associations (Pestoff, 1982). Furthermore, state actors in some of these nations have gone as far as legally compelling firms to create price and production associations, as was the case, for example, in Germany during the two World Wars (Marburg, 1964; Feldman and Nocken, 1975). In all of these countries, state policy has had a salutary effect on the formation of price and production associations.

In contrast, the American state has displayed an exceptional enmity toward price and production associations since the early twentieth century (for example, NICB, 1925; Foth, 1930; Whitney, 1934; Galambos, 1965; Hawley, 1966; Cuff, 1973; Himmelberg, 1976; Chandler, 1977; Schmitter and Brand, 1979; Keller, 1980, 1981; Skocpol and Finegold, 1982; Lamoreaux, 1985). While state agencies have at times promoted the construction of associations, such efforts were temporary, short-lived expedients; emerged as responses to tremendous economic or political upheavals such as war and the Great Depression; and represented radical departures from the policy of consistently abstaining from encouraging associational formation. In fact, the American state has vigorously opposed the formation of price and production associations. Committed to liberal principles, and actively pursing antitrust policies, the courts, the Federal Trade Commission, the Justice Department and the US Congress have produced a legal and political environment which is quite hostile to the price and production association, and which has led American business to avoid studiously even the hint of an attempt to control competition via associative behaviour. Thus, state policy in the US has functioned to suppress the formation of price and production associations in all but a few sectors.

In sum, the transaction cost approach provides little leverage for explaining the initial emergence of price and production associations. First, the shift from markets to collective self-regulation of competition via associations is driven not by transaction cost economizing, but rather by strategic and distributional concerns. Moreover, this governance form is created to regulate non-contractual relations among competitors; and its emergence hinges less on transactional characteristics than on industry-level characteristics. Further, state policy – a factor bracketed by TCE's separation of economics and politics – plays a central role in generating variation in the extent and rate of associational formation.

Organizational development The construction of agreements regarding price, production and so on does not exhaust the life history of the price and production association. As noted earlier, the creation of associations exposes industry members to new kinds of problems, subjects firms to new kinds of pressures, and spurs a process of organizational development. In particular, newly formed associations are frequently forced to (1) deal with members who cheat on their agreements; (2) contend with new entrants; and (3) modify prices, market shares and production quotas when business conditions change (for example, Galambos, 1965; Chandler, 1977; Lamoreaux, 1985; Kikkawa, 1988). To resolve these problems, firms have sought to fortify their associations' governance capacities, have delegated rights and powers to full-time professional staffs, and have instituted a variety of bureaucratic controls. In some cases, associations have gone as far as forming selling 'syndicates' which purchase members' output, sell it at a fixed price and distribute the proceeds according to a quota system; in other cases, associations have organized 'money pools' which tax overproducers and subsidize firms which produced below quota; and it is hardly unusual for associations to seek state aid, either in the form of protective tariffs, and/or of laws which ban new entry, make membership compulsory and which grant associations rights to regulate investment (Jones, 1922; NICB, 1925; Chandler, 1977; Kocka, 1980; Levy-Leboyer, 1980; Streeck and

Schmitter, 1985; Jacek, 1987; Daviet, 1988; Pierenkemper, 1988; Turner, 1988).

TCE is quite well placed to explain these developments. To begin with, the initial formation of the price and production association is a process whereby like firms *create* exchange relations amongst themselves. It is a contracting operation in which firms agree to perform in a particular way – to maintain a minimum price, produce at a certain percentage of capacity, restrict sales to a particular locale, and so on – in exchange for a commitment from other firms to perform in the same or similar manner. Moreover, *the organizational innovations that emerge as associations become institutionalized represent vehicles through which these newly created exchange relations are monitored, regulated and maintained.* For example, inspection services, reporting requirements and information-gathering departments serve important surveillance functions and enable associations to monitor the extent to which members comply with agreements and sustain contractual commitments. Similarly, structural features such as money pools, selling syndicates and special departments charged with levying fines and organizing boycotts all operate to provide the association with the means to enforce contracts, ensure that members abide by the terms of their agreements, and selectively punish cheaters. Further, forecasting services, grievance procedures, patent stockpiles, and compulsory membership allow the association to manage changes in business conditions, contain conflict among the transacting parties, and prevent outsiders from disrupting the transactional nexus. In short, the structural features connected with the development of the association constitute devices whereby members manage interfirm agreements, subject intra-industry transactions to administrative controls, and regulate directly the exchange relations they have created amongst themselves. For this aspect of the price and production association's life history, TCE's claim that the transaction is the basic unit of analysis is clearly warranted.

The record regarding the structural reform of the price and production association also confirms TCE's claims concerning the problems, forces and motives which prompt actors to supplement or displace contractual relations with more developed, hierarchical and authoritative forms of control. First, *the emergence of associations transforms the problem of regulating competition into a problem of contracting, and subjects participants to pressures and difficulties of a transaction cost nature.* As seen earlier, newly formed associations frequently have to contend with defection and free-riding. On the one hand, association members often try to gain short-term advantages by producing above quota, selling below the fixed price, or by otherwise reneging on their contractual commitments, On the other hand, outsiders seek to profit from artificial scarcity and high prices by entering the market, refusing to join the association, and by selling output just below the cartel price. Both of these strategies represent instances of 'self-interest seeking with guile' which exposes associations to the hazards of opportunism, and which make negotiating, expanding and maintaining the nexus of interfirm agreements extremely difficult. Such difficulties are often compounded by the fact that the limits on rationality prevent associations from monitoring compliance, keeping track of new entrants, and anticipating changes in market conditions that could render interfirm agreements maladaptive.

More generally, the process of organizing and maintaining a price and production association often involves significant transaction costs. Firms have to communicate to each other their intentions and understandings of the situation; negotiate and renegotiate the terms under which they will co-operate; provide one another with assurances that they will abide by their agreements; and monitor and enforce compliance. These operations can consume a great deal of time and resources, especially where the limits of bounded rationality are reached and incentives for opportunism are present. In short, many associations find that bounded rationality and opportunism produce serious contracting problems, generate substantial transaction costs, and undermine the efficacy of collective self-regulation.

Furthermore, *associations deliberately institute the types of organizational innovations just discussed in order to resolve these problems, that is, to overcome the difficulties and reduce the costs involved in making, regulating and adjusting intra-industry transactions.* By forming inspection departments, developing forecasting services, and delegating surveillance functions to a full-time professional staff, associations and their members seek to enhance their information-processing capabilities, and thereby to economize on bounded rationality. Further, firms solicit state assistance, attempt to make membership compulsory, institute grievance procedures, organize selling syndicates, money pools and the like in an attempt to contain intra-industry conflict and safeguard members from the hazards of opportunism. More generally, firms centralize association operations, create specialized governance structures, and delegate rights, resources and powers to full-time association officers in order to reduce transaction costs. By reorganizing the association in this manner, firms not only simplify the tasks of incorporating new members, managing adaptation to changing conditions and maintaining the integrity of the transactional nexus, but they also relieve themselves of the burden of having to maintain separate contractual relations with each and every other member of the association. Put simply, the organizational development of the price and production association is driven by transaction cost economizing.

Finally, the historical record indicates that TCE correctly specifies some of the conditions under which firms embark on a path of structural reform. Uncertainty clearly plays an important role. Market turbulence, sudden and unanticipated declines in demand, and/or rapid change in the composition of the industry generate renewed pressures for price competition; strain associations' forecasting, regulatory and adaptive capacities; and thereby prod members to introduce organizational innovations (for example, Chandler, 1977; Lamoreaux, 1985; Pierenkemper, 1988). The frequency of transactions – or more properly, the duration of the interfirm agreements – also appears to affect the likelihood of organizational development. Where overcapacity is a chronic problem, firms face the prospect of having to maintain the association over a long period of time, and thus experience powerful pressures for creating specialized governance structures and hiring full-time association staffs (for example, Galambos, 1965; van Waarden, 1987). Further, asset specificity contributes to structural reform, although the ability to redeploy assets may have contradictory effects. On the one hand, high asset specificity may have a 'lock in' effect and produce incentives for organizational development. On the other hand, low levels of asset specificity make it easier for outsiders to enter the market, a problem that plays a major role in prompting firms' efforts to fortify their associations' governance capacities (for example, Lamoreaux, 1985; Kikkawa, 1988).

Nevertheless, a full specification of the conditions under which organizational development takes place requires us to go beyond TCE's particular formulations, as the structural reform of the price and production association frequently hinges on the characteristics of the industry involved. The level of fixed costs, for example, plays an extremely important role in promoting associational development (for example, Becker, 1971; Chandler, 1977; Lamoreaux, 1985). As fixed costs increase, firms experience intense pressures to keep their plants 'running full', more frequently succumb to the price-cutting temptation, and find that highly centralized and well developed associations are required to maintain the transactional nexus. Also affecting the likelihood of structural reform are the size and number of firms in the industry (for example, Galambos 1965; Feldman and Nocken, 1975; Streeck and Schmitter, 1985; Turner, 1988). Where firms are large and few in number, they are generally able to maintain associational discipline via informal and decentralized means. But where firms are small and numerous, transaction costs increase, informal associations prove unable to monitor or enforce compliance, and firms turn to more formalized and centralized associational forms. Finally, the costs and difficulties involved in regulating inter-industry transactions increase as members are divided by 'rival projects' such as ethnicity or region, when there is substantial project heterogeneity, or when firms in an industry use different processes or confront different costs and constraints (for example, Galambos, 1965; Feldman and Nocken, 1975; Schmitter, 1986; van Waarden, 1987). In short, the magnitude of contracting problems, the costs of governing intra-industry transactions, and the extent to which firms fortify their associations' capacities are largely determined by industry-level characteristics which lie outside TCE's present formulations.

Overall, the evidence regarding the organizational development of the price and production association confirms TCE's core claims and insights. Once associations are in place, intra-industry transactions become important, and members find themselves exposed to problems of contracting, that is, to limits, pressures and constraints that figure centrally in the transaction cost approach. Moreover, these difficulties produce interests in resolving contracting problems and in reducing transaction costs, interests which lead firms to transform the organizational structure of the association and institute devices which regulate intra-industry exchange relations. Further, TCE does specify some of the conditions under which firms fortify associations, although the model must be extended to incorporate the role that industry-level factors play in generating transactional difficulties and precipitating structural reform.

Reproduction or death   The last set of processes to be considered involve factors and forces which promote or undermine the longer-term survival of the price and production association. Of particular interest here is the extent to which the collective self-regulation of competition displaces – or is displaced by – alternative governance forms.

TCE presents two kinds of argument regarding the conditions under which governance forms are reproduced. The first argument maintains that the reproducibility of governance forms hinges on their transaction cost consequences, that is, on whether or not they provide actors with more opportunities to economize on transaction costs than do alternative governance forms. When firms achieve a more efficient or 'discriminating' match between governance structures and underlying transactions, they can realize considerable cost savings. These savings, in turn, allow firms to outperform their less efficiently organized rivals, and to increase their chances of survival in the competitive process. Over 'intervals of five to ten years', such competitive processes effectively 'perform a sort between more and less efficient modes and . . . shift resources in favor of the former' (Williamson, 1985: 22–3). In short, governance forms survive because they are 'fitter', that is, more efficient ways of regulating transactions than alternative forms, and are thus better able to withstand the selection processes involved in economic competition.

A second argument emerges from a series of comments on the history of American railroad cartels (Williamson, 1985: 159–60, 277–9). According to these comments, the railroad cartels were disbanded first, because they encountered severe auditing limits and thus could not determine whether or not members had complied with agreements; and second, because they were unable to localize discipline, selectively punish opportunism, and overcome powerful incentives to cheat. Implied here is the more general claim that the survival of collective self-regulation hinges on the extent to which the association is able to monitor and enforce interfirm agreements.

The historical record regarding the reproduction or death of the price and production association poses serious problems for both of these formulations. To begin with, competition is not a constant. It is variable, an endogenous factor or constraint that is an object of struggle and strategic behaviour. In fact, price and production associations in some countries have sometimes been quite successful in reducing and even eliminating competition for long periods of time (for example, Feldman and Nocken, 1975; Keller, 1981; Grant, 1985; Pestoff, 1987; Kikkawa, 1988). Thus our models cannot simply assume that competitive pressures sort out governance forms, even in the long run.

Furthermore, while the evidence supports TCE's claim that the survival of the price and production association depends on its capacities to enforce inter-agreements, these capacities are directly and fundamentally determined by political factors. More specifically, comparative analysis indicates that the extent to which associations were able to forge agreements within an industry, impose discipline on members, cope with the problem of new entrants, and displace market governance ultimately depends on state structures and state policies – that is, on factors largely ignored by TCE.

As noted earlier, the American state has strenuously opposed the regulation of competition by price and production associations (Naylor, 1921; Jones, 1922; NICB, 1925; Foth, 1930; Whitney, 1934; NAM, 1942; Galambos, 1965; Hawley, 1966, 1981; Cuff, 1973; Himmelberg, 1976; Chandler, 1977; Schmitter and Brand, 1979; Keller, 1980, 1981; Skocpol and Finegold, 1982; Lamoreaux, 1985). Courts and regulators refused to make cartel agreements legally binding; state and federal legislatures passed antitrust laws, including the 1890 Sherman Act that declared illegal 'every contract, combination . . . or conspiracy, in restraint of trade'; and the Supreme Court rendered decisions from 1895 to 1925 which dissolved associations, fined members, and which placed cartel practices (output limits, price fixing, market division) and their instruments (joint selling, boycotts, pools, exclusion) under a ban of law. While federal agencies have at times advocated associational forms of governance – notably the War Industries Board during the First World War, Hoover's policies within the Commerce Department in the 1920s and the NRA in the early New Deal – departmental rivalries, separation of powers and other structural features of the US political system prevented these agencies from achieving more than partial, short-term successes. Overall, with a few exceptions – for example insurance, agriculture, and professional sports – the structure and policy of the American state have generally functioned to support liberal principles, and to deprive associations of the rights, resources and capacities needed to organize effective cartels.

Since the American state barred associations from making price and production agreements, from enforcing discipline and from erecting barriers to entry, American business began in the 1890s to search for other means of controlling competition. Firms in highly fragmented sectors such as lumber and cotton experimented with scaled-down associations which eschewed central direction in favour of product standardization, uniform cost accounting and 'open price' schemes which sought to stabilize competitive relations indirectly by eliminating 'waste', by restricting competition to price, and by providing firms with the data needed to make independently price and output decisions that would reduce overcapacity and the likelihood of price warfare (Jones, 1922; NICB,

1925; Whitney, 1934; Galambos, 1965; Hawley, 1981). Firms in more concentrated sectors – such as railroads, petroleum and steel – abandoned price and production associations; turned to alternative institutional arrangements for managing competitive relations including the trust, the holding company and the horizontal merger; and ultimately achieved some degree of stability via the price leadership afforded by oligopolistic structures (Chandler, 1977; Keller, 1980; Lamoreaux, 1985). In both cases, the American state's hostility towards the collective self-regulation of competition rendered the price and production association non-reproducible, and precipitated a shift towards alternative governance forms.

In contrast, British state policy before the Second World War tolerated price and production associations and effectively slowed the pace of corporate consolidation (Schmitter and Brand, 1979; Hannah, 1980; Keller, 1980, 1981; Turner, 1988). While British courts sometimes decided against attempts to impose cartel provisions on members, they imposed no general ban on cartel agreements, vigorously defended the freedom of contract, and consistently ruled that contracts among associations and third parties were binding even when they involved restraints on trade. Moreover, there were no British antitrust statutes until the 1948 and 1956 Restrictive Practices Acts. In France too, the state was far less opposed to cartel associations than was the case in the US, and there were even instances when state-owned enterprises joined associations (Keller, 1980, 1981; Daviet, 1988).

Yet it was Japan and a few continental countries that departed most dramatically from liberal principles and the US antitrust tradition. In Germany, government support of price and production associations before the Second World War '[resulted in a] degree of cartelization unmatched elsewhere' (Keller, 1981: 61; Marburg, 1964; Feldman and Nocken, 1975; Keller, 1980; Kocka, 1980; Poensgen, 1983). Courts and legislatures sustained boycotts and rebates, held that price, production and market sharing agreements were legally binding and in the public interest, and thereby placed the power of the state firmly behind associational governance. Further, state agencies actively promoted cartels and occasionally compelled non-members to join associations. It was not until 1957 that the German government imposed a general ban on cartels. Passed partly in response to Allied pressures, the 1957 Cartel Law limits firms' abilities to form associations; yet it contains exceptions, and has sometimes been used to support quotas, syndicates, and rationalization cartels.

Like its German counterpart, the Japanese state actively

sustained the collective self-regulation of competition before the end of the Second World War, particularly in the 1930s when the passage of supporting legislation prompted and even compelled firms in a large number of industries to form or reorganize price and production associations (Kikkawa, 1988; Miyamoto, 1988). While this practice was curtailed when the Allies imposed on Japan the Antimonopoly Act of 1947 – an act which prohibited cartel agreements and which banned associations from limiting entry, restricting member activities and so on – the Diet and the Ministries have since weakened this statute significantly by passing laws that permit whole classes of price and production associations and by supporting the use of hundreds of rationalization, depression, export, import and small business cartels (Caves and Uekusa, 1976; Magaziner and Hout 1980). State policies have also promoted the reproduction of price and production associations in Switzerland, the Netherlands, Sweden and Austria. By granting associations rights to compel participation and regulate members' investment decisions, the state in these countries has effectively promoted the long-term use of the price and production association (Pestoff, 1982; Traxler, 1985; Jacek, 1987; Farago, 1987; van Waarden, 1987).

In sum, comparative historical analysis reveals that state policy toward economic governance plays an important role in determining the extent to which price and production associations (1) persist over time, and (2) displace or are displaced by alternative governance forms. Where governments opposed the collective self-regulation of competition, the price and production association proved non-reproducible, and firms either turned to weaker forms of associational control or sought to control competition through trusts, holding companies, horizontal mergers and oligopolistic structures. But where governments supported this regulatory mode, associations' long-term survival prospects were dramatically enhanced; firms turned more slowly to and relied less heavily on the horizontal merger, and opted instead to supplement and even displace market governance of competitive relations via centrally regulated associational behaviour. Thus, TCE's failure to incorporate the state into its analysis leaves it unable to account for the cross-national, cross-sectoral and over-time variations in the reproductive histories of the price and production association.

Conclusion

Can transaction cost economics explain trade associations? Focusing on one associational form, our analysis indicates (1) that different factors and forces operate at varying points in the price and production association's life history, and (2) that TCE's applicability and explanatory power critically depends on the aspect or phase of this life history that is under consideration. With regard to the *organizational development* of the association, the evidence largely confirms TCE's core concepts and propositions. The transaction is the basic unit of analysis; bounded rationality and opportunism expose association members to problems of contracting; and the structural reforms of the associations are driven by an interest in transaction cost economizing. Furthermore, TCE correctly specifies some of the factors which promote structural reform, although the model must be extended to describe fully the conditions under which these reforms are undertaken. Above all, firms create more developed and hierarchical forms when transaction costs are high, and when prior forms prove incapable of managing adaptation to changing circumstances and selectively punishing opportunism. Thus our analysis shows that TCE has provided us with a set of variables and propositions that explanations of associational development can only ignore at great peril.

However, our analysis also demonstrates that TCE cannot explain either the *initial emergence* or the *ongoing reproduction* of the price and production association. Firms create these associations for strategic and distributional purposes, that is, to enhance their market power and shift the risks and burdens of adjustment on to their exchange partners. Moreover, while firms mobilize this associative strategy in order to regulate relations in which they find themselves vulnerable to the strategic behaviour of others, the relations at issue do not involve prior transfers of goods and services, and the extent to which firms find themselves vulnerable does not depend on the nature or properties of exchange relations. Instead, the principal object of the price and production association is to regulate horizontal relations among non-transacting competitors, and the shift from markets to collective self-regulation is far more sensitive to industry and political factors than it is to characteristics of transactions. Finally, state policy toward economic governance – a factor ignored by TCE – plays a far more important role than competition and transaction cost economizing in determining whether or not price and production associations displace alternative forms and persist over the long run. Thus, TCE's core concepts and propositions do not account for the rise and reproduction of price and production associations.

While further research is required, our analysis indicates that TCE's ability to explain trade associations is limited. Strategic considerations often dominate associative behaviour; non-transactional relations figure centrally in associational governance; and the state plays a fundamental role in determining the extent to which transactional and non-transactional relations can be subjected to collective self-regulation. Note, however, that we do not conclude that TCE should be rejected. The considerable insight it provides into certain aspects of the trade association's life history; the fact that the study of governance is still in its adolescence; and the ongoing refinement of the transaction cost framework militate against such a hasty conclusion. Instead, we conclude that a complete account of the rise, development and persistence of the trade association requires us to retain many of TCE's core concepts and insights, and incorporate its claims within a more general theory of the factors, forces, motives and contextual conditions that underlie governance structures and their transformation.

Notes

In writing this chapter, we are very indebted to Philippe Schmitter, who more than anyone else has put the study of trade associations on the research agenda of those who are interested in the governance of capitalist societies. We would also like to thank Oliver Williamson, Bo Gustafsson, Masahiko Aoki, Wolfgang Streeck, William Coleman, Wyn Grant, Leon Lindberg, Charles Halaby, David Stark, Lauren Edelman, Ann Miner, Terry Amburgey, Robert Freeland, and the participants in the SCASSS conference on 'The Firm as a Nexus of Treaties' for their comments and support. Errors, omissions and misrepresentations are, of course, the authors' responsibility.

1. For an overview of the structure and function of trade associations, see Schmitter and Streeck (1981). On trade associations in the US, see Jones (1922), NICB (1925), Foth (1930), Whitney (1934), NAM (1942), Galambos (1965), Hawley (1966, 1981), Becker (1971), Cuff (1973), Himmelberg (1976), Chandler (1977), Skocpol and Finegold (1982), Staber and Aldrich (1983), Lamoreaux (1985); in the UK, Hannah (1980), Turner (1988), Davenport-Hines (1988); in Canada, Coleman (1985); in France, Levy-Leboyer (1980), Daviet (1988); in Germany, Marburg (1964), Feldman and Nocken (1975), Kocka (1980), Poensgen (1983), Streeck (1983), Pierenkemper (1988); in Switzerland, Farago (1985); in the Netherlands, de Vroom (1985), van Waarden (1985); in Austria, Marin (1983), Traxler (1985); in Japan, Kikkawa (1988), Miyamoto (1988); in Sweden, Pestoff (1982). For a comparison of the US and UK, see Schmitter and Brand (1979); Germany and the UK, Grant and Streeck (1985); Canada and the UK, Coleman and Grant (1984); Belgium, Canada, France and the UK, Boddewyn (1985); and for associations in the food processing industries of Canada and Europe, see Coleman (1987), Jacek (1987), and Traxler (1987).

2. Williamson has recently argued that cultural differences account for the fact that Japanese firms rely on subcontracting far more heavily than their American counterparts (Williamson, 1985: 120–3), an argument that indicates that he

recognizes the role that broader social factors play in selecting governance forms. Yet these arguments are largely ad hoc, and while devoting considerable time to criticizing the assumptions which underlie the legal and political regulation of the economy (Williamson, 1975, 1985: 365–84), Williamson has made little effort to incorporate the state into his theoretical framework.

On the role of the state in shaping the development of associations, see Schmitter and Streeck (1981); Streeck and Schmitter (1985); Jacek (1987); Pestoff (1987); van Waarden (1987).

References

Becker, William H. (1971) 'American Wholesale Hardware Trade Association, 1870–1900', *Business History Review*, 45: 179–200.

Boddewyn, J.J. (1985) 'Advertising Self-regulation: Organizational Structures in Belgium, Canada, France and the United Kingdom', in Wolfgang Streeck and Philippe C. Schmitter (eds) *Private Interest Government*, pp. 1–43. Beverly Hills: Sage Publications.

Caves, Richard and Masu Uekusa (1976) 'Industrial Organization', in Hugh Patrick and Henry Rosovsky (eds) *Asia's New Giant*, pp. 459–523. Washington, DC: The Brookings Institute.

Chandler, Alfred D., Jr (1962) *Strategy and Structure*. Cambridge, MA: MIT Press.

Chandler, Alfred D., Jr (1977) *The Visible Hand*. Cambridge, MA: Harvard University Press.

Chandler, Alfred D., Jr (1980) 'The United States: Seedbed of Managerial Capitalism', in Alfred D. Chandler, Jr and Herman Daems (eds) *Managerial Hierarchies*, pp. 9–40. Cambridge, MA: Harvard University Press.

Coleman, William (1985) 'Analyzing the Associative Action of Business: Policy Advocacy and Policy Participation', *Canadian Public Administration*, 28: 413–33.

Coleman, William (1987) 'Agricultural Policy and the Associations of the Food Processing Industry', in Wyn Grant (ed.) *Business Interests, Organizational Development and Private Interest Government*, pp. 151–65. Berlin: Walter de Gruyter.

Coleman, William and Wyn Grant (1984) 'Business Associations and Public Policy: A Comparison of Organizational Development in Britain and Canada', *Journal of Public Policy*, 3: 209–35.

Coleman, William and Wyn Grant (1988) 'Business Cohesion and Political Influence: A Study of General, Intersectoral Associations'. *European Journal of Political Research*, 16: 467–87.

Cuff, Robert D. (1973) *The War Industries Board: Business–Government Relations During World War I*. Baltimore: Johns Hopkins University Press.

Daems, Herman (1980) 'The Rise of the Modern Industrial Enterprise: A New Perspective', in Alfred D. Chandler, Jr and Herman Daems (eds) *Managerial Hierarchies*, pp. 203–23. Cambridge, MA: Harvard University Press.

Daems, Herman (1983) 'The Determinants of the Hierarchical Organization of Industry', in Arthur Francis, Jeremy Turk and Paul Willman (eds) *Power, Efficiency and Institutions*, pp. 35–53. London: Heinemann Educational Books.

Davenport-Hines, R.P.T. (1988) 'Trade Associations and the Modernization Crisis of British Industry, 1910–35', in Hiroaki Yamazaki and Matao Miyamoto (eds)

Trade Associations in Business History, pp. 205-26. Tokyo: Tokyo University Press.

Daviet, Jean-Pierre (1988) 'Trade Associations or Agreements and Controlled Competition in France, 1830-1939', in Hiroaki Yamazaki and Matao Miyamoto (eds) *Trade Associations in Business History*, pp. 269-95. Tokyo: Tokyo University Press.

de Vroom, Burt (1985) 'Quality Regulation in the Dutch Pharmaceutical Industry: Conditions for Private Regulation by Business Interest Associations', in Wolfgang Streeck and Philippe C. Schmitter (eds) *Private Interest Government*, pp. 128-49. Beverly Hills: Sage Publications.

Farago, Peter (1985) 'Regulating Milk Markets: Corporatist Arrangements in the Swiss Dairy Industry', in Wolfgang Streeck and Philippe C. Schmitter (eds) *Private Interest Government*, pp. 168-81. Beverly Hills: Sage Publications.

Farago, Peter (1987) 'Retail Pressure and the Collective Reactions of the Food Processing Industry', in Wyn Grant (ed.) *Business Interests, Organizational Development and Private Interest Government*, pp. 166-79. Berlin: Walter de Gruyter.

Feldman, Gerald and Ulrich Nocken (1975) 'Trade Associations and Economic Power: Interest Group Development in the German Iron and Steel and Machine Building Industries, 1900-1933', *Business History Review*, 49: 413-45.

Foth, Joseph Henry (1930) *Trade Associations: Their Service to Industry*. New York: Ronald Press Company.

Galambos, Louis (1965) *Competition and Cooperation: The Emergence of a National Trade Association*. Baltimore: Johns Hopkins University Press.

Granovetter, Mark (1985) 'Economic Action and Social Structure: A Theory of Embeddedness', *American Journal of Sociology*, 91: 481-510.

Grant, Wyn (1985) 'Private Organizations as Agents of Public Policy: the Case of Milk Marketing in Britain', in Wolfgang Streeck and Philippe C. Schmitter (eds) *Private Interest Government*, pp. 182-96. Beverly Hills: Sage Publications.

Grant, Wyn (1987) 'Introduction' in Wyn Grant (ed.) *Business Interests, Organizational Development and Private Interest Government*, pp. 1-17. Berlin: Walter de Gruyter.

Grant, Wyn and William Coleman (1987) 'Conclusions', in Wyn Grant (ed.) *Business Interests, Organizational Development and Private Interest Government*, pp. 208-27. Berlin: Walter de Gruyter.

Grant, Wyn and Wolfgang Streeck (1985) 'Large Firms and the Representation of Business Interests in the UK and West German Construction Industry', in A. Cawson (ed.) *Organized Interests and the State*, pp. 145-73. London: Sage Publications.

Hannah, Leslie (1980) 'Visible and Invisible Hands in Great Britain', in Alfred D. Chandler, Jr and Herman Daems (eds) *Managerial Hierarchies*, pp. 41-76. Cambridge, MA: Harvard University Press.

Hawley, Ellis (1966) *The New Deal and the Problem of Monopoly*. Princetown: Princetown University Press.

Hawley, Ellis (1981) 'Three Facets of Hooverian Associationalism: Lumber, Aviation, and Movies, 1921-1930', in Thomas K. McGraw (ed.) *Regulation in Perspective*, pp. 95-123. Cambridge, MA: Harvard University Press.

Himmelberg, Robert F. (1976) *The Origins of the National Recovery Administration: Business, Government and the Trade Association Issue, 1921-1933*. New York: Fordham University Press.

Hollingsworth, J. Rogers and Leon Lindberg (1985) 'The Governance of the American Economy: The Role of Markets, Clans, Hierarchies, and Associative Behavior', in Wolfgang Streeck and Philippe C. Schmitter (eds) *Private Interest Government*, pp. 221–54. Beverly Hills: Sage Publications.

Jacek, Henry J. (1987) 'Business Interest Associations as Private Interest Governments', in Wyn Grant (ed.) *Business Interests, Organizational Development and Private Interest Government*, pp. 34–62. Berlin: Walter de Gruyter.

Jones, Franklin D. (1922) *Trade Association Activities and the Law: A Discussion of the Legal and Economic Aspects of Collective Action through Trade Associations*. New York: McGraw Hill.

Keller, Morton (1980) 'Regulation of Large Enterprise: United States Experience in Comparative Perspective', in Alfred D. Chandler, Jr and Herman Daems (eds) *Managerial Hierarchies*, pp. 161–81. Cambridge, MA: Harvard University Press.

Keller, Morton (1981) 'The Pluralist State: American Economic Regulation in Comparative Perspective, 1900–1930', in Thomas K. McGraw (ed.) *Regulation in Perspective*, pp. 56–94. Cambridge, MA: Cambridge University Press.

Kikkawa, Takeo (1988) 'Functions of Japanese Trade Associations before World War II: The Case of Cartel Organizations', in Hiroaki Yamazaki and Matao Miyamoto (eds) *Trade Associations in Business History*, pp. 53–83. Tokyo: Tokyo University Press.

Kocka, Jurgen (1980) 'The Rise of the Modern Industrial Enterprise in Germany', in Alfred D. Chandler, Jr and Herman Daems (eds) *Managerial Hierarchies*, pp. 77–116. Cambridge, MA: Harvard University Press.

Lamoreaux, Naiomi R. (1985) *The Great Merger Movement in American Business, 1895–1904*. Cambridge: Cambridge University Press.

Lembruch, Gerhard (1977) 'Liberal Corporation and Party Government', *Comparative Political Studies*, 10: 91–126.

Levy-Leboyer, Maurice (1980) 'The Large Corporation in Modern France', in Alfred D. Chandler, Jr and Herman Daems (eds) *Managerial Hierarchies*, pp. 117–60. Cambridge, MA: Harvard University Press.

Magaziner, Ira and Thomas Hout (1980) *Japanese Industrial Policy*. Berkeley: University of California Press.

Marburg, Theodore (1964) 'Government and Business in Germany: Public Policy toward Cartels', *Business History Review*, 38: 78–101.

Marin, Bernd (1983) 'Organizing Interests by Interest Associations: Associational Prerequisites of Cooperation in Austria', *International Political Science Review*, 4: 197–216.

Miyamoto, Matao (1988) 'The Development of Business Associations in Pre-war Japan', in Hiroaki Yamazaki and Matao Miyamoto (eds) *Trade Associations in Business History*, pp. 1–45. Tokyo: Tokyo University Press.

NAM (National Association of Manufacturers) (1942) 'Review of T.N.E.C. Monograph No. 18: Trade Association Survey', in John Scoville and Noel Sargent (compilers), *Fact and Fancy in the T.N.E.C. Monographs*, pp. 260–73. NAM.

NICB (National Industrial Conference Board) (1925) *Trade Associations, Their Economic Significance and Legal Status*. New York: National Industrial Conference Board.

Naylor, Emmett Hay (1921) *Trade Associations, Their Organization and Management*. New York: Ronald Press Company.

Ouchi, William G. (1980) 'Markets, Bureaucracies and Clans', *Administrative Science Quarterly*, 25: 129–41.

Perrow, Charles (1981) 'Markets, Hierarchies and Hegemony', in Andrew H. Van de Ven and William F. Joyce (eds) *Perspectives on Organizational Design and Behavior*, pp. 371–86. New York: Wiley.

Pestoff, Victor (1982) 'The Organization of Business Interests in the Swedish Food Processing Industry'. Paper presented at the 'Organization of Business Interests' conference, Wroxton, St. Mary, Banbury, Oxfordshire.

Pestoff, Victor (1987) 'The Effect of State Institutions on Associative Action in the Food Processing Industry', in Wyn Grant (ed.) *Business Interests, Organizational Development and Private Interest Government*, pp. 91–116. Berlin: Walter de Gruyter.

Pfeffer, Jeffrey and Gerald R. Salancik (1978) *The External Control of Organizations*. New York: Harper and Row.

Pierenkemper, Toni (1988) 'Trade Associations in Germany in the Late Nineteenth and Early Twentieth Century', in Hiroaki Yamazaki and Matao Miyamoto (eds) *Trade Associations in Business History*, pp. 233–61. Tokyo: Tokyo University Press.

Poensgen, Otto H. (1983) 'Between Markets and Hierarchies', in Arthur Francis, Jeremy Turk and Paul Willman (eds) *Power, Efficiency and Institutions*, pp. 54–80. London: Heinemann Educational Books.

Schmitter, Philippe C. (1986) 'Neo-corporatism and the State', in Wyn Grant (ed.) *The Political Economy of Corporatism*, pp. 32–62. London: Macmillan.

Schmitter, Philippe C. and Donald Brand (1979) 'Organizing Capitalists in the United States: The Advantages and Disadvantages of Exceptionalism'. Unpublished paper presented before the American Political Science Association.

Schmitter, Philippe C. and Wolfgang Streeck (1981) 'The Organization of Business Interests: A Research Design to Study the Associative Action of Business in the Advanced Industrial Societies of Western Europe'. Discussion Paper IIM/LMP 81–13, Berlin: Wissenschaftszentrum.

Skocpol, Theda and Kenneth Finegold (1982) 'State Capacity and Economic Intervention in the Early New Deal', *Political Science Quarterly*, 92: 255–78.

Staber, Udo and Howard Aldrich (1983) 'Trade Association Stability and Public Policy', in R.H. Hall and R.E. Quinn (eds) *Organizational Theory and Public Policy*, pp. 163–78. London, Sage Publications.

Streeck, Wolfgang (1983) 'Between Pluralism and Corporatism: German Business Associations and the State', *Journal of Public Policy*, 3: 265–84.

Streeck, Wolfgang and Philippe C. Schmitter (1985) 'Community, Market, State – and Associations? The Prospective Contribution of Interest Governance to Social Order', in Wolfgang Streeck and Philippe C. Schmitter (eds) *Private Interest Government*, pp. 1–29. Beverly Hills: Sage Publications.

Traxler, Franz (1985) 'Prerequisites, Problem Solving Capacity and Limits of Neo-corporatist Regulation: A Case Study of Private Interest Government and Economic Performance in Austria', in Wolfgang Streeck and Philippe C. Schmitter (eds) *Private Interest Government*, pp. 150–67. Beverly Hills: Sage Publications.

Traxler, Franz (1987) 'Patterns of Associative Action', in Wyn Grant (ed.) *Business Interests, Organizational Development and Private Interest Government*, pp. 18–33. Berlin: Walter de Gruyter.

Turner, John (1988) 'Servants of Two Masters: British Trade Associations in the First Half of the Twentieth Century', in Hiroaki Yamazaki and Matao Miyamoto (eds) *Trade Associations in Business History*, pp. 173–98. Tokyo: Tokyo University Press.

van Waarden, Frans (1985) 'Varieties of Collective Self-regulation of Business: The Example of the Dutch Dairy Industry', in Wolfgang Streeck and Philippe C. Schmitter (eds) *Private Interest Government*, pp. 197–220. Beverly Hills: Sage Publications.

van Waarden, Frans (1987) 'Sector Structure, Interests and Associative Action in the Food Processing Industry', in Wyn Grant (ed.) *Business Interests, Organizational Development and Private Interest Government*, pp. 63–92. Berlin: Walter de Gruyter.

Whitney, Simon N. (1934) *Trade Associations and Industrial Control. A Critique of the N.R.A.* New York: Central Book Co.

Williamson, Oliver E. (1975) *Markets and Hierarchies: Analysis and Antitrust Implications*. New York: The Free Press.

Williamson, Oliver E. (1981) 'The Economics of Organization: The Transaction Cost Approach', *American Journal of Sociology*, 87: 548–77.

Williamson, Oliver E. (1985) *The Economic Institutions of Capitalism*. New York: The Free Press.

Williamson, Oliver and William G. Ouchi (1981a) 'The Markets and Hierarchies and Visible Hand Perspectives', in Andrew H. Van de Ven and William F. Joyce (eds) *Perspectives on Organizational Design and Behavior*, pp. 347–70. New York: Wiley.

Williamson, Oliver and William G. Ouchi (1981b) 'A Rejoinder', in Andrew H. Van de Ven and William F. Joyce (eds) *Perspectives on Organizational Design and Behavior*, pp. 387–90. New York: Wiley.

Young, Brigitta, Leon Lindberg and J. Rogers Hollingsworth (forthcoming) 'The Governance of the American Dairy Industry: From Regional Dominance to Regional Cleavage', in H. Jacek and W.D. Coleman (eds) *Regionalism, Business Interest Associations and Public Policy*. Florence: de Gruyter.

Notes on the Contributors

Bo Gustafsson is Director of Economic Studies at the Swedish Collegium for Advanced Study in the Social Sciences in Uppsala and Professor of Economic History at Uppsala University.

Oliver E. Williamson is Transamerica Professor of Business, Economics, and Law at the University of California, Berkeley.

Masahiko Aoki is Henri and Tomoye Takahashi Professor of Economics at Stanford University and Professor of Economics at the Institute of Economic Research at Kyoto University.

Jacques Crémer is Professor of Economics at the Virginia Polytechnic Institute and State University, Blacksburg, VA.

Matti Pohjola is Acting Professor of Economics at the University of Helsinki and Senior Scientific Advisor at the Labour Institute for Economic Research in Helsinki. He formerly held various research and teaching positions at the Academy of Finland, the University of Tampere and the University of Helsinki.

Michael H. Riordan is Professor of Economics at Boston University. His research concerns the economics of vertical integration, procurement contracting and regulation, and other topics in industrial organization.

Kurt Lundgren, a civil engineer in chemical technology, is a teacher at the Swedish Center for Working Life and at the Economics Department of Stockholm University. He is currently working on his doctoral thesis in economics 'Aspects of the Economics of Learning' in which technological development is analysed from an economic, institutionally oriented perspective.

Torger Reve is Professor of Organization Science at the Norwegian School of Economics and Business Administration and senior research fellow at the Norwegian Research Centre in Organization and Management, Bergen, Norway. His research has concentrated on interorganizational relations and economic theories of organization.

Henry Hansmann is Professor of Law at Yale University. He is the author of a number of articles on the law and economics of non-profit and co-operative organizations, and is interested generally in the economic analysis of legal rules and institutions.

Kazuo Koike is Professor of Economics in the School of Business Administration at Hosei University, Japan. His publications include a recent book, *Understanding Industrial Relations in Modern Japan*, published by Macmillan (in English) 1988.

Ronald J. Gilson is Professor of Law at Stanford Law School and Director of the Law and Business Program at Stanford Law School. Both he and Robert H. Mnookin are engaged in an ongoing study applying the tools of finance and economics to an investigation of the structure of the legal profession.

Robert H. Mnookin is Adelbert H. Sweet Professor of Law at Stanford Law School and Director of the Stanford Center on Conflict and Negotiation.

Erik Berglöf is currently a John M. Olin Visiting Scholar at the Harvard Law School Program in Law and Economics. He is also affiliated with the Institute of International Business at Stockholm School of Economics. His publications include a recent report, 'Ownership and Control over the Firm – A Comparative Study of Financial Systems' (in Swedish) published by a Swedish government commission (1988).

Håkan Lindgren is Head of the Banking History Project in the Department of Economic History at Uppsala University and Associate Professor at the Institute of Economic History, Stockholm University. His publications include *Corporate Growth. The Swedish Match Industry in its Global Setting* (Liber, 1979).

Herbert Gintis is Professor of Economics at the University of Massachusetts at Amherst. He is the co-author, with Samuel Bowles, of *Democracy and Capitalism* and is currently working on the Microfoundations of Political Economy, a topic on which he has written several articles.

Karl Ove Moene is Professor of Economics at the University of Oslo. His international publications include articles on unemployment problems, investment under uncertainty, bureaucratic interaction and collective wage bargaining. He is currently working on problems related to unemployment and income determination in economic systems with different ownership structures. With Jon Elster he is the editor of *Alternatives to Capitalism* (1989), Cambridge: Cambridge University Press.

Marc Schneiberg is an organizational sociologist in the Department of Sociology at the University of Wisconsin-Madison. He is interested in studying organizations in a variety of economic sectors both within and across countries.

J. Rogers Hollingsworth is Professor of History and Sociology and Chairperson, Program in Comparative History, University of Wisconsin-Madison. His interests lie in the political economy of Western Europe and North America. Among his publications are *The Political Economy of Medicine: Great Britain and the United States* (1986) and *The Consequences of State Intervention* (1989).

Index

Index compiled by Jackie McDermott

QMW LIBRARY
(MILE END)